In the Beginning, Woman Was the Sun

Weatherhead Books on Asia

Front cover of the inaugural issue of *Seitō* (September 1911)

In the Beginning, Woman Was the Sun

THE AUTOBIOGRAPHY OF A JAPANESE FEMINIST

Hiratsuka Raichō

Translated, with an introduction and notes,

by Teruko Craig

Columbia University Press
New York

This publication has been supported by the Richard W. Weatherhead Publication Fund
of the East Asian Institute, Columbia University.

Columbia University Press

Publishers Since 1893

New York   Chichester, West Sussex

Translation copyright © 2006 Columbia University Press

Copyright © 1992 by Hiratsuka Raichō

Originally published as GENSHI, JOSEI WA TAIYŌ DE ATTA, 1971–1972; paperback edition, 1992.

Vol. 1 & Vol. 2 by Ōtsuki Shoten, Tokyo

English translation rights arranged with Ōtsuki Shoten
through Japan Foreign-Rights Centre

Library of Congress Cataloging-in-Publication Data

Hiratsuka, Raichō, 1886–1971.

[Genshi, josei wa taiyō de atta. English]

In the beginning, woman was the sun / Hiratsuka Raichō ;
translated with an introduction and notes by Teruko Craig.

p.   cm. — (Weatherhead books on Asia)

Includes bibliographical references.

ISBN 0–231–13812–1 (cloth : alk. paper)

1. Hiratsuka, Raichō, 1886–1971. 2. Feminists—Japan—Biography. I. Title. II. Series.

HQ1762.5.H56 A3   2006

305.42092—dc22

[B]   2005046630

Columbia University Press books are printed on permanent
and durable acid-free paper.

Printed in the United States of America

c 10 9 8 7 6 5 4 3 2 1

Contents

Introduction

> In the beginning, woman was truly the sun. An authentic person. Now she is the moon, a wan and sickly moon, dependent on another, reflecting another's brilliance....

Thus did Hiratsuka Raichō (1886–1971) announce the publication of *Seitō*, Japan's first literary journal created by women for women. By invoking the image of a lost sun, Raichō was calling out to Japanese women to reclaim their sense of self-worth, reaffirm their creativity, and fulfill their human potential. *Seitō* would serve as a forum for the full expression of women's awakened self-awareness. The year was 1911; Raichō was twenty-five.

Nothing in Raichō's early life foretold her future as a leader in the women's movement. Her father was a high-ranking official at the Audit Board of the Meiji government and a member of the small coterie that framed the Meiji constitution. Fluent in German, for a time he taught that language at the First Higher School. Her mother was well born, the daughter of a family that had furnished physicians to a Tokugawa branch house. Raichō—the pen name she adopted in 1911—was born Hiratsuka Haru in 1886, three years before the promulgation of the constitution. Indeed, her earliest memory was of being taken by her grandmother to see the festivities surrounding the occasion.

As the second daughter of an upper-class Tokyo family, Raichō grew up in privileged circumstances with the family expectation that she would marry well and live comfortably. Even as a child, however, she was stubborn and given to what she later called—in English—a propensity to "inwardness." She attended local public schools, and in 1898, entered Ochanomizu, an elite girls' high school attached to the Tokyo Women's Higher Normal School. She excelled in her studies. It is probably not significant that she and a small clique of classmates called themselves the "pirates." It is more telling that she occasionally walked out of morals class, a sign of her impatience with the school's emphasis on womanly virtues. She took private lessons in *koto* and the tea ceremony—traditional "marriage arts" considered indispensable for middle- and upper-class girls.

Raichō entered Japan Women's College in 1903. In Japan at that time, only a tiny fraction of one percent of women received a higher education. Her father had opposed her application to the college, but relented on the condition that she enroll in the home economics department. She spent most of her school years auditing courses on Western philosophy, Western art, and Japanese and European history. She also began a serious practice of Zen Buddhism, which, she later claimed, gave her an inward freedom and an awareness of the unlimited possibilities of life. She graduated at age twenty in 1906, a year after Japan's victory in the Russo-Japanese War, the event that marked the nation's coming of age as an imperial power.

A victory over a major Western nation would have been unimaginable forty years earlier. At the time of the Restoration (1868), Japan, long isolated from the world, was still divided into "feudal" daimyo domains, and its economic and military foundations were weak. The new Meiji government set out to transform the country. It centralized political authority, abolished the samurai class, began conscription, mandated universal primary education, established a cabinet and a new judiciary, and in 1889, promulgated a constitution. It also embarked on an extensive program of industrialization. Private initiatives soon matched those of the government.

Along with such political and economic changes, by the time Raichō entered college, Japan had also undergone a cultural and social revolution that led to an intellectual and moral ferment in society. The first wave of cultural change came during the 1870s and was known as the Civilization and Enlightenment movement. The first public discussion of women's issues began at this time. The members of the Meiji Six Society (Meirokusha), all men, criticized the low estate of women in the Japanese family system and called for reform. University students read translations of Adam Smith, Bentham, Darwin, Spencer, Mill, and Rousseau. Newspapers and journals popularized democratic ideas. A second, overlapping wave was the Freedom and People's Rights movement of the late 1870s and 1880s. Among the activists in this movement for representative government were a few women, such as Kishida Toshiko and Fukuda Hideko, who delivered public speeches calling for women's rights and "a single standard of sexual morality." During the decades before and after the turn of the century, Christian women's societies also presented arguments against prostitution and concubinage and in favor of a more Western moral code.

From the second half of the 1880s, the once revolutionary Meiji government took on a more complex character. It continued to emphasize modernization, but it also began to stress elements of Japanese tradition. Nowhere
was this more evident than in measures affecting women. The government
continued to press for universal primary education; by the turn of the century,
virtually all school-age children, boys and girls alike, were learning to read
and write. In 1899, it passed a law requiring at least one girls' high school in
each prefecture. At about the same time, it also approved of the establishment
of private and public three-year colleges for women, though none was given
university status. The formation of such institutions and the entry of educated
middle-class women into the workforce led, almost inevitably, to a new social
consciousness among women.

The government was also concerned about social stability; indeed, the
stated goal of public girls' high schools was to educate "good wives and wise
mothers." Rejecting a more liberal code, it affirmed the subordinate status of
women in the 1898 Civil Code. Among other restrictions, a wife could not
enter into a legal contract without her husband's permission or share in his
estate after his death. Adultery was a crime for a wife but not for a husband.
In the event of a divorce, the wife had no custody rights over the children.
Two years later, under Article 5 of the Police Security Regulations, women
were prohibited from joining political organizations and holding or attending
political meetings. Fukuda Hideko and other women socialists petitioned the
Diet for its revision. A partial amendment was passed by the Lower House in
1906, but was defeated by the nonelective Upper House on the grounds that it
was "detrimental to female virtue."

Raichō was keenly aware of these inequities, but she was intent on culti-
vating the inner self. Even after graduating from college, she lived at home.
She continued her practice of Zen, studied English, read books at the Ueno
Library, and in 1907, joined a woman's literary group started by Ikuta Chōkō,
a translator and graduate of Tokyo Imperial University. The next year, Raichō
became involved in an unconsummated affair with one of the group's lecturers, a married man. The affair was reported in the newspapers and the man
divulged the thinly veiled details in a novel, which became a best-seller. Overnight, the daughter of privilege became a figure of scandal. It does not exag-
gerate to say that the incident was a major turning point in her personal life.

Raichō bore the brunt of the ensuing public criticism. Undaunted, and
still undecided about her future, she pursued her religious practice and studies even more zealously. Then, in 1911, Ikuta Chōkō urged her to begin a
monthly literary journal for women. She accepted the challenge, though
somewhat reluctantly. Chōkō suggested that she name the journal *Seitō*

(*Bluestocking*). The term, first applied derisively to a group of unconventional women in eighteenth-century England who met to discuss literature, had a defiant ring to it. To defray the initial printing costs, her mother gave her 100 *yen* from the money that had been set aside as her dowry. The dowry was no longer necessary, since a normal, that is to say arranged, marriage had become unlikely.

The journal immediately attracted attention. Other women's magazines were already in existence, but they were mainly devoted to practical advice on home and family. *Seitō* was the first to call for women's spiritual revolution. Among its contributors were Yosano Akiko, Tamura Toshiko, and Okamoto Kanoko, who wrote fiction and poetry, and others who translated Chekhov, Maupassant, and Anatole France. Within two years of its founding, the journal began to shift from literature to larger issues affecting women, and became identified with candid discussions of female sexuality, chastity, and abortion—topics scrupulously avoided by other women's journals of the era. Several issues of *Seitō* were censored. The private lives of some of the contributors—their easy involvement in love affairs, their defiance of moral and social convention—also gave the journal notoriety as the "training school" for "New Women" or "made-in-Japan Noras." In 1914, Raichō herself began to live openly with her younger lover, an artist named Okumura Hiroshi, with whom she had two children out of wedlock in 1915 and 1917. (Their relationship was monogamous, and they married in 1941.)

Raichō was never physically strong, and in January 1915, pleading ill health, she relinquished control of the journal to Itō Noe, a younger colleague. Circulation was already declining, and the journal collapsed early the next year when Itō began an affair with the anarchist writer and activist Ōsugi Sakae. *Seitō* barely lasted five years, but by encouraging women to speak out and assert their selfhood, it gave fresh impetus to the nascent feminist movement in Japan.

The story of Raichō's life to 1917, as she herself related it, is presented in this translation. For the remainder of her life, until 1971, I have appended a moderately detailed translator's afterword. With one exception, there is no need to discuss her later life here. The exception is her founding of the New Women's Association in 1920, Japan's first women's organization to call for female suffrage.

After Raichō withdrew from *Seitō* in 1915, it was almost as if she had turned her back on the women's movement. She lived quietly at home with Okumura and her children. Along with some financial help from her parents, she supported her family by writing articles for leading journals such as *Chūō kōron* and *Fujin kōron*. During these years, as the mother of two young children, she daily faced the conflicting demands of work and family, and her concern for women's spiritual awakening and personal issues gradually turned to questions of social reform. She felt that mothers with young children deserved government aid, and in 1918, engaged in a prolonged published debate with Yosano Akiko, who thought otherwise. A visit to textile mills in Nagoya in 1919 convinced her that women must act collectively to gain political rights and achieve social reform.

In turning toward reform, Raichō moved in step with the times. In 1916, a women's division had been established in the Yūaikai, the first national labor union, which had been formed in 1912. This was not surprising, since women workers in textile mills accounted for more than half of Japan's industrial labor force. The following year, thousands of workers at steel mills and shipyards went on strike demanding higher wages. In the summer of 1918, riots broke out across the country to protest soaring rice prices. Troops had to be called in, and the Terauchi cabinet resigned. In 1919 the Yūaikai leadership was taken over by socialists, who also formed unions for tenant farmers.

During the same years, intellectuals also wrote in support of reform. Minobe Tatsukichi, a scholar of the Tokyo Imperial University law faculty, attacked the notion of an absolute state. Even the emperor, he argued, was not an absolute authority but an organ of the state and subject to its laws. Yoshino Sakuzō, another scholar at the same institution, wrote and campaigned in favor of parliamentary reform and party cabinets. Expectations for a genuine party government rose throughout the country, and in 1918, Hara Takashi became the first "commoner" prime minister, the first who was not a member of the domains that carried out the Meiji Restoration. Although Hara extended the suffrage, it did not meet the popular demand, and opposition parties called for universal manhood suffrage and held political rallies throughout Japan.

In 1920, after a five-year hiatus, Raichō reemerged as a leader in the women's movement. Soon after her visit to the textile mills in Nagoya, she enlisted the aid of Ichikawa Fusae and formed the New Women's Association (Shinfujin Kyōkai). The primary goal was social reform, and to that end, the association demanded women's suffrage. As a first step, it petitioned the Diet for the revision of Article 5 in the 1900 Police Security Regulations, and was partly successful: in 1922 the Diet amended the law, giving women the right to hold and attend political meetings, but not to join political organizations or to vote. Late that year the association was dissolved. The New Women's Association was short-lived—Raichō herself withdrew in 1921—but it had proven that by working together through legal channels, women could bring about political reform.

Hiratsuka Raichō is chiefly remembered for her pioneering role in Seitō. Her autobiography recounts the striking array of emotional and intellectual factors that led her to this initiative, and later, to the formation of the New Women's Association. Raichō was complex. She was at once idealistic and elitist, fearless and vain. While she lacked staying power and was often erratic and inconsistent, she was brilliant, an iconoclast in a conformist society and a perceptive observer of its foibles. The force of her personality, her articulate writings, and her life-long quest for self-transcendence and self-actualization make her the most compelling, and the most appealing, of Japanese feminists. Her autobiography is the record of an extraordinary person who inspired Japanese women to reclaim their hidden sun.

The Text

This book is a translation of volumes 1 and 2 of *Genshi, josei wa taiyō de atta* (*In the Beginning, Woman Was the Sun*). The two volumes represent the portion of the four-volume edition (Ōtsuki Shoten, 1971–73) that Raichō herself wrote.[1] I have used the paperback edition published in 1992. The pagination differs slightly from the 1971–73 hardcover edition.

The autobiography originated as an oral narrative.[2] As a result, it tends to be repetitious and digressive. When Raichō repeats herself, I have taken the liberty of eliminating some of the redundant information. In some instances I have omitted details that seemed unnecessary or irrelevant; each omission is noted. I have also corrected chronological inconsistencies.

Also, rather than using the chapter headings and subheadings supplied by the publisher, I have supplied my own. Brackets indicate information I have added to clarify the narrative. Parentheses and ellipses are as they appear in the original text.

The names in the translation are given in the Japanese fashion, family name first. I refer to women by their first names and men by their family names. Raichō, in her autobiography, usually refers to younger women by their first names and older women by either their first or last names. She refers to men by their last names and to authors by their pen names. For women who are variously cited by their maiden or married names, I give the names by which they are better known, or as they appear in biographical dictionaries, for example, Yamakawa Kikue rather than Aoyama Kikue.

I leave ages in the Japanese count, according to which a child is one on the day of its birth and two the next New Year's Day. (This does not mean, however, that all Japanese regard January 1 as their birthday.) By this reckoning Raichō, who was born on February 10, 1886, was two on January 1, 1887. When Raichō inadvertently uses Western count, I note it accordingly. I have converted year periods (Meiji: 1868–1912; Taishō: 1912–1926; Shōwa: 1926–1989) to their Western calendrical equivalents.

Familiar Japanese words like "kimono" and "samurai" are not italicized. Other Japanese words are italicized on first appearance and after that left in roman type. Japanese long vowels are indicated by macrons. Macrons are omitted for familiar place names such as Tokyo and Osaka.

Acknowledgments

I owe thanks to many: Ōtsuki Shoten for permission to translate volumes 1 and 2; Yoneda Sayoko, Ishizaki Shōko, Ikegawa Reiko, Yamamoto Hiroko, and Sakai Hiromi—scholars with an interest in Raichō who answered my frequent queries. Also: Jan Bardsley, who let me read her manuscript before its publication; Janine Beichman, Michael Burtscher, Hiroko Cockerill, Kuniko Yamada McVey, Kathleen Molony, Nakamura Masanori, Sumiko Otsubo, William Woehrlin, and Yokozawa Kiyoko. Haruko Iwasaki gave me invaluable help with passages I found opaque. Jennifer Crewe expedited the publishing process. My greatest debt is to Phyllis Birnbaum for her enthusiasm and generous suggestions on prose style, and to my husband, Albert Craig, for his warm encouragement, thoughtful advice throughout the project, and technical assistance.

In the Beginning, Woman Was the Sun

1

Childhood

My Earliest Memories

Pushing and shoving, the people around me scramble for space. The street is congested from Hanzōmon to the embankment in front of the Imperial Palace and as far as the Hibiyagahara parade ground. The noise from the crowd sounds like the surging sea. I hold on to my grandmother—she is carrying me piggyback—and take a timid look over her shoulder at the parade ground. Through the profusion of bobbing heads, I make out a procession of floats to the side. There is a life-sized figure of a doll standing on one of the floats. Perhaps it is Jinmu, the first emperor of Japan. All this I can see dimly in my mind's eye. The float must have been decorated with something bright and shiny because even now, in this earliest of memories, it shimmers like a distant star. (Records state that there were as many as 107 floats in Tokyo that day.)

Another scene is superimposed on the first: a procession of "foxes" dressed for a fox wedding slowly makes its way along a street. Lining the street is a tall black fence with posts set up at regular intervals. I have no idea where we are—I was barely four—but this is probably a back street behind the government buildings in Marunouchi. There are only a few spectators, so I am able to see everything up close—the masqueraders covered from head to toe in deep yellow robes, the ears on their masks sticking straight up. The distinctly yellow image of the foxes against the coal black fence remains with me to this day. I also vaguely remember standing on the corner of a busy street where I looked up at a big arch decorated with bunting.

The skies were clear that day, but the streets were probably slushy, since I learned later that snow had fallen the previous day. My sister Taka must have been with us too. She was a year older than I and would have been carried by Kiyo, her wet nurse. Kiyo was a cheerful, talkative young girl who wore her hair in the *ichōgaeshi* style.[i] For some reason, they do not figure in my memory.

This day that I remember was Empire Day, February 11, 1889, but the festive atmosphere in Tokyo had little to do with the commemoration of the nation's founding by Emperor Jinmu. That very morning, the Imperial Constitution of Japan had been promulgated in the presence of military and civil officials at a solemn ceremony in the Imperial Palace. By sheer coincidence, my earliest memory is of a city celebrating the country's first modern constitution. And just one day earlier, I had observed my third birthday.[ii]

⊙ ⊙ ⊙ ⊙ ⊙

My family lived in Sanban-chō in the Kōjimachi (now Chiyoda Ward) section of Tokyo. Aside from my father and mother, my family consisted of my grandmother, my father's younger sister [Ai], my sister and me, my sister's wet nurse, and a maid. My grandmother, who died in 1919 at age eighty-four, was then in her early fifties.[iii] Healthy and active, she liked going out, especially with her adored grandchildren, and on an occasion like this, she certainly would not have stayed at home. And since my sister's wet nurse was a typical Tokyo native in her enthusiasm for seeing new sights, she also would have insisted on accompanying us.

But there was another, more personal reason for my grandmother to join the public celebration: her only son—my father—had actually played a role in drafting the constitution. My father was proficient in German, so he had been hired by the House of Councilors (Sanji-in) in 1882. He had served in the legal affairs department as interpreter and translator for Hermann Roesler, the German scholar invited to draft a commercial code. Under Roesler's kind tutelage, my father read widely in German law and was asked by Itō Hirobumi, [prime minister and] chairman of the constitutional committee, to work with him, Kaneko Kentarō, Itō Miyoji, and others in drawing up a constitution. My grandmother knew this, of course, and had looked forward to the day with more than ordinary joy and pride, even though she did not know anything about the contents of the document.

---

[i] A simple hairstyle favored by women in downtown Tokyo. Raichō makes frequent mention of women's hairstyles, which correspond to their class, age, and marital status.

[ii] By Japanese count Raichō became four on January 1, 1889, but her third birthday was of course on February 10 of that year. See introduction for discussion of Japanese reckoning of ages.

[iii] Raichō's grandmother actually died in 1918.

That same night, I went with my parents and sister to see the fireworks at Hibiyagahara.[iv] My father held me while I watched in utter delight as the display burst high in the sky. Then, unexpectedly, one of the fireworks exploded ahead of schedule and sent a shower of sparks over our heads. The startled crowd scattered and my father sheltered me in his arms and ran from the spot, but I could still see the sparks grazing my shoulders. The shock and terror of that moment stayed with me for years. I always hated fireworks, and to avoid them, I went to shrine festivals only during the day. Young relatives used to come and stay overnight to watch the annual display at nearby Yasukuni Shrine, but even when they teased me about being a coward, I refused to go. I was content to listen to the boom and crackle in the safety of my home.

My Family

My father, Hiratsuka Sadajirō, and my mother, Tsuya, had three daughters. The first child, Ine, was born in 1883, but contracted measles and died of pneumonia. Fond of boiled beans, she had just learned to say *mami*—her way of saying *mame* [the Japanese word for beans]—when she succumbed to the disease. I was often told I looked like her.

The second child was born on January 30, 1885. This happened to be the holiday honoring Kōmei [the father of the reigning Emperor Meiji], and the child was accordingly named Taka.[v] I was the third child, born on February 10, 1886, the nineteenth year of Meiji. I was named Haru.[vi] My mother had hired a wet nurse for my sister as soon as she found out she was pregnant. She had never been strong, and, exhausted from having two babies in a row, she stopped nursing me soon after my birth and gave me condensed milk instead.

I was a healthy child, chubby, my arms creased with rolls of fat. I was slow to speak, however, and my mother secretly worried that there was something seriously wrong. Even now, I speak slowly and have trouble projecting my voice, so I may well have been born with a physical impairment of some kind. As the youngest, I grew up a cherished child, secure in the love of my family.

In May 1887, a year after I was born, my father [who was now at the Audit Board] was asked to accompany his superior, Viscount Watanabe Noboru, on

---

iv In her much shorter 1955 autobiography Raichō writes that her father was in Germany at the time of the promulgation of the constitution and that she went to see the fireworks when she was four or five, after he returned to Japan (*The Path I Took* 7–8).

v "Taka" is a variant reading for the *kanji* "kō," as in Kōmei.

vi "Haru" is a variant reading for "mei," as in Meiji. Raichō sometimes drops "ko," a common suffix for girls' names.

a tour of Europe and the United States to study accounting laws. He returned at the end of the year I turned three, and until then there were only women in the house.[vii] In my father's absence, my mother began studying English. As the wife of a government official at the forefront of the Civilization and Enlightenment movement who was moreover studying abroad,[viii] she had to keep up with the times. She attended classes at the Sakurai Girls' School in Nakarokuban-chō. The school, headed by Yajima Kajiko, the former president of the Japanese Christian Women's Temperance Union, had a number of foreign women on its staff. I imagine that my mother's decision to study English was not hers but my father's, since he no doubt thought that women as well as men should know English.

My mother also took lessons in knitting and Western-style sewing and embroidery at the Girls' Trade School in Hitotsubashi. When she was away at school, my grandmother took over; I am sure she was the one who changed my diapers, among other chores. One of my greatest pleasures was to go with my grandmother to my mother's school to deliver her lunch. Because of my mother's frail constitution, the lunch always included milk, which was sold at only one store, the Hokushinsha in Iida-chō, and came in cone-shaped tin cans rather than the glass bottles of today. On these trips my grandmother dressed me in Western clothes, which were then still a novelty. I do not know if this is why my mother's classmates and foreign teachers made a big fuss over me. I enjoyed all the attention, but I also felt a bit self-conscious.

My mother also began wearing Western clothes, with her hair arranged in tight curls over her forehead. She was small, but the style suited her delicate build and pale oval face. Dresses at the time had stiff shoulders, a narrow waist that required a corset, and a bustle padded with cotton. These dresses, which were sewn with intricate pleats and gathers, extended to the floor—one never saw a woman's stockings—and were highly impractical. Women always wore hats—mostly bonnets, but sometimes hats with narrow brims and sprigs of artificial flowers. Needless to say, Western attire was limited to the upper and middle classes and went out of style before it caught on with the general public.

I distinctly remember our house in Sanban-chō. It was on the right side of a street that ran off a busy thoroughfare just opposite Yasukuni Shrine and between the trolley stops at Kudanzaka and Hitokuchizaka. There was a cotton-

---

[vii] Raichō must mean three by Western count, that is to say, her father returned to Japan in December 1889. This would explain her later account of the souvenirs of the Eiffel Tower and the Paris Centennial Exposition, which opened in January 1889.

[viii] A movement during the 1870s and 1880s to strengthen Japan by adopting Western ideas and institutions.

spinning shop on the corner, and anyone walking by could hear the ping and whir of the looms. The house had a modest gate of unvarnished wood and to one side, a tall maple tree that provided shade in the summer. The first floor had an entrance hall, a Western-style parlor, my father's study, a room for my mother, another for my grandmother, a dining room, and a maid's room. The second floor had only one room, which was completely Japanese-style and used when guests came to play *go* with my father or stayed overnight.

My father's study reflected the Westernizing spirit of the times. It had a large floral carpet, tables, chairs, and on one wall, a shelf crammed with the collected works of Goethe and Schiller, an anthology of poems by Heine, and other books by Western authors. The books, purchased in Germany, looked impressive in their leather bindings and gold-lettered spines. Hanging from the ceiling was a glass lamp—another foreign purchase—with a bird's nest painted on its surface. Some of the eggs had already hatched, and the chicks, their yellow beaks wide open, were waiting impatiently for the bee in the mother's mouth. I thought the scene enchanting and never tired of looking at it.

As I look back, I find it puzzling that my father—not yet thirty, a lower-grade bureaucrat at the Audit Board with no inheritance—could afford a house such as ours, and a maid and wet nurse to boot. Was everything much cheaper back then? And speaking of being puzzled, I must mention all the gifts my father brought back from his trip. For my mother, there was a hand-operated sewing machine—an object of beauty decorated with intertwined gold, red, and green leaves; a gold filigree bracelet; a cameo ring; a gold pin set with turquoise stones; leather gloves of different lengths in white, cream, and brown; and an assortment of dresses. My sister and I each received a toy sewing machine that could sew dolls' clothes, a big rubber ball with painted scenery, and a child's peep show made in France. My peep show had a view of the Eiffel Tower; my sister's, a panoramic view of the Paris Centennial Exposition. My father, who had visited the tower and exposition, brought back a photograph album of the exhibition as well.

We also received big dolls. Mine was dressed in pink and my sister's in pale blue. Other gifts were music boxes, silver bracelets, necklaces made of two strands of coral beads, and matching dresses. One dress, of pink velvet with a floral design, had beige trim on the bodice, a satin sash, and a matching bonnet with a tie. Another was made of stiff silk like the kind produced in Kai Province, with blue and white checks. There was another dress of deep rose, which was embroidered in the same color on the collar and cuffs. My father also brought back bolts of fabric. For himself, he bought a gold ring with his monogram; a gold pocket watch and chain with a mechanical pencil attached to one end; a pince-nez; binoculars; a pistol; a cane with a sword hidden inside; the German books mentioned earlier; reproductions of paintings; and photos of sculpture and architecture. The gifts for his younger sister were much the same as my mother's. At a time when things Western were worshipped indiscriminately, my father must have stretched all his resources to make the purchases. He was by no means extravagant, but he was fond of his family and no doubt watched every penny during his stay abroad. It now occurs to me that my mother may have brought a dowry, but of course, such matters were never mentioned.

My Grandmother Yae

With our mother away at school, my sister and I turned to our grandmother for company. In fact, as a child, I was closer to her than to anyone else in the family, and will say without hesitation that my grandmother Yae, who clung to her regional dialect to the day she died, had a strong, if not the strongest, formative influence on me. I know nothing about her family background, apart from the fact that she was born in 1833, in the Wakayama domain. Since she lost her husband early on and had two young children, she had to struggle to make ends meet. Fortunately, she was a born optimist and a hard worker who couldn't keep still for a minute. Compared to my mother, who was somewhat cool and formal, my grandmother was open, down-to-earth, and had a common touch. She was totally unconcerned about her personal appearance.

The grandmother I see in my memory is a small, elderly woman, her hair cut short, wearing a man's kimono held in place at the waist with a black satin half *obi*. She was not particularly literate—what she knew was mainly from hearsay. She regularly consulted one book, however, an old-fashioned manual on the Tōkyūjutsu school of physiognomy. I do not know when or how she became interested in its teachings, but the school had been founded in 1834 by Yokoyama Marumitsu, who believed that the earth was governed by the ancient Chinese zodiac and people's characters were determined by the zodiacal sign under which they were born. Thus, he said, human beings should find out their good points and bad, their strengths and weaknesses; cultivate themselves accordingly; and strive for spiritual enlightenment and peace.

Armed with this knowledge, my grandmother claimed she could tell a person's character and temperament just by his birth date and facial features. I often saw her take out a sheet of paper with a picture of a face and fill in the physical characteristics. I was too young to understand what all this meant, but I still remember the strange drawings. I also remember seeing her get up early, open the wooden shutters, and sit down to meditate. As she meditated, she breathed deeply at measured intervals, but this too, I gather, was part of the founder's teachings. She occasionally took her daughter—my aunt Ai—to meetings of the Tōkyūjutsu school. My parents were totally uninterested.

On the days my mother went to classes, my grandmother usually took us to the grounds of the Yasukuni Shrine. She carried me on her back and Kiyo carried my sister. Occasionally we went farther, cutting across the riding grounds with its bronze statue of Ōmura Masujirō and continuing to the Fujimi Elementary School in Fujimi-chō. When we passed the residence of the royal family of the Ryūkyū Islands, we often caught a glimpse of the men in their exotic attire—kimono worn in reverse, right side over the left, and long silver pins stuck in their tightly coiled hair. Another excursion took us uphill toward Kudanzaka, past the so-called Lower Shrine—now the Ushigafuchi Park—and down to the Trade Exhibition Hall at the foot of the hill. Still another route took us in the opposite direction, to the west. Following a street behind the shrine toward Dote Sanban-chō, we emerged on the embankment of the outer moat of the Imperial Palace and gathered herbs growing under a big pine tree. Close by was another thickly branched tree called the Hanging-by-the-Neck Pine, but this we carefully avoided.

One of our favorite trips was to a shop on the street that ran in front of the main entrance of Yasukuni Shrine. It specialized in *ezōshi*, and in an age when children's books were unheard of, these booklets with brightly colored illustrations gave us much pleasure. Prominently displayed in the shop were prints by Kunisada, Kuniyoshi, Toyokuni, and other masters. Some of the prints were on a single sheet, but others spread over double or triple sheets. Famous actors and beauties of the demimonde were depicted—subjects deemed unfit for children—but several prints, with captions like "Things in Vogue," were of people playing the koto, performing the tea ceremony, or viewing flowers at Ueno Park. There were also prints designed to encourage children to read. One had a picture of a dog, cat, and mouse, and printed below in the *hiragana* phonetic script were the words "bow-wow," "meow," and "squeak." Another had a goldfish, turtle, and cow, and a line that read "goldfish, stray turtle, moo-moo cow." Still another, with a picture of frogs, read "Three frogs leap, hop, hop, hop." The shop also sold patterned paper for origami and paper dolls. In a word, this was a place not to be missed.

I often begged my grandmother to take us to Chidorigafuchi, an inlet of the palace moat where there were ducks, geese, grebes, and a host of other waterfowl. I liked watching the ducks best of all. Sometimes floating, sometimes paddling, they swam neatly in a row or waddled up onto the opposite shore and nestled perfectly still on the sun-dappled grass, as if they were taking a nap. I grouped them according to size—Group One, Group Two, Group Three, just as I had seen the teachers do in my sister's kindergarten class. Once in a while, we spotted a *mogutcho* or *kaitsumuri*, a small, black, scruffy-looking bird, which quickly dove beneath the water and kept us waiting until it finally came bobbing up to the surface again.

The outer moat of the palace was more shallow, but we often saw a white egret near Ichigayamitsuke. I was fascinated, for the bird never seemed to move. One afternoon, I decided to keep watch until it did move, thinking that the bird and I would have an endurance match. After I took up my position on the grass bank, I watched and waited. The bird grew fainter and fainter in the gathering dusk, at last turning into a pale white spot floating in the darkness. My grandmother said it was getting late, and I reluctantly went home. We returned the next day to see if the egret was still there, but it had vanished without a trace. I thought, oh, so the bird moves, after all. But I felt betrayed and gazed disconsolately at the empty shore. My sister said the egret had to stay still in order to catch an unsuspecting fish, but to me, the egret would always be a distant, unfriendly bird unlike the ducks.

We also went to Hie Shrine to see the monkeys and about once a month to Ginza to buy rice crackers at a shop called Matsuzaki. The crackers, which were always included in our mid-afternoon snack, came in all sizes and shapes: "Ogre's Feather Fan," larger than a grown-up's face; "Plover," in the shape of a bird in flight and frosted with sugar; rectangular crackers made with egg and decorated with lined patterns; thick half-moon crackers flavored with *miso*; hard crackers wrapped in *shiso* leaf, and many more.

On the way to the store my grandmother entertained us with stories. When we passed the Sakuradamon Gate of the palace, for example, she invariably told us about the Shogunate Elder Ii Naosuke, or Ii Kamon-san, as she called him, who had been assassinated on that very spot, on the third day of the third month, by disgruntled samurai from the Mito domain. Then, on our way home, which took us past a small waterfall near Sukiyabashi Bridge, we always stopped to rest under a willow tree on the grassy embankment of the moat. After a few minutes of watching the geese, my grandmother would look into a large paper bag, take out some crackers, and say in her Wakayama dialect, "We'll save the big ones for later." She doted on us and could not wait to give us a treat. Years later, I heard that Matsuzaki was still in business in the same location behind what is now the Hattori Clock Store, so I went there for old times' sake. The store was small and quite ordinary, not at all as I remembered it. Gone was the wide front, with its spacious earthen entranceway. Gone, too, were the men who sat shoulder to shoulder in the dimly lit back room, bending and weaving as they shaped and toasted the crackers. I could not believe it was the same store.

We made other excursions to Zōjōji Temple in Shiba, Suitengū in Nihonbashi, and Sensōji Temple in Asakusa, as well as to various fairs at temples and shrines. Our grandmother was in good health and full of energy, happy to take us out on any pretext.

Ancestors

I was my grandmother's pet. I slept with my mother at first, but after a while moved to my grandmother's room. It was the only room in the house with a charcoal foot-warmer built into the floor, and as soon as the weather turned cold, my sister and I snuggled under the quilt on top and asked her to tell us stories. Besides those familiar to all Japanese children, she told us stories from her native Wakayama: about the priest Kiyohime[, who fell in love with the priest Anchin and pursued him relentlessly in the form of a snake]; the fabulously rich merchant Kinokuniya Bunzaemon[, who cornered the market for tangerines and lumber in Wakayama]; the famous Ashibe rice crackers made in the province. She also talked about Shirahama, Kumano Shrine, the waterfall at Nachi, and other scenic sites, but she most often told the story about Miura Daisuke,[ix] the warrior in the children's counting song who lived until he was 106. At the end she invariably said, "Miura Daisuke's our ancestor, and that's why we all live so long in this family. The two of you are going to live until a hundred, do you hear, and I intend to live just as long, too." As I mentioned, she lived until she was eighty-four.

As I later found out, my grandmother's story about our ancestry was not altogether nonsense. According to the family genealogy in my possession, our ancestor Miura Daisuke Yoshiaki was a warrior based in Miura, Sagami Province during the twelfth century. A kinsman, Miura Tameshige, who was in service to the Kamakura shogunate, was given land in the village of Hiratsuka as a reward for subduing bandits in the Hakone Mountains; this is the source of our family name. Tamehiro, a seventh-generation descendant of Tameshige who was lord of Tarui Castle in Gifu, entered the service of the great warlord Toyotomi Hideyoshi [in the late 1500s] and remained loyal to the Toyotomi family after Hideyoshi's death. Killed in the epic Battle of Sekigahara [1600], he left behind a farewell poem: "I little regret forfeiting my life for the sake of honor / Knowing this world of ours will vanish in time too."[x]

Our direct ancestor, Hiratsuka Tamekage, was Tamehiro's younger brother. Tamekage was taken captive at Sekigahara, but instead of submitting meekly, he insulted the victor, Tokugawa Ieyasu, to his face. Much impressed, Ieyasu released Tamekage and had him enter the service of [his son] Yorinobu, the daimyo of Wakayama. Tamekage then arranged to have his dead brother's

---

[ix] Miura Daisuke (Yoshiaki) was a retainer of Minamoto Yoritomo, the founder of the Kamakura shogunate. Daisuke died in battle in 1180, at age 89, but Yoritomo, who visited his grave 17 years later, thought Daisuke had died more recently—which would have make him 106, hence the saying, "A crane lives a thousand years, a tortoise, ten thousand, and Miura Daisuke, one hundred and six."

[x] "Tame," as in his name, also means "for the sake of."

three sons enter the daimyo's service, and with their future assured, he withdrew from office and became a Buddhist priest. Having no children of his
own, Tamekage adopted Kanbei, the youngest of his brother's children. All
future first sons in the family would thenceforth be called Kanbei.

Tamekage's grave is at Honkeiji, a temple just outside the city of Wakayama.
The grave is on a small hill, just behind a small shrine dedicated to Kannon, the goddess of mercy. According to family legend, Tamekage donated
the money for the shrine when he was told in a dream to honor a small gold
statue of the goddess that a dying bandit had given him. The statue is said to
be deep inside a well under the shrine floor.[1]

My grandfather Hiratsuka Tametada was the eighth Kanbei. He served
the daimyo of Wakayama like his forefathers, and on the eve of the Meiji
Restoration (1868), he was put in charge of domain soldiers sent to Kobe to
protect foreign residents [from xenophobic samurai]. In 1871, the new Meiji
government abolished feudal domains and stripped samurai of their hereditary stipends. Worried about his future, my grandfather decided to leave his
ancestral home and seek his fortune in Tokyo, the nation's new capital. He
handed over his entire estate, including some 1,000 *tsubo*[xi] of land, to his son
and two daughters by his deceased first wife, and left for Tokyo in 1872. He
took his second wife—my grandmother Yae—and their two children with
him; he was penniless.

I am inclined to think that my grandfather had another reason for going
to Tokyo, namely, to extricate himself from the tangle of family relations. A
glance at the family tree reveals an unusual number of daughters and a succession of sons-in-law who were adopted into their wives' families. My grandfather himself had been born into the Kondō family, hereditary physicians to
the daimyo of Wakayama. He was adopted by the Hiratsuka family, who had
no sons, and married the oldest daughter.[xii] She died, leaving him with three
children. His new wife then had two children—my father and Aunt Ai—com-
plicating matters even further. Not for nothing was my grandfather known
to say, "So long as you've got three cups of bran to your name, don't ever be
adopted into your wife's family as a son-in-law."

In any event, when the time came to leave, all he said was, "We're off to see
the sights in Tokyo." He never returned. My father, born in 1858, was fifteen at
the time. As he recalled, they took a boat from Wakayama in the morning, but

---

[xi] *Tsubo* = 3.31 square meters.

[xii] In the absence of a male heir, it was common practice to adopt a son and have him marry the eldest
daughter. The son-in-law (*muko yōshi*), who was regarded as a direct lineal descendant of the family,
eventually inherited the family property and was responsible for the welfare of the family members.

due to engine trouble, reached Osaka in the middle of the night instead of at two in the afternoon as scheduled. The next day, they transferred to a boat for Tokyo, but it stopped to help a foreign ship that had run aground in Kumano Bay. By the time they arrived in Shinagawa Bay, they had been traveling for five full days.

My grandfather, in effect, had run away from home and now had to support his family. He went to see a cousin, Tsuda Izuru, who was the head of the Army Accounting Bureau. He was invited to live in a house on Tsuda's estate in Kōjimachi and became responsible for overseeing the extended household. My father was also put to work as an attendant at the front entrance.

Prior to the Restoration, Tsuda had played a leading role in reforming the Wakayama military on the Prussian model. When the new Meiji government heard about this, he was recruited by [Minister of the Right] Iwakura Tomomi to assist the government's modernization programs. Tsuda found the atmosphere in the government office too constricting, however, and spent most of his time at the Army Officers' Club in Kudanzaka-ue. The two-story structure was formerly the residence of a shogunate retainer and had a fine view, so in the summer, he would have his subordinates join him there. Before long, my father was asked to work as an office boy.

My Father

My father's early education was completely traditional. Growing up in Wakayama, he had learned to read and write at a local temple school. As the son of a samurai, he then attended the domain academy and studied the Chinese classics and military arts, including swimming, which he practiced in the Kinokawa River. But now at the office, he noticed that someone called Matsumi, who was from Wakayama and knew German, was highly valued despite his low rank. For example, whenever a decision had to be made, the men in the normally rank-conscious office would turn to him for advice: "Could you tell us how it's done in Germany?" My father made up his mind to study German because he felt that would surely help him make his way in the world.

Since they were from the same domain, he asked Matsumi to teach him the language. As my father soon discovered, the man could read but could not speak German. So my father enrolled at a private school in Surugadai, where the language was taught in a more systematic manner. To earn money for tuition, he went around selling the salted beans he had roasted at home while studying his grammar book. Determined to master German, he persuaded his father to part with some 200 yen he had stashed away and then took the entrance examination for the newly established Foreign Language School. This was in 1875; the decision determined the course of his life.

The school was organized into ten grades, each lasting a half year. Degrees were granted after five years. My father was allowed to skip three times and by the end of three and a half years, he was ready to graduate. In the meantime, my grandfather had fallen sick and run out of money. My father felt he had to withdraw, but the principal, who recognized his abilities, appointed him to the staff with a monthly salary of 25 yen. According to my grandmother, my grandfather's illness had been diagnosed as tympanites, or what is now called chronic peritonitis, but she herself was convinced that he had been put under a curse. One of the houses owned by the Tsuda family was said to be haunted, and my grandfather, who thought this "complete nonsense," had gone to the house, spent the night, and been stricken soon after.

My grandfather lingered on for two years. The daily cost for his medicine came to 14 *sen*, or more than 4 yen a month. On my father's salary, it was a staggering sum.[xiii] Yet my father was devoted to his father and arranged to have him seen by Dr. Edwin Baelz, of whom it was said, "If you've been seen by the doctor, you can die without any regrets." On that doctor's advice, my grandfather was taken to the University Hospital. Even at the lowest rates, the fees amounted to 35 sen a day, including meals and medicine. To earn extra money, my father worked as a copyist in his spare time. Tacked on the front window of the house was a sign that said, "Documents copied. 6 *rin* for one sheet of paper with 10 lines, 20 characters to a line."

After my grandfather's death, my father entered government service. He started out as a clerk at the House of Councilors, transferred to the Ministry of Agriculture and Commerce and then to the Ministry of Foreign Affairs, and in 1886, the year I was born, transferred to the Audit Board. In the following year, he made his trip abroad. Toward the end of his life, my father told me that the monies for the trip had come from a secret cabinet fund. He also said that on the eve of departure the head of the delegation had been expressly instructed by Prime Minister Itō to pay special attention to the accounting laws in Prussia. Quite possibly, the draft of the constitution, with its heavy reliance on the undemocratic Prussian charter, had already been completed.

On his return, my father worked tirelessly on the draft of the new auditing regulations. He stayed at the Audit Board for a total of forty years, until his retirement in 1924, at age sixty-six. The busiest period in his career was during the Sino-Japanese (1894–1895) and Russo-Japanese (1904–1905) wars, when

---

[xiii] 1 *yen* = 100 *sen* = 1000 *rin*. In 1873 a bowl of sweet azuki bean soup cost 3 sen. In 1875 a bowl of buckwheat noodles cost 1 sen 2 rin.

he was sent to Taiwan, Korea, Manchuria, and Siberia to audit colonial and military finances. At the outbreak of World War I, he was sent to the islands in the South Pacific that had come under Japanese rule. His work was not the sort to attract attention but was demanding nevertheless.

Although German was the only subject he studied formally, my father was widely read in law and economics. Besides his official duties, he taught German at the First Higher School, gave the first course in accounting at the Army Paymaster School, and helped found the German Association School. At the end of his career he was second in command at the Audit Board, a testament to his abilities. In fact, because he lacked the proper academic credentials, a special ordinance had been issued to allow him to fill the position. When the top post eventually became vacant, my father was expected to fill it, but his lack of credentials again became a problem, and at that point he resigned.

My father had a prodigious memory. He liked to tell the story about how, when he had served as an interpreter in Germany, he had translated an entire lecture faultlessly, without taking a single note. He was also proud of having met Bismarck. Among the books he wrote were *Introduction to German*; *A Primer of German Grammar*; and *Lectures on Auditing*. He also translated (with Hirata Tōsuke) Bluntschli's *Lehre vom modernen Staat*; (with Terada Yukichi) Eheberg's *Grundriss der Finanzwissenschaft*; (with Hirata Tōsuke and Shinagawa Yajirō) Roscher's *Nationalökonomik des Ackerbaunes und der verwandten Ur-productionen* and *Nationalökonomik des Handels und Gewerbfleisses*. His intellectual curiosity was boundless, yet with all his responsibilities and interests, he was also a family man, always willing to play with his children.

My Mother

My mother's maiden name was Iijima Tsuya. Born in 1864, she was the third daughter of Iijima Hōan, a physician in service to the Tayasu, a branch house of the Tokugawa family. Her father was actually born into the Takano family, who also served the Tayasu as doctors of traditional medicine, but he, his wife, and three daughters had been adopted into the Iijima family when the first Iijima Hōan died, leaving a small son. It was said that the lord of Tayasu himself had had a hand in these arrangements.

The second Iijima Hōan, that is to say, my maternal grandfather, was exceedingly fond of drinking. He was also a man of excellent taste and an accomplished poet. A discolored glass-plate photograph shows an amiable old man dressed in a casual kimono and a little square cap, the kind worn by tea masters and the like. Hōan had no sons, so he encouraged his daughters to study the arts from an early age. My mother, the youngest, learned reading, writing, and the abacus at a temple school, and at age five began dancing lessons. She took lessons in chanting Tokiwazu ballads, and by the time she was seventeen—when she married—she had received a special name from her teacher in recognition of her skill.

For generations, the Iijima family had lived in Tokyo, or Edo, as it was formerly called. With a black gate in front, the house in Hongō Maruyama-chō looked out on a street that ran from Hakusan-ue to the First Higher School (now the site of the Agricultural Department of Tokyo University). The grounds were spacious and the style of life was equally comfortable. Despite this, my maternal grandfather was quite willing to give his youngest daughter's hand in marriage to my father, an impecunious clerk living in a cramped row house. There was another offer from a distinguished family, but my grandfather had been won over by my father's character and declined. A poem he wrote on the occasion of my parents' wedding has been preserved. It is written on pale green paper with elegant brushwork and says something to the effect that the fields of young rice shoots will in time yield a bountiful harvest. The oldest daughter was married to a minor bureaucrat. The second had married "for love." Disowned and forbidden to enter the house for years, she later fell upon hard times, and, childless, came to live with us. My parents looked after her to the very end.

Of the three daughters, my mother made the best marriage, or so it would seem. Privately, she may have thought otherwise. For one thing, she barely understood her mother-in-law, who persisted in speaking her impenetrable Wakayama dialect. For another, she had been obliged to adjust to a completely new way of life and give up her own interests, since my father, a man of irreproachable rectitude, frowned on anything that had to do with the arts. Two splendid samisen[xiv] she had brought as part of her dowry hung untouched in the storeroom; dancing was out of the question. Deprived of what she most enjoyed, she could not have found married life easy.

To make matters worse, my father was extremely devoted to his mother. Before leaving for work in the morning, and again on returning home, he would go straight to her room, bow down on the tatami floor, and pay his respects. Since his mother came first in all things, my mother must have been in constant fear of doing something wrong. And then, there was my father's sister—the "little mother-in-law"—who was sunny and outgoing but doubtless difficult in her own way. As was expected of women of her generation, my mother made great efforts to deny rather than express herself. My father,

---

xiv A three-stringed instrument played with a plectrum like a banjo.

I am sure, appreciated his docile, virtuous young wife. Among the items left by my parents is a handbook for the tea ceremony that my father copied for my mother. Bound by silk thread, the worn cover bears the words, "Sixteen Rules for the Tea Ceremony; Shelf for Tea Utensils." Inside, the pages of fine Mino paper are covered with my father's precise brushstrokes, the margins illustrated with pictures copied from the original. The last page reads, "Copied on the fifteenth day of September, 1892." Each time I take it out, I like to picture my parents in my mind's eye—my father, full of tenderness for his young wife; my mother, happy in his affection.

My mother was a classic Edo beauty, small-boned and refined. With her thin, well-shaped nose and slender, pale face, she was much better looking than her mother, whom I know only from a photo. By the time I was born, my maternal grandparents had already died, and Iijima Teian, my mother's adoptive brother, had succeeded to the family profession. Once or twice a year, I went with my mother to visit her family home and spent the hours watching the helpers chop and grind the medicinal herbs. Compared to our home, which was an urban middle-class dwelling with many Western trappings, their house was old-fashioned and gloomy. I remember being startled by the sight of Teian's wife sitting by a hibachi and puffing away on a long-stemmed metal pipe.

The future of traditional medicine was uncertain, so Teian sold most of the property to build a clinic that offered both traditional and modern medicine. Plans went awry, and when I knew him, he was rather unsuccessfully practicing medicine of the old school. Teian was unusually well-built, gentle, and good-looking, with a pale face framed by dark hair. It was rumored that he received a constant flow of love letters from women in the neighborhood. Teian never forgave himself for losing the family property. He started drinking heavily and died of heart disease in his forties, leaving behind four children. My father, with his strong sense of family duty, took in the oldest son and daughter and made sure that they received a proper education. But this happened much later, when I was in high school.

◎ ◎ ◎ ◎ ◎

Life at home was quiet and orderly, with not a harsh word spoken, not a voice raised. My mother took pride in keeping a neat house. Dressed in a kimono of soft silk and a black everyday obi casually tied with the ends loose, she moved about with the grace of a trained dancer, instructing the maid and wet nurse in her clear, bright voice. She was not a tireless worker like my grandmother, but fastidious, in the true Tokyo manner. Before guests arrived—the parlor, needless to say, was immaculate—she always checked herself in front of the mirror.

Her concern for personal appearance extended to the children and even the maids. She also tended to stress form for form's sake. My grandmother was the exact opposite. A commoner to the core, she thought nothing of stripping herself to the waist in hot weather. My mother found this highly distasteful but could hardly complain. Again, when we went out, my grandmother always carried me piggyback, but this was beneath my mother's dignity. Later, when I was old enough to walk on my own, my grandmother and I walked everywhere—I have her to thank for my sturdy legs—whereas my mother always hired a rickshaw.

Kiyo, my sister's wet nurse, accompanied us whenever our grandmother took us out. Bursting with health, she had been hired because of her abundant breast milk. She wore her luxuriant black hair swept up in an ichōgaeshi, and her face, though faintly pockmarked, had a fresh, clean look, accented with a dab of bright red lipstick in the center of her lips. She came from the old downtown district, so in a sense she was an outsider, but she was cheerful, openhearted, and liked by everyone. My sister refused to let her out of her sight and would go looking for her, wailing if she disappeared for a minute. Kiyo stayed with us for a long time; in fact, my sister was still nursing at age four. My mother's milk was thin, so I was weaned early, though I remember sharing Kiyo's milk from time to time.

My father's younger sister Ai was like my grandmother, sunny and constantly on the go. Too absorbed in her classes and social life, she paid little attention to her nieces. She attended a girls' high school in Sanban-chō that had Buddhist affiliations and was headed by a famous priest called Shimaji Mokurai. After graduation, she took lessons in knitting and sewing at the same school my mother had attended and made dresses for my sister and me. On the very rare occasions when someone spoke loudly, it was usually Aunt Ai arguing with my grandmother.

My father called my sister and me Taka-kō and Haru-kō.[xv] My mother called us Neh-chan and Haru-chan, as did our grandmother.[xvi] We called our parents Ototchan and Kā-chan; Grandmother was Obā-chan. In high school, we switched to Otō-san and Okā-san, more formal terms not in wide use earlier.

My father seemed to be especially fond of me, his youngest, and played with me whenever he was free. Getting out a go board, he would say, "How

---

[xv] The "kō" for Taka-kō and Haru-kō is not the "ko" for "child" used in many girls' names, but the "kō" for "lord," as in Itō Hirobumi-kō (Prince Itō Hirobumi). This playful use of the term is like a Western father calling his daughter "Little Princess."

[xvi] Diminutive for the suffix *san. Neh* is a variation of *ane,* or older sister.

about it, Haru-kō?" and teach me how to play Five in a Row. My mother sometimes joined us, though she preferred to play *shōgi*[xvii] with my father. Having learned to play as a young girl, she was proud of her skills and often beat him. She hated losing and would insist on playing until she won. My sister and I would watch them, ignorant of the rules but amused to see our ordinarily submissive mother change into another person as she gave vent to her accumulated frustrations. At the end of the game, my father would say, "Mommy won, Mommy won, that's all for today," and, in a good mood, put away the pieces. He also taught my sister and me how to play 21 and Old Maid. During the New Year holidays, we played cards for hours, although as I think back, I wonder how my father found the time.

In winter, my sister and I sat by the hibachi or the Western-style stove and listened to our father tell stories. I have forgotten most of them, but they were usually set in a Western country—Grimm's fairy tales, Aesop's fables about the stupid donkey or the greedy dog, the story about William Tell. Not only was he an accomplished raconteur, he also seemed to have an endless fund of stories. My mother's stories were mostly anecdotes—about the time she was frightened when forces loyal to the Tokugawa shogunate fought against government troops at Ueno, or about the woman who'd been tricked by a fox lying in wait under a tree in front of Lord Abe's residence in Nishikata-machi. I believe the tree is still standing.

As a struggling young student, my father had had little time for relaxation of any sort, but now he practiced archery, went fishing, and, accompanied by a guide and dog, hunted rabbits in the Chichibu Mountains. On display in his study were stuffed specimens of several animals he had caught—a woodpecker, a flycatcher, and something I found particularly gruesome, a flying squirrel with its limbs stretched out, as if in midair. In fact, one of the maidservants claimed that the flying squirrel had crawled up her leg when she was trying to light the kitchen hearth. No amount of explaining by my mother would change her mind, and she finally left us.

Then, odd as it may seem, my father liked to knit. My mother had taught him, of course, but in his spare time, he would take out four metal needles and knit his own socks. Thorough and meticulous by nature, he used an especially strong yarn called Scotch and reinforced the heels and toes with double yarn. One winter, he noticed my chapped hands and made a pair of red mittens with white horizontal stripes and openings for the fingertips. As he handed them to me, he said with a smile that I was not to tell anyone at school that he had made them. Immensely pleased, I wore them all the time. In comparison

---

[xvii] A board game like chess.

to my mother's stitches, which were loose and droopy, my father's were even and dense; one could be certain that the things he made would never lose their shape. He also darned his fishing nets, using a small bamboo needle and applying a coat of persimmon juice afterward [to prevent the threads from decomposing].

My father had several nicknames for me. One was "Red-faced Kintoki" because I not only was chubby as a baby but also had ruddy skin.[xviii] Another was "Blowfish," because I would purse my lips and pout whenever I was out of sorts. If we happened to see a lantern in the shape of a blowfish at a shrine fair, he would immediately point to it and say, "Oh look, there's Haru-kō."

My sister Taka was a child in every sense of the word, brimming with energy and singing lustily in a loud voice. In contrast, I was withdrawn and as close-mouthed as a clam. Unable to talk back, I was always the loser in fights. I even have a memento of one of our fights—a faint mark on my forehead made by scissors. I wonder—was she trying to cut my bangs?

In other respects, too, we were poles apart. I was a poor eater; barely able to finish half of my mid-afternoon snack, I would give the rest to my sister. She almost never became sick, while I frequently came down with a fever, sometimes as high as 102 degrees. A doctor would be sent for immediately, and after he administered an enema, I would quickly recover, as though nothing had happened. Also, my sister was emotional and short-tempered, talkative and outgoing, a consequence of having been born in the Year of the Rooster, according to my grandmother. I was born in the Year of the Dog, and by the same reasoning lacked charm and was unsociable. As a result, I was cautioned to be particularly careful. Whatever the explanation, my sister and I were completely different in both character and temperament.

I suffered from headaches, too. "A headache at your age? How impertinent!" The family would either laugh at me or dismiss it as something I had inherited from my father. In retrospect, I think my headaches may have been caused by our mostly Western-style food, which had an excess of animal protein, though my sister seems not to have been affected. We had a steady diet of milk, eggs, and fish, and very few vegetables, which were supposedly difficult to digest because of their high fiber content. Apples and tangerines were about the only fruit we ate, aside from pears, which we merely sucked for the juice. Watermelon and other members of the melon family were strictly forbidden to children on the grounds that they caused cholera.

I was a well-behaved child, but I could be stubborn. One of my tricks was to run away when my mother threatened to lock me up in the parlor for

---

[xviii] A mythic child-hero born with reddish-brown skin and superhuman strength.

being naughty. Just as she was about to turn the key to the door, I would say, "I have to go to the toilet," duck under her arm, and take off. Perhaps I was not as shy as everyone thought. My motor skills were excellent, and later, at school, I was able to skip rope, race, bounce a ball, twirl a top, and juggle beanbags as well as the other children, despite being smaller and less developed. I was always in a good mood, but once I started crying, I apparently gave the family a hard time.

The only time I went out with my mother was to visit her family. I do not remember going with her anywhere else. In deference to her husband and mother-in-law, she seldom went out on her own, and besides, she was probably reluctant to leave the maid in charge of the house. When she did go out, it was usually to attend meetings of the Greater Japan Women's Education Society. On rare occasions, my mother went with my grandmother and Aunt Ai to shop for kimono. The more reputable stores at the time were Echigoya in Suruga-chō, Amazakeya in Ichigayamitsuke, Isetan in Kanda Matsuzumi-chō, and Matsuzakaya in Ueno. I sometimes went along. As I remember, Echigoya (the present Mitsukoshi) had a broad exterior and just inside the entrance, there was a large room where the clerks conducted business on the tatami floor. On one visit, we were led to a separate room and served a delicious meal after we had finished shopping, but this was probably special for the sale season.

Sundays were for family outings, now common enough but considered unusual at the time. Our destination varied according to the season: Ueno Zoo, the amusement center in Asakusa Park, Koishikawa Botanical Garden, the chrysanthemum display at Dangozaka. We walked until we were exhausted, and took a rickshaw the rest of the way. I was delighted when my parents hired a two-passenger vehicle that enabled me to sit on my mother's lap with my sister at her side. We also went to buy plants at shrine fairs—those close by were at the Nishichi Fudōsan Temple and Hitotsu no [Yotsugi no] Inari, and those farther off, at Bishamonten in Ushigome Kagurazaka. Now and then, after supper, we walked to the Trade Exhibition Hall, on this side of Manaita Bridge, to buy toys and stationery. At first, I had no trouble keeping up with rest of the family, but after a while, I came to a dead stop in the middle of the street. "What's the matter, tired?" my father would ask. "I'm not walking," I would declare and refuse to take another step. "Come on, it's only a little bit more." My father would try to put me in a good mood, but to no avail. Once I made up my mind, nothing on earth could budge me, and in the end my father had to carry me until I consented to walk again.

Diagonally across from the Lower Shrine at Yasukuni was a pet shop that sold songbirds, mynahs, parrots, and occasionally, pugs and monkeys. We could hear the parrots calling out people's names. Next to the shop was the

Suzuki Photography Studio, an impressive Western structure whose proprietor was said to have taken pictures of the empress, the crown prince, and other illustrious people.

At home, my sister and I amused ourselves with games our mother taught us: juggling beanbags, bouncing a ball, playing *ohajiki*,[xix] stringing beads, folding origami, and paper dolls. My mother usually left us alone, but when I was sick, she sat by the bed and fashioned bracelets and rings with beads of many colors. This was to keep me company, of course, but I think she enjoyed herself, too.

My mother was very clever with her hands and often spent her spare time sitting at the embroidery frame set up in her room. She hemmed and embroidered all her kimono half-collars and handkerchiefs, as well as her sister-in-law's. Displayed in her room was her graduation project at the trade school, a large, framed embroidery of a pair of male and female golden pheasants. But when it came to making paper dolls, no one could match Kiyo. As we watched in awe, she deftly created the head on the end of a chopstick with a piece of cotton and inserted it into a neatly folded sheet of patterned paper. My sister and I always divided the finished products equally.

Another cherished memory from childhood is a secret I shared with my sister. A black wooden fence separated the garden in back from the *yose* entertainment hall behind us. If we peered through a knothole or gap in the slats, we could see some of the performances. In one magic show, a prettily made-up girl was enclosed in a large wooden box, which was then covered with a lid and pierced repeatedly with a long spear. The magician opened the box and the girl emerged unscathed. We also saw men spinning tops in the style of the Matsui Gensui school and a puppet show by performers of the Yūki family.

There were also various dramatic scenes. One was from the act in the Kabuki play, *An Exemplary Tale of Womanly Virtue,* in which Omiwa goes to the villain Iruka's mansion to look for her lover and is killed. Another was a reenactment of the eruption of Mount Bandai in 1888. Against a backdrop of plumes of fiery smoke, people ran back and forth across the stage, one woman clutching a headless child. I was terrified.

Kiyo shared our secret. In fact, in all likelihood, she was the one who suggested we take a peek in the first place. Brought up in downtown Tokyo, she was fond of yose, plays, and other entertainments. She wanted to take us next door, but my father would not allow it, so she had probably come up with the idea.

[xix] A game like marbles.

We had a pond in the garden, barely 6 feet square but large enough for my sister and me to float our paper dolls on pieces of board. One day I tossed in a board I had found in the storage room and jumped on it. The board sank to the bottom and I was thoroughly drenched. My sister laughed: "Haru-chan, how can you be so stupid!"

The pond was also home to the tadpoles we had scooped out of the pond at the Lower Shrine. They soon turned into tiny baby frogs, which hopped around the garden, some with their tails still attached. I still happily recall that moment of great excitement.

Kindergarten

I started kindergarten at Fujimi Elementary School in Fujimi-chō in the spring of 1890; I was five. My sister had started the previous year. Our grandmother accompanied us at first, but later we went on our own, cutting through the riding grounds of Yasukuni Shrine. From kindergarten through high school, my sister and I went to school together each day. We wore Western clothes to school—matching dresses, shoes, and hats—and for more formal occasions, such as national holidays, kimono of Yūzen *crepe de chine* and purple satin *hakama*.[xx] But even when we dressed in kimono, we always wore laced-up leather shoes and felt hats with narrow brims, a bizarre combination but in line with the prevailing tendency to blend East and West. Apart from a girl whose father owned a Western-style restaurant called Fujimiken and another girl called Takahashi Olga, whose mother was German, we were the only students to wear Western clothes.

The kindergarten was divided into three classes. The teachers, all of them young and single, wore kimono of understated design, dispensed with hakama, and arranged their hair in a simple Western style.

The first songs we learned in kindergarten were:

> Around goes the pinwheel, turning with the wind.
> Never stopping, never stopping, round and round it goes.
> Around goes the water mill, turning with the water.
> Never stopping, never stopping, round and round it goes.
>
> It's opened, it's opened,
> Oh, what is opened?

[xx] A divided skirt worn over a kimono.

The lotus flower is opened.
But the moment it opened,
It closed up again.
It's closed, it's closed,
Oh, what is closed?
The lotus flower is closed.
But the moment it closed,
It opened up again.

We held hands as we sang, going around in circles. By the 1920s, when my own children attended kindergarten, the repertoire of children's songs had vastly expanded, but in the late 1880s and early '90s, the number of songs was still limited. Some of the other songs I remember from childhood are: "Is It Mist, or Is It a Cloud?" "Butterfly, Butterfly," and "Spring, with Its Brocade of Flowers." But these I learned in elementary school, from a songbook bound in silk thread that may have been the first one put out by the Ministry of Education.

Besides songs and games, we also learned how to make things. Much of this, I believe, was Froebel's influence.[xxi] We constructed things with blocks and boards; folded origami; cut, pasted, and wove strips of colored paper in various designs; made little objects with beans and straw. For some reason, we were never taught how to draw.

A loner to begin with, I felt even more shy and withdrawn when participating in these group activities. While the others played happily together, I looked on from a corner. I did not mind or feel particularly lonely; I was simply not interested in playing with the other children. At home, too, I disliked having grown-ups hover over me and preferred being alone. But in kindergarten, everyone was expected to join in. And more than anything, I dreaded having to perform in front of others.

I am sure I was shy from birth, but there was another reason—my inability to speak loudly because of the minor impairment of my vocal cords. Unable to sing lustily like my classmates, I hated singing. Also, like my mother, I was slight of build, and much smaller and frailer than my classmates. In contrast, Takahashi Olga was big, healthy-looking, and good-natured, though not especially pretty. She brought her lunch in a basket, which always included fruit—an apple, persimmon, or tangerine. I envied her.

I was curious about her, so one day, on the way home—she lived close to school—I stopped by for a visit. The house was Western-style, not too large

---

[xxi] Friedrich Froebel (1782–1852), German founder of kindergarten education who stressed self-generated activity and play.

but with simple, clean lines. (I think her father was a university professor.) Her mother brought out some homemade cookies and started talking to us, but all of a sudden, without warning, she slapped her big hands on both of our heads and pushed us together. We happened to be standing, and I barely reached Olga's shoulders. Her mother burst out laughing, evidently finding this funny. I was nonplussed and shocked, too, that a mother could be so physically strong and rough. I never went to Olga's house again.

Some of my other classmates were Uehara Kise, who later became a close friend in high school; Yanagita Takako, who married [the eminent folklorist] Yanagita Kunio; and the granddaughter of [the politician] Tani Kanjō.

There was a girl in my sister's class who was fat and had a round face. Just once, I went with my sister to her house in Ichiban-chō. I learned later that she was the daughter of the Protestant minister Uemura Masahisa, which would mean that Uemura Tamaki [, the famous opera singer,] was her elder sister.

Some fifty years later, at a wake for Yamada Kakichi, I happened to see Yamashita Sensei, one of my teachers in kindergarten. She recognized me at once, and said that on the occasion of her mother's sixtieth birthday, my grandmother had collected pieces of silk cloth from the parents and sewed a jacket as a gift.[xxii] In spite of her age, Sensei served on the local board of education; she was still dedicated to the education of small children.

Elementary School

My birthday came before April 1, and [under the existing regulations,] I entered Fujimi Elementary School at age seven.[xxiii] Unlike schoolchildren today, we had no homework, nor did we prepare or review our lessons. At most, we practiced calligraphy, making a fair copy of what we had learned at school. My mother rarely said a word about schoolwork, but on one point she was adamant: women, she insisted, must have good handwriting. For practice we used special paper, writing with water instead of India ink, and using the same paper as soon as the writing dried. Absorbed in play one day, my sister and I completely forgot about our calligraphy, and as punishment were ordered to trim the morning glory vines on the back fence.

---

xxii The completion of five zodiacal cycles, that is to say, a person's sixtieth birthday, is considered a cause for celebration; a red sleeveless jacket like a child's is worn to signify the beginning of a new cycle.

xxiii Then, as now, children born before April 1 are allowed to enter school a year earlier. In 1892, the year Raichō entered elementary school, attendance for school-age children was 36.5 percent for girls and 71.5 percent for boys.

I have before me a copy, or rather, a photo of a letter I wrote in calligraphy class. Addressed to a classmate's mother, it is written on two sheets of paper lined like the grid on a go board and marked "For the use of the second grade, Fujimi Elementary School." The letter is in the old epistolary style: "This is to inquire about your recent state of health. I entreat you to take good care of yourself. The newspaper you requested has been forwarded to you. Please read it at your leisure." This was a classroom exercise, of course, but I am amazed that a child of eight was able to write like this. Times have changed indeed.

The principal's name was Yamazaki. A remote presence, he had almost no contact with the students. My teacher, Takahashi Sensei, was a man. All the other teachers were women, but for some reason this middle-aged man had been assigned to the first grade. I could not warm up to him, since even to a child like me he seemed listless in speech and movement. Classes were easy but school was boring. My grades were uniformly good. I frequently helped the other children, in particular, a pale, sickly girl called Okumura, who sat in front of me and needed help in arithmetic. Her father owned a printing shop, and as a token of her appreciation, she gave me a packet of assorted paper, some brightly colored, other sheets glossy white or flecked with gold or silver.

My memories of elementary school have dimmed over the years, but my activities on the way home have remained fresh in my mind. I always went to school directly, but after classes, I would dawdle on the riding grounds at the Lower Shrine and look for grasshoppers and crickets in the tall grass or inspect the bugs that had fallen down from the lampposts. Then there were the stalls on the street that ran through the center of the shrine grounds. Feast day or not, hawkers and entertainers plied their trades. There was an old man who drew pictures on the ground near the cannons in front of the bronze statue of Ōmura Masujirō. Scooping up a handful of colored sand—red, blue, green, and yellow—he would let it sift through his fingers and draw a cartoonlike picture, all the while keeping up a steady patter. He did this with the utmost ease, and whenever someone tossed him a coin or two, he would erase the picture and start all over again. There was another man who engaged in elaborate swordplay to entice passersby into buying a salve that supposedly stopped toothaches or eased the pain, should extraction become necessary.

I have mentioned catching tadpoles in the pond at the Lower Shrine. In summer I also caught cicadas. Perched high up in the branches of the ancient cherry trees and the same color as the bark, they were difficult to catch. I would hit the trunk with all my might, hoping some would fall down, but they would drone on unperturbed. A classmate who lived several doors down the street—her father was a policeman—invited me to go with her to catch cicadas. Her mother volunteered to come with us and showed me a long stick covered with birdlime at the tip. "Just take a look, young miss," she said. "We should be able to catch a lot with this." My mother, however, refused to let me go. In her opinion, catching cicadas was strictly for boys.

The shrine was thus very much a part of my childhood, more so than school. The enormous black bronze *torii* at the main entrance, each pillar of which was at least 12 feet in circumference and 46 feet high, must have made a deep impression on me. According to family lore, whenever I heard of something big, I would say, "But is it as big as the torii at Yasukuni?"

I also saw my first Noh play and sumo match at the shrine. The play was held at night in the field behind the main shrine, the stage illumined by blazing pine branches. One of the performers kept throwing paper streamers onto the floor, so the play was probably *Earth Spider*. Horse races were also held at the shrine, but since I do not recall any, I was probably too timid to go. I was afraid of crowds, and for good reason. Sometime earlier, my grandmother and I had gone to a fair at the shrine, and just as we left the grounds, we ran into a mob of people on a narrow side street. My clogs were lost in the crush, I was certain I would be trampled, and my grandmother kept shouting, "Please don't push, there's a child here!" A policeman finally came to our rescue, but the frightening experience, together with the memory of fireworks, has left me with a lifelong aversion to crowds.

⊚ ⊚ ⊚ ⊚ ⊚

In 1894, when I was in third grade, we moved to Hongō Komagome Akebono-chō and I transferred to Seishi Elementary School in Nishikata-machi. The old neighborhood had become crowded with new houses, many of them geisha houses and cheap rooming houses for students. In fact, the area was now known as Geisha Town, and my father had presumably decided to move the family to a more peaceful and wholesome environment.

A minor incident may have also contributed to his decision. A large two-story rooming house had been built on the other side of the fence on the northern edge of our property, and since one of the windows directly faced a window on our second floor, my sister and I could see right into the room. We happened to be gazing idly out of the window one day when a lodger tossed us an empty cigarette pack, the "Sunrise" or "Pinhead" brand. Much to our delight, there was a glossy print of a half-naked Western beauty inside the pack. Incidents of a similar nature followed, and when we finally told our mother, we were soundly scolded.

There was another reason for moving to a less congested area: Tokyo had been badly jolted during the Great Nōbi Earthquake two or three years earlier, and we had been obliged to seek refuge on the shrine grounds. But the most compelling reason no doubt was my father's decision to teach German part-time at the First Higher School, which had relocated to Komagome Oiwake-chō.

The house in Sanban-chō had been taken apart and reassembled on the property, some 600 tsubo of land that had been cleared of tea bushes. Beyond, tea fields stretched as far as the eye could see. The layout of the house remained the same: on the south side was the front hall, the parlor with its big Western-style windows, the bedroom that also served as my mother's sitting room, my grandmother's Japanese-style room, the toilet, and the bath-room. On the north side was a room for a live-in student, my father's study, the storeroom, the dining room, the kitchen, and the maid's room. On the second floor was the Japanese-style room. With no children's room to speak of, my sister and I put our desks and school things in a tiny room adjoining the storeroom.

The yard in front of the house was enclosed by a hedge and bamboo fence and had a miniature rock garden and several maple trees. The back yard was planted with persimmon, peach, and plum trees and had a small flower gar-den at one end. In one corner was a mound of earth for my father to practice archery on. The rest of the property was used to grow vegetables and the tea bushes that had been left to make tea for our own use.

Out in the countryside, it was not unusual to see pheasants, turtledoves, and other wild birds foraging for food. On summer nights we heard the haunting hoot of the owl, unseen and yet so close. Huge, ungainly bullfrogs lurked here and there. Grasshoppers and crickets, which we had to buy in the city, came uninvited into the house and sang all night outside the mos-quito net. I even discovered an *aodaishō* snake stretched out on the sill of the toilet window. I was startled, but after several encounters, became quite used to it.

Back at the house in Sanban-chō, we had awakened to the sound of bugles coming from the Konoe regimental headquarters at Takebashi. Here, we woke to strange shrill cries that pierced the early morning air. We wondered what they could be, but then learned that this was the sound of cranes being fed at Rikugien, the estate of [the industrialist] Iwasaki Yatarō. Enchanted with my new surroundings, I scarcely thought of the grounds at Yasukuni Shrine, much less of my friends at the old school.

The vegetable patch was my grandmother's domain. She knew a great deal about farming and worked long hours with the maid, who came from a farm-ing family in Nerima. For backbreaking work like pulling out the roots of tea bushes, she hired an old farmer. My sister and I joined her now and then, hap-pily weeding, thinning out *daikon* and other greens, getting rid of insects, and gathering the season's harvest. My grandmother also grew sesame and azuki beans. The sesame plants bore pretty, purplish pink blossoms, but the leaves were often infested with caterpillars—fat, mottled, and unspeakably repulsive. Everyone else was squeamish, so I took on the job of getting rid of these and felt quite pleased with myself.

I sometimes accompanied my grandmother to a seed shop in Ōji Asukayama. She was knowledgeable about seeds, too—what to plant, where, and when—which leads me to believe that she came from peasant stock and had grown up in the countryside and not the castle town of Wakayama. Only a person with experience could have handled a hoe with her skill.

With the coming of summer, we could hear the voices of women picking tea leaves in the nearby fields. At our house, too, everyone helped, competing to see who could pick the most. We piled the leaves on straw mats spread out on the earthen kitchen floor, and when we had a sufficient quantity, a professional came to sort the leaves into three grades and roast them. The maid sometimes roasted the tough leftover leaves for everyday use. Summer was also the season for strawberries. We picked these by the basket day after day. Few people ate strawberries at the time, so my mother made jam, which she stored in glass jars.

On Sundays in autumn and winter, my father went hunting. Setting out early with his gun, he would roam the fields near Ōji and Akabane and return before dark with his catch—usually a pheasant, a brace of turtledoves, and several brown-eared bulbuls.

My mother was the only one who seemed out of place in the new surroundings. She disliked gardening and was little inclined to help out, since soiling her hands and feet with dirt probably went against her nature. As before, she paid scrupulous attention to her personal appearance and made sure that her children observed the rules of etiquette. Even in the countryside, it was important to open and close the doors quietly, line up one's clogs neatly in the entryway, and eat in the prescribed manner.

Seishi Elementary School

My new school was a complete change from my old school in Sanban-chō. At the old school, the teachers had mainly been women. Now, they were all men, except for the sewing teacher, who was an elderly woman with a rust-colored complexion, an abundance of wrinkles, and hair pulled back in a tight little bun. I was disappointed by her looks, but when I took her class, she praised me effusively, saying I was more than ready to sew a lined kimono. I was her pet. In contrast to the old school, where the atmosphere was progressive and urban middle-class, the school at Akebono-chō was more working-class, simple and old-fashioned, if somewhat lacking in refinement.

My teacher Nikaidō Sensei was a sturdy-looking young man of medium height with dark skin and a prominent nose. When he took attendance, he read our names without the polite ending "san," and if anyone failed to respond with a vigorous "yes," he would reprimand the child, or worse, make the student stand in the hallway. Since I had a small voice, it was a torment for me to answer. Also, each time I answered a question, he would tell me to speak up. So after a while, I stopped raising my hand even when I knew the answer and regretted more than ever my inability to speak clearly.

Cleaning the classroom was part of the daily routine. We took turns doing this, straightening the desks and chairs and getting down on our hands and knees to mop the floor with wet rags. In winter, the only source of heat was a small hibachi in the corner, and in dictation class, our fingers were often too numb to hold a pencil. The school had no indoor gym or auditorium large enough to hold all the students, so on national holidays, ceremonies would be held outside on the playground, even in the middle of winter. Exposed to the biting wind, we would stand at attention, our heads bowed, our toes freezing, as the principal read aloud the Imperial Rescript on Education.[xxiv] We endured this as a matter of course and would never have dreamed of complaining. At the conclusion of the ceremony, we always sang an anthem. [On November 3,] it would be "On this most auspicious day His Majesty was born…" or [on February 11,] "Mount Takachiho, its peak wreathed in clouds.…" The teachers then distributed red and white rice cakes and we headed happily home.

Field Day was held at nearby Asukayama. The entire school also went on hikes, usually from Asukayama to the Takino River or Dōkanyama, and once in while farther afield to the ferry crossing at the Arakawa River. For these excursions, we packed our lunch boxes with sushi rolls with sweetened gourd strips tucked inside, or rice balls with a pickled plum in the center and bonito flakes sprinkled on top. As a rule we did not take sweets, though just once the school gave us sweet buns as a treat.

The principal at my old school had always worn a black suit and neatly parted his hair in the middle. In contrast, the principal at Seishi—his name was Naruse—wore his hair clipped short and dressed in a kimono, a hakama

---

[xxiv] Edict issued in 1890 by Emperor Meiji. Regarded as the basic guideline on educational policy until the end of World War II, it stressed traditional virtues such as loyalty to the emperor, love of country, filial piety, and respect for elders. The rescript was committed to memory by all schoolchildren and read aloud by school principals on national holidays.

[xxv] A short jacket worn over a kimono.

of striped Kokura cotton, and a black cotton *haori*[xxv] dyed with his family crest on the back. I think he was already quite old.

School was easy. I almost never opened my books and was always at the head of my class, dropping to second place only once, when I received a bad grade in singing. On the way home one day, I peeked at my report card. The teacher had written, "It has come to my attention that the child avoids talking with her classmates and seems to dislike playing with them. You would be well advised to talk to her about this." I burst into tears and wished I didn't have to show it to my parents. At home, my father tried to console me: "It's nothing to cry about." But the tears kept flowing, and the next day, too embarrassed to show up with my eyes swollen, I stayed at home.

As I reflect on it now, I realize that Nikaidō Sensei was the first person in my life to see into my character—my preference for solitude and for seeking freedom within an inner world. But at the time I resented being scolded for not speaking in a louder voice. I only gradually realized that he liked me and was genuinely concerned about my welfare. In time I grew to like my new school, too.

I noticed the children at school liked to suck on strips of cinnamon bark. Mint was another popular flavor. Before classes, I would see them lining up at a stationery store to buy small bundles of cinnamon bark, tiny glass tubes filled with cinnamon or mint water, or pieces of rice paper saturated with the same liquid. Swapping their purchases during recess also seemed to be part of the fun.

The girls played much the same games as they did at the old school—oha-jiki, juggling beanbags, bouncing balls—but here, they played squatting on the hallway floor. I excelled at all of these, but was unable to juggle three beanbags at the same time. Determined to master this, I practiced on my way to school and back, and once, to my mother's great displeasure, took the bags out of my kimono sleeve and started throwing them up in the air while we were eating.

Making our own beanbags was also a great pleasure. My sister and I scoured the house for pieces of cloth and sorted them into two piles according to size and shape—one to make bags for ordinary use, the other for special occasions. Impatient by nature, my sister sewed quickly, with big, uneven stitches. I was slow but careful, my seams firm and straight, my beanbags better shaped. I should mention that one event on Field Day involved running and juggling beanbags at the same time.

For bouncing games we used small rubber balls. In one game, you were supposed to bounce a ball and quickly pass your other hand over it before it bounced back. Instead of passing your hand, you could swing your leg, but this we never tried. We wore kimonos, and my mother would have disapproved of such tomboyish behavior [in our ladylike attire].

We also liked making our own balls. For this, we needed rubber balloons, which cost from half a sen to 10 sen and came in all sizes and colors. We blew one up to a suitable size, wrapped it with a thin layer of cotton, covered the entire surface with double-twisted white thread, and as a final touch, decorated it with threads of different colors. Impatient to try out my new ball, I would run to the parlor—the room with the highest ceiling in the house—bounce it with all my might, and twirl myself around, shouting, "Go around once!" before it came down. I then made another turn and shouted, "Go around twice!" and spent many happy hours playing by myself.

Another game we played required much manual dexterity. It involved holding a bundle of about 10 bamboo sticks—each polished smooth and measuring about 7 by 1/3 inches—in the palm of your hand, next flicking your wrist so that the sticks all landed on the back of the hand, and then carefully sliding them one by one, right side up, onto the tatami. Whoever did this without any mishap received a "bonus" and was allowed to continue until she made a mistake. Once you learned the trick, it was surprisingly easy. I was good at this, though my small hands were a distinct disadvantage.

I also played "Hiding Rubbish," a perfect game for little girls. When a friend came to play, we took turns hiding tiny pieces of rubbish in the cracks of the shingled fence in the front yard. The other person had to find these pieces, but I soon discovered that it was better to rely on instinct than on vision, and to this day, I have a knack for finding lost objects.

The Sino-Japanese War

The war with China began [in July 1894], and the country was swept up into a military fervor: children sang patriotic songs—"Smite them, punish them, down with the Chinese!"—extra editions of newspapers announcing victories were sold to the incessant jangle of little bells, and victory parades were hastily organized. At school, we were kept informed of developments on the front, but even so, we were stunned to hear that our own teacher had been drafted. For a time Nikaidō Sensei did not come to school, but one day, to our great surprise, he appeared before us resplendent in his Konoe Imperial Guard uniform. He had probably been called up for short-term duty to teach the other soldiers. The children ran up with shouts of joy and clung to him in excitement. I was happy to see him, too, but as usual, I stayed back and watched from a distance.

I wanted to know more about the war, but as there was no reading matter for children at the time, I glanced through *Illustrated Customs* (*Fūzoku gahō*), a magazine my parents regularly purchased. I looked mainly at the illustrations, which were undoubtedly products of the artist's imagination and fre-

quently quite ridiculous. I remember one cartoon of a Japanese soldier pulling the pigtail of a hapless Chinese soldier.

After the war, the teacher talked to us about the return of the Liaodong
Peninsula. In simple terms we could understand, he explained at length how,
despite its victory, Japan had been forced by Russia, Britain, and France to
return its rightful acquisition. Turning to the blackboard, he wrote in large
characters, "Sleep on firewood, lick the liver of bear."[xxvi] He erased the
words immediately, but even now they are etched in my memory. Some of
the phrases he used, like "pressure from world powers" and "Western aggression in Asia," were beyond our comprehension, but we listened intently and
resolved in our hearts that, come what may, we would rise to the defense of
our country. For a long time afterward, a map of East Asia with the Liaodong
Peninsula colored in red hung on the classroom wall.

I remember the war with China far more vividly than the war with Russia [,
which took place nine years later]. This was no doubt because I was still a child,
innocent and impressionable, but Sensei may have influenced me. In any event,
the forced return of the Liaodong Peninsula was a great shock to the Japanese
and caused much indignation. Still, for the first time in its history, Japan had
fought a war against a foreign power, an important one at that, and won. People
today would be hard pressed to imagine our joy and pride at the time.

One of our family possessions is a scroll with a poem written by Itō Hirobumi. Inscribed to my father, the scroll is dated October 31, 1895, the day
the Chinese paid the Japanese delegates in London the first installment of
their war indemnities. That very same day, Viscount Watanabe, my father's
superior at the Audit Board, invited Prime Minister Itō, the army and navy
ministers, and other officials to the Kōyōkan in Shiba to give a report on war
expenditures. At the banquet afterward, my father asked Itō to write something for him.

As my father recalled, Itō was in the best of moods. "The prime minister
immediately called for a brush and inkstone, and after I unrolled the paper,
he told me to hold it steady and in one flourish finished writing the poem." Itō
had evidently composed the poem in his youth when he was plotting to over-
throw the Tokugawa shogunate. The large characters are brushed in faint ink.
The first line says, "A spirit of daring pervades the skies" and ends "A hero is
present in this company." One can easily imagine the scene—Itō jubilant, his
subordinates no less elated, everyone toasting and congratulating one another.

[xxvi] *Gashin shōtan*, a phrase based on the story of two rival rulers of ancient China who underwent great
hardships and privations in preparation for taking revenge on each other. The teacher was telling the
students that Japan would one day have its revenge on the interfering powers.

No one, I suppose, gave a thought to the dead, the wounded, or the grieving women and children.

Other Childhood Memories

The Sakai, a former daimyo family, lived in Koishikawa Hara-machi, on the other side of the main street in Akebono-chō. Their son attended my school, and from time to time the children in the neighborhood were invited to a slide show in their garden. With a war going on, the slides inevitably showed battles, but some depicted earlier events, such as the Korean independence movement led by Kim Ok Kyun and the Tonghak Rebellion.[xxvii] One slide showed Ōtori Keisuke, the Japanese minister to Korea, speeding off to an unidentified destination in his carriage. I also saw my first movie at one of these gatherings. It was primitive, to say the least: a train pulled into a station, and then some of the passengers got off and walked on the platform.[xxviii] The children were nevertheless delighted.

I am sure these events were no more than a diversion for the head of the family, but even so, it was friendly of him to invite the commoners in the neighborhood. He must have been progressive, too, with egalitarian instincts, since he sent his son to the local school rather than to the Peers' School [for sons of the nobility]. But unlike the other children, "His Young Lordship," as he was addressed, commuted in a rickshaw. Dressed in a kimono of fine silk, with a white kerchief wrapped around his neck, he looked frail and was to the end a sad and solitary figure.

The boys at school wore cotton kimono woven with stripes or a *kasuri*[xxix] pattern and hakama for ceremonial occasions. The girls wore kimono made of double-stranded cotton or ordinary Meisen silk. In the lower grades they wore short *sanjaku-obi*, and in the higher grades half-width obi of regular length made of merino wool. The daughters of tradesmen tied their obi in a *kainoku-chi*, in the shape of a shell, while those from the more affluent families tied them in a *tateyanoji*, with a horizontal loop and then straight down. Everyone wore straw sandals with hemp soles.

[xxvii] Rebellion in 1894 fomented by the antiforeign reformist Tonghak sect in Choson dynasty Korea and used as a pretext by the Japanese for the Sino-Japanese War.

[xxviii] Almost certainly, Raichō saw *The Arrival of a Train*, an early documentary by the French filmmaker Louis Lumière.

[xxix] Tie-dyed cloth with a splashed pattern.

⊚ ⊚ ⊚ ⊚ ⊚

From summer through autumn, we looked forward to a series of shrine fairs. The closest was at Fuji Shrine, or "Ofuji-san," in Komagome. Farther away were those at Hakusan Shrine in Koishikawa, Nezu Shrine in Nishisuga-chō, and Forty-six Thousand Kannon in Dangozaka.[xxx]

My mother took great pains with our appearance for these occasions. The day before, she would comb our hair in front in straight bangs, then arrange the hair in a *momoware* or *chigomage*, with the hair on the side and back swept up into two big loops on the top of the head and held in place with strips of red and white paper. I had hair that was thin and limp and tended to frizz, so every night, before going to bed, she would straighten it with hot water, apply a thick, sticky liquid made of leaves of the *binnankazura* vine, and tie a cloth band around my head. She had done this ever since I started to wear my hair in bangs, and I simply hated it. "That's enough, that's enough," I would say, but no matter how much I protested, she refused to give in. My father and grandmother had wavy hair, but no one seemed to care about them; it was unfair. Without question, the nightly routine is one of the more unpleasant memories of my childhood.

On the day of the fair, my sister and I always wore matching kimono that my mother had ordered specially. One was an unlined crepe kimono patterned with pink *nadeshiko* flowers, another, a mauve crepe kimono with a vertical kasuri pattern. To complete the outfit, we wore a red merino wool obi and red lacquered clogs with red thongs. I suppose only a girl would remember such details.

As children we were strictly forbidden to handle money, but fairs were an exception. The amount was small, 30 sen at most, but we could hardly wait, since we were allowed to spend it any way we wanted. We usually bought seedpods of the *hōzuki* plant [which we blew up after puncturing a hole and taking out the seeds]; ornamental hairpins; barrettes; pouches; small, decorated boxes; patterned paper; and goldfish, which were actually *medaka*. Our purchases were quite ordinary, no different from those of other girls, but for us, exploring the stalls with our friends was pleasure enough.

There was one stall that sold trinkets unavailable elsewhere—hairpins topped off with glass beads, for example. The beads were filled with water, and a couple of tiny red and green gourds or flecks of gold leaf would be float-

---

[xxx] Popular name for Kōgenji Temple, after the number of visits supposedly required for a prayer to come true.

ing inside. The hairpins were for summer use, and as we walked by, the stall keeper would call out, "Put one of these on and I guarantee, it'll cool your head and get rid of all headaches." I bought one, but when I showed it to my mother, she said the bead would break easily and I would get hurt. I put the pin away, but took it out now and then, much preferring this hairpin to the expensive ones from my parents, which had gold and silver tassels.

The owner at another stall beckoned the children in a singsong voice: "Step right up. Anything you want for just 5 sen. Take your choice." Like other girls my age, I was fond of collecting pretty boxes, so after carefully examining what he had to offer, I bought one made of plaited straw.

The straw snakes and roasted barley cakes were the biggest attractions at the Fuji Shrine. The snakes were supposed to ward off diseases and evil spirits, but I preferred the cakes, which came in sturdy paper bags with twisted paper handles and a picture of Mount Fuji in blue on the side. Just thinking about them now, I can almost smell the aroma of roasted barley.

The fair at the Nezu Shrine, which included a display of big floats, was the most elaborate. As residents of Akebono-chō, we were considered parishioners, but the shrine was some distance away, so we were less attached to it than to the Fuji Shrine or Forty-six Thousand Kannon.

I must have been in fourth grade when my father took me fishing for the first time. We went to a pond that drew water from a canal near the Edogawa River in Koishikawa, but I am sure we went more for my amusement than for his. In fact, the old man in charge must have been informed ahead of time, because the moment we arrived, he said, "Now that the little miss is here, I'll throw in some more red carp." I once caught a carp so big that my father had to help me reel it in, but then he said it was unfit to eat and too large to keep at home, and I reluctantly threw it back. After that, every carp I saw looked pitifully small in comparison.

I enjoyed fishing, and during high school accompanied my father on his fishing trips, eventually earning the nickname "Creel Carrier." Some of the fish we caught were tuna, roach, *haze*, goby, *ayu*, and prawn. My sister, who already considered herself a young lady, disdained fishing altogether.

I shall mention one other memory from childhood—my first and last koto recital. The recital was to be at Ibumurazakura, a restaurant in Ryōgoku. My sister and I were playing "Yachiyojishi," but the piece had one short passage where I had to sing by myself. I had resisted doing this from the very beginning, but my teacher and mother had made up their minds; I had no choice but to go through with it. Our mother had ordered matching kimono for the occasion—pale purple silk crepe with a white herringbone pattern. Needless to say, she had straightened my hair the night before. On the day of the recital she arranged our hair, painted our faces and necks with white paste powder, and dabbed rouge on our lips and the outer corners of our eyes. She was determined that her children look their prettiest.

My mother called for a rickshaw. It was raining, and I felt more and more nauseated because the hood was raised and the obi was bound tightly around my waist. When we finally arrived at the restaurant, my sister was, as usual, in good spirits. It was our turn to play. I felt trapped and heartily wished I had never come, but half in tears, I somehow finished the piece. "Oh, aren't they sweet." "They must be twins." The whispered compliments made me even more miserable. We stayed to hear the advanced students play "Chidori," "Kumano," and other pieces, but I was utterly bored and could hardly wait for the rickshaw to take us home.

My sister and I had begun lessons when we were still living in Sanban-chō. Our mother had taught us at first, taking us through simple pieces like "Sakura, Sakura" and "Kurogami," but after we finished "Rokudan," she decided to send us to a professional. She was a beautiful and refined widow who wore her hair in the style of widowed samurai women. Through her good offices we were then accepted as students by her own teacher, Hagioka Kengyō, a master of the Yamada school. We saw him a couple of times at most and were mainly taught by his students. It was not that I disliked the koto. I liked playing "Rokudan," for instance, which required no singing. But I had never asked for lessons and had taken them solely because my mother thought that koto was part of a girl's education. In any event, I neglected practicing and sometime in high school gave it up altogether, having earned only a "middle grade" certificate.

2

High School Years

I turned thirteen in 1898, and in April I entered the high school attached to the Tokyo Women's Higher Normal School. Located in the Ochanomizu section of Tokyo, the school was then, as now, more commonly called Ochanomizu Girls' High School.

The elementary school system at the time consisted of a four-year lower-level course and a four-year higher-level course.[i] Girls generally entered high school after completing two years of the secondary course, a step that was taken in stride, with none of the stress seen among students today. In my class, only three girls went on to high school. I was the only one to go to Ochanomizu. The other two, with whom I competed for first place, went to the Prefectural Girls' High School in Koishikawa Takebaya-chō. Several girls went to a school in Hongō Yushima, which taught Japanese-style sewing and qualified students to teach the subject in elementary school. Besides Ochanomizu and Prefectural Girls' High School, there was the Peeresses' High School for the daughters of upper-class families, and private schools such as Jogakkan, Atomi Jogakkō, Meiji Jogakkō, and Ferris Jogakkō, which was in Yokohama. The only schools for girls beyond high school were the Tokyo Higher Normal School (which trained high school teachers) and the coeducational Music Academy in Ueno. Three-year colleges for women like Japan Women's College, Joshi (later Tsuda) Eigakujuku, Joshi Isen (a medical college), and Joshi Bijutsu (fine arts) were established in the early 1900s.

I was not particularly elated about going to Ochanomizu; I merely followed my father's wishes. As a government official, my father had probably never thought of sending his daughter to a private or missionary school. Also,

---

[i] At the time, compulsory education was for four years.

my sister had entered the same school the year before. The times were more carefree, and so I made no special preparations for the entrance examination. On the day of the examination, as well as for the entrance ceremony, I went all by myself. Like everyone else, I took this for granted, though admittedly, I was a bit nervous on the day of the examination.

The examination, which covered the entire range of academic subjects, must have been easy, since I remember nothing about it. We also had to demonstrate our sewing skills by sewing the right sleeve for a lined kimono. I had not learned this at school, so I was at a loss at first, but eventually figured it out.

Used to having male teachers, I was surprised to see a young woman acting as proctor. She was pretty, with a face as round as an *okame* mask[ii] and hair mounded in a matronly *marumage* and held in place with a piece of bright red cloth. The woman, Yahagi Sensei, would be my teacher for five years, the entire duration of high school. As I soon learned, she was a graduate of the Higher Normal School and had recently married Yahagi Eizō, a law professor at Tokyo Imperial University.

School uniforms were yet to be adopted, and like other high school students, the girls dressed in kimono, hakama, and leather shoes. My own choice was a kimono of either Meisen silk or double-threaded cotton and a purple cashmere hakama. I later switched to a maroon hakama, a more popular color. Some of the students wore kimono without hakama and tied their obi in a tateyanoji or kainokuchi. A few dressed in Western clothes. When the male instructor had us do bar exercises and other exercises to correct our posture in gym class, the students in kimono simply tucked up their long sleeves with cloth bands. Then, for dancing, we untied the bands and moved around fluttering our sleeves. Gym class, in short, was yet another example of the peculiar blending of East and West, the old and the new, which prevailed at the time.

As to hairstyle, the students in the lower grades wore their hair straight down the back, and those in the higher grades in a simple *sokuhatsu* or in a more elaborate style like momoware or *tōjinmage*. I wore my hair with bangs in front, the hair on top gathered with a ribbon, and the hair on the sides hanging loose, or braided and tied with a ribbon of the same color. I had ribbons of various widths and colors—purple, brown, black, moss green. From time to time I also stuck a barrette decorated with a red rose in my hair.

The majority of the students at Ochanomizu came from upper- and middle-class families. In my own class, several were from former daimyo and court

---

[ii] Mask of a woman's face, with a wide forehead, tiny nose, full cheeks, and a smile.

families and many from the new nobility—bureaucrats, military officials, and businessmen who had been elevated to the peerage because of their contributions to the Meiji state. There were also students whose fathers were scholars or educators, well established but of more modest means. As the daughter of a plain-living, low-ranking government official, I belonged to the lowest tier. The students, then, represented a fair sample of girls whose fathers had led the country in a time of rapid change. Because of this, a certain air of privilege, an aura of bureaucratic correctness, pervaded the school. In speaking to one another also, the students used excessively polite language; for example, they referred to themselves as *"watakushi,"* rather than the more informal *"watashi"* or *"atashi."*

Physically I was still undeveloped. In a schoolwide physical examination, I was told that I barely weighed 58 pounds and that my lung capacity was half that of others in my age group. My appetite remained poor, and the teacher felt moved to point out that I did not bring enough food for lunch. I did not suffer from a particular malady but was simply less developed than my peers. In my second year, when the teacher spoke to us about menstruation, I had no idea what she was talking about. The opposite sex did not interest me at all.

"Haruko, it's really too bad you weren't a boy"—so my grandmother had said from the time I was a child. I was undeniably dark-skinned and by inclination a tomboy. Though he never talked about this, my father also seemed to have a different set of expectations for each of his two daughters. Did he perhaps see in me the son he never had? After all, I was the one who went fishing with him and carried his wicker creel. And so, despite my attendance at an all-girls school, I continued to behave like a young boy and was treated as such by the family. My sister, meanwhile, was growing more ladylike by the day.

My mother shared my grandmother's opinion. She would look at my face and sigh, saying, "Oh, if only you were a boy." According to my mother's standards of female beauty, my eyebrows were too thick, eyes too big, nose too prominent, and lips too full. Everything was in excess; I would have been better off as a boy. Also, as I mentioned, I took after my father and had wavy hair. I was hopeless.

Even at school I was teased about my glossy dark skin and nicknamed Rakan-san.[iii] My friends had another name for me—Hamu-chan. Our home economics text had mentioned a brand of smoked ham called Lacan [?], and since my thin braids resembled a pig's tail and "Lacan" sounded like "rakan," Haru-chan had become Hamu-chan. The second nickname would stay with me long after graduation.

---

iii *Rakan* (Arhat): A Buddhist sage usually depicted with dark skin.

Drawing on her knowledge of Tōkyūjutsu, my grandmother often analyzed my face. "You've got a good face, that's for sure. Now, if only your eyebrows weren't so close together. And your eyes—they're too close to your eyebrows. If you don't watch out, you're going to turn into a very stubborn person." Then, having detected a few stray hairs on my eyebrows, she would say, "This doesn't bode well for girls. It means you're the kind of person who finds it hard to say yes to a superior." In the years that followed, I was often reminded of her words. Her prediction was not entirely off the mark, or had she already seen into my character?

Singing apart, classes at Ochanomizu were easy. I was always first or second in the class. Mathematics was my best subject. In algebra class, I competed with a girl from Fujimi Elementary School to see who could come up with the simplest equation first. I was also good at sewing and calligraphy and received regular praise from my teachers and classmates.

The calligraphy teacher, Okada Kisaku, was well known in his field and taught at the Higher Normal School also. We used a copybook with his calligraphy, which was relaxed and free of affectation. A big man already advanced in years, he had a longish, pockmarked face and at first glance could be quite intimidating. But he was actually very kind, and his habit of stuttering was endearing. Still, whenever he praised me, spitting and stumbling over his words, I could hardly keep from laughing. Basking in his praise, I bought my brushes at a well-established shop called Gyokusendō, and for a while even thought of becoming a calligraphy teacher myself.

In art class we painted in the traditional style, copying the pictures in our textbook, line for line, on thick patterned paper or glazed Mino paper. Our teacher, Araki Jippo, was the adoptive son of Araki Kanpo, a famous artist who taught at the Higher Normal School. Jippo was young and gentle, almost effeminate, and though we admired his father, I am afraid we did not take him seriously.

For my graduation project I painted a picture on silk of Nakosonoseki [the old barrier station famous in poetry]. I copied my picture from a book, of course, and poorly too, but it was displayed along with other graduation projects. On looking closely at the painting, I discovered to my dismay that it had been completely retouched by the teacher. The term "freehand sketching" was then unknown, and only rarely did we draw from real life. We were instructed to copy the pictures in our textbook faithfully, thinning the ink, mixing the paint, and varying the tones exactly as we were told. I was clever with my hands, so my grades were good, but I knew that I was creating not art but some kind of sham. In spite of my art classes, I never learned to appreciate the beauty, verve, and power of a line drawn with a brush, nor the subtle shadings of light and dark.

I have mentioned that singing was a sore point. Making matters worse was my inability to read music. The girls who came up from Fuzoku, the elementary school attached to Ochanomizu, had learned the solfège system and sang do, re, mi, fa. I had learned to read notes by numbers—*hi, fu, mi, yo, i, mu, na*[iv]—and was thus incapable of singing along with the rest of the class. I also had difficulty transcribing the music the teacher wrote on the blackboard. Even now, with the exception of the C major scale, I do not know how to read music.

The teacher herself was very nice. A graduate of the Music Academy at Ueno, Hayashi Sensei dressed in subdued kimono—she wore hakama only for school ceremonies—used no makeup, and combed her hair in a simple ichōgaeshi. She gave me a B. Her successor, a young woman straight from the academy, gave me a C, my first C ever. I was crushed.

English was an elective, and students could take sewing instead. On my parents' advice, I took sewing, as did my sister. A couple of years later, we decided on our own to learn English and went for private lessons at the home of a missionary school graduate who taught at the Prefectural Girls' High School. We next switched to Shibata Sensei, a graduate of Dōshisha in Kyoto, and started with volume 1 of the *National Reader*, a text then in wide use. Still unmarried, Shibata Sensei used rough language, and her brisk and matter-of-fact manner bordered on the masculine. But we liked her, since she was so different from the stiff and formal teachers at school. Her teaching method was typical of the time: the students lined up to take their turns, listened to her read a passage in a steady monotone, read the same passage, and then translated it. My sister and I made little headway, and since I started on the wrong foot, I had trouble learning English later on.

I cannot remember whether it was my sister or I who asked our parents for permission to learn English. But I do know for a fact that it was the first time either of us had gone out of our way to make such a request. I was not consciously aware of it, but this may have been my first act of resistance to my father's growing conservatism. Ten years earlier, he had insisted that his wife and sister study English; he was now of the opinion that women didn't have to know English.

My father was not alone in his new attitude, for by the mid-1890s, a general reaction to Westernization had set in, especially of the kind exemplified by the fancy dress balls at the Rokumeikan Hall. Japan was once again to be "pure," and in the wake of the war with China, the calls for a return to traditional values and a more assertive nationalism had become more strident.

[iv] Alternate way of counting one, two, three, four, five, six, seven.

Even before the outbreak of the war, the Western-style parlor in our home had been made over into a room with a tatami floor. The reproductions of Western paintings on the sliding doors had been taken down and replaced with paper with Japanese designs. My mother no longer wore dresses, and instead of curled bangs, she arranged her hair in a traditional marumage. My sister and I had also forsaken our dresses and wore kimono, with our hair done in Japanese style. Furthermore, within a year or two of the issuance of the Imperial Rescript on Education, the painting in the parlor of a half-nude Western beauty had disappeared and was replaced by a framed copy of the rescript written in the brushwork of my mother's calligraphy teacher. My father was an upright government servant, and for him this was undoubtedly the meet and proper thing to do.

A more ominous sign of the times was the new Civil Code, which was promulgated in 1898. The old code by Boissonade had been introduced in 1890 but was never enforced because of opposition from scholars who claimed it would "lead to the demise of loyalty to emperor and parents." No less disturbing was the 1900 Police Security Regulations, which succeeded the 1890 Law on Public Meetings and Political Associations. The provision banning women from all political activities not only deprived women of equal political rights but also ensured the continuance of the feudalistic family system.

My own school was a case in point. It had been founded in 1872 at the height of the Civilization and Enlightenment movement as the private Tokyo Girls' High School. The school had then been attached to the Tokyo Women's Normal School in 1882, and when the normal school became the Tokyo Women's Higher Normal School in 1890, it had been designated as the practice-teaching school and put under the direct supervision of the Ministry of Education. As such, the school's philosophy was based on the perpetuation of the traditional family system, its immediate goal the education of young girls who would become "good wives and wise mothers," as the phrase went. To enforce this educational policy, the Girls' High School Act of 1899 emphasized practical subjects such as sewing, home economics, needlework, and etiquette, rather than academic study and general culture.

At Ochanomizu, students were expected to behave in a circumspect, maidenly manner and observe the rules of etiquette. In this respect, the school was no different from my home. If we happened to meet the etiquette teacher in the hall, we had to come to a full stop, put our feet together, and bow as we had been taught in class. Our own teacher, Yahagi Sensei, was a model of good manners. A classic Kyoto beauty with flawless skin and a beautiful voice, she was unfailingly cool and correct. Her classes, on the other hand, were deadly dull and devoid of any rapport with the students. Regardless of what class she was teaching, she followed the text to the letter, not once mentioning reference books or outside reading. We merely had to memorize the text, a method hardly calculated to make us think on our own, let alone discover the joy of learning. It was my great misfortune to study every single subject with her for five straight years—literature, mathematics, history, geography, science. I do not know how the students endured this, though they were probably incapable of questioning her teaching.

Then again, she may not have been entirely to blame, for she herself had been taught in the same stultifying manner at the Higher Normal School. This school, which had been established by the government to train high school teachers, had a feudalistic, Confucian educational philosophy and teaching methods that were rigid and formalistic. Several years later, I was not at all surprised to find the following sentence in the school's "Statement of Guiding Principles": "Inasmuch as Heaven and Earth differ in virtue and yin and yang differ in action, the girls at this school are to be educated in conformance with their inborn nature." Small wonder that education at the Higher Normal School was of such poor quality.

Apart from the classes, life at school was pleasant. In gym class we were taught how to dance the cotillion and the quadrille, a vestige no doubt of the Westernizing craze of the Rokumeikan days. Divided into groups of eight, we formed two lines and faced each other, picked up the folds of our hakama and curtsied, then danced in 4/4 time to the piano music. Dressed as we were in long-sleeved kimono, hakama, and leather shoes, we must have looked odd indeed, but no one seemed to give it a second thought.

The students at the Higher Normal School seemed to like dancing, too, and during lunch hour, we would see them practicing in the gym. They also did Swedish gymnastics, something their teacher, Iguchi Aguri, had studied in the United States, and I would watch in fascination as she taught the complicated moves, dressed in her black gym shorts. The school encouraged sports, and unlike elementary school, furnished a wide variety of equipment. I had good motor coordination, so I tried everything—tossing rings, swings, swinging on a rope, and tennis. I particularly enjoyed tossing rings. Using two sticks shaped like drumsticks, a classmate and I would toss a bamboo ring back and forth, keeping it in the air until the muscles in our right upper arms became sore.

Classes continued to be boring. Perhaps in reaction to this, I became a tennis enthusiast in my third year even though I had no special affinity for sports. I was small and not very strong, so I was not a very good player, but I enjoyed myself and spent many hours on the court. Normally I was not competitive, but I hated losing at tennis. I bought a racket at Mimatsu, a sporting goods store near the main gate of Tokyo Imperial University, and practiced in the garden, hitting the ball against the wooden shutters over and over. My mother complained, but I refused to give up. To compensate for my size, I was determined to perfect my stroke—a mean slice that would send the ball curving off course—and in no time my right forearm was knotted with muscles.

Away from the court, I had little contact with my tennis partners, who had all graduated from Fuzoku and tended to have aristocratic tastes. Sturdily built and strong, they effortlessly drove the balls over the net, but I still preferred to play with them rather than with less skillful players. One of my tennis partners was the daughter of Kikuchi Dairoku, the minister of education. She was tanned, with big, round eyes, unaffected, and did not care at all about how she looked. Actually, she reminded me of a naughty little boy. To everyone's surprise, she was the first one in the class to marry and become a mother. Her husband was Minobe Tatsukichi [the famous constitutional scholar]; her son Ryōkichi later became governor of Tokyo. Other tennis partners were the daughters of Baron Mekada Tanejirō, of the politician Katō Takaaki, and of someone named Adachi, who was said to own a coal mine in Hokkaido.

My classmates included daughters from daimyo families like the Tokugawa, Nanbu, and Ikeda. Tokugawa [Masako], who commuted from Koume in Mukōjima, was probably the daughter or granddaughter of Yoshinobu, the last shogun. The young ladies of the nobility came to school in rickshaws and accompanied by their servants. In all other respects, they spoke and dressed like everyone else. They seemed to dislike sports and usually gathered under a tree during recess and watched the others play. Their grades were said to be mediocre.

I sensed a subtle tension, if not outright antagonism, within the class between two groups: those who came from Fuzoku without taking an examination, and those who came from ordinary public schools. The first group was upper class and elitist, the second more middle class and made up of girls whose fathers were scholars, educators, and low-ranking bureaucrats. The upper-class girls tended to stick together and keep their distance, while the girls in the second group secretly looked down on them and made no effort to be friendly. The tension continued throughout high school.

School Friends

I made several close friends. Kobayashi Iku was from a school attached to the high school but separate from Fuzoku. Her family situation was complicated. She had been given up for adoption early on, and that may have been why she seemed mature beyond her years. She also had inner resilience, a mischievous streak, a quick mind, and a sharp tongue. Everyone in the class liked her, except for Yahagi Sensei, who treated her coldly, even maliciously. Iku was not what you would call a straight A student—her academic record was uneven—and since she came from a relatively poor family, her clothes were probably not up to Sensei's standards.

Another friend, Ichihara Tsugie, had taken the entrance examination with me. Her father was the mayor of Yokohama, and since I had never been to Yokohama, I went to visit her. I shall never forget my first glimpse of the harbor. The huge foreign ships docked on both sides of the pier seemed to stretch forever into the sea. We climbed to the top of Nogeyama and then walked around Chinatown, or Nankin-machi, as it was called. Crowded and dirty, the neighborhood had none of the Chinese restaurants that line the streets today. We also went to Isezaki-chō, which even then was a bustling amusement quarter. Everything about the city was exotic, and we walked the entire day, taking in the sights and exchanging girlish confidences.

Tsugie was an accomplished koto player. A student of the Yamase school, she had already received a certificate in recognition of her advanced level. She considered her koto playing a social grace rather than a future profession, and after graduation, she attended a school attached to the Higher Normal School that trained kindergarten teachers. She taught at the school kindergarten—one of her charges was Yahagi Sensei's child—and afterward moved to the new kindergarten at Japan Women's College in Mejiro. She hoped to continue in her job, but was forced to quit by her parents and siblings, who thought an unmarried working daughter would adversely affect the marriage prospects of younger siblings.

My third friend was Uehara Kise, whose father was the principal of the Music Academy at Ueno. She had already decided to enter the piano division of the academy and commuted to a branch of the academy in Hitotsubashi. She avoided all sports, physical work, or activity that might hurt her hands, and as a result she always looked pale. Quiet, intelligent, good at mathematics, and with a logical turn of mind, she was more the serious, hardworking achiever than the naturally gifted artist. Thanks to Kise, I attended several performances at the academy, which boasted the only orchestra at the time. It was pitifully small, with a limited range of instruments, and performed once a year at the annual graduation ceremony. Many of the instructors at the school were foreign, with names like Keble, Heidrich, and Junger.

One other friend, Nagata Sono, studied the violin. I attended concerts with her, too—a piano recital by Kōda Nobuko and a violin recital by Andō Kō. Opera was then unknown; the singer Miura Tamaki made her debut several years later. Sono attended the academy after graduation but died when she was 29. She was very bright, with a talent for mathematics. I will always regret the early death of this quiet and self-assured person.

My friends and I would get together on any pretext—to gather herbs at the Arakawa River, pick primroses at Toda Bridge, view flowers at Koganei or the foliage at Takino River, or walk around the Koishikawa Botanical Garden. We took our lunch for longer trips, since proper middle-class girls were not supposed to go to places that served food. An adult woman might have a bite at a sushi shop or stop for a bowl of sweet azuki bean soup, but even this was considered the exception and not the rule. It was unheard of for a well-bred young girl to go into an eatery alone.

When we were together, we talked about whatever was on our minds. Our conversation was neither focused nor conclusive, yet we spoke earnestly and thought things through as much as was possible for girls our age. It turned out that Iku's adoptive father had been indicted on charges of fraud. She was in despair, and to cheer her up, we met at a field near Hongō Kikusaka. But, overcome by the gravity of the situation, we could not stop ourselves from bursting into tears. Mostly, we talked about the future. We all agreed that marriage and family, the vaunted ideal of "good wife and wise mother," was not for us. We would find jobs and be independent at all costs.

Here I will skip ahead several years. Because of her family circumstances, Iku attended the tuition-free practical arts division of the Higher Normal School and taught sewing and home economics. She married a young naval officer, and since he was frequently away on duty, she accepted a position at a girls' high school in Nagano Prefecture. She went with her adoptive mother, whom she looked after for many years. A hardheaded realist, she told me years later that she had married a naval officer knowing he would be absent most of the time.

Tsugie, as I mentioned, was forced to give up her job as a kindergarten teacher. She was then bullied into marrying a younger colleague at her father's bank. The couple set up house near her family, but she found life dull and empty. Fond of children but with none of her own, she showered her affections on her nieces and nephews. Her husband, too, was a disappointment. As she once confided, "He's always going off somewhere to drink. You would think he'd drink at home. I told him that if he wanted the company of geisha, he could always invite them home—as many as he wanted. Drinking and partying at home shouldn't be all that difficult to arrange. But he said it just wouldn't be the same…." I regret to say that she died in middle age.

Kise entered the piano division of the Music Academy, as planned. She quickly established a reputation for technical brilliance and for a time was hailed as a genius, but she stopped giving recitals after marrying an electrical engineering student at Tokyo Imperial University. He had lived at her home and tutored her in algebra and geometry. Her husband, fortunately, played the piano and shared her passion for music. For Kise, being the principal's daughter may have been a disadvantage. Some of the students were bound to be jealous, and she herself may have wondered whether she had the stamina to survive in the cutthroat world of professional artists. Marriage and family offered an easy way out. Also, like me, she had a delicate build and was not particularly robust.

My friends and I eventually went our separate ways, but as young girls, we were united in our opposition to conventional views on marriage and the ideal of womanhood that was foisted on us at school. We purposely neglected our appearance, little caring whether our faces were sunburned or not. Part of this, I am sure, was in reaction to the daughters of the nobility and wealthy families, who were unduly preoccupied with their looks and came to school elaborately coiffed and dressed. All their talk of dances and card parties—a popular pastime with a segment of the upper and middle classes—was not only tedious but beneath contempt. We would not have dreamed of attending such functions.

Frustrated and bored by the classes, we felt as though our youthful desire to stretch our minds was being nipped in the bud. Then, in our third-year history class, we learned about the Wakō, the Japanese pirates who pillaged the Chinese and Korean seacoasts from the thirteenth to the sixteenth century. We were immediately captivated and stirred by their spirit of adventure and wild audacity. As a result, we immediately formed our own "Pirates' Band." We came up with this idea on the spur of the moment when we were in a playful mood, but it was at least an outlet for our mounting dissatisfaction. The members of the band were Iku, Tsugie, and myself, plus Kise and Sono, whom we more or less dragged in.

In June 1901, the year after we formed our band, the politician Hoshi Tōru was stabbed to death by Iba Sōtarō, a fanatical reactionary. Hoshi, who had been a leading member of the Seiyūkai party and head of the Tokyo Municipal Assembly, had recently been criticized harshly by his political enemies and the public for the underhanded methods he had used to strengthen his faction. His murder was of course linked to the power struggle between the parties and the oligarchs who were entrenched in the government.

Our understanding of politics and Hoshi's position was hazy at best, but all the same, we were shocked, even indignant. In spite of rising criticism, he had remained true to his convictions, and in our naïve way we admired his self-confidence and willingness to take risks; we felt he deserved our sympathy. Indeed, compared to our teachers, with their suffocating moralizing, we considered him far from any kind of villain. On the contrary, we believed him "as flawless as an angel's robe."

On a hot summer's day, Iku, Tsugie, and I decided to visit Hoshi's grave. We walked as far as the ferry crossing at Yaguchi, but then we remembered that this was the spot where Yoshioki, Nitta Yoshisada's son, had been trapped in his boat and killed. We stopped to pay our respects at the shrine built in his honor.[v] Hoshi's grave was at the Ikegami Honmonji Temple. We made an offering of white lilies, and since this was our first time in the area, we walked around, absorbed as usual in heated conversation. For all our indignation, the visit to Hoshi's grave was really an excuse for another outing.

The three of us remained friends after graduation. Iku was clever at thinking up nicknames, and I like to think that I was influenced to a degree by her playful, fun-loving character. She was the one who thought of my nickname Hamu-chan, and she continued to address me as such in her letters.

Forming the Pirates' Band was one way of deflecting my growing dissatisfaction with the school. My next step was to boycott morals class—the class I hated the most. Yahagi Sensei taught it, of course, reading the text in her usual droning manner. Bound in Japanese style and with a dark pink cover, the *Morals Textbook for Girls* was a dry-as-dust compendium of dos and don'ts in the style of the *Greater Learning for Women*.[vi] It held up as models of feminine virtue the nun Matsushita Zenni, a paragon of frugal living; the wife of Yamanouchi Kazutoyo[, who gave her entire savings of gold coins to her warrior husband to buy a horse]; the mother of Kusunoki Masatsura[, who bid her son follow in his father's footsteps and fight to the death for Emperor Godaigo]; Princess Tachibana, the consort of Prince Yamato Takeru, who threw herself into Sagami Bay [to appease the sea god so that her husband could proceed with his military expedition]; and Kesa Gozen, who defended her chastity with her life. They were all totally irrelevant to the everyday lives of high school girls.[vii] The teacher never took the time to discuss the examples or to ask us questions. Instead, she merely rephrased the text, which was written in stilted classical Japanese.

So just as class was about to begin, I would calmly leave the room without a word, as if it were the most natural thing to do, and go straight home. My mother never questioned me about my early return, nor did my grandmother, who said, "Oh, you're home early," and left it at that. Among my classmates, Iku was the only one to make a comment: "Hamu-chan, you really did it, didn't you!" I am sure that I was not the only student bored to tears, but I was the only one who walked out. My ability to do this calmly, without any trepi-

---

[v] Father and son were medieval warriors faithful to Emperor Godaigo during a military uprising.

[vi] *Greater Learning for Women* (*Onna daigaku*): Attributed to the Confucian scholar Kaibara Ekiken (1630–1714), the book defined the proper behavior for women and was widely read during the Tokugawa period (1600–1868).

[vii] All the examples are from the Middle Ages, or in one case, Princess Tachibana, from prehistoric times.

dation, must have meant that deep within me was the intransigent child who refused to speak when she was displeased. This is not to say that, as a child, I was deliberately contrary. No, it was a question of resisting what had been forced upon me. My resentment at having to submit to my mother's attempts to straighten my hair was another instance. What was so wrong with having curly hair?

Oddly enough, I was never reprimanded by the teacher, who was normally so strict, and this despite the fact that I was skipping morals class at a school supposedly dedicated to educating "good wives and wise mothers." The simple fact was that the teacher liked some students and disliked others. She was mean to Iku, but she had liked me from the very beginning. My grades were always good, and I was polite, just the sort of student who appealed to her. I should also mention that the handwriting and spelling in my tests and compositions were neat and correct, and my notebooks (we had to make our own) were meticulously made, the pages precisely folded and aligned, the thread binding firm and secure. There was nothing she could find fault with. I was an outstanding student even by her exacting standards.

Sensei took several maternity leaves during my five years at Ochanomizu. The other teachers and upper-level students from the Higher Normal School took turns substituting for her, and my friends and I, eager to see a new face, rejoiced whenever she became pregnant. We privately referred to her pregnancy as "expansion" and childbirth as "explosion," and if we thought she was being unusually short-tempered or nitpicking, we would nod knowingly to one another and whisper, "Oh dear, looks like another expansion," as if the whole thing was a joke. We did not know anything about such matters, but at a time when women were expected to be good wives and wise mothers, Sensei must have struggled to teach long hours and perform her duties as a housewife and mother.

By far, the most memorable event in high school was the visit of Empress Shōken, the present empress dowager, in October 1897.[viii] To make sure that nothing went wrong, the entire school rehearsed for days. We were in the midst of music class when Her Majesty came into the room. Because of my small size, I was in the front row and was able to observe her closely. The empress was much smaller than she appeared in her photographs, with a delicate build and a thin face of great refinement and beauty; her ladies-in-waiting paled in comparison. She wore a mauve gown with a trailing hem, and when she listened to us sing, she stood so motionless that I thought she would stay rooted to the spot forever. I found this almost uncanny. I could stare at

---

[viii] Raichō says Meiji 30 (1897), but she must mean another year, since she entered high school in 1898.

her only because we looked straight ahead while we sang. Earlier, when we had lined up at the gate to welcome the empress, we had been told to bow deeply and not to raise our heads under any circumstances.

Rain or snow, my sister and I always walked to school and never found the distance of about 2 miles too long or arduous. In fact, except for the daughters of the nobility and rich families, who commuted by rickshaw, all the students walked. In good weather we wore kimono, hakama, and leather shoes. In rain or snow, we used an umbrella and wore a cotton raincoat and high wooden clogs. No matter how cold, we never wore overcoats, and at most covered our shoulders with thick knitted woolen shawls and our heads with hoods. Instead of carrying a bag or briefcase, we wrapped our books in a *furoshiki*[ix] and hoisted it on our shoulders if it rained.

My sister and I could choose between two routes to school. We could take Hongō-dōri, walk past Kichijōji Temple through the fresh produce market and on to Oiwake-chō, past the First Higher School and the main entrance of Tokyo Imperial University to Hongō Sanchōme. Or we could go from Koishi-kawa Hara-machi to Hakusan, take a right turn at the gate in front of the First Higher School, go past the main entrance of Tokyo Imperial University, and follow Hongō-dōri. The intersection near the main entrance of the university was lined with shops. Other than carts, rickshaws, and the occasional bicycle, there was almost no traffic.

When we took the second route, we often stopped by a small stationery store called Keiseidō. Takashima Beihō, a newcomer in Buddhist studies who was known for his sharp tongue, had set up the business for his older sister, and he would be sitting inside reading books or working on a manuscript. A few years later, after I started Seitō, Beihō asked me to write a preface for his book *Storefront Zen* (*Tentō Zen*). I knew he was critical of *Seitō* and the "New Women," but for old times' sake, I agreed.

On our way to school we often saw the First Higher School and Tokyo University students in their square black caps with thin white bands. Apart from the very few who wore uniforms, the students at the university dressed in kimono of striped or kasuri cotton, hakama of striped Kokura weave, and crested haori of dark blue or black cotton fastened with long ties of braided white cotton, the tips of which they sometimes flung over their shoulders. The more extravagant students sported ties made of white wool yarn. They wore either unvarnished clogs or *Satsuma-geta*,[x] and tucked a cotton hand towel into the waistband of their hakama. Thus attired, they walked at a deliberate

---

[ix] Square piece of cloth used for wrapping and carrying objects.
[x] A heavy clog made of a single piece of wood.

pace, sticking their chests out and taking their time. Since my sister and I walked quickly, we easily passed them.

We were proud of our ability to walk fast and counted how many people we managed to overtake. One morning, our father told us to leave the house earlier and walk more slowly. Apparently, the elderly custodian at the First Higher School had talked to him about us: "I can't believe how fast your daughters walk. I see them on my way to work now and then, but I just can't keep up with them." My father must have thought we were trying to get to school on time, when we were simply having fun walking as fast as we could.

Usually students entered the school grounds through the main gate facing Ochanomizu Bridge, but we preferred the shorter route that took us through the back gate on Yushima-dōri. Diagonally across from the back gate was the Saisei Gakusha, a private medical school founded in 1876 and the only one of its kind. The school was coeducational, and we occasionally saw a couple of women students coming out of the front gate with the men. The men looked bad enough—rough and crude, like a bunch of political henchmen—and the women not much better. I never cared for vain women, but I found their slovenly appearance highly offensive. By coincidence, Yoshioka Yayoi was a graduate of the school. If I had known how much suffering she and the other women had been made to endure by the contemptuous male students and the widespread prejudice against women doctors, I would have been more sympathetic [when she criticized me later].[xi]

On snowy days, we took the longer route so as to gaze at the scenery from the bridge. The canal was much deeper then, and looking at the snow-covered trees on the banks and the clear water flowing below us, we momentarily believed that we were in a remote forested valley. Lingering for a last look, we made a dash for the gate, and after classes, stopped again for one more look.

There were no trolley cars or other means of public transportation at the time, so to save our mother the trouble of coming all the way to Hongō to shop, my sister and I sometimes did errands on the way home. We went to Aokidō, a store that dealt in imported luxury goods; a pharmacy called Uryū; Kaneyasu, a store that sold pots and pans and other household items; Echigoya, which sold thread; and Okano, a confectioner. If we were going to koto lessons, we also stopped to buy candy for our grandmother at Saruame, an old store where two men made *sarashiame*[xii] out on the street, shouting in time with each pull.

[xi] Yoshioka Yayoi (1871–1960): Founder of Japan's first medical college for women. She later refused to support Raichō when she founded the New Women's Association.

[xii] A taffylike candy.

Our family members were steady customers of Aokidō, which delivered purchases to our house. For our father, there were deliveries of liquors and cigars; for guests and children, cookies, wafers, chocolates, and other fancy sweets. But to be truthful, I hated shopping. I felt shy about going into a shop and asking for something, so I usually stood silently behind my sister and let her make the purchases.

Life at Home

I shall now describe my life at home during high school. My father's younger sister Ai was married in 1891 or 1892, when we were still living in Sanban-chō. Her husband, Ōuchi Ushinosuke, worked at the Audit Board, where my father also worked. They had four boys and three girls in quick succession, and to help out, my grandmother often went to her daughter's house or brought back several children. The Ōuchi family then moved to Taiwan, and later to Manchuria.[xiii] When the two older boys were ready to enter middle school, they came to live with us. My sister and I felt as though we had suddenly acquired two younger brothers.

The son of my father's half-sister in Wakayama and the son of his half-brother in Osaka also lived with us at the time. Enrolled respectively at the German Association School and the Academy of Fine Arts at Ueno, they earned their keep by receiving visitors at the front door and performing other such errands.

My father's half-brother, the present head of the main branch of the Hiratsuka family, had run into financial difficulties after my grandfather's sudden departure for Tokyo. Forced to sell the property left by my grandfather, he had gone to Osaka and used the money to open a small factory that made ornamental hairpins. My grandfather had been born a Kondō, and descendants of that side of the family also lived in Osaka, where they made personal stamps and seals to earn a living. Like so many others in a period of unprecedented change, my relatives had had their share of hardship, yet in one way or another they had landed on their feet. But no one had achieved this as successfully as "Sada-san," now an important official in Tokyo. Surely he would not mind taking in a young relative or two? That was what families were for. My father could hardly refuse.

[xiii] Taiwan became a Japanese colony as a result of the Sino-Japanese War (1894–1895). After the Russo-Japanese War (1904–1905), Japan acquired the Russian lease on the Liaodong Peninsula and the Russian-built railway in Southern Manchuria.

In a household as large as ours, life was often hectic. At mealtimes, for instance, the room would be crowded, since everyone sat in front of individual trays, though my sister and I shared a tray, as did my mother and grandmother. The maids served the meals, which were the same for everyone except my father, who had one or two special dishes to go with his evening sake. He was also the only one who had a Western-style breakfast—buttered toast, black tea, milk, and slices of cheese. This was better for his poor digestion, he claimed, but probably he had never been fond of the usual rice and miso soup. He was also very particular about the bread, which had to be from Sekiguchi, in Mejiro, or from Charisha, in Tsukiji. When neither was available, he ate oatmeal instead.

Despite the flurry of activity at home, my mother always looked cool and unruffled. Maids were easily affordable; the pace of life was unhurried. Also, apart from special items, most purchases could be made at home. The fishmonger came to the kitchen door with his stack of trays balanced on a pole; the vegetable man came around with his cart. The bean vendor announced his arrival with the tinkling of bells; the bean curd man, with a toot on his little horn. One man sold roasted beans that were still warm, while others sold young plants, medicine, and bamboo poles for hanging laundry. Then there were the men who sharpened knives or mended clogs, smoking pipes, barrels, umbrellas, pots, and pans. Thus, most daily needs could be satisfied at the doorstep.

I do not remember my mother ever wearing a *kappōgi*, the sleeved wraparound apron used today. For housework, women either tied up their kimono sleeves with cloth bands or wore a simple apron. Some wore a blue cotton jacket with tight sleeves called a *mukimiya*, but this was considered somewhat uncouth and was shunned by urban middle-class housewives. The jacket was worn mainly by housewives in the downtown merchant district.

⊚ ⊚ ⊚ ⊚ ⊚

One of my fondest memories of life at home is the New Year's holidays. On the morning of the first, my father seated himself in a rickshaw pulled by two men and went off to the Imperial Palace to pay his respects. Then he made the obligatory round of New Year's greetings, which took at least three days. In the meantime, the front gate, with a decoration of pine branches to one side, was left open for guests. A small lacquer tray for calling cards was placed at the entrance, where a maid or one of our young live-in relatives was in attendance. My mother instructed that person about who should be invited in and who should be sent away with a word of thanks. The person in charge would be in for a scolding should an important visitor be turned away by mistake. The steady flow of visitors usually lasted until the seventh.

For New Year's we had both traditional and Western food. A family specialty was something called "punch," a beverage resembling the present-day cocktail. I do not know what the ingredients were, but I remember watching my mother as she mixed the assorted liquors and fruit juices under my father's supervision. The dishes varied little from year to year. A favorite of mine was *fukaden*—meatballs with all kinds of delicious stuffing inside. Some of the regular callers were particularly fond of the Western dishes served after the customary sip of sweet rice wine, and since my grandmother had to have her special New Year's dishes too, the kitchen was in an uproar at the end of the year. On the thirty-first, my mother and the maids often cooked all night.

During the New Year's holidays, we played cards in the evenings. My father, who liked competitive games, was especially fond of cards and knew a variety of games. Everyone's favorite was 21, for which we used go stones as chips—white standing for 10, black for one. We also played a simplified version of *hanafuda*.[xiv] My father excused himself, however, when we played 100 Poets.[xv] My sister and I also went outside and hit a shuttlecock back and forth with a paddle. Ping-Pong was just beginning to be popular, but it was considered a game for children and not the fierce sport of today.

⊚ ⊚ ⊚ ⊚ ⊚

The summer after I entered high school, we spent our first vacation at the seashore. Going somewhere to escape the city heat was still a luxury, so my father must have dug deep into his pocket to give the family a treat. We rented lodgings in Hayama, on the southern coast of Kanazawa Prefecture. That was my first view of the open ocean. Nowadays, when I go to the shore at Hayama and watch the waves lap monotonously at my feet, the sea seems more like a part of the garden surrounding the imperial villa. But when I first saw the ocean, I was overwhelmed, as though my very being were being crushed by the water's elemental force. Wave upon wave came crashing in, the restless sea heaving like a living creature. Even now, I remember my knees shaking as I felt the water's power course through my body, a vital, living force that seemed to rule the universe.

[xiv] Game played with twelve sets of four cards, each card printed with different flowers representing the seasons. The object of the game is to collect as many cards as possible by matching suits.

[xv] 100 Poets (*Hyakunin isshu*): Game played with 100 cards, each with the final line of a *waka* poem by a different poet. The cards are placed face up on the tatami, and as a designated person reads aloud the opening line of a poem, the players compete to see who gets the card with the correct final line first.

A villa owned by Viscount Inoue Kowashi was near our lodgings. His daughters and their foreign governess, Alice, stayed there. One daughter, Fuji, who sat directly behind me in class, was rumored to be the child of the viscount's concubine, but she was bright and a good student. Anyway, Alice offered to teach me how to swim. When I met her at the beach for lessons, wearing a white calico outfit my mother had sewn on the machine, I felt terribly self-conscious, for, apart from some hardy foreigners, very few people and certainly even fewer women bathed in the ocean. But there I was with Alice, a foreigner conspicuous in her bright red suit, with her pale thighs bared for all to see.

The family of one of my father's younger colleagues had also taken lodgings in Hayama. They had two pretty daughters old enough to have just finished high school. The daughters had brought their bathing suits—which looked more like nurses' uniforms—but we had never seen them on the beach. Puzzled, we asked them why. "Oh," they said, "we're too embarrassed to go during the day, so we go at night." By then, I had overcome my embarrassment and fear of water, and thanks to Alice, had learned to swim and had even come to enjoy it.

My father did not swim. He preferred to fish, either using a rod and tackle or casting a net. I acted as his assistant, not because I felt I had to but because I still liked his company. A stream on the grounds of the imperial villa emptied into the sea, and fishing from the bridge one day, we caught gobies, instead of the usual prawns and little eels. I was delighted, especially since my haul was twice the size of my father's. When I boasted about this, he looked at me and said something I shall never forget. "You know, a goby is just about the stupidest fish there is. It's really very, very stupid." He then fixed a dish of goby marinated in vinegar, saying the fish tasted best when it came from a stream that flowed into the sea. The dish long remained a favorite with me, even though I was teased for liking something that was served with sake.

My sister did not join our fishing expeditions. Fish, she said, were smelly, and worms slimy and repulsive. But I did not hesitate to pull the worms apart and put them on the hook, just as I had seen my father do. In fact, from the time I was little, I was fascinated by crawly things—potato worms, caterpillars, inchworms, even snakes. I liked touching them and examining them up close. I once raised some silkworms a classmate had given me, and often wondered why my sister shuddered and turned away whenever she saw me pick one up.

My Aunt's Family

As I mentioned, my aunt's family had gone to Taiwan, and rather suddenly at that. My grandmother was inconsolable—her only daughter, her precious

Ai, living in a strange, far-off land. But my uncle, who attended the same language school as my father and worked at the same office, was intensely ambitious. Given to grandiose talk, he had chafed at having to work at a staid government job. So after the war with China, when Japan embarked on a large-scale program of military expansion, he decided to make the most of future opportunities and had the good fortune to be handpicked by Gotō Shinpei to serve under him in Taiwan. Gotō himself, the head of the Bureau of Civil Affairs at the Home Ministry, had been appointed by General Kodama Gentarō, the governor-general of Taiwan since 1898. Despite the efforts of past governors-general—Admiral Kabayama Sukenori, General Katsura Tarō, and General Nogi Maresuke—the future of Taiwan was uncertain. There had even been talk of selling it. For the next eight years, the general and Gotō worked together to put the colony on a firmer footing.

By all accounts, my uncle served his superior exceedingly well, and he was named head of civil affairs in Dairen when Gotō became the first president of the Southern Manchurian Railway. All in all, my uncle did very well for himself, and his career as a top colonial official was no doubt a source of great satisfaction. But this came at a price. To begin with, there was the matter of his children's education. As I mentioned, his oldest son had been sent back to Japan to attend middle school. Sitting at the desk next to mine, the young boy studied for his entrance examination but soon got bored and went off to see my grandmother on the slightest pretext. So I made up my mind to take him in hand: I would think of him as my younger brother and help with his studies. One day, I noticed that he had made a mistake in a simple calcula-tion—decimals or fractions, I've forgotten which—and I blurted out, "If you can't even do this, you'll never get into middle school!" The poor boy burst into tears, but to everyone's joy and relief, he passed the examination.

Before long, the second son and then the third entered middle school. My aunt decided to return to Tokyo to be with her children, and naturally, my grandmother was overjoyed. But while his family was away, my uncle took up with a geisha who had gone to Manchuria to work. The woman moved in, ran the house, and eventually bore him several children. With two rival fami-lies, there were bound to be complications. Even a born optimist like Aunt Ai suffered for years. Yet, seen against the larger, more tragic chain of events precipitated by Japan's aggression on the continent, I suppose the breakup of the family was a minor incident.

◎ ◎ ◎ ◎ ◎

Besides studying the koto, I also took lessons in the tea ceremony. The tea master was a middle-aged man who came from Nagoya once a month to

teach at the home of my maternal great aunt in Hongō Sanchōme. I hated
the lessons at first, but since I was with my sister and cousin and later with
a close classmate, I minded less and less. There was one problem: the tea
master always dressed formally in a kimono, short brown haori, and white
or sometimes gray *tabi* socks, but there was something about him—the way
he walked and went through the motions of the ceremony—that made me
want to laugh. I did not feel like laughing, of course, when it was my turn to
prepare tea. What exactly did I find so funny? I was at that giggly stage, but
I think the incongruity of the situation affected me—the teacher's solemn
show of teaching, his insistence on our mimicking his every gesture, and his
not once explaining to us the inner meaning of the ceremony.

Among the students was a young doctor, a graduate of the Saisei Gakusha.
He was a little eccentric and regularly appeared with a purple *fukusa*[xvi] peeking out of the breast pocket of his suit. When his turn came to prepare the
bowl of tea, he handled the fukusa in such a clumsy manner that I started gig-
gling, the other students joined in, and even the reserved middle-aged ladies
covered their mouths and discreetly looked the other way.

I admit my attitude was less than serious, but I am glad I took lessons.
Though it might have been superficial, the knowledge I gained, together
with the rules of etiquette instilled by my mother, stayed with me through
the years, and, I believe, gave my movements a measure of calm grace. Years
later, when I began *Seitō*, Otake Kōkichi, who was one of my colleagues, used
to comment on the elegance of my carriage and the way I moved my hands
and fingers.

A new German teacher at the First Higher School often came to the house,
and each time my father would tell me to prepare a bowl of green tea. My
mother, on her part, would bring out an array of kimono and obi. The man
was probably lonely, living all by himself in a strange land, or he was interested in observing family life in Japan. In any case, I kept wishing he wouldn't
come, and was particularly annoyed when he overstayed his welcome on the
day of the Festival of Dolls and I had to play the koto. For a German, he was
unusually slight and mild-mannered, and to my father's evident pleasure, said
my father's students all had excellent pronunciation.

A subject much discussed at the time was the need to reform girls' clothes.
The traditional kimono hampered physical activity, and the times called for
a kimono better suited to an active life. To solve this problem, an Association
for the Reform of Girls' Clothing had been formed by Hatoyama Haruko,
Yamawaki Fusako, Shimoda Utako, Miwada Masako, and other prominent

---

[xvi] Handkerchief-sized piece of silk cloth used in the tea ceremony.

educators. The problems were obviously the kimono's tendency to come open at the hem, the long sleeves, and the constricting obi, so predictably, most of the proposed designs featured an upper garment with tight sleeves and a skirt divided like a hakama.

I was influenced by all the talk and decided to make my own outfit. I sewed tiny pleats at the opening of the sleeves of a summer kimono and wore it the next day, the only one to wear a self-proclaimed "reformed kimono" at Ocha-nomizu. Schools in the outlying provinces were reported to have adopted the shorter Genroku-style sleeve, but those in Tokyo, and particularly my school, remained averse to the idea.

My Growing Resistance to My Father

Looking back over my high school years, I am surprised by some of the things that fired my imagination. One was a burning desire in my fourth or fifth year to climb Mount Fuji, a sentiment perhaps akin to my earlier impulse to make a hero out of Hoshi Tōru. I had never been interested in mountains, but had somehow made up my mind to climb the mountain I considered the most sacred in Japan, indeed, in the entire world. In addition, admiring articles about women who scaled the peak had appeared in the newspapers.

I decided to go during the summer vacation and by myself. I started collecting information about Mount Fuji—pictures, photos, maps, poems, newspaper articles. Poring over guidebooks, I plotted my course: I could take either the approach from Yamanashi Prefecture or the one from Gotenba, on the old Tōkaidō highway. I took notes assiduously. I now believed myself to be an authority on Mount Fuji. I decided to shoot the rapids at Fujikawa, too. With a map of Japan spread out on the floor, I contemplated other trips. My desire to climb Mount Fuji had become a passionate desire for travel itself.

When summer vacation came, I mustered my courage to ask my father for permission. Our relations had cooled, and I could no longer talk to him in a free and easy manner. There was no specific reason for this; it was rather the aura he projected of absolute authority. His long years as a bureaucrat and his steady rise in the hierarchy had turned him into a different person. His bearing, even his facial expression, bore the unmistakable stamp of a government official, and I rebelled against this subconsciously.

As I half expected, my request was turned down. "Of all the stupid ideas! It's no place for women and children to go." The look of scorn and pity on his face was extremely unpleasant. Nowadays, a daughter in a similar situation surely would protest. But at the time, nothing approaching what we now call a dialogue between father and child existed. Disappointed as I was,

I had no choice but to obey, and blinking back the tears, I silently withdrew from his room.

I seethed with resentment. How could he do this to me? If I had had money, I would have gone off without his permission. Fortunately or not, I did not have any. My mother had been brought up in a samurai family and frowned on handling money. Nor did she believe in giving it to her children. In our family, children were taught not to ask what something cost; I could not possibly have scraped up enough money for a trip.

My mother tried to console me, but to no effect. I frittered away the entire summer fuming. I was somewhat mollified in the fall, or it may have been the following spring, when I went to visit my sister, who had been diagnosed with pleurisy and sent with my grandmother to recuperate at an inn in Odawara. The inn was near the old Tōkaidō highway, which went through Mount Hakone, so, together with a member of the Pirates' Band, I climbed the road leading up to the pass, suitably shod in rough straw sandals.

My Reading

I first became interested in reading during my third year of high school. One reason for my late start was that, unlike older, established families who owned a set of the Chinese classics or picture books from the Tokugawa period, we had very few books. My grandfather, as I said, had left behind all his possessions when he came to Tokyo. There were the foreign books in my father's study with their impressive gold-stamped titles, but of course I was unable to read them. We also had the Hakubunkan editions of Japanese classics like *The Adventures of Hakken*, *Shanks' Mare*, and *The Life of Toyotomi Hideyoshi*, but these I looked at mainly for the pictures. I leafed through the magazines the family purchased—*Miyako no hana*, *Taiyō*, *Fūzoku gahō*, and *Marumaru chinbun*, the last, a magazine that featured satirical cartoons of current events. Even the daily newspapers hardly seemed worth more than a passing glance. My lack of interest in reading was fairly typical of high school girls at the time, or at least typical of the students at Ochanomizu.

My mother subscribed to the journal of the Greater Japan Women's Education Society. The members of the society, which was headed by a member of the nobility called Mōri Yasuko, were upper and middle class. Serving on the board were Shimoda Utako, Hatoyama Haruko, Yamawaki Fusako, and other leading educators. The journal had a pink cover with a design of cherry blossoms, but since I do not remember the contents, I probably never read it.

I have more or less forgotten the books we read at school. We were given no guidance about our outside reading, and we would not have thought of going to a library or bookstore. On the street from Hongō Sanchōme to Haruki-chō there were stores specializing in medical texts, but none that sold magazines or new books for the general public. And even if there had been such a store, I strongly doubt a high school girl would have gone inside to browse.

The first book to stir my interest was Frances Hodgson Burnett's *Little Lord Fauntleroy*, which I read in my third or fourth year of high school. The Japanese translation was published by Hakubunkan, but I remember most vividly the photograph of the translator, Wakamatsu Shizuko, rather than the plot or Cedric, the main character. Wakamatsu Shizuko's plain hairstyle and eyeglasses, her earnest, youthful face radiating intelligence and religious conviction—the total effect was refreshingly different from the teachers at school. I was drawn to her at once, though I made no attempt to learn more about her or her husband, Iwamoto Yoshiharu, who was the principal of Meiji Girls' School and founder of the magazine *Jogaku zasshi*.[xvii] *Little Lord Fauntleroy*, in fact, had first been serialized in that magazine around 1890.

Meiji Girls' School was a so-called missionary school that had been founded in 1885 by a group of Christians led by Kimura Kumaji and his wife. Unlike other such schools, it was run entirely by Japanese. In its founding charter, the school stressed the importance of equal education for men and women:

> Since boys and girls in civilized countries attend school together and are educated freely in the same manner, girls have been shown to be the equal of boys in both intelligence and knowledge and, indeed, are at times superior. For this reason, men do not look down on women but treat them with courtesy and respect. This is not the case in our country, where there is an immense difference in the way boys and girls are educated.... Because of their parents' lower expectations and the paucity of opportunities, girls, however intelligent or ambitious they may be, are confined to their homes and are at most allowed to read and study after finishing their chores. Again, owing to age-old customs, people are of the opinion that book learning is of no use to women and that Western books, in particular, can only lead to frivolity. A woman's place, they claim, is in the home. Consequently, Japanese women are limited in outlook, ignorant in dealing with people outside their family, and deficient in helping their husbands and managing their homes. Since this is the situation at home, they, of course, fare worse in the outside world. Among strangers, they are hesitant and fearful, mute like puppets.... The inequality between men and women shames us deeply before the Westerners, and the situation will not change until women are allowed to develop their minds.

[xvii] Founded in 1885, *Jogaku zasshi* (*Girls' Education* magazine) was Japan's first magazine for young women.

In those days, it was exceptionally courageous of the school to affirm the inherent equality of men and women. In addition, the school was Christian but did not try to proselytize among the students. Attracted by its progressive spirit, young girls came from all over the country to study there. Graduates included Yamamuro Kieko, Hani Motoko, Sōma Kokkō, and Nogami Yaeko. Each woman, capable in her own right, served as proof of the excellence of the school's educational philosophy. Had I known of the school and the magazine, my spiritual awakening might have come sooner.

I began to read more seriously in my third and fourth year. Some of the books I read were the Min'yūsha series of *The Lives of Great Western Men*, which included people like Carlyle, Byron, and Goethe. Carlyle I found rather dull, but I was enthralled by Byron—his heroic exploits on behalf of the Greek independence movement, his utter disregard of social convention, his aristocratic good looks. (Each volume had a picture of the subject on the cover.) I also read a book called *The History of the World*, which covered Japan as well as China.

My Sister

By contrast, my sister's interests were more literary. Under the influence of a student teacher from the Higher Normal School, she read widely and worked on her writing, imitating the ornate style then in fashion. She even read *Teikoku bungaku* [a literary magazine put out by Tokyo Imperial University]. Her interest in literature was shared, and no doubt encouraged, by our cousin Michinaga, who was living with us at the time.

Michinaga was the eldest son of Teian, the adoptive head of my mother's family, who had drunk himself to death, leaving behind his wife and four children. Michinaga had finished his studies at the German Association School and was then at the Foreign Language School, specializing in German. His room near the front entrance was filled with books, among them *Tangled Hair* (*Midaregami*), Yosano Akiko's first collection of poems, and copies of *Myōjō*.[xviii] He also had a copy of *Portrait of a Demon of the Literary World* (*Bundan shōmakyō*), a poorly printed book revealing Akiko's love affair with Yosano Tekkan and his liaisons with other women. It was probably at my cousin's suggestion that I read *The Lives of Great Western Men*. My sister borrowed his copy of Takayama Chogyū's *Takiguchi, The Lay Priest* (*Takiguchi nyūdō*)

[xviii] Poetry journal founded in 1887 by Yosano Tekkan, the leader of the New Poetry Society (Shinshisha) and Yosano (Hō) Akiko's future husband.

and was apparently deeply moved by the historical romance, but I quickly tired of its flowery style and gave up after a few pages.

Too young and immature to understand literature, I looked with disapproval, even disdain, upon my sister's absorption in novels and poetry. I was aware of the publication of *Tangled Hair* in 1901—I was in my fourth year—and the ensuing controversy [over Akiko's frank depiction of sexual love], but the subject struck me as lacking in seriousness and did not interest me in the least.

My sister often talked late into the night with Michinaga, and I would frequently be sent to deliver a message: "Mother says it's getting late and time for you to go to bed." But now and then, I sat down and joined their conversation, little suspecting that my sister had fallen in love with her cousin.

My parents became aware of the growing intimacy and decided to take drastic action: Michinaga was banished from the house. My sister, not to mention my cousin, must have been devastated. She never talked to me about it, and I refrained from intruding upon her private feelings and thoughts. I was incapable of imagining her deep pain, but from that time on, I noticed a subtle change in my sister.

In the summer of 1900 [1901], soon after my cousin's sudden banishment, my parents adopted Yamanaka Yonejirō, the son of a farming family in Wakayama. This was on the understanding that he would eventually marry my sister and become the legal heir of the Hiratsuka family. At the time of his adoption, Yonejirō had just graduated from Wakayama Middle School.[xix] He entered the First Higher School the following spring and moved into the dormitory. He later studied German law at Tokyo Imperial University, was graduated with high honors, and became a government official. For the Hiratsuka family, especially for my father, he was the ideal heir.

Our relatives in Wakayama had arranged the adoption. The principal at the school had assured them that the boy was brilliant. Brilliant, no doubt, but to me he seemed old beyond his years, too complacent, with none of the sparkle of young men in Tokyo. My mother told me to address him as "Elder Brother," but I could not warm to him. With his thick country dialect and stiff, grown-up manner, he could have been an alien from another world. In my view, his adoption had been a mere expedient.

Even after moving into the dormitory, my adoptive brother came home on Sundays, but he was always treated like a guest, so I could not bring myself to think of him as a brother, much less appreciate my parents' relief and sat-

---

[xix] At the time, boys attended six years of elementary school and four or five years of middle school (*chūgakkō*), then went either to a three-year vocational college (*senmon gakkō*) or to a higher school (*kōtōgakkō*) for three years before entering a university, where they studied for three years to earn the degree of *gakushi*.

isfaction at having settled on an heir. I did not even attempt to understand the emotions of my sister, whose heart had been broken and whose future husband had been forced upon her.

The Opposite Sex

Looking back, I am appalled at how innocent and backward I was about relations between the sexes. Indeed, only after I finished college and began reading novels did I become dimly conscious of the opposite sex. Until then, I remained totally indifferent to such matters.

There was a girl in my class called Katō Nobu. Pretty, with a thin, pale face, refined manners, and a touch of daring chic, she later married Dohi Shunsho, who belonged to Tsubouchi Shōyō's Literary Arts Association and achieved fame as Japan's first Hamlet. Unlike the other girls at school, she was interested in literature and once talked to me about Namiko, the heroine in *Hototogisu*.[xx] One day, I overheard her talking about a boat race she had seen at Mukōjima. The race was between students on the rowing team at Tokyo Imperial University, but in her description she dropped hints and insinuations, so I wondered, why all this excitement over a boat race? My father, who was also teaching German at the First Higher School, frequently acted as coxswain for the crew, but he never invited me to a race; nor was I especially interested in going. Most girls, I suppose, would have been delighted.

I remember a minor incident from my college days a couple of years later. I went with my adoptive brother to visit my sister, who had suffered a relapse and was staying at a sanatorium in Chigasaki. We were walking alone on the shore one evening when he inexplicably took hold of my hand. We continued to walk, my hand in his, but other than thinking this unusual, I do not remember being particularly conscious that I was alone with a man.

As a young girl, then, I had virtually no contact with the opposite sex. My father was the legal guarantor for some students at the First Higher School and Tokyo University, and they came to our house now and then. There were also the male relatives who lived with us off and on, but needless to say, not one roused even a passing interest.

From early on, I seem to have been predisposed to the theoretical and philosophical aspects of life, rather than to emotional and literary concerns.

[xx] A novel by Tokutomi Roka. Namiko, who suffers from tuberculosis, is forced by her mother-in-law to divorce her husband, a naval officer who is away on duty. Namiko dies soon after. First serialized in the *Kokumin shinbun* from 1897 to 1898, it was published in book form and became a best-seller.

Perhaps I inherited this trait from my father, or perhaps he influenced me, but I am convinced that even as a young girl I had a strong vein of seriousness in my psychic makeup. This became more evident as I was gradually drawn to philosophical and religious questions.

⊚ ⊚ ⊚ ⊚ ⊚

I was now in my fifth and last year at Ochanomizu. Sitting next to me in class was the daughter of Dr. Murakami Senjō, a noted scholar of Buddhist studies. A sober girl in sober clothes, she was not the type to draw attention to herself. I happened to see an announcement in the newspaper about a lecture by her father and decided to go. This took no small degree of courage, since high school girls normally did not attend public gatherings without a grown-up. The lecture was at the Kinkikan in Kanda; the occasion, a commemoration in honor of either Shinran or Hōnen.[xxi] I had never before heard a talk on Buddhism, or for that matter, attended a public lecture by myself. Since I was accustomed to the dreary classes at school, I was deeply impressed by both the talk and the rapt attention of the audience. Dr. Murakami himself looked like a weathered old peasant, and I am sure he was a kind and interesting father.

One of the requirements at school was public speaking, so several days later, when my turn came to stand on the podium, I gave a rehash of the talk. Tokugawa Masako, who was the other speaker, gave a speech on the Nihilists in czarist Russia, a rather peculiar choice for the granddaughter of a former shogun. I was pleased with my speech. Ordinarily hesitant to speak in front of others, I was impelled by some inner force to share what I had heard. I have no doubt that Dr. Murakami's talk was a vital factor in bringing me closer to religion and philosophy.

[xxi] Both Shinran and Hōnen were important religious figures of medieval Buddhism.

3

College

Eager to pursue my awakening interest in religion, ethics, and philosophy, I
made up my mind to apply to Japan Women's College, which had just opened
[in 1901]. My more immediate reason was a book I had read by Naruse Jinzō,
the school's founder and president. *Women's Education* (*Joshi kyōiku*, 1896),
written on the eve of his campaign to found a college for women, set forth his
views on the need for such an institution. I do not remember where or how
I obtained the book, and as I had told no one of my plans to go to college, I
certainly could not have borrowed it from a friend. In any event, Naruse had
founded the college amid vehement opposition—people said it was either too
early or completely unnecessary—so I may well have heard of the controversy
and picked up a copy out of curiosity.

Naruse's ideas on women's higher education were highly original. He had
first studied the theoretical and practical aspects of women's education in the
United States, and then modified his findings to fit the reality of Japan's past
and present situation. His basic philosophy was to educate women first as
human beings; second, as individuals; and third, as Japanese citizens. After
he described his ideas, he gave specific proposals on the intellectual, moral,
physical, and practical education of young women. Stifled and frustrated as
I was by the rigid and formalistic education at Ochanomizu, his ideas captivated me, and without consulting anyone, not even my mother, sister, or
friends, I decided to apply. Of the three fields offered—Japanese literature,
English, and home economics—I hoped to study English.

I spoke to my father. To my great surprise, he opposed my plan outright:
"Too much learning is bound to make a woman unhappy." And this, from
a man who had been sent abroad to study by the Meiji government. My
father, sad to say, was no more enlightened than other members of society
who opposed women's higher education. I shall never forget his concluding

remark: "A parent's duty to a daughter ends with high school." My sister, who had finished school the previous year, was content to busy herself with lessons in the koto, violin, and German; poetry composition; and studying *The Tale of Genji*. My father saw no reason I should not do the same; women were supposed to do what they had always done—stay at home and manage the household. Given his categorical refusal, there was little I could say.

Secretly, I had no intention of obeying my father. Whatever the consequences, I decided to just go ahead and apply. Unlike the time I was forbidden to climb Mount Fuji, I was adamant about my decision. I was prepared to defy my father, the embodiment of patriarchal authority, and there is no question that my grim determination to carry out my plan was an implicit criticism of him.

At home, my father had never been known to seek anyone else's opinion. Even in so minor a matter as gardening, he routinely ignored my mother's suggestions and did exactly as he pleased. Our garden was supposed to be modeled on Arashiyama in Kyoto, but this too had been his one-sided decision. It also bothered me that my mother, even when unconvinced, always went along meekly. This is not to say that my father was more high-handed than most men at the time. He was kind and attentive to his family, a conscientious husband and father. Moreover, he took care of his personal needs, and unlike other husbands, never asked my mother to set out his clothes. He left the finer details of managing the house to her, as well as the responsibility for disciplining the children. As a child, I hardly remember being scolded. Yet, over time he had become a distant figure, a father with whom I could no longer speak in a carefree manner.

Had my father exercised his paternal prerogatives in a more arbitrary fashion, I might have been more openly rebellious, for I had always resisted the notion that a natural hierarchy existed among human beings. Still, there was a distinct tendency in our family to stress hierarchy and defer to seniority, although it was not as pronounced as in the families of professional military men. In speaking to my grandmother, for example, my father used language that was more polite and deferential. And I doubt he ever bowed to anyone at home, apart from my grandmother and the portraits of their majesties in the second-floor alcove, to which he paid daily obeisance.

My request to go to college was summarily rejected. My mother, however, knew only too well how stubborn I could be and interceded on my behalf. She succeeded in convincing my father, and I was given permission on the condition that I specialize in home economics and not English literature. I graduated from Ochanomizu in March 1903; I was seventeen [by Western count]. Aside from those who went on to the high school's two-year upper division, only a handful of the forty graduates continued their formal education: three went to the Higher Normal School, one to its training school for kindergarten teachers, one to Tsuda Eigakujuku, and two to the Ueno Music Academy. I was the only one to apply to Japan Women's College. Except for the colleges that I mentioned, institutes of higher learning were all closed to women.

I sent away for a brochure. There were no entrance examinations, and only a high school certificate was necessary. I sent for application forms, filled them out, and made all the arrangements on my own.

⊙ ⊙ ⊙ ⊙ ⊙

I entered college in April 1903 as a member of the third graduating class. I walked through the gates of the campus in Mejiro, my heart dancing with anticipation. In every respect, the students were different from those at high school. Bewildered and confused, I felt as though I had tumbled headlong into the world of grown-ups. Among the students were women who had taught at elementary school for several years, mothers, widows, and house-wives, even a middle-aged woman whom the students addressed as "Auntie." Many came from the provinces and wore their hair and kimono without any sense of style, and spoke in dialects that struck me as boorish—a far cry from the elegant attire and polished accents of the girls at Ochanomizu. Surrounded by these rough-mannered classmates, I felt lost, as if I were sur-rounded by foreigners.

Because of my new milieu, I decided that I would at least try to look like a grown-up. I took out the shoulder tucks sewn into my kimono, got rid of my purple kimono and hakama from high school days, and wore kimono with a more understated pattern of thin stripes or kasuri weave and a dark brown or olive-colored cashmere hakama. I also changed my hairstyle. Instead of tying my hair with a wide ribbon, or arranging it in the popular "Marguerite" style, with bangs in front and the hair swept up at the sides, I wore braids, looped up and tied with a narrow brown or black ribbon.

Unlike at Ochanomizu, none of the students wore Western-style clothes or bothered to arrange their hair in the cumbersome traditional style. Their tastes were simple and rustic; several students wore homespun cotton kimono and hakama. Only the commuters showed any signs of vanity; the rest were unconcerned. Rather than being disappointed, I was heartened to be among classmates who seemed more mature and serious.

The home economics department had an enrollment of close to a hundred and was the largest in the college; Japanese literature was the smallest. Our first assignment was to determine the seating arrangement. In keeping with the school policy of "Self-governance and self-study," we tried to do this on our own, but confusion reigned, and we had to ask the more knowledgeable students from the high school attached to the college to guide us. In contrast, the teachers at Ochanomizu had not suggested even once that, instead of looking to them for guidance, we should work things out by ourselves.

The new students assembled once a week to hear Naruse Sensei give a two-hour lecture on practical ethics. In his first lecture, he talked about the school's educational policy and how we should pursue our studies and academic research. His emphasis on creativity and studying on one's own, his opposition to rote learning and indiscriminate accumulation of facts, were a complete change from the force-fed education in high school. There were to be no examinations, no grades, no failures; the only requirement was a graduation thesis. The college was in every sense ideal.

Each day brought yet another new experience; I was overwhelmed. But it was Sensei's course on practical ethics that stirred me to the depths of my soul. Not what you would call an orator, he had an impassioned delivery, his voice rising and falling as he spoke, and this I found riveting. He sometimes talked for three hours until he had finished what he had to say, and by the time we left the lecture hall, it was often dark.

Sensei was originally from Yamaguchi Prefecture. After teaching at Baika, a Christian high school for girls, in Osaka, he was ordained as a minister and went to the United States to study.[i] On his return he became the principal of Baika and built up its reputation. But he had long hoped to found a women's college, and at the time I entered, he had just realized his life's ambition. He burned with idealism, his every word like a spark of fire. I had been frustrated about my inability to describe exactly what I did not like in my high school experience, but now my frustration gradually disappeared as I listened to him speak of his ideals and beliefs concerning women's education, even though he tended to get carried away. In Naruse Jinzō, I found for the first time in my life a person with a generous vision regarding women, a person whom I could truly respect and admire.

The lectures on practical ethics were meant as a starting point for our spiritual education and as such covered a wide range of subjects—religion, philosophy, ethics. These lectures also gave Sensei an opportunity to describe his view of the world and his religious convictions. He was a devout Christian and a minister by calling, but he never preached, despite the presence of many of his former students from Baika who were Christian. To the contrary: he was quite bitter about the prejudices and dogmatism of organized Christianity and warned us not to fall into the error of so many sentimental women who sought easy solace in churches and other religious institutions.

---

[i] Naruse Jinzō (1858–1919) studied at Andover Theological Seminary and Clark University from 1891 to 1893.

According to a history of the college, Sensei had arrived at his views on religion during his studies in the United States: "God is not God for one nation or for one people. He is impartial. He belongs to all people. Thus it is that from ancient times to the present, He has governed all nations, all peoples, all creation in a like manner. Those who do not accept this truth go against His will." Based on his firm belief in a universal God and an all-encompassing religion, he later established the Concordia Association [in 1912].[ii] His universalistic view of religion and the founding spirit of the college were essentially one and the same.

By now a fervent admirer of Naruse Sensei, I took copious notes, asked questions in class, and sought him out afterward in the hallway. With a deep furrow between his brows, he looked high-strung and unapproachable, but patiently answered my questions. He may have lacked personal charm—his sunken cheeks and bristly moustache certainly did not help—but he was pure in thought and character, his inner strength and vitality like an incandescent flame. I could not but respond to him with all my heart and soul.

Walking to school, a distance of about two and a half miles, was a pleasure, too. Illumined by oil lamps early in the morning, the streets were empty of vehicles except for a few rickshaws. (Gaslights were introduced after the Russo-Japanese War.) I walked rain or shine, and I savored every minute, not at all burdened by the distance. In fact, walking to school at my own pace while taking in the scenery is one of my fondest memories of those days. There were the verdant rice fields at the foot of Nekomatazaka, the egrets in the bamboo grove beyond, the red gate in front of Gokokuji Temple, Mount Fuji soaring in the distance, the gingko trees with their golden leaves.

I had noticed that life at college centered on the dormitory. The proctors, or "leaders," as we called them, urged me to move in. They said that the spirit of the school could be fully appreciated only by living on campus. It was true that the majority of the students came from out of town and that commuters tended to be treated like stepchildren. So in my second year, against my parents' objections, I moved into the dormitory.

The dorm, which was located to the rear of the campus, consisted of a row of seven attached wooden houses built in traditional style. Each house, or ryō, constituted a "family" of twenty or so members, including the younger students in the college high school, with a senior student or female teacher presiding as "housemother." Now and then, a house would invite other houses for a "family conference," at which time the students in home economics

---

ii "Concordia Association" is the college's official translation for Kiitsu Kyōkai. "Kiitsu" literally means "returning to oneness." The association was founded to promote peace and understanding among nations.

would be called upon to cook special dishes and demonstrate the correct way to behave in polite society.

I was assigned to House Number 7. Under the supervision of the dormitory head, Hirano [Hama], a third-year student, acted as housemother. My classmate Ideno Ryū and I were selected as "leaders." Ryū, who came from Nagano Prefecture, was a graduate of the college high school. On first meeting her, I had been impressed by her poise and firmness of character, but as I came to know her better, I began to doubt her qualifications as a leader. Narrow-minded and unwilling to listen to others, she was good at parroting Naruse Sensei's ideas, but despite her air of superiority, she had obviously never thought about them deeply. One of the more active leaders in the dorm was Inoue Hideko, a home economics student who later became president of the college. Considerably older—she was said to be married—capable, and efficient, she spoke in a clipped, precise manner and gave the impression of being more neuter than feminine.

It had been my decision to move into the dorm, but I was soon disillusioned. Four students occupied an eight-mat room, and it was impossible to study sitting face to face across a shared desk. On top of this, we were expected to attend meetings for "self-improvement" in the evenings. If we went to all these meetings, we would have been unable to do our work. I did not want to waste a minute, so I skipped the meetings and stayed in my room reading, organizing my notes, writing in a diary, or just sitting still, lost in my thoughts. I was promptly criticized; according to the other leaders, I was being selfish, and my behavior showed a disregard for the group. To the fanatic devotees of the Naruse cult, a student who neglected meetings and buried herself in books was an egotist, or worse, a hopeless heretic.

But hadn't Sensei himself repeatedly stressed the importance of self-reliance, self-control, and creativity? If we were to apply ourselves to our studies, shouldn't we be given enough time? The endless round of meetings made no sense at all. They were supposed to foster group spirit, but as far as I could tell, the discussions were meaningless, since the most talkative students claimed all the attention with their superficial views.

At one meeting I happened to attend, the older students asked us to discuss our impressions of the practical ethics class. At another meeting, we were asked to make a confession of our religious beliefs. The poor students with nothing to say had to make something up on the spot, and I suspect that few confessions of faith were genuine. Those who could rattle off some choice clichés were trusted and admired, while those who were true to themselves were invariably ignored.

I avoided meetings as much as possible but faithfully attended classes. Courses required for students in home economics were Practical Ethics

(Naruse); Ethics (Asō Shōzō); Pedagogy (Yumoto Takehiko); Applied Psychology (Matsumoto Matataro); Child Psychology (Takashima Heisaburō); Physiology (Ōsawa Kenji); Applied Chemistry (Nagai Nagayoshi); Hygiene (Miyake Hiizu); Law (Okuda Yoshito); Biology (Watase Shōzaburō); and Economics (Nakazawa Keizō).[iii] Added to these were classes in Japanese cooking (Akabori Minekichi); French cooking, taught by Yamazaki Buhachiro, a former chef at the French legation; and American cooking, taught by someone called Yanagisawa, a wiry, fast-talking elderly man who had run a restaurant in a train station somewhere in the United States.

Cooking classes were held two afternoons a week for the entire duration of college. I slipped out as soon as I finished taking notes and escaped to the library or audited courses in the humanities. I saw no point in staying, since the actual cooking was done by a select few while the others merely looked on. I either timed my return so that I could at least sample the food or sat reading at the back of the classroom until the food was ready. I had never been fond of cooking—it took too much time. I did learn how to bake, and at home, I persuaded my sister to help me make cookies, sponge cakes, or pies, which were then consumed by the family with exclamations of appreciation. My sister's favorite flavor was lemon, mine vanilla.

We were allowed to audit classes in the humanities, so whenever I could, I attended those I particularly enjoyed: History of Western Thought (Asō Shōzō); History of Western Art (Ōtsuka Yasuji); History of Japan (Okabe Seiichi); Western History (Ukita Kazutami); and Classical Chinese (Ichimura Sanjirō). Dr. Ōtsuka, who also taught at Tokyo Imperial University, was married to Ōtsuka Kusuoko, the author of the poem sequence "One Hundred Visits to the Shrine." Whenever he lectured, the hall overflowed with students eager to see his slides of paintings by Raphael and Michelangelo. His wife came to attend an event, and I remember admiring her from afar.

The school did not go on organized hikes or sightseeing trips. Field Day was an important event, and at the college, where physical education was a requirement, Naruse Sensei hoped to set up a separate department that would conduct systematic research on this subject. The curriculum included gymnastics, competitive sports, and all kinds of calisthenics to improve posture. We even had a class for self-expression, which, together with bicycling, was unique to the college. Wearing long gowns with tucks and gathers that resembled the long tunics of ancient Greece, we glided and gestured in time

---

[iii] Many of the lecturers were leading figures in their fields and on the faculty of Tokyo Imperial University.

to the piano. The purpose of the exercise, devised by Shirai Kikuo Sensei, was to express one's inner feelings through bodily motion, but it was almost embarrassing to watch, especially since the garments did not look good on the students, who mostly came straight from the provinces. The pace of the class was much too languid for my taste, so I skipped it.

Field Day was in the autumn. Held with great fanfare, the event was open to the public and attracted enormous crowds well into the 1920s. In 1903, the year I entered, it was on October 24 and attendance climbed to more than 5,000. Starting the day before, the students in home economics were busy making sandwiches and cookies for the invited guests, but there were more people than expected and we had to make curried rice at the last minute.

By far the greatest attraction of the day was the bicycle demonstration. At a time when few women rode bicycles, the school put special emphasis on the sport and kept ten or more bicycles on hand. The girls, wearing matching kimono and hakama, advanced in one line or divided into two. Then they circled the ground and picked up red and white balls with a long scoop. The spectacle never failed to draw thundering applause from the crowd.

Basketball was also unique to the college. Personally introduced to Japan by Naruse Sensei, the sport was eminently suited to the school policy of encouraging competition between groups rather than individuals. In fact, anyone who stood out from the crowd was generally looked upon with disfavor. I joined the home economics team in my first year, and along with the other members, wore a belted blouse, bloomers, long black stockings, and canvas shoes. Our first match was against the humanities team, but we were roundly beaten, even though we had practiced for days. As we walked off the court, the tears came trickling down my cheeks, not so much because we had lost, but because I had not been in good condition and was unable to do my best. Mortified, I hid myself in a classroom.

Sometime after the match, I saw a group photo of the team. We were standing in a line in front of the hoop, but I was so small in comparison to everyone else that I could have been mistaken for a child. Clearly, I was never meant to play the game. I quit then and there.

I participated in one other group activity that year. The students in the humanities department had decided to create *tableaux vivants* from the novel *Takiguchi, The Lay Priest* and were looking for someone small and slight to play the part of the heroine, Yokobue. Presentations of scenes from history and literature were very popular, and since all I had to do was to dress up in a costume and stand still—there was no need to talk—I volunteered. But this, too, was my first and last time.

I React Against Authority

Although unhappy with dormitory life and critical of the leaders, I was devoted as ever to Naruse Sensei and eager to absorb all he had to offer. Indeed, I shall be forever grateful that I was given the opportunity to come into direct contact with his charismatic personality and extraordinary magnetism. The experience was invaluable for my spiritual growth. And Sensei, for his part, seemed to have taken notice of me, for without question I was an exceptionally determined student.

I was not alone in worshipping Sensei. My fellow students were no less fervent, but to my surprise and disappointment, they did not appear to be particularly interested in their studies. I took notes conscientiously and rewrote them after class, but they seemed content just to sit back and listen. Not that it mattered, since there were no examinations.

Take Asō Sensei's lectures on the history of Western philosophy. He began with the Greeks, talking about Thales, who claimed the world was made of water; Anaximenes, who said it was air; Heracleitus, who said it was fire; and another thinker who said it was all three plus earth. He also spoke about Heracleitus's theory that all things were in constant flux, but that an unchanging principle called "logos" also existed. Hungry for more information, I rushed to the library after class and read books by Kuwaki Gen'yoku, or it may have been Ōnishi Hajime. But I was the only one to do this. There was not even one other student who showed the same intellectual curiosity.

The boarding students were particularly remiss. Perhaps they should not be blamed, because, after all, "service" and "sacrifice" came first and anyone caught at her desk was made to feel guilty. Or, to put things in a more positive light, those students had more than enough to do absorbing Naruse Sensei as a person as well as his precepts, and so had little time or energy to spare for serious study.

Something else baffled me. I do not know why, but the home economics department was considered the stronghold of Sensei's teachings, and the students were distinguished from the rest and expected to lead. For instance, whenever an eminent visitor came, we had to prepare the food. There would be tumult in the kitchen, and predictably, the student who worked the hardest—and by that I mean the one who showed the most group spirit—would be singled out for praise. Service to a benefactor was automatically considered to be service to the school, and in turn, to God and society. I found this hard to swallow, and resisted inside myself and did as little as possible.

But even more distasteful was Sensei's attitude toward the benefactors. His displays of gratitude were so blatant that I pitied him. On one occasion, he thanked a visitor fulsomely in front of the assembled students, not once but over and over. Under ordinary circumstances, he did not smile, but then he did his best to put on a smile, which was more like a grimace.

In a way, I understood his predicament. Private schools depended on these benefactors, especially a women's college founded in the face of strong opposition. I realized that the college finances were straitened, but did he have to stoop so low? And why did he express his gratitude in a way that seemed to ask the students to do the same? Much as I sympathized with him, I could not subdue my negative reactions. Monthly tuition was 3 yen, boarding fees, 4 1/2. Unlike today, parents were not asked to make extra contributions, so running a college may have been more difficult than I could have imagined.

The main benefactors were leaders in the business world like Iwasaki, Mitsui, Sumitomo, Shibusawa, Morimura, Hirooka, and Dokura, and political figures like Itō, Ōkuma, Konoe, and Saionji. Benefactors occasionally came to give talks, but what they said was usually superficial and full of platitudes; not a single one earned my respect or admiration.

Ōkuma Shigenobu, already old, was particularly arrogant and patronizing. His views on women's education were utterly dismissive of women. According to him, they had to be educated not for themselves, but because their continued ignorance would be a national disgrace. Furthermore, if women did not keep up with men, who had already made great strides, they would not only be useless as helpmates but actually would be a hindrance and ultimately detract from Japan's national strength.

Another equally disagreeable visitor was Hirooka Asako, the wife of the head of the Kajimaya merchant family in Osaka. Known for her business acumen, she had apparently worked hard for the college at the time of its founding. In an access of zeal, she began haranguing the students, and worse, chided Naruse Sensei to his face. On another visit, she had the gall to tell the upper-level students in home economics that theories were not worth anything and that they would be better off sticking to practical subjects. The woman may have been a benefactor, but she prattled on in such a self-satisfied, bullying tone that I did not feel an ounce of gratitude.

My Search for the Meaning of Life

As I grew increasingly disenchanted with the college, my enthusiasm for Sensei's lectures also began to wane. It was as if I were recovering from a prolonged bout of drunkenness. When he was lecturing, his clenched fists raised, his heart and soul in every word, I was momentarily swept away. But afterward, on rereading my notes, I often felt strangely let down—a chill would come over me, as if I were sitting next to a hearth of dying embers. Without

Sensei's living presence, his words and ideas lost all their persuasive power and became lifeless.

Toward the end of my second year or the beginning of my third, Sensei lectured on empiricism, the leading Western philosophical theory in those days. He first talked about Descartes' apothegm, "I think, therefore I am," then spent many hours explaining Comte's positivism and James's pragmatism. His lectures were no doubt meant to prevent his young charges from falling prey to pernicious current ideas, or again, to stop them from seeking emotional solace in dogmatic organized religions. But his lectures also reflected his new interest in positivism. I knew he liked to keep abreast of intellectual trends abroad and regularly purchased books at Maruzen.

According to Sensei, Comte divided the development of human thought into three stages: the theological, the metaphysical, and the positive, or empirical. Human beings had already passed through the first two stages and were presently in the third; they should thus discard old ideas and construct a scientific, empirical worldview and philosophy. I listened intently, and while I had no objection to Comte's emphasis on experiential knowledge and the formulation of laws from observed phenomena, I was not persuaded that such a philosophy would fulfill my own nascent spiritual aspirations. All the same, I was thirsty for knowledge; eager to know more about Comte, I went to the library and searched for books on his approach to sociology and the system of moral beliefs based on positivist ideas. They satisfied my intellectual curiosity, but failed to stir me. At this stage in my life, I was attracted more to thinkers like Spinoza, the nontheist intoxicated with the notion of God; Meister Eckhart and his vision of mystic union with God; and the German idealist thinker Hegel and his doctrine of Absolute Being.

Within the college, Sensei's views on ethics were regarded as the "voice of God," beyond dispute and absolutely binding. Students went around echoing his phrases: "We must be more empirical," or "The age of metaphysics is over." And no sooner did they hear a lecture on Comte or Jamesian pragmatism than a new catchphrase was on their lips: "Knowledge unrelated to real life is irrelevant," or "Knowledge without practical application is useless."

I found it deplorable that utilitarianism and pragmatism in the narrowest sense had taken hold of the school. When Sensei claimed the age of metaphysics was over, he was saying that dogmatism prevented human progress, and was warning his students not to see everything from a limited Christian perspective. (There were many Christians at the college.) But his words were insufficiently understood, and worse, the students in the home economics department were claiming that those in the humanities, especially in Japanese literature, were hopeless anachronisms and of no use to the advancement of human society. By contrast, they were attuned to everyday life, actively involved, and concerned with religion.

In such an atmosphere, a student who buried herself in books, especially books unrelated to empiricism, was immediately branded an apostate and a dangerous subversive. We were forbidden to read Nietzsche, Tolstoy, and other writers whose extreme, unsound ideas were deemed harmful to susceptible young minds. The dormitory head once took me to task for reading such a book. She was intolerant of any idea that did not come straight from Sensei—in spite of the fact that she herself was incapable of grasping his true meaning. Though I remained circumspect in my behavior, I had by then also been singled out as the ringleader of the metaphysical clique and had been admonished by upper-level students (one was Inoue Hideko, who, as I mentioned, later became college president) to reconsider my ideas. This did not change my resistance to their narrow-minded pragmatism and their propensity to exclude those who did not agree with them.

In any case, I had acquired a passion for reading and devoured books. As I look back now, the college library was pitiful, and, no doubt reflecting Sensei's past interests, its holdings were mainly concerned with Christianity. Still, the library was better than nothing, and in my spare time, I would run over there or skip classes and spend the whole day reading. One night, after lights-out at nine-thirty, I sneaked into the dining hall and read by candlelight, but the dormitory head caught me, and I was reprimanded.

My reading was unsystematic and focused on religion, philosophy, and ethics; I was not interested in literature or science. Some of the books I read were: Kuwaki Gen'yoku's *Outline of Philosophy* (*Tetsugaku gairon*) and *General History of Western Philosophy* (*Seiyō tetsugakushi gaisetsu*); Ōnishi Hajime's *History of Western Philosophy* (*Seiyō tetsugakushi*); Oka Asajirō's *Lectures on Evolution* (*Shinkaron kōwa*); and in translation: the Bible; Renan's *Life of Jesus*; Dante's *Divine Comedy*; Bunyan's *Pilgrim's Progress*; Milton's *Paradise Lost*. I also read a book about Tolstoy's views on life and religion, periodicals such as *Rikugō zasshi* (*Cosmos* magazine), published by the Unitarian Church, and *Shinjin* (*New Man*), put out by the Hongō Church. Among the contributors to *Shinjin*, I particularly admired Tsunashima Ryōsen's articles.

Then I read other articles by Inoue Tetsujirō, Motora Yūjirō, Nakajima Rikizō, Kuwaki Gen'yoku, Takayama Chogyū, Tobari Chikufū, Anesaki Chōfū (Masaharu), and other scholars in *Journal of Philosophy* (*Tetsugaku zasshi*) and *Lectures of the Teiyū Ethical Society* (*Teiyū rinri kōenshū*), which were published by Tokyo Imperial University. It was in the latter journal that I read with great interest about the debate between Nakajima Rikizō and others on the question of motivation as an ethical problem, a topic then under heated discussion. It was also in that journal that I first read about Ibsen's play, *A Doll's House*. Though it would be some time before Nora became the subject of wide controversy, the long article by Kuwaki made a strong impression. My first encounter with Nietzsche and Schopenhauer was also in the school library.

Even as I read indiscriminately, my restless mind teemed with questions: What is God? What am I? What is truth? How should one live? I thought I was the only person obsessed with the ultimate questions of human existence, but to a greater or lesser degree, other young Japanese were also searching for a new philosophy of life. Indeed, from about the time of the war with Russia, a youthful vibrancy and romantic spirit had enlivened the world of thought as intellectuals were increasingly drawn to religious and ethical issues. Nietzsche's philosophy was particularly popular. This was largely due to Takayama Cho-gyū, who wrote on Nietzsche's theory of the aesthetics of the instinctive life and glorified the medieval Buddhist monk Nichiren as the embodiment of the Nietzschean heroic ideal. The essays on religion by Tsunashima Ryōsen also had an enthusiastic following. Thinkers vied with one another to propound their ideas on religion and ethics and recent converts to Christianity also translated works like Tolstoy's *My Confession* and *What I Believe*.

The shocked reaction of young people to the death of Fujimura Misao, the eighteen-year-old philosophy student who threw himself into the Kegon Falls at Nikkō, or the deaths of so many youths who followed his example,[iv] can only be understood in the context of this intellectual ferment. Caught between the dissolution of the old feudal ethic and emergent nationalism and militarism, racked with doubts and apprehension, young Japanese gravitated toward religion and philosophy in their search for the meaning of existence and for inner peace.

At the college, students were discouraged from embracing religious beliefs other than those professed by Naruse Sensei. Nonetheless, a few attended services elsewhere. Some went to Fujimi Church, for instance, where Uemura Masahisa was pastor, or to Chikazumi Jōkan's house in Hongō Morikawa-chō to hear his lectures on *Tannishō*[, the compilation of the sayings of Shinran]. One Sunday, half out of curiosity, I accepted a boarding student's invitation to go to the Hongō Church in Ikizaka. This was my first exposure to a Christian milieu; I had read the Bible but never attended a service.

The church had a large contingent of men and women students. The pastor, Ebina Danjō, delivered the sermon, and I listened attentively along with

---

iv In May 1903 Fujimura, a student at the First Higher School, committed suicide after carving a note on a nearby tree declaring that he had chosen death because the truth was beyond all understanding.

the rest of the congregation. I was not one to do things halfheartedly, and so, clutching my black leather-bound Bible, I started going to church every Sunday. I also attended Uchigasaki Sakusaburō's lectures on the Bible. Drawn instinctively to the Psalms, I read them over and over and memorized my favorite: "As the hart panteth after the water brooks, so panteth my soul after Thee, oh God."

Ebina's sermons were very popular among the young students. He was an eloquent and polished speaker with a commanding presence. Solidly built, he had a big, flat face, bushy black beard, and booming voice. He was too polished for my taste, however, almost glib. As a speaker, Naruse Sensei was much more inspiring. I would get excited about something Ebina said for a moment, but feel afterward that he had not really answered my questions. He also spent an inordinate amount of time talking about chastity—there were many women in the congregation—and possibly because war with Russia was expected any day, he kept hinting at some kind of compromise with the nationalistic state ideology. But I was not interested in these matters; I was seeking God. I did take a look at his book, A New Life for Imperial Japan (Teikoku no shinseimei), but as I remember nothing about it, I must have disagreed with what he said.

I had another objection to the idea of God as defined by Christianity, that is, its positing of a transcendent being high above the heavens in opposition to lowly man, a creature conceived in sin and the embodiment of sin. If God were truly God, supreme and absolute, there should be nothing to oppose him. I preferred to think that God was not transcendent but immanent in the universe, that he was the ground of being for all of nature, including humankind, and that we all resided within God, the Absolute Being.

Finally, I noticed in the general attitude of the church members an emotionalism perhaps peculiar to Christians. In trying to win over potential converts, they would say, "There's no need to understand—just believe. Believe and be baptized." I could only react negatively to such an argument; I had to be persuaded by logic and reason.

A quiet elderly woman, of a sort often seen among Christians, came up to me one day and urged me to be baptized. "Be baptized first, and I assure you, faith will follow." I could not bring myself to do this. The mere thought was horrifying; I would be deceiving myself, Christ, and God. I dodged her request: "Please let me think this over for a while. I'd like to go over things more carefully in my mind. Once I see that there's no other path to spiritual peace, I promise you that I'll ask to be baptized." This was not the only time I was pressured. I soon tired of it and stopped going to church. My time could be more profitably spent reading the Bible at home. I never went inside a church again, although I did read Uchimura Kanzō's Studies on the Bible (Seisho no kenkyū).

My brief association with the Hongō Church had its compensations. After the service there were talks by famous people. I vividly remember one guest, the writer Tokutomi Roka, who spoke on Higuchi Ichiyō. Roka still looked like a student, and instead of speaking from the lectern, he sat on a chair he had brought down from the platform. He spoke slowly, in an offhand, confidential tone, and when he praised Ichiyō's descriptive passages in her novel *Takekurabe*, he seemed to be talking to himself. I had not read the novel but was strangely moved.

Another guest was Kinoshita Naoe, the author of *Confessions of a Husband* (*Ryōjin no jihaku*), who spoke passionately about Tanaka Shōzō and the scandal surrounding the pollution caused by the copper mines in Ashio.[v] Only dimly aware of the incident, I was much disturbed to hear the details. Anesaki Masaharu also came to talk about his recent travels in Europe. He was thin and tense, the picture of a young intellectual, but I cannot remember what he said.

⊚ ⊚ ⊚ ⊚ ⊚

For a while, I had felt a vague physical discomfort. Had the stress and anxiety of my single-minded search for the true God taken a toll? Or had the hypertropic sinusitis for which I'd had an operation flared up again? I went to see the school doctor. He told me I was suffering from nervous exhaustion and possibly from Basedow's disease[, a malfunction of the thyroid gland]. I had done very little exercise since moving on campus, and so I took up tennis again, playing during lunch hour and at other free moments.

One of my partners was Naganuma Chieko, who had entered one year after me. She later married Takamura Kōtarō and become widely known through *Chieko-shō*, the series of poems he wrote about her. She was shy and withdrawn, too timid to look at anyone in the face, her voice barely audible. But she was good at tennis, hitting the ball just over the net, and had a powerful serve. I often wondered where she got her strength. She rarely spoke, and since I was just as taciturn, we played tennis together but never had a sustained conversation. Chieko was also in the home economics department, but she seemed uninterested in her classes and spent most of the time roaming the school grounds with her box of watercolor paints or riding a bicycle on the athletic field. (I shall say more about her later.)

I suddenly came down with a fever. The diagnosis was paratyphoid, and I was immediately sent home. I had cajoled my parents into letting me board at

---

[v] The politician Tanaka Shōzō (1841–1913) was a champion of the peasants whose livelihood was threatened by the pollution of nearby rivers and fields by toxic effluents from the Ashio Copper Mines in Tochigi Prefecture.

the school and felt somewhat embarrassed, but I had had my fill of dormitory life and welcomed the excuse to move out.

Still recuperating from my illness, I had a second operation for my sinusitis at the Okonogi Hospital near Ochanomizu. Then, from the end of December until New Year's, I spent a few days with my father at an inn on the Odawara coast. Responsible for auditing military expenditures, he had been putting in long hours at the office since the outbreak of the war with Russia [in February 1904] and was much in need of a rest. In addition, he had been diagnosed with diabetes. Away from Tokyo and the inevitable onslaught of New Year's visitors, he would be able to relax. My mother, who thought the mild sea air would do me good, told me to accompany him.

Confined to one room alone with my father for the first time in several years, I felt the distance that had opened up between us more acutely than ever. I had been close to him until my second or third year of high school, but now I found we had nothing in common to talk about. Had I spoken to him about what was uppermost in my mind—my spiritual turmoil—he would not have understood. It was not that I positively disliked him or could not stand the sight of him. After all, he was my flesh and blood. Rather, I disliked the odor of officialdom that clung to him. This odor became more pronounced as he advanced in the bureaucracy and gained more honors. I would turn away in disgust when an expression typical of a government functionary flickered across his face. He was not the only person who wore this expression—I had noticed the same look on his colleagues who came to the house. It was as if the dregs of long years of government service had settled into the lines on their faces.

I am digressing, but some years later, when I came across a photograph of Mori Ōgai, I instantly recognized the expression on his face—the same as my father's and typical of Meiji bureaucrats. I was surprised, since he looked so different from the author I had imagined from reading his books. This may be the reason I did not visit him years later, even though he expressed support for Seitō, and subsequently, the New Women's Association.

I am not sure how or when I came to react against worldly authority, even lose all respect for it. I have to say that I felt the same aversion to my father that I did to Ōkuma and the other benefactors of the college, though the intensity of my feelings differed. My aversion to authority has lasted to this day, and will probably stay with me until the end of my life.

My father was fond of go and occupied his time playing on a board he found at the inn. I did not know how to play go, but since I knew Five in a Row, he challenged me to a game now and then. As a child, I had been quite good and even beaten him once or twice. But I was in no mood to compete and became so absent-minded that he would say, "Are you sure you want to make that move?" I quickly took back the stone, but as his stones spread out over the board, I wondered whether there was any point in playing.

Our walks on the shore were equally irritating. My father was not interested in walking for the sake of walking, and since the wind could be quite chilly even in Odawara, he always wanted to quit right away. Instead of returning with him, I kept walking at a furious pace and got back to the inn just as he was having his evening drink. I had always preferred my own company, but now, condemned to be with my father, I counted the minutes until we could return home.

⊚ ⊚ ⊚ ⊚ ⊚

Classes resumed. No longer a boarding student, I walked to school with my sister, breathing in the crisp morning air. My sister, I should mention, had entered college a year after me and enrolled in the Japanese literature department. This was not her decision but my father's. She and I were only a year apart, and my father had always treated us even-handedly. Since he had allowed me to go to college, he no doubt believed that it was his parental duty to let her go, too. I had received permission on the condition that I specialize in home economics, but my sister had consented to go only if she was allowed to study Japanese literature. (My father's policy of equal treatment extended to our clothes, food, possessions, school, and private lessons. Not surprisingly, people often mistook us for twins.)

My sister seemed unimpressed by Naruse Sensei's classes on practical ethics, or for that matter, by all the talk about school spirit. Her sole concern was literature—the lectures by Togawa Zanka, Shioi Ukō, and Sekine Masanao; the poetry writing class taught by Miyake Kaho, a woman writer then as famous as Higuchi Ichiyō; literary discussions with like-minded friends. But then in her second year, she was diagnosed with first-stage tuberculosis and had to withdraw.

As a child my sister had been healthy and sturdy. She'd had a mild case of pleurisy soon after finishing high school and spent some time with my grandmother in Odawara, but we assumed she had completely recovered. The tuberculosis diagnosis came as a blow. Even now, I often wonder whether her poor health was in some way connected with the cruel and arbitrary separation from her cousin. Unable to utter a word of protest, could she have internalized her grief and despair? Michinaga, in the meantime, had graduated from the Foreign Language School, and after teaching German at Chiba Medical School and Kansai University, had accepted a job at the Seventh Higher School in Kagoshima. He never returned to Tokyo. I am certain he was deeply hurt, too. My father probably thought he was only exercising his normal paternal prerogatives and never gave the matter a second thought.

My sister was sent to Nanko-in, a sanatorium in Chigasaki under the management of Dr. Takada Kōan, one of the doctors at the college. She was lonely at first, but was soon joined by her classmate Yasumochi Yoshiko, and together they passed the hours composing waka and haiku. After she recovered, she spent some time on the coast with my grandmother.

Years later, my sister established contact with Michinaga. Retired and living in Moji, he happened to see me on a program that Osaka Television had arranged for my seventy-second birthday. He got in touch with my sister, and until his death in 1962 at age eighty, the two corresponded.

◎ ◎ ◎ ◎ ◎

The war with Russia was in its second year. The entire nation had rallied to the war effort, and at school some of the students volunteered for work rolling bandages and making cheer-up kits for the soldiers at the front. Wrapped up in my world of abstract ideas and grappling with the same questions as before, I made no effort to help.

By this time, two antiwar poems had appeared: "Brother, Do Not Die" by Yosano Akiko and "A Hundred Visits to the Shrine" by Ōtsuka Kusuoko.[vi] I was acquainted with Kusuoko's poem, but not with Akiko's. The college refused to have anything to do with the kind of literature associated with [her husband's journal] *Myōjō*, which was not surprising given the lineup of old fogies in Japanese literature. Uchimura Kanzō, Sakai Toshihiko, Ishikawa Sanshirō, Kōtoku Shūsui, and others associated with the *Yorozu chōhō* newspaper had also ignited a public controversy when they announced their opposition to the war. Again, at a meeting of the [antiwar] Socialist Society (Shakaishugi Kyōkai) at the YMCA, the police had come out in force, and when in the middle of Kōtoku's speech they ordered the meeting closed, a fistfight broke out. But at that stage in my life, these events could have taken place in another world, for all I knew.

[vi] Ōtsuka's poem was published in the January 1905 issue of *Taiyō*. In her poem she admits that when she visits a shrine, she prays more for her husband who is at the front than for her country. "If I were asked which is more precious, my country or my husband / I would only shed tears and not answer...." Yosano's poem sequence, which was subtitled "To My Younger Brother in Despair," was published from September 1904 to January 1905 in *Myōjō*. At the time, her younger brother was in Port Arthur, the scene of bitter fighting. The poem begins with the lines: "Oh, how I weep for you. Brother, do not die. Did your parents bring you up to kill someone with a sword? Did they bring you up to die at twenty-four?"

As a general policy the college steered students away from current political or social issues and tried to erect a barrier between the school—the ideal society—and the real world, isolating them from baleful outside influences. As a result, the students—including me—only glanced at the newspapers, if they looked at all, though inevitably news of developments at the front reached our ears. My father often returned late at night, after a full day of auditing military expenditures. We also received word that my Aunt Ai's brother-in-law, an army officer, had been killed in action at the Battle of Port Arthur. So we must have talked about the war at home, but strangely enough, I remember the earlier war with China more vividly.

It was now the spring of 1905. Reports of the impending arrival of the Russian Baltic Fleet stirred the country, and while people could talk of nothing else, I had reached a momentous turning point in my inner life: I had read an article by Tsunashima Ryōsen called "My Encounter with God" (*Yo ga kenshin no jikken*).[vii] The article was in a library copy of *Shinjin*. I had long admired Tsunashima's writings, mostly theoretical discussions on ethics and religion, in *Shinjin* and *Rikugō zasshi*. But this article was different; it was based on his own spiritual experience. He had written a deeply felt, searingly honest account of how he had come face to face with God. For a journal article it was unusually long, and as he explained in his prefatory remarks, he had written it not for readers who had already undergone a serious religious experience but for those who earnestly hoped to find God and enter into the life of the spirit. As I turned the pages, I literally held my breath, absorbing every word and oblivious to my surroundings. When I came to the following passages, I was overwhelmed with the realization that I had been searching for God in the wrong way.

> Verily have I seen God. Verily have I seen Him face to face ... entered a realm in which I myself have become God. I give thanks for this, for this utterly confounding, utterly unexpected state of consciousness received directly from God, without the slightest mediation of the testimony or experience of people in the past.... My religious beliefs had been mainly formed by putting my trust in the person of Christ and the prophets, or again, by accepting the validity of their powerful spiritual awareness. Not based on what I myself had experienced, my beliefs were shallow and puerile.
>
> ...As I immersed myself more deeply in the life of the spirit, I resolved to cast aside all past testimony and rely on myself to hear the voice of God. My earnest

---

[vii] Tsunashima Ryōsen (1873–1907): Religious philosopher and literary critic. Ryōsen, who suffered from tuberculosis beginning in his early twenties, wrote the article two years before his death.

quest to find Him was not in vain. Not once, but many times over, I felt His radiant presence in the deepest chambers of my soul. The God I encountered was no longer the God of old, a conventional timeworn image, an abstract ideal. And yet, I thought, might there still not be a thin veil separating me from the God whose presence I felt so vividly?

...But this no longer is the case. The God of heaven and earth has manifested Himself, as glorious as the noonday sun. God is now a living reality, marvelous and wondrous. Oh, what a blessing!

Reading the article, I realized the futility of filling my head with the words and ideas of others who had made the same quest, or of trying to find the true God, the authentic self, in a world of abstraction that lacked any personal experience. Yet concretely, what must I do in order to come face to face with the living God, to attain true faith and unshakeable peace of mind? It was all very well to say that one should get rid of preconceptions and excessive intellectualizing, "immerse oneself in the life of the spirit," or "listen with earnest desire for the voice of God," but to my great distress, I had no idea how to proceed.

Zen Buddhism

One day, not long after this, an errand took me to my old dorm and on a sudden impulse, I decided to visit Kimura Masako, a classmate with whom I was not particularly friendly. On her desk was a copy of *One Wave in the Sea of Zen* (*Zenkai ichiran*), a tract written by Imakita Kōsen, the first *kanchō* of Engakuji in Kamakura.[viii] Intrigued by the old-fashioned woodblock printing, I leafed through the pages. A phrase caught my eye: "Seek the Great Way within yourself. Do not seek it outside of yourself. The wondrous force that wells up within you is none other than the Great Way itself." Adrift as I was in the world of abstraction, the words were like a direct warning.

I saw another phrase: "Many are those who know their natures but few who see into their natures. To know one's nature is merely to know Heaven. To see into one's nature is to gain Heaven." The tract, in two fascicles, was apparently a Zen Buddhist critique of Confucianism, in particular the virtues set forth in *The Analects, The Greater Learning,* and *The Doctrine of the Mean.* In wild excitement I borrowed the book and hurried home. Even now, years later, I

[viii] *Zenkai ichiran:* Treatise written by Imakita Kōsen (1816–1892) in 1862. *Kanchō:* A new title instituted in the early Meiji for the chief abbot of a Zen temple. Engakuji: A temple of the Rinzai sect of Zen Buddhism founded in the thirteenth century.

wonder what made me stop by Masako's room—I hardly knew her. We had very different characters and personalities. But joined by our mutual interest in Zen, we remained close friends until the day she died. A strange, strange bond, indeed.

Masako was exceptionally tall and had a muscular build that made her a champion on the basketball court and a star of the bicycle team. With her broad cheekbones and long, tilted eyes, she could be quite intimidating at first sight, but she had a supple voice, which she would modulate at will, depending on her companion. She was also practical and open-minded, with sound instincts—my exact opposite in every way. A student of Zen for some time, she had already achieved *kenshō* and been given the religious name Ekoku.[ix] She talked to me about Zen and *zazen*, the practice of introspection that called for quiet sitting and concentration on a given problem. She said that religious enlightenment—kenshō—could be attained by steadfast adherence to this practice. As I understood it, the state of heightened awareness achieved in kenshō seemed the same as Tsunashima Ryōsen's epiphanic experience of God. At last, I knew what I had to do.

Several days later, Masako took me to Ryōmō-an, a hermitage in the middle of the rice fields in Nippori. I recall that this was in the early summer of my third year of college. At Ryōmō-an—the "Hermitage of Forgetting Both"—it was possible to cast aside both illusion (*maya*) and enlightenment. The head of the hermitage was Shaku Sōkatsu-rōshi, the Dharma successor to Shaku Sōen-rōshi, second *kanchō* of Engakuji.[x] Still in his thirties, Sōkatsu-rōshi had already established a reputation as a brilliant teacher. He lived alone. Gotō Sōseki, a student at Tokyo Imperial University with unsophisticated country ways, served as his attendant. Most of the people who came to the hermitage were students at the university. Each one struggled with questions about human existence and looked so grim that the air crackled with tension.

The first requirement was an interview with Sōkatsu-rōshi. Following Gotō's instructions, I waited my turn in a room at the end of the hall. I had ready the designated sum of money suitably wrapped in paper. I struck the gong twice and, with both hands clasped to my chest, walked slowly to Rōshi's room. I opened the sliding doors in a crouching position and after I closed them, I pressed my palms together in greeting. I next made three prostra-

---

[ix] *Kenshō*: Literally, seeing into one's nature. An approximate synonym for *satori*, it is considered the first stage of religious enlightenment.

[x] *Rōshi*: Literally, "elder teacher"; usually translated as "Zen master." Title bestowed by a master when he thinks a disciple has attained religious understanding equal to his own and experienced genuine satori. Dharma successor (*hossu*): A monk or priest who is given permission by his master to carry on his teachings.

tions with my hands turned upward on the tatami and sat down approximately three feet from Rōshi.

At the end of the interview I was given permission to train with Rōshi and assigned my first *kōan:*[xi] What was your original face before your parents were born? "What was your face before you were born, before your parents were born, yes, even before the sun, moon, and stars came into existence? Go over there, have someone teach you how to sit properly, and work on it." After saying this with barely a word of explanation, he shook a small handbell and dismissed me. I was utterly confused but could not do anything but leave the room.

I asked Gotō to teach me the correct sitting posture, and without further ado, I sat down on the cushion to practice zazen. A completely new world had opened up—a world with its own rules and regulations. From that day forward, I practiced zazen and embarked on an arduous, endless journey in search of my true self. It was truly a fateful day.

A zazen session usually lasted [from forty-five to sixty minutes,] the time it took for an incense stick to burn. Between sessions, we met with Rōshi on a one-to-one basis. We were not allowed to reveal what took place at the meeting or which kōan we had been assigned. During the meeting, we were supposed to report to Rōshi any insight we might have gained about the kōan, but more often than not, as soon as we entered the room, we would be told to work harder and be dismissed with a shake of the bell. Indeed, it was said that Rōshi could tell how much progress we had made by the mere sound of the gong, the fall of our footsteps, the way we opened the sliding doors and bowed.

One day, soon after I started zazen, Gotō took me aside. "I must lodge a complaint," he said with an unusually stern expression on his face. Apparently, among my schoolbooks, he had noticed a copy of *Tetsugaku zasshi.* "Don't read that kind of thing. If you're going to read, read the biography of a famous monk." I had begun zazen with the earnest hope that it would lead me to a personal experience of the truth. I knew I was supposed to clear my head of all previous ideas, but I had been carrying around the philosophy journal out of habit. That is why he rebuked me. I was annoyed—he had no business meddling in my affairs—but then I thought about it further and realized that he had spoken to me out of kindness.

Gotō was studying philosophy at Tokyo Imperial University. He later took the tonsure and was certified as Dharma successor to Sōkatsu-rōshi. He

---

[xi] Variously translated as "case" or "conundrum." A terse statement that cannot be understood by ordinary logical reasoning. Employed chiefly by the Rinzai sect of Zen Buddhism to jolt the practitioner into a deeper state of consciousness and ultimately to attain satori.

trained many students and served successively as head abbot of Myōshinji and Daitokuji, the great monastic centers in Kyoto. Gotō Zuigan-rōshi, as he was known, passed away some years ago, but each time I heard his name, I remembered the young layman who had scolded me.

A weeklong *sesshin* was held once a month at Ryōmō-an. During this period of intense training, we sat for hours in the meditation hall and were permitted to see Rōshi several times a day. We also listened to *teishō*, Rōshi's commentaries on the sayings of famous Zen masters. The first talks were on sayings from *The Eternal Lamp of Zen* and *The Record of the Zen Master Daie*.[xii] Since I remember nothing about the talks, I must have been in a complete daze. As I became accustomed to sitting, however, I became more focused, and by the time Rōshi spoke on the *Rinzairoku*, I was able to absorb his every word.[xiii] I was moved to the depths of my being, but I shall speak of this later.

On ordinary days, we were allowed to see Rōshi between five and six in the morning, the time he recited the sutras. In winter I would wake up in the dark while the family was still asleep and slip out of the house with a lighted lantern. From Akebono-chō I walked down Dangozaka, past Zenshō-an—a Rinzai Zen temple associated with the master swordsman Yamaoka Tesshū— and then through Yanaka to Nippori. At that hour the streets were deserted, but I never felt frightened or lonely. Eyes fixed straight ahead on the road, I walked on with determination, my mind focused on my kōan.

I went to classes after the zazen sessions, but once in a while I stopped by the Mejiro Fudōsan and spent the entire day meditating in the main hall. If visitors became too intrusive, I retreated to a small, unlit chapel dedicated to Aizen Myōō. I was familiar with the temple because I had previously gone with some of the boarding students to hear the resident Shingon monk lecture on the *Jikkanshō*, the writings of [the medieval religious leader] Kōbō Daishi.

With each passing day, I found myself better equipped mentally for sitting and concentrating. I was even complimented on my sitting posture, but I made no progress at all on the kōan about my "original face."

I knew that Inoue Sakiko, a classmate in the home economics department, had recently begun training with Nakahara Nantenbō-rōshi. She had struck

---

xii *The Eternal Lamp of Zen* (*Shūmon mujin tōron*): An introduction to the thought of the great Zen master Hakuin Ekaku (1686–1769) by his most important disciple Tōrei Enji (1721–1792). *The Record of the Zen Master Daie* (*Daie Zenji sho*): A collection of the writings, sermons, talks, and verse of the twelfth-century Chinese Zen master Dahui.

xiii *Rinzairoku* (*The Recorded Sayings of Rinzai*): Rinzai (d. 866; Chinese, Linji) was the founder of the Rinzai school of Zen. Consisting of sermons and descriptions of his life and encounters with other Zen masters and students, this is considered the most authoritative and influential text of the basic principles and practices of Zen Buddhism.

me as naïve and simpleminded, with no particular interest in intellectual or religious matters, but at her very first sesshin—she missed school for a week—she had attained kenshō. I was flabbergasted, especially since she was not the type to practice zazen. In fact, she herself had admitted that she had started at the insistence of her fiancé, a Zen enthusiast with a degree in medicine who had stipulated that she practice zazen and attain kenshō as a condition for marriage. They hoped to be married right after her graduation. Sakiko had not trained of her own free will, but even so, I could see a profound change—the look on her face, the way she held herself. She had always reminded me of a pretty little Western doll, but now her face, noticeably thinner, gave off an ethereal glow and her large eyes held a pure, clear light. Actually quite small, she even seemed taller, with a new gravity of presence.

I thought about Sakiko, and came to the conclusion that kenshō or *satori*—whatever you called the heightened state of awareness—was attainable for all seekers, but the path leading to attainment, the distance, the degree of difficulty, differed with each person. I did not think that someone like myself would ever experience *tongo*, a sudden awakening; I would have to work at my own pace, with perseverance and patience.

◎ ◎ ◎ ◎ ◎

I still had to think about school. Graduation was fast approaching, and I had already missed the thesis deadline. The halls were filled with an air of feverish excitement as student meetings became more frequent. Since I was as always the outsider, with no close friends to speak of, and by now the acknowledged school eccentric, I looked on with a cold eye.

The meetings dealt with topics such as "the mission of women privileged with a college education" and "the need for graduates to behave with discretion." This was to be expected, I suppose, considering the small percentage of women who went to college and the continuing prejudice against women's higher education. Also, college women at the time were definitely more serious and imbued with a greater sense of mission than their counterparts today. The majority, of course, wanted to be wives and mothers who would create an ideal home environment. (Some of the students were already married.) A few planned to return to their home provinces and dedicate themselves to educating young girls. Others talked of acting as mentors to Chinese women who were studying in Japan or of going to China to teach. Still others said they intended to remain at the college for the rest of their lives and work on behalf of the school, Naruse Sensei, and the alumnae association. Then there was the lone student who claimed that, despite its pretensions to higher education, the college had failed to prepare her for a professional career that would enable her to live independently. She decided to study medicine and become a doctor. (After several attempts to pass the medical board examinations, the woman committed suicide some years later.)

I attended one of these meetings and was asked about my future plans. "Since I have yet to know my true self," I replied, "I do not know what my mission or purpose in life is. For the time being, I think I will study English and classical Chinese." Of course, I made no mention of my interest in Zen. But, to be frank, all their blustering about the responsibilities of educated women struck me as presumptuous. With just three years of college, what did they hope to accomplish?

The only requirement for graduation was a thesis. My classmates had thrown themselves into this task months earlier, while I, in contrast, had been striving day and night to empty my mind of all previous knowledge. The mere thought of writing a thesis was painful. But I was determined to finish college, if only to satisfy my parents. The thesis had to be short, something I could write quickly. Having neglected my studies in home economics, I was incapable of writing about child-rearing practices, education, and other topics related to food, clothing, and shelter. I only felt informed about the knowledge I had gained from my three-year quest for the true God.

I decided to write on the evolution of man's idea of God. I drew on my spiritual experience, and, to give my thesis a semblance of objectivity, I set this within the context of the historical development of religion. The thesis was a perfunctory job—I have even forgotten the title—but since beginning zazen, my mind had become transparently clear, so that once I began, the rest was easy. My unorthodox thesis was accepted, and in March 1906, I was "sent out into the world" as a member of the third graduating class of Japan Women's College. By Japanese count I was twenty [twenty-one]. I have no memory of the graduation ceremony or what the diploma looked like. I must not have been interested or in any way moved by the occasion.

4

The Years After College

My immediate goal was to improve my English. I was eager to read books in the original, and though I had taken some English courses in college, I was not at all ready to read on my own. Unbeknown to my parents, I enrolled in the second year of the preparatory division of Tsuda Eigakujuku. As a matter of fact, I had taken the entrance examination while still in college. I had chosen the easier exam for the preparatory division to make sure I would pass and advance to the college proper the year after.

I left the house each morning saying I was going to the library and went straight to the school, near the British embassy in Kōjimachi. Then, on the way home, I stopped by the Nishō Gakusha to attend Mishima Chūshū's lectures on classical Chinese. I had audited Ichimura Sanjirō's course in college but needed to improve my skills in order to read Zen texts, many of which were in classical Chinese. To pay tuition for both schools, I used my allowance from my parents and the money I earned taking shorthand [a skill I acquired during the summer of my third year].

The Nishō Gakusha was also in Kōjimachi. The school, founded by Mishima in 1877, specialized in teaching classical Chinese. Mishima himself was elderly but in good health and taught classes on *The Book of Poetry*. His son and others on the staff lectured on canonical works such as the *Four Books* and *Five Classics*, *Outline of the Eighteen Histories*, *Wenxian*, Sima Qian's *Historical Records*, *Eight Writers of the Tang and Song Dynasties*, *Zhuangzi*, *Laozi*, *Han Feizi*, and *Sunzi*. Attendance was voluntary. Students went to class at their own convenience. None of them mingled socially, so I left the school as soon as my classes were over. The only other female student was a middle-aged woman who looked like a schoolteacher and seldom came. Everything about the school was antiquated—the building, the benches, the long table at which we sat elbow to elbow. But it was quiet and orderly, the only distraction the occasional clatter of the students' wooden clogs.

During the summer I had taken a course on shorthand at a trade school for girls in Ichigayamitsuke and additional lessons at the home of the instructor. I studied shorthand for the simple reason that after graduation, I resolved to do as I pleased and live as an independent being. At the very least, the skill would free me from worrying about having enough to eat. Stenography was also fairly mechanical and left me enough energy to pursue my larger goals. Marriage was never an option. The instructor, Niwa Tatsuo, who worked as a stenographer at the Upper House of the Diet, had great hopes for me and urged me to become a professional. Of course, I had no such intention. For my first assignment, I recorded two speeches at the graduation ceremony of the trade school. I have forgotten how much I was paid, but I do remember my great pleasure in earning money for the first time in my life. I was also sent to Professor Motora Yūjirō's home in Hongō Nishikata-machi to transcribe his lectures for his experimental psychology course at Tokyo University.

Soon after enrolling at the Eigakujuku, I went to see the president, Tsuda Umeko. I told her of my plans to both work and study and asked her to call on me if she needed a stenographer. She looked at me uncomprehendingly, as if I had made the strangest request. She had lived in the United States for many years and knew all about that country, but very little about the realities of life in Japan. She also seemed naïve about the ways of the world, and probably thought I was eccentric.[i] Tsuda Sensei was probably in her early forties, but she looked closer to fifty and seemed difficult to get along with. By comparison, Kawai Michiko Sensei, who had just returned from the United States, was young, and in her Western clothes, moved about with an air of brisk competence. I attended several of her classes but found her Japanese speech oddly stilted, with a hint of a foreign accent.

Classes mainly consisted of conversation, taught by foreign women; memorization; and dictation. The texts were dull and devoid of content. In short, the school offered the narrowest kind of language training. The teachers were uniformly demanding and the students diligent in preparing their work and completing their assignments. In marked contrast to the students at Japan Women's College, no one seemed to be self-motivated or interested in studying for the pleasure of it.[ii]

---

[i] Tsuda Umeko (1864–1929): In 1871, along with four other young girls, she was sent by the government to study in the United States. She stayed until 1882, returned to Japan, then studied at Bryn Mawr College from 1889 to 1892. Tsuda founded her school in 1900.

[ii] Raichō contradicts her earlier statement about the lack of intellectual curiosity on the part of the students at Japan Women's College.

The school was effective in teaching the students to pronounce English correctly, to understand foreigners, and to carry on everyday conversation. But I was not interested in speaking to foreigners or going abroad; my sole purpose in attending the school was to learn to read English with ease and accuracy, and as soon as possible. The school clearly did not meet my needs, so after a while, I began skipping classes, arriving late, or leaving early, each time running into petty rules more appropriate for schoolchildren.

Now and again, we had to memorize poems and passages from books as homework. I was unwilling to waste the time at home, so I did this work on my way to school, which took me well over an hour. Repeating the lines over and over, I walked from Akebono-chō to Hakusan, Yanagi-chō, and Kasuga-chō, past the artillery arsenal (a huge red brick building where I could see a crowd of workers in green uniforms out in front each morning) across Suidō-bashi Bridge, up Kudanzaka, and then to Ichiban-chō in Kōjimachi. My efforts were futile. Inarticulate to begin with and unable to project my voice, I would always have much trouble with recitation and conversation.

I became more and more dissatisfied with the school, so one day, on a mischievous impulse, I lit up a cigarette in the classroom. Emboldened, I smoked after classes—never during—or at lunchtime, as the other students, who were three years younger and just out of high school, looked on in open-mouthed amazement. Oddly, my bad behavior never became an issue.

At age eighty-four, I still smoke. I have no recollection of when or how I picked up the habit. Could someone have offered me a cigarette during a break in a zazen session? I am quite certain I started after college. At home, I smoked secretly at first, in the privacy of my room. I preferred cigarettes with filtered tips like Shikishima or Yamato and was never tempted to smoke cigars like my father.

I withdrew from school in the middle of the term. This was a shame in a way, since the school was supposed to be difficult to get into. The following year, in January 1907, I transferred to the Seibi Women's English Academy in Iida-chō.

Meanwhile, despite my full schedule of classes and occasional shorthand stints, I continued to attend zazen sessions at Ryōmō-an. If anything, I was more dedicated than ever. I also noticed that my chronic headaches and sinus trouble had disappeared completely. I could even speak with greater ease. I felt wondrously light; I would walk for miles and never tire. I rarely dreamed and could get by with a few hours' sleep. All this was almost certainly because my mind had been purged of mundane distractions and had become much clearer. My mother and grandmother were delighted to see the improvement in my health. Yet no matter how long I meditated, the kōan about my original face continued to elude me.

Early one morning, after having stayed up all night meditating in my room, I went to Ryōmō-an as usual. When my turn came to see Rōshi, I simply could not bring myself to go. I stood up to leave, but then a small, elderly woman with short hair spoke to me: "Go ahead and see Rōshi." I replied, "But I have nothing to say to him even if I do go to see him. I'm going home." "Ah, but you see," the woman said, refusing to give up, "when Rōshi receives you for an interview, he is no ordinary mortal. He's a mirror polished to perfection. It doesn't matter if you have nothing to say. Go and see him. Just sitting all the time won't do you any good."

"A mirror reflecting a mirror"—I felt a surge of courage, struck the gong twice, and walked down the hall to Rōshi's room.[iii] The woman who spoke to me had apparently been practicing Zen for years. She was refined and at the same time, something of a busybody. I shall forever be indebted to her for guiding me on my spiritual journey, though I never learned her name.

Others who came for the morning session were Sasaki (Sōkeian) Shigetsu (he was later certified and went to the United States to teach Buddhism) and his lover Eshō; a Tokyo University student called Tago Ichimin (he became a high official at the Home Ministry) and his wife, a student at my college. The daughter of a well-known English teacher, [Frank] Eastlake, was said to come regularly on her bicycle, but I never had the chance to meet her.

It was sometime during the weeklong sesshin [in July 1906]. As was the custom, we raised our hands in prayer and recited the Four Vows together before Rōshi's talk: "Sentient beings are numberless. I take a vow to save them. The deluding passions are inexhaustible. I take a vow to destroy them. The Gates of Dharma are manifold. I take a vow to enter them. The Buddha way is supreme. I take a vow to complete it."[iv]

We next recited Hakuin Zenji's Chant in Praise of Zazen: "Sentient beings are intrinsically Buddha. It is just as it is with ice and water. Apart from water, there is no ice. Apart from sentient beings, there is no Buddha...." We came to the last lines: "At this moment, what is there more for you to seek, with Nirvana itself manifest before you? This very place, this is the Lotus Land; this very body, this is Buddha."[v] Then, just as I was about to place my hands on my lap, tears as large as hailstones came pouring down my face. Whenever I cry, I do so in private, choking back the tears. But now, I was crying shamelessly in front of everyone. I could not believe it. These were not tears of sadness, not tears of grateful reverence for Hakuin's words. No, I was crying because I had

---

iii "A mirror reflecting a mirror," without even the shadow of an image between, i.e., mind and object are one and the same.

iv The translation is taken from Sasaki, *Zen Dust*, 36.

v The translation is taken from ibid. 251. The entire text may be found on 251–253.

broken free of my finite self and reached a state of pure awareness. My whole being had exploded in a flood of tears. I had never experienced this wondrous, strange state before.

Nor shall I ever forget Rōshi's commentary on the *Rinzairoku*. Close to sixty years have passed since then, but I will try to set down the gist of his words: The Buddha has three types of bodies—the Essence body, the Bliss body, the Transformation body—but these distinctions are nothing but names and have never really existed. The true source of the Buddha is none other than the person who is actually listening to this talk. Look at the person, the True Man without rank, without shape or form, yet who truly exists. If you are able to discern this, you are no different from the Buddha. Do not ever release your grip on this. Everything that meets your eyes is this. There is no one among you who cannot attain enlightenment.

Even now I can hear Rōshi's clear, strong voice: "Upon this lump of reddish flesh sits a True Man with no rank. Constantly he goes in and out of the gates of your face. If there is anyone here who does not know this for a fact, look, look!"[vi] His voice pierced me like a jolt of electricity, and in that instant I said to myself, "I understand!" Later I heard talks by many Zen masters, but none as compelling as the talk by Rōshi that day.

At another session, Rōshi spoke on the Four Procedures of Master Rinzai: "Sometimes I take away man and do not take away the surroundings. Sometimes I take away the surroundings and do not take away the man. Sometimes I take away both man and the surroundings. Sometimes I take away neither man nor the surroundings."[vii] I also remember other talks to this day.

I had finally attained kenshō. I was confirmed by Rōshi and given the religious name Ekun. My kenshō was not a so-called tongo. It had come after more than six months of intense sitting and amounted to a gradual awakening that culminated in a 180-degree turn, a spiritual revolution, an upheaval of the greatest magnitude. I had been reborn. I was a new being. My first birth had been of the flesh, unwilled and outside of my awareness. My second birth was of my true self, born from my efforts to look into the deepest level of my consciousness. I had searched and searched and at last found the entrance to the Great Way of True Life.

Unable to contain my joy and unwilling to go home, I walked the whole day and paid no heed to where I was going. From Nippori I walked along the rice fields to Mikawashima, and from there, to the ferry crossing at Odai and

---

[vi] The passage is from the *Rinzairoku*. I have based my translation on Watson, *The Zen Teachings of Master Lin-chi*, 13. The "lump of reddish flesh" refers to the body and the "gates of the face" to the sense organs and the intellect.

[vii] The translation is from Sasaki, *Zen Dust*, 157.

on to Nishiarai. I was oblivious to fatigue; I felt disembodied. The Zen texts had not deceived me when they had declared, "Mind and body are one," or "One must let the mind and body fall away." And when Sakyamuni declared, "Above the heavens and below the heavens I am the only honored one," he was not exaggerating but speaking from the truth of experience. What is God? What am I? How does a person relate to God, the One and the Many? The philosophical questions that I had wrestled with had been resolved in one flash. I felt emptied and indescribably exhilarated.

A great change came over me. I found myself eager to explore the intricate web of human relationships, an aspect of life I had ignored until then. I went with Masako, my friend and guide in Zen, to theaters and yose halls, to Shintomiza, Meijiza, Kabukiza, and Misakiza to see Kabuki plays. We often stood in the gallery because we were short of money and time. Everywhere I went was a totally new world for me, everything I saw was enjoyable—the young girls performing plays or reciting *gidayū* ballads to the accompaniment of samisen, the acrobatic acts by the Egawa Troupe. We even plotted our route so that we could walk through the licensed pleasure quarters at Yoshiwara and the disreputable neighborhood of Ryōunkaku, the twelve-story building in Asakusa Park. Then, depending on the season, we went to see the cherry blossoms at Asukayama and Koganei, the wisteria flowers at Kamedo, the foliage along the banks of the Takino River, the peonies at Yotsume, the irises at Horikiri, or the bush clovers at the Hagi Temple in Yanaka. No matter what the distance, we walked and walked, taking our lunches to save money. Our only extravagance was a sweet dumpling, an arrowroot rice cake, or some other local specialty.

My days were full: there was daily zazen, English and classical Chinese classes, trips to the Ueno Library and the Ōhashi Library in Niban-chō. I took on assignments in shorthand, and if I heard of an interesting lecture, I rushed to attend it. I went from one pursuit to the next, as though borne on a swift current, with energy to spare. Never again, in all my days, did I live on such a heightened plane of spiritual awareness or feel so vibrantly alive.

My mind was crystal clear, limitlessly expanding. My body was marvelously light, as though it did not exist. I never tired. I walked all day and stayed up until one or two in the morning. Life was full of pleasure, beauty, and joy. I overflowed with psychic energy.

Masako was now my closest friend and confidante. Straightforward and never intrusive, she always seemed to know exactly what I was thinking. Although she was not especially interested in philosophy or literature, she was ambitious in her way, and no doubt had taken up zazen as preparation for some life work she had in mind. She was closemouthed about her family, though she did mention once that her father was an army officer who had been decorated in the Russo-Japanese War and greatly admired General Nogi [, an army commander during the war]. When she spoke of her father, she usually exaggerated his shortcomings—he seemed to be extremely stubborn—and said she hoped to escape from the clutches of her family, go to the United States, make lots of money, and set up a fund for women's causes. After listening to her, I was also tempted and went with her to seek advice from Abe Isoo, the Waseda professor who had taken the university baseball team to the United States. Masako also went to see Shimanuki Hiradayū, a fervent Christian who had founded the Rikkōkai Society to help people emigrate. Her plans came to nothing, but since she was determined to do something worthwhile, she was studying English and accounting.

Masako lived out in Ōji, so she came in by train to meet me at the Ueno Library, or later, at the Kaizenji temple in Asakusa. We then set off, dressed alike in short-waisted kimono, hakama, and wooden clogs, and tramped around the city like a pair of scampering mice. Despite my mother's objections, I still wore a hakama though I was no longer a student. I found an obi too constricting and besides, a hakama was better for zazen. I kept my hairstyle simple, parting my hair to one side or down the middle, twisting it into a bun in the back, and fastening it with two imitation tortoiseshell combs. I also shunned makeup, applying at most "Baelz Water" [a lotion invented by Dr. Edwin Baelz]. One item I never failed to carry was a small dagger in a white case, which I tucked under my hakama. I had come upon the dagger at a small hardware store in Surugadaishita and purchased it on the spot because the finely honed blade seemed symbolic of the intensity of my mind at the time.

Rumors of our escapades eventually reached the college, and before long, we received a summons from Inoue Hideko, the head of the college alumnae association, and were duly reprimanded: tramping around town in wooden clogs sullied the reputation of the school; we were to wear leather shoes. But solid wooden clogs were ideal for the streets of Tokyo, and ignoring the woman's protests, we continued to dress as we pleased.

Except on holidays, I spent all my waking hours away from home. My mother rarely questioned me. She knew I went to the library. She also knew that I went somewhere in Nippori to meditate, but she seemed uninterested in what sort of place it was. I burned incense and practiced zazen in my room, but she never asked what zazen was like, and I did not volunteer any information or say a word about my kenshō. In fact, my mother completely refrained from asking the usual questions about where I was going and what I did. Considering that I was a daughter living at home, I was given the greatest freedom imaginable in those days. My father, too, seemed reluctant to pry into my affairs. In retrospect, I find this puzzling. Was there something about me that kept my parents at arm's length? All the same, if I happened to return late at night, I stopped outside their room to say I had come home and made a hasty retreat to my room.

I sometimes wonder whether my parents were disappointed to have a daughter who never consulted them or asked their opinion, who never showed interest in what she ate or took pleasure in receiving a new kimono. And yet, for all that, they seemed to trust me completely. They also relied on me, rather than on my sickly older sister, for matters large and small. I may not have always behaved as they wished, but they definitely saw me as a dependable daughter. Years afterward, when my father drew up his will, he disclosed to me—not, as might be expected, to his older daughter or his adoptive son—where he kept it, along with other pertinent information. Several years later, when I came under harsh public criticism for a certain indiscretion, their trust in me never wavered, even though the outside world may have thought that they disapproved of my behavior.

My Sister's Marriage

My sister recovered from her illness, and my adoptive brother was due to graduate from Tokyo Imperial University. In the winter of 1906, the two were married as planned. In the days leading up to the wedding, my sister talked happily with my mother about her bridal kimono and acted as though she had gotten over her bitter disappointment in love. To all appearances, she was yet another young woman looking forward to a new life. Of course, no one ever knew how she really felt.

The reception was held at the Seiyōken in Ueno. Instead of the usual elaborate bridal hairstyle, my sister wore her hair in a modest pompadour and fastened it with a hairpin decorated with white flowers. Her kimono was similarly understated, with sprays of large white lilies on the hem. In the parlance of the day, she was very much the "up-to-date" bride. My kimono was less formal, with shorter sleeves and a design of chrysanthemums and swirling water against a background of purple and madder red. To match the kimono, my mother had chosen a rather ostentatious cream-colored obi, but I persuaded her to let me wear a hakama.

The entertainment was provided by Yanagiya Kosan and En'yū, professional raconteurs who were no doubt chosen by my father. My parents asked me to make the arrangements for the restaurant as well as for the entertainment, and when I finally found Kosan's house on a back street in Fujimi-chō, I was surprised that he was so small and courteous. One of my sister's college friends also played a piece on the piano.

The wedding went smoothly, though my sister was disappointed not to see her old wet nurse Kiyo. She had married a master carpenter, and whenever she came to see us, she looked happy, her hair arranged in a marumage and her teeth dyed black.[viii] On each visit she reminded us to invite her to my sister's wedding, but then she abruptly stopped coming, and when my sister wrote to her, the letters were returned stamped "Address Unknown."

My grandmother was overjoyed now that my sister was married and my adoptive brother firmly established as legal heir to the Hiratsuka family. My parents also seemed relieved and satisfied. As for me, I had done my share in the wedding preparations, but my sister's marriage bore no relation to my world, and I knew in my heart that I would never follow in her footsteps; nor was I the least bit inclined to do so.

I was spared the usual pressure to marry. Just once, my mother said, "I'll say this much because it's my duty as a parent—," but otherwise, she never brought up the subject. My father was the same. Indeed, with only two daughters, he may have wanted to keep me at home. My mother may have had her reasons, too. Perhaps she would not have declared herself dissatisfied with her marriage, but she may have found it less than fulfilling. Accomplished in dance and music, she had married into a family that was not only uninterested in the arts but actually forbade them. And it could not have been easy to defer to her mother-in-law at every turn.

I remember the time when Mrs. Itō Chūta, the wife of a famous architect, came to visit my mother. I went into the parlor to serve tea and overheard my mother. "I've been telling my daughter she should marry, but she doesn't seem at all interested." At this, Mrs. Itō had begun to talk about her own marriage. She had been a teacher at the Higher Normal School, but since she was convinced that women were meant to marry, she had quit her job and married. Yet even now she wondered whether she had made the right choice. My mother kept nodding in sympathy, and I made a mental note of what a woman seemingly settled in happy domesticity had said in a moment of confidence.

The newlyweds moved into the house my parents had built for them in the field behind ours, and I took over the two rooms formerly occupied by my adoptive brother. The rooms, in Japanese style, were in a wing off the front entrance and were sufficiently isolated to be quiet at all times. The view of the rock garden in front was another plus. I set up my study in the smaller, three-mat room with a large round window and used the four-and-a-half mat room for sleeping and zazen. I kept the larger room simple, with a single

---

[viii] Married women often dyed their teeth using a liquid made from iron filings soaked in tea or vinegar. This supposedly made them attractive.

vase in the alcove, an incense burner beside it, and two hanging scrolls that
Sōkatsu-rōshi had inscribed at my request. Mounted on cheap paper—all I
could afford—one scroll read, "I prize highly the long swords drawn by the
soldiers of Great Yuan." The other read, "Like a flash of lightning they slash
at the spring wind." As my friend Nakanishi Godō told me years later, the
phrases were from a poem by Bukkō Kokushi (Mugaku Sogen), the founder
of Enryakuji, who was threatened by soldiers of the Yuan army when he was
still living in China.[ix]

I was immensely happy—a room of my own, free from outside intrusion. I
liked to think that I had suddenly left home and become independent. Refreshed,
I resolved to throw all my energy and will into study, zazen, and work.

⊚ ⊚ ⊚ ⊚ ⊚

Let me return to my training in Zen. Since attaining kenshō in the summer
of 1906, I had passed one kōan after another in quick succession. Buoyed by
the momentum, I was poised to redouble my efforts, but then I learned that
Sōkatsu-rōshi was taking Gotō Sōseki (Zuigan), Sasaki Shigetsu, and other dis-
ciples to the United States to spread the teachings of Zen Buddhism. I was
crushed, especially since Rōshi expressly forbade me to train with anyone else
while he was away. Too disheartened to look for a new teacher, I wandered from
temple to temple listening to lectures by Daikyū, Sōei, and other Zen masters.

One day, I happened to go with Masako to the Rinshō-in in Hongō to hear
a talk by Sakagami Shinjō-rōshi, the abbot of Seikenji temple in Okitsu (Shi-
zuoka Prefecture). I do not have the faintest recollection of what he said, but I
shall never forget my first impression. The elderly Rōshi had a face like a pug,
but he was austerity itself, without a trace of ill will, spite, or unctuousness. I
was attracted to him at once, and upon learning that he held sesshin at Kaizenji, the Rinzai sect temple in Asakusa, I went to see him without any formal
introduction and received permission to train with him. I had been working
on the kōan "Empty-handed, yet holding a hoe," and since I was fairly confident that I understood it, I asked Rōshi to pass me. He ignored my request and
told me to work on "Jōshū's oak tree in the courtyard," the thirty-seventh kōan
in the *Mumonkan*.[x]

[ix] Sogen was telling the soldiers that there was nothing to be gained by killing him since he had already
attained Nothingness.

[x] *Mumonkan* (*The Gateless Barrier*; Chinese, *Wumenguan*): Collection of 48 kōan compiled by the
Chinese Zen master Wumen Huikai (1183–1250). The thirty-seventh kōan: On being asked by a
monk what Bodhidharma brought over from India, i.e., what is the Dharma, or Universal Law, the
Zen master Jōshū (Zhaozhou) replies, "The oak tree you see in the courtyard."

The sesshin at Kaizenji was for the benefit of the Nyoidan, a group of students from the Tokyo Higher Commercial School (now Hitotsubashi University), and in the absence of a resident abbot, Shinjō-rōshi was asked to come in from Okitsu once a month. The temple had been prominent in the past and patronized by daimyo and nobles, but it had fallen into disrepair—the roof leaked, the tatami were soggy and rotting. In the hope of restoring the temple's former glory, the abbot at Engakuji had appealed to former parishioners and sent Nakahara Shūgaku, a capable young monk, to serve as acting resident abbot. Since one of his duties was guiding the students, he encouraged them in their practice by monitoring their zazen sessions. Masako and I were not allowed to sit with the students, so we meditated in a separate room and joined them afterward for Rōshi's talks.

The temple was near Asakusa Park in a busy section of downtown Tokyo, but it had spacious grounds all around and was quiet and peaceful. There were also a number of empty rooms where students could sit anytime, so even when there was no sesshin, I often stopped by on my way to and from the Ueno Library. Masako and I also met for lunch there before setting off on our expeditions.

Seibi Women's English Academy

As I mentioned, I began studying English at the Seibi Women's English Academy in January. The school operated under the auspices of the Universalist Church and was headed by a minister named Akashi. Classes were held inside the church building, which had beautiful stained-glass windows. Masako also attended—she took courses in practical English—but because of our different schedules, we rarely saw each other at the school. Most of the students were high school graduates; my class, the most advanced, had only ten members. Unlike at Tsuda Eigakujuku, we were not required to memorize long passages, conversation class was separate, and attendance was voluntary. The reading assignments were also much more interesting: *The Sorrows of Young Werther* by Goethe (taught by Ikuta Chōkō); Andersen's *Fairy Tales* (Sōma Gyofū); Dickens's *Cricket on the Hearth*, and Tennyson's *Enoch Arden*, the last two taught by other teachers. We covered a great deal of material since the teachers merely read and translated the passages. There were no examinations, and I could pick and choose my classes. In every way, the school suited my purposes perfectly.

Both Ikuta Chōkō and Sōma Gyofū had graduated from university a year or so earlier. Chōkō was the dandy and gentleman of the two, dressed impeccably in a suit, hair neatly parted and the tips of his little moustache twirled at a sharp angle. In contrast, Gyofū looked shabby in his old kimono, but he was kind and unpretentious, if somewhat finicky and moody, with a gentle manner that was typical of timid people. The staff was solidly made up of Tokyo Imperial University graduates; as a graduate of Waseda, he was the only exception.

One day, I went to visit Sōma Sensei with a classmate. I had told her that Sensei had recently been married and she had insisted on going to his house with a wedding gift. The woman, a former geisha in Yoshiwara, was at least fifty and looked much older than my mother. She was rather funny, and in Chōkō's class on *Werther*, she would ask questions that left the rest of us laughing while Chōkō, looking more serious than ever, would patiently give an explanation she would understand. At the house in Mejiro, Sensei's wife came out to greet us. She was a classic beauty, with even, doll-like features. We had hoped that Sensei would tell us about his life as a newlywed, but instead, he talked about the controversy surrounding *Waseda bungaku*'s advocacy of Naturalism. He was associated with the journal, and I gathered from what he said that literary circles were petty and cliquish. I should mention that, perhaps because I was older and more educated than the others in the class, Sensei treated me more as a friend than as a student.

◎ ◎ ◎ ◎ ◎

Chōkō had long been interested in women's writing, and in June, he formed a study group called the Keishū Literary Society.[xi] He gave lectures and enlisted the services of his friend Morita Sōhei, as well as Yosano Akiko, Togawa Shūkotsu, Hirata Tokuboku, Baba Kochō, Sōma Gyofū, and others associated with the New Poetry Society. Young women who did not attend the school were also allowed to join. Needless to say, I joined at once. Since achieving kenshō, I had become thoroughly tired of anything abstract or theoretical. I could not bear to look at another book on German idealism. I was now interested in the actual, live world and the complexities of human society.

About fifteen members met once a week after class. Among the first lecturers, Yosano Akiko talked about *The Tale of Genji* and corrected the poems we submitted; Baba Kochō spoke on the modern European novel; Morita Sōhei talked of Greek tragedy; and Ikuta Chōkō spoke on the art of the novel. I doubt anyone was paid.

Yosano Akiko presumably came because of her connection with the New Poetry Society. She was also Chōkō's neighbor. Frankly, I was taken aback when

---

[xi] *Keishū* means "accomplished women."

I first saw her. I had read *Tangled Hair*, and I imagined that the author of those wild, uninhibited poems would be dazzlingly glamorous. The woman who stood before us looked as if she had been dragged into the classroom against her will. Cringing beside Chōkō, she had the forlorn expression of someone who hated speaking in front of an audience. I felt so sorry for her that I wanted to avert my eyes. Her kimono was wrinkled from constant wear, her hair haphazardly tied in a bun with the tip of a black cord hanging limply down from it. Akiko had obviously been plucked from a whirl of domestic chores and deposited just like that in our midst. Everything about her—her big face, which crinkled when she smiled, her short, stubby neck, and her wide shoulders—was different from what I had imagined, or for that matter, from the woman I knew years later. And when she lectured, she mumbled in the Kansai dialect, as if she were talking to herself. I doubt anyone understood her.

I submitted my first attempts at poetry—about ten waka—and received an encouraging comment. One of my poems apparently appeared in the October 1907 issue of *Myōjō*, but I do not remember this. Several other poems appeared in the final issue of the magazine, but these were sent in by Chōkō, who kept a copy of some of my poems. They were all embarrassingly amateurish and certainly not worth a second look. Personally, I preferred Gyofū's understated style to Akiko's and asked him to look at my poems, too. As a result, I became friendly with him and heard some of the inside gossip about the New Poetry Society and the financial difficulties of the Yosano family. Once I heard about Akiko's travails, I understood why she looked so different from the poet I had pictured in my mind.[xii]

Literature was still unexplored territory for me, since I started reading works like Mori Ōgai's *Minawashū* [a collection of his translations of Western works] and *Sokkyō shijin* [his translation of Andersen's *Improvisatoren*] only after I achieved kenshō. Now, as a member of the study group, I acquired a new interest in foreign literature and read every translation I could get hold of. On Chōkō's advice I also read English translations of Turgenev and Maupassant to get a sense of good prose style, and on my own, tried my hand at translating the prose poems of Turgenev and Poe.

My reading of Japanese literature also became more systematic. I drew up a list of representative works, jotted down the catalogue numbers at the National Library, and read through them one by one: the poetry anthologies *Man'yōshū* and *Kokinshū*, *The Tale of Genji*, *The Pillow Book*, *Tales of Idleness*, *The Ten-foot Hut*. I owed a great deal to Aoyama (Yamakawa) Kikue, who had joined our group after seeing a notice in a newspaper. She was a

---

[xii] Yosano Akiko (1878–1942) was then the mother of four young children.

graduate of the [Second] Prefectural Girls' High School and a student at the Training Center for Japanese (Kokugo Denshūjo), and so she was formidably well read. She seemed to know everything about the classics.

I assumed Kikue was about my age, but was surprised to learn that she was seventeen or eighteen, three or four years my junior. She looked unhealthy with her sallow, pinched face, and her cotton kimono were invariably dark and somber, the woven design so subdued as to be barely visible. In fact, nothing about her suggested youth or maidenly charm. To tell the truth, she was physically unattractive, but once she spoke, her precise diction, the sharpness of her observations, and her penetrating intelligence were immediately obvious. Kikue later turned to politics, but at the time she was engrossed in literature and probably contemplating a career in writing or teaching Japanese literature. She was particularly fond of Higuchi Ichiyō and seemed to know everything she had written.[1]

I was intrigued by Kikue, and one day, on the way to see my shorthand teacher, I stopped by her home in Dote Sanban-chō. I have forgotten what we talked about—no doubt the usual gossip about the teachers in the study group—but I distinctly remember the gloomy old house, the room cheerless in its lack of color and adornment, the air dank and chilly, as if the fire had gone out and would never burn again.

My First Kiss

At this point in my story I shall have to make a confession: I committed an unconscionable blunder from sheer stupidity and ignorance, though at the time it seemed a most natural thing to do. As usual, I had gone to Kaizenji to meditate. The weather was cold, so it must have been early in 1907. I sat in the mortuary chapel of one of the parishioners, a long and narrow room with a row of memorial tablets. I soon entered a state of profound stillness, and suffused with unutterable peace and quiet, I lost track of time. By the time I got around to checking, it was already eight or nine in the evening. I quickly stood up. It was pitch dark inside, but seeing a gleam of light in the direction of the temple office, I made my way through the shadowy rooms and hallway.

Nakahara Shūgaku, the young monk who had come to serve as acting resident abbot, was in the office reading a book by the gas lamp. He looked up, surprised, and said, "Oh, you're still here." He lit a candle, led me to the side entrance of the empty kitchen, and opened the door. The night air, as well as my heart and mind, were filled with a luminous calm. I felt as though I were on the ocean floor striding through the gentle undulating waves. I looked at

Shūgaku—a priest clad in indigo robes, a band of the same hue tied neatly around his waist, holding a flickering candle. Or rather, I saw a young monk, as pure and innocent as a novice. On an impulse, I kissed him without a moment's hesitation. I stepped out into the cold wind and hurried home.

Several days later I went to the temple as usual. Shūgaku was waiting for me. "Why did you do that the other day?" he said and suddenly kissed me. "I've already talked to the old man (Shaku Sōen-rōshi) about it. I'm going to marry you." I was aghast. Marry me? How did he jump to such a conclusion? Wasn't he being impetuous?

When I told him I had no such intention, he was furious. "So you were making fun of me. Or were you just trying to seduce me?" He was different from ordinary mortals in the way his emotions came tumbling out so straight-forwardly. He refused to listen. "All right, if you don't want to marry a priest, I'll give it up. I can always pull a rickshaw. Supporting you would be the easiest thing in the world." He rolled up his sleeves and thrust out his arms, taut and muscled from years of physical labor in the monastery. He was proposing in earnest, with a naïveté that made me wonder if he was joking.

Shūgaku could rage and fume, he could accuse me of trying to seduce him, but I felt absolutely no need to apologize. I had had no such intentions in mind; there was nothing I could conceivably want from him. In the lingering quietude of meditation, I had merely expressed my appreciation for his kindness in letting me out. It had been a kind of "thank you" and "good-bye." As far as I was concerned, he was the one at fault for misinterpreting my gesture.

At least, that is what I thought at the time. But now, looking back, I wonder what induced me to do such a thing. I had acted on the spur of the moment, completely spontaneously. Had I been reading too many foreign novels? Had something in *Young Werther* affected me subconsciously? Whatever the reason, I had been stupid not to think of the consequences: I had shocked a young monk who had spent months and years practicing the strictest austerities, sequestered from the world.

Alarmed and upset, I finally talked to Masako and asked her to intercede. She succeeded in calming him down, but Shūgaku took a while to recover his peace of mind. We agreed to act as though nothing untoward had happened and sat together in meditation, but before a third of the incense stick had burned down, he would get up abruptly and leave. He was also irritable, scolding the young helpers for no reason; he drank to excess; and, sharp-tongued to begin with, he became more sarcastic still.

Yet remarkably enough, the incident brought the three of us closer, for both Masako and I were fond of Shūgaku. Direct, uncomplicated, innocent of pretense, he possessed a pure humanity that was immensely likeable. We confided in one another and shared an occasional meal. At Shūgaku's urging,

I had my first taste of sake. I discovered the pleasure of sharing food and drink with others. Perhaps I took after my father, but I discovered I could drink quite a bit and enjoy it, without feeling the slightest effect. We never drank in public, however.

Shūgaku was born in Sendai and, having lost his father early on, he had been adopted by Nakahara Nantenbō-roshi, the abbot of Zuiganji in Matsushima. He entered the priesthood, trained with Shaku Sōen, the chief abbot at Engakuji, and in due course received *inka*,[xiii] the Dharma seal of approval from his master. And it was Sōen, "the old man," as Shūgaku affectionately called him, who had ordered him to go to Kaizenji and revive its fortunes.

By the time I started going to the temple, Sōen had already retired from the abbacy and was living in seclusion at the Tōkeji in Matsugaoka. He came to Tokyo once in a while and stayed at the temple, but since he seemed rather remote, I had never talked to him. He was close to Shūgaku, more like a father to him than a Zen master.

Like Shūgaku, Shaku Sōkatsu, my rōshi at Ryōmō-an, had trained with Sōen. This made them brothers in a way. They were close in age, too, but no two people could have been more different. Trained by the same rōshi, they presumably passed the same set of kōan and attained satori in the same manner. Yet Sōkatsu had been designated the Dharma successor; he had been certified as a teacher and given a temple where he could instruct students and laypeople with the full dignity of his office. Shūgaku, in contrast, gave no indication of wanting to become a teacher. Certainly, he was devoted to the students who came to the temple, but he still dressed like a novice in blue cotton kimono and black robe. As he went about his tasks, he tossed off jokes and sarcastic remarks with abandon. I should mention that he was quite ugly, too, though I for one did not mind, since his rough features seemed to fit his personality. Indeed, as our friendship deepened over time, I found myself powerfully drawn to the man, or should I say, to what lay hidden in the core of his being. Also, despite our misunderstanding, I continued to attend the monthly sesshin at Kaizenji and to meet with Shinjō-rōshi for interviews.

⊚ ⊚ ⊚ ⊚ ⊚

In the meantime, on Chōkō's recommendation, the study group had put together a magazine of writings by the members. This magazine, meant for private circulation, was really no more than a collection of handwritten manuscripts bound together with thread. It had the potential to become a full-

---

[xiii] Certification from the Zen master that a disciple has passed the requisite number of kōan.

fledged women's magazine like the future *Seitō*, but things did not turn out that way and, as I shall describe later, I bore a large share of the blame.

My own contribution was my first fictional effort, "The Last Day of Love." Still feeling the aftereffects of kenshō, I was full of psychic energy and confident of endless possibilities. Above all else, I felt fearless, even brazen. I dashed off the story, made a clean copy with my brush on ruled rice paper, and immediately handed it in. The story was purely imaginative. I have forgotten the details, but it was about a young college graduate who ends a love affair and asserts her independence by taking a teaching job away from Tokyo. I had not originally intended to portray such a woman, but the plot had come out that way naturally.

The only other member to submit fiction was Yamakawa Kikue. She wrote with fine, precise brush strokes on ruled paper, and her story had an elegant style reminiscent of her favorite author Higuchi Ichiyō. I forgot the contents, but when I met her sometime afterward, she told me that she had written about a family whose household belongings were seized by a bailiff because the father had failed to pay a debt. Her own family had met such a fate, and she had written the story from the perspective of the young daughter.[2]

The year drew to a close, and late in January 1908, I received a long letter from Morita Sōhei, one of the lecturers. It was a critique of my story, but I did not even dream of the consequences. Morita, who had been a close friend of Chōkō's from the time they were at the First Higher School together, had probably been coaxed into talking to our group. His subject was Greek drama, but his lectures were far from polished. Grabbing the desk with both hands, he looked down and muttered to himself, as if embarrassed. Compared to Chōkō, who was suave, quick-witted, and thorough, Morita, with his large head and bulky body, was awkward and full of flaws. He seemed vulnerable, yet had his own charm. I attended his lectures but had never talked to him.

The letter was written with skillful brush strokes in faint ink on a roll of rice paper. But it was not a critique of my story so much as a message of wholly undeserved praise; never before had I received such a strange letter. I sent a reply right away, using the same kind of writing paper. He answered, and thus began a relationship that would quickly develop in an entirely unforeseen direction. Ever since attaining kenshō, I had felt an overwhelming sense of the plenitude of life, as though I were living in a realm of absolute freedom where Subject and Object were one. I feared nothing. I was also curious to see what would happen.

A meeting about the magazine was going to be held at Chōkō's home in Sendagaya. I had been invited, and knowing that I had never been to the house, Morita wrote to say that he would be happy to take me; I was to wait for him at Suidōbashi Station. I went as instructed, and together we boarded a train on the Kōbu Line. The train pulled into Sendagaya Station, but Morita showed no signs of getting off. He ignored my remonstrations and remained in his seat, wrapped in sullen silence. I thought to myself, "Aha, I've been tricked," and was suddenly seized with a childish desire to pay him back in kind. What would happen would happen.

I stayed in my seat. We got off at the end of the line at Nakano without having exchanged a word. I thought of a remark made by one of the lecturers: "That Morita—in college he was so smitten by a gidayū performer that he followed her all the way home." We spent the rest of the afternoon walking aimlessly on the country roads in Nishiaraiyakushi, and after dark, returned by train to Kudan. We then went to the Fujimiken, a restaurant I remembered from childhood. One of the oldest Western-style restaurants in Japan, it was owned by the father of a kindergarten classmate.

As we sat eating, Morita opened his furoshiki and took out a small book with a dark green cover. It was an English translation of Turgenev's *Smoke*. The group had read excerpts, since Chōkō believed that the book was eminently suitable for aspiring women writers: not overly serious for a Russian novel, it had just the right touch of romanticism, a beautiful style, and sensitive descriptions of nature. We had also been given summaries of Turgenev's novels and told to read to them in English translation. But instead of discussing *Smoke*, Morita kept talking about D'Annunzio, in particular, his *Triumph of Death*. He greatly admired the book. In fact, he seemed obsessed by it, for whenever we met later, he would bring it up.[xiv]

Among other things, Morita mentioned a flower described in the book, a certain species of wild lily that bloomed in the desert under the hot tropical sun. The flower withered within hours, but anyone who looked inside the petals would find an insect, dead from the intoxicating perfume. "That's what it says in the book. Isn't it wonderful?" He launched into an extravagant paean to passion, but then, in a clearly false display of abject humility, he accused himself of being a miserable man, shallow and frivolous, incapable of love or jealousy. I had not read D'Annunzio's book, so I later bought a copy at Nakanishi (the only store besides Maruzen that carried foreign books) and looked up the passages Morita had mentioned. The book was then relatively unknown but would become popular among literary youth.

We finished our meal, but instead of going our separate ways, we took a train to Ueno Park. Although I realized I had been tricked, I had done everything Morita had suggested up to that point, and going to Ueno was no differ-

---

[xiv] *The Triumph of Death* (1894) is about Georgio Aurispa, a wealthy young Italian, who falls hopelessly in love with Hippolyta, a married woman. They escape to a hideaway in a small village on the Adriatic, but Georgio, having become convinced that death is the only way to escape from his own sensuality, takes Hippolyta on a walk near a cliff and plunges them both into the sea.

ent. Once there, I was on home ground. Not only had I cut across the park on my trips to the Ueno Library and Kaizenji but I had also traced and retraced the paths while working on my kōan. I knew every inch of the place.

On that cold and moonless night, we wandered hand in hand in the dark woods, far removed from any lamppost. I felt at one with the surroundings, happy and content. Morita kept slipping and stumbling on the exposed roots of the trees, his unwieldy body in danger of losing its balance any minute as we made our way to a lookout spot. I sat down, using a familiar rock as a bench, and motioned to him to join me. We watched the city lights flickering in the distance, but then he suddenly got up and sank to his knees. He started kissing the hem of my hakama like a medieval knight paying homage to a lady. Next he took hold of my hand and after kissing it, began nibbling the tips of my fingers, two or three at a time. I stayed perfectly still, letting him do as he wished, but to me, his gestures seemed forced and devoid of genuine emotion. He seemed to be merely mimicking love. Furthermore, I had been with him all day and had been intrigued and amused by his behavior, but I had never once felt in my heart the truth of Morita the man.

Why, I thought, this man isn't one bit serious. My patience gone, I stood up and said, "Sensei, can't you be serious for once! I detest insincere behavior. Be more serious, will you!" I flung myself against him. As Morita confessed later on, my counterattack caught him completely caught off guard, and he was shocked and dismayed. I have to admit I was surprised, myself.

One morning, a couple of days later, Morita took me to a *machiai*.[xv] Had my outburst at the park led him to think I was a woman of passion, as volatile as a volcano? (In a sense, all human beings are like volcanoes, but my spiritual training and powers of concentration may have made me seem more passionate and intense than I actually was.) And did he conclude that I was experienced with men, that I was no longer a virgin? And did he plan to find out about all this himself?

I had never been to a machiai. In fact, I was like other sheltered girls raised in uptown Tokyo and had only a vague idea about the purpose of such places, despite my college education. The machiai, a small house with a lattice door, was on a back street in Sanban-chō, near where I grew up. "I should tell you that I come here once in a while with Ikuta," Morita told me before going in. "He goes to church and prays and sermonizes with a pious look on his face, but he's really a hypocrite. Let's go inside—we can't just stand here like this." I followed him in, believing this was one of the geisha houses that had sprung up in my old neighborhood.

[xv] A house used for assignations.

Inside, all was quiet, not a geisha or customer in sight, no sign of anyone bringing us cups of hot tea. We sat facing each other across the only hiba-chi in the room, puffing our cigarettes without uttering a word. To break the awkward silence, I said, "Is there a geisha here that you and Ikuta Sensei are particularly fond of?" Morita merely grimaced. He went into the next room and whispered to the maid, "Just leave those there for now." He came back and sat down, but in a few minutes got up again and started carrying in some futon from the next room. He flung away his jacket, and lying down on the futon, he murmured, "Why don't you lie down, too?"

I may have been ignorant, but I was not stupid. I had a dim sense of what was on his mind and shot back at him: "There's no point in asking me. I am neither woman nor man. I transcend such distinctions." He burst out laugh-ing. "Not a woman? You don't expect me to believe that, do you? You shouldn't tell lies, you know." His words cut me to the quick. He had no idea what I was talking about. I had blurted out those words but I had not lied, nor had I made up something on the spot. I had spoken the truth, a hard-earned truth that I had verified with my own being. I was not about to let anyone accuse me of telling a lie. Hurt and angry, I could feel the tears rush to my eyes.

"All right, all right, you don't have to sleep with me if you don't want to. I just wanted to test you because you were so bold the other night at the park." He got up and sat beside me. After apologizing for bringing me to the machiai, he asked me not to think ill of him. "Ah, you're like ether, you're a transparent white plume of smoke. Yes, that's what I thought when we were at Ueno." He kept talking while I remained silent. He then started asking me questions. Had I read a lot of novels? Had I ever fallen in love? Had I ever felt sexual desire for a man? I weighed each question and gave my answers: yes, I had recently begun to read novels and found them interesting; no, I had never fallen in love but from my reading could imagine what it was like and was not entirely incurious about the opposite sex; yes, I was aware that there was such a thing as sexual desire but had yet to experience it myself.

"Well," he said, "it's impossible to live without love or sexual desire. With-out them life would be 'Mu'—Nothingness. And you say you've never felt such a desire?" "Nothingness would suit me fine." My remark led to a further exchange on the question of sexual desire, but I held my ground. "I know perfectly well that sexual attraction is a vital instinct for the preservation of the species. I'm not denying its existence or saying it's immoral or unclean. All I'm saying is that I've never had such feelings." I was not lying. I had honestly never been conscious of such a desire, but Morita did not seem to believe me, or at least did not seem willing to accept my statement.

We finally left the machiai, without touching the beer that someone had brought us. Once outside, Morita started apologizing again—he shouldn't have brought me to a place like this, I was not to worry, he wouldn't tell anyone, and so on. Highly offended, I told him, "Where I go is none of your affair. I am I, and I certainly don't need you to protect me." And why, I wondered, was this man, who had most certainly seduced many women, worrying about what people thought? Worse still, why was he assuming that I was the sort of person who would worry? For a minute I truly despised him.

I returned home. A letter from Morita was waiting for me. He had written in response to a letter I had sent immediately upon returning from the park that night. He had written large characters in hasty brush strokes on a roll of Mino rice paper. "How very prompt you have been in analyzing the situation," he began, and then went on to describe Sappho, the poet who was thwarted in love and leaped into the sea from the Leucadian Rock, and Hypatia, the woman philosopher of Alexandria who was persecuted by Christians and slowly scraped to death by seashells. Women, he wrote, were the most beautiful at the moment of death, and for this reason, he intended to kill me. As an artist and a disciple of Beauty, he was determined to see me, the fairest of all, in my last moments. His letter read like a student exercise in composition, but I was nevertheless taken aback. I made a detailed entry in my diary and sent him a copy with the heading, "My Thoughts for the Day." For the day had been truly eventful, and thanks to Morita, I now knew the difference between a geisha house and a machiai.

Three or four days later, I attended a meeting of the Keishū Literary Society. By then, the membership had dwindled to four or five. Chōkō and Morita finished their lectures, and as we were sitting around the stove, Morita handed me a piece of paper. "Here's the answer to the question you asked the other day." I had no idea what he was talking about, but took the paper with a nod and went straight home. It was a letter written in pencil.

My love for you has me in its tenacious grip. I think of you day and night. I long for you. All this because I know my love for you is hopeless, no matter how much I turn it over in my mind. The day will never come when you will return my love. If this is truly love, was there ever a love so hopeless? I do not know. I do not know. I do not know what I should do. Where can I go? Where can I go to escape? Love is its own punishment and so I must resign myself to submitting to this emotion while living under your cold gaze. Still, the letter you sent the other day is more than I can bear. If anyone else had written those words, I would have called such cruelty an attempt to make light of things.... You are destined to die young. Someone like you cannot hope to live long, cannot ever hope to live long.

(I have quoted verbatim a letter from a novel that Morita wrote later, but it is substantially the same as the one he sent me.)

I objected to his saying that, after reading my letter, he wanted to call "such cruelty an attempt to make light of things." I wrote back immediately, asking if he had made such remarks because of my lack of interest in society and total indifference to conventional morality, customs, and rules of etiquette. I wrote, half in explanation and half in self-justification, that the world of "Nothingness," which encompasses all contradictions, was my world, and that, free of suffering and desire, this world transcended death. Also, indirectly, I alluded more than once to his declared intention to kill me and see me at my most beautiful.

Besides exchanging letters, we took long walks. Morita usually took the initiative; I, rarely. Once in a while, we ran into each other on the street. We tended to go to places I knew—Ueno Park, Yanaka, and Nippori. We were in Ueno Park one evening, sitting on the same rock, when he started praising *The Triumph of Death* again. "Picture this scene. Georgio is waiting for his mistress Hippolyta at their love nest, and he's instructed the young girls in the village to throw wild broom flowers upon the path leading to the house. Hippolyta arrives and walks up the path, crushing the golden petals with her tiny feet, just like the Madonna in a miracle story. Isn't it wonderful? Compared to this, all the writing by the Naturalist school in Japan is soiled, gloomy, and shabby. What they write isn't fiction, it isn't even literature."

He continued in the same vein, criticizing the Naturalist writers of the Waseda group, but just as he started expounding his theories on aestheticism and neo-Romanticism—his own preference—a policeman appeared on the scene and began asking questions. Visibly flustered, Morita gave his name, address, and profession. "I won't tell you the woman's name, and I would appreciate it if you didn't ask." The policeman turned nasty. "Didn't you say you were a middle school teacher? What's a teacher doing with a woman at this time of day?" I intervened at this point and gave my name and address. "You're probably lying," he said. "Well, if you think I'm lying," I retorted, "why don't you take me home?" At this, the policeman finally left. The moment the policeman disappeared from sight, Morita laughed. "I really admire you!" He was trying to hide his discomfort over the trivial incident, but the state of my mind at the time made me find the whole encounter unaccountably funny. And I now knew that he taught English at a private school called Ikubunkan.

Morita lived in Hongō, in a house in Maruyama Fukuyama-chō that was said to have belonged to Higuchi Ichiyō's family. The house was at the end of a narrow alley off a street I took each morning, and now and then, from the corner of my eye I would see him in his kimono, cleaning his teeth at a well

---

xvi Morita Sōhei (1881–1949) had fathered a child by his common-law wife.

out in front. Naturally, I pretended not to see him and hurried on. I had no interest in his living arrangements, though I had heard him say he had sent his family back to his home village and wanted to be free of them forever.[xvi] ·

One morning, I had extra time, so on a whim, I stopped by his house. An elderly woman who looked as if she came from the downtown district answered the door, and in a few minutes, Morita appeared and invited me in. But something about the expression on his face, his attitude, in fact, the house, told me that I should not have come. I also noticed a young woman's kimono with a bright red lining in what was probably Morita's room. The old woman served us tea, but her stare seemed to ask me what was I doing there. "Sensei, I'm afraid I've intruded on you, coming like this in the morning without warning." I mumbled an excuse and left without taking a good look at the house once inhabited by Ichiyō.[3]

The woman did not look like Morita. I wondered if she might be his wife's mother, but as I learned sometime later, she was the mother of his second "wife." With his family away in his home village, he had taken up with a dancer from downtown Tokyo.

I did not see Morita for several days. The study group held a party at a teahouse in Ueno Park, but there, too, we pointedly avoided each other. For one thing, we were both busy—I with the monthly sesshin and the occasional shorthand job, and he, no doubt, with his work and family affairs. I did receive a letter, however. (As I will describe later in my narrative, all his letters were destroyed, so I shall set down what I remember.) His letter, as always, was written in a beautiful script.

> When it comes to you, I think I am capable of murder. This is because I have no way of expressing my love for you aside from killing you. I shall kill you. But I myself will not die. I am an artist, a writer. I must see for myself what happens to me, study my psychological state after I commit the act. And so I intend to escape, escape as far as I can.

Then, for a change, instead of *The Triumph of Death*, he wrote about the central character in Dostoevsky's *Crime and Punishment*.

Ten days passed before I saw Morita at a meeting of the Keishū Literary Society. He looked alarmingly pale. As we walked together afterward and headed toward our respective homes, he faltered over his words in telling me that he was thinking of giving up the lectures. If he did, he would be unable to see me. He was also thinking of going to China in the near future. I listened, half in disbelief, but then he started talking about *Crime and Punishment*, the novel he had mentioned in his last letter. By this time we were walking toward Ueno Park almost by habit. He seemed fascinated by Dostoevsky's depiction of Raskolnikov's psychological motives for murdering the old female pawnbroker, and possibly with this in mind, he burst out, "I'll kill you, and afterward live out my days in a lone cell in a snowbound Sakhalin jail, observing the changes in myself." He spoke excitedly, as if this were the only way a serious writer could live. Listening to him, for a moment I was carried along by his words, but then I thought of how much his thinking had changed since our first meeting.

He continued to talk about Dostoevsky—how he had been an epileptic, how the illness was always associated with genius, and how Hippolyta in *The Triumph of Death* suffered from it. He sounded as if he wished I were an epileptic, too, though I could have told him that even a Zen initiate achieved the transcendent clarity of vision, the kind of ecstasy supposedly experienced by epileptics before an attack. But I did not want to dampen his enthusiasm, so I held my tongue. This was not the only time Morita behaved strangely, yet I was charmed and attracted by his obsessive love, his wild imaginings about literature, his muddleheaded good nature, even his physical ungainliness. These stirred my latent, irresponsible sense of mischief.

◎ ◎ ◎ ◎ ◎

On the twenty-first of March, Morita put his plan into execution. I was totally unprepared. Even now, I fail to understand why he was in such a hurry to settle things between us. Was he trying to test me again, putting me to the ultimate test? Did this have something to do with his family? Or had his creative urges become so fierce that he could no longer wait?

In any case, we arranged to meet at the Kaizenji before going for our customary walk. I was also supposed to meet Masako on a small business matter, so I went early in the morning and meditated in one of the rooms until she arrived. We talked, and I told her that Morita was expected shortly. She and Shūgaku were the only ones who knew about Morita and me. By then Shūgaku had recovered from that unfortunate incident. He was completely at ease with me, and we related to each other as friends. When I'd told him about Morita and myself in a moment of mischief, he had taken it in stride and even made a pun about our names. "Sōhei, did you say? The two 'hei'— Kusahei and Heitsukamei—can you beat that!"[xvii] He pinched his nose when he said this, but I detected a note of caution, as if he were trying to tell me that writers nowadays were not to be trusted.

[xvii] Sōhei and Hiratsuka Haru can mistakenly (in this case, deliberately) be read Kusahei and Heitsuka Mei. This involves a pun on "breaking wind."

Morita arrived in a while, looking drawn and ashen. We set off, and as he walked ahead in silence, I struggled to keep up. When we reached Kuramae, he told me to wait outside and went into a shop that sold guns. The moment I saw the look of despair on his bloated face as he came out, I felt as if I had been struck violently in the chest. He had decided to go through with it, after all.

"They were willing to sell me a gun but no bullets," he told me. "In that case," I said, "my father has a pistol in his study and I'm quite sure it's loaded. I'll go home and get it." I said this in order to get the weapon but, more important, to settle my affairs. I went home immediately.

In all my life, I do not think I have ever accomplished so much in such a short time as I did that day. I finished a batch of shorthand assignments and mailed them off, wrapped my diaries, old manuscripts, and letters in a large furoshiki, and then went to the local rickshaw stand to have the package delivered, together with a brief farewell note, to Kimura Masako. (I would have aroused suspicion if I had I burned the papers at home; Masako, who was my closest friend, knew all about Morita, and could be trusted to carry out my wishes.)

I headed home, but to my surprise, I saw Morita coming my way. His eyes cast down, he stumbled and lurched about in obvious turmoil and anguish. He looked up, startled, and said, "You can't imagine how terrible it was waiting for you. And one more thing—could you bring all the letters I sent you, and come as soon as you can?" We settled on a new time and place to meet, and after assuring him that I would be there without fail, I ran home.

The twenty-first happened to be the feast of the vernal equinox. My mother had decided to make sweet rice dumplings, and in a stroke of bad luck, she asked me to help. Feigning nonchalance, I worked alongside the maid, but was secretly waiting for a chance to get hold of my mother's dagger. The dagger, together with a tiered lacquer box for inkstone and brushes, was a wedding gift from the Tayasu family. I had long coveted the dagger. It was beautiful, with an oxidized silver chase on the blade and a black leather case. I managed to get it from her bureau, but did not have the courage to steal my father's pistol.

I quickly put my rooms in order. All I had to do was to change my clothes. I still had an hour until ten, when we were supposed to meet, so I sat down to meditate for the last time in my room. I lit an incense stick in the white porcelain burner. Except for the steady hum of the gas lamp overhead, it was as quiet as the dead of night; not a sound came from my parents' wing of the house.

By temperament and habit, I have always been able to concentrate on whatever I do. I had focused all my energies on preparing for my escape the entire day, and, inexcusably, had not once thought about my parents or my grandmother. At the very least, I had to leave my father a note. I took out my pen and jotted down three lines: "I shall carry through my life convictions. I shall have fallen for my cause. No one else is to blame."[4] The words had come to me unbidden. I put the piece of paper in my empty desk drawer where it would be easily found. In the morning, my family would be shocked, angered, and saddened to find me gone, but the note, I hoped, would forestall any speculation about who was responsible for my death.

I quickly changed into my clothes: a dark green silk kimono with a woven design of white kasuri and thin stripes, a cashmere hakama of the same color, a crested haori of grayish-blue patterned silk, a black twill wool overcoat. I tucked two daggers under my hakama—the one I had stolen from my mother and my own. I also had Morita's letters in a furoshiki and a small purse with 20 or 30 yen.

I slipped out of the house through one of the wooden shutters I had purposely left open. To avoid being heard, I crossed the garden barefoot and put on my shoes after closing the back gate. The night was clear and a full moon was suspended in the sky. I made my way through the grounds of Tenso Shrine in Komagome, down Dōzaka, uphill to Tabata, and toward a teahouse called Tsukubaen. Bathed in the silvery rays of the moon, I walked up the deserted tree-lined path with a light step and light heart. The bare boughs of the zelkova trees cast their shadows on the moon-bleached pavement, weaving a delicate tracery of light and shade. The image is etched indelibly in my memory, for I felt extremely tense as I embarked on a great adventure.

Morita was waiting for me, drinking sake by the dim light of a gas lamp. He stood up and apologized. "Sorry to be drinking—waiting for you was such a strain." We left the teahouse and arrived at Tabata Station just as the last train pulled in. I had no idea where we were going, nor was I particularly interested. On the way to the station Morita had asked whether I wanted to go to the sea or the mountains, and, picturing a vista of snow-capped mountains, I immediately said, "Mountains." I may have also been thinking subconsciously of the harrowing last scene in *The Triumph of Death*[, in which Georgio and Hippolyta leap off a cliff into the sea]. But as I found out afterward, he had already purchased two tickets to Nishinasu.

The train went only as far as Ōmiya. We had no choice but to spend the night at a dilapidated inn in front of the station. Morita looked strained and downcast. I, on the other hand, had renounced everything, and felt an enormous sense of relief welling up from deep within me. And strangely enough, memories of childhood, silly, foolish things, kept floating back. I thought of my father and mother, who had been extraordinarily permissive and tolerant. Still, as a daughter who wished to live without restrictions as an independent being, I felt the very notion of family and parent weighing heavily upon me like an invisible monster.

In a while Morita's spirit seemed to lift, as if he had sensed my lightness of heart. "There's still a lot of time until morning," he said. "We should get some sleep." But I was in no mood to sleep; I wanted to savor each passing moment. "Please go ahead—you must be exhausted. Don't mind me." I was used to staying up all night, and both mentally and physically, I was too tense to sleep that night of all nights.

Morita must have thought I was worried about what he might do, and to put me at ease, he began talking about his childhood home in the countryside. "There was a brothel nearby, and I starting going there when I was a young boy. I've been dissolute ever since, and now I'm impotent. You have nothing to worry about. Get some sleep." What he said did not concern me, mostly because I only half understood what he was talking about. I made no comment and sat by the hibachi, adding bits of charcoal to the meager fire. In the end, Morita kept me company all night. Huddled near the hibachi, we spent the time talking in a rundown country inn, without even a cup of tea to warm us, but not for a moment did I feel the cold or wish the hours would pass more quickly.

Early the next morning, we took the first train to Nishinasu. Our next destination was Shiobara, but we could only get there by horse or by rickshaw, so we hired a rickshaw and arrived just as the sun was about to disappear behind the snow-covered mountains. I was fully prepared to climb the road and follow its path deeper and deeper into the mountains, but Morita was against this. We had to eat, he said, and since we did not know the terrain, we would get lost in the dark. We decided to spend the night at an inn. The servants said that the road, which went all the way to Obana Pass and beyond to Aizu, was buried in several feet of snow. They also warned us that this was the avalanche season.

That night, I gave Morita the dagger I had stolen and the packet of all the letters he had sent me. He set the packet aside without so much as a glance. He looked drained, utterly exhausted. I thought, this Georgio doesn't even have the strength to look at the love letters he's written. All he could do was soak in the hot spring at the inn and crawl into bed.

The next morning, I urged Morita to make an early start. We headed straight for the pass, but the road soon turned into drifts of snow. I was small and light and had no trouble, but Morita, who was overweight, sank into the snow with each step he took. He had never done any sports at school, nor had he ever exercised; since he could barely move his bulky body, I sometimes had to stop and pull him along. We had some distance to cover before we reached the pass, but as soon as we came to an open field above a deep valley, Morita gasped out, "I can't go another step," and collapsed to the ground. He took a bottle of whiskey from his pocket, gulped down several mouthfuls, poured the rest of the liquid on the letters, and set them on fire.

But there was something wrong. [I had asked him to bring all the letters I had sent, but] the packet containing my letters was half the size of his, and my letters had always been much longer. I said nothing and stared into the flames.

(When Morita had asked me to bring his letters, I immediately thought of the scene in *The Triumph of Death* when Georgio reads the love letters that Hippolyta has brought to their hideaway on the sea.)

All of a sudden, Morita cried out, "I'm a coward! I can't kill anyone! I thought if it were you, I could do it, but I just can't." Without even removing the dagger from the sheath, he threw it down into the valley. I was seized by a confusion of emotions—a surge of anger, a sense of bafflement and frustration. I suppressed the impulse to follow the dagger into the snowy depths of the valley and looked down helplessly.

It was already getting dark. Curled up on the snow, Morita kept wailing about how he was a spineless coward, and how he was going to die in a ditch like a beggar as soon as he ran out of money. What had happened to the "artist," who had vowed "to live out my days in a lone cell in a snowbound Sakhalin jail, observing the changes in myself"?

The time had come for me to take charge. Until then, I had been completely passive, acceding to Morita's every wish. At this point, we reversed our roles. I told him to get up. We had to reach the pass; living or dying was no longer the issue. I started walking. He followed grudgingly, though from time to time, I had to retrace my steps and pick him up. The sun had set, but we could still see by the light of the snow. "I give up. I can't walk." Morita refused to move.

We were at a clearing. On one side, the mountains were rapidly receding into the dark. I spotted a clump of bushes and brushed off the snow. Next I cleared a space under the twisted lower branches. We would spend the night here and I would watch over Morita. I took off my coat and spread it on the ground. We sat as close together as possible, but the cold crept up and penetrated our bones. Exhausted and still under the effects of the whiskey, Morita soon nodded off into sleep. I stayed awake, afraid he would freeze to death.

A full moon as bright as a mirror hung high in the deep blue sky. Illumined by its rays, the chiaroscuro of glistening snow and dark folds of the mountains suggested a host of banners unfurling soundlessly from the heavens. Overwhelmed by the majesty of the scene, I thought I had entered the kingdom of the dead and was sitting alone in a palace of phosphorescent ice and snow, unencumbered by body or mind. I had not forgotten Morita. In fact, I shook him from time to time, but he merely blinked his eyes, oblivious to the sublime grandeur of nature.

With the first light of dawn, the mountains assumed a completely different aspect. We started walking, aiming for the pass. I urged Morita to keep up with me, but unable to find a road, we lost our way. Then, unexpectedly, two men who looked like hunters emerged from the trees ahead. They turned out to be policemen who had been sent from the Utsunomiya Police Station to search for us. They told us to leave the mountain at once. Bears lurked in the area, and avalanches were also a danger.

We followed them meekly, not in the mood to resist. On the way down, they pointed to the tracks of a big bear. We had spent the night near the same spot but did not say a word. By then I had started to wonder about how the men knew where to look, and so quickly at that. (I learned later that on the night of our departure Morita had mailed a postcard to Natsume Sōseki from Tabata Station saying he was going on a trip.)[xviii]

The policemen took us to an inn. To our great surprise, Chōkō was waiting for us. We were even more surprised when my mother appeared minutes later. She had been waiting since the day before at the Utsunomiya Police Station. I had absolutely no desire to talk to Chōkō, let alone my mother. Since I couldn't flee or hide, I resolved to at least maintain my composure. I was also immensely relieved to see my mother calm and serene, with no visible signs of mental strain or fatigue.

That night, I slept in the same room with my mother for the first time in many years. Lying side by side in the tremulous glow of the old-fashioned oil lamp, I wondered if I was dreaming. "I'm afraid you won't be able to go home now," she told me in low voice. "If Father refuses to take you in, what will you do?" I tried to put her mind at ease. "Mother, please don't worry. I can teach or take shorthand. I'm quite capable of fending for myself." "Yes, but will anyone hire a woman who ran off with a man? You really don't know a thing about the world, do you?" There was nothing I could say in reply.

She asked about what Morita and I had done since I left home. "And what about your physical condition—are you all right?" For my mother, the question no doubt had serious implications, but I misunderstood her completely: "I'm not a bit tired. A day or two without sleep or food doesn't bother me at all. It was hard for Morita Sensei to climb the mountain, but thanks to zazen, I was all right." "Oh," was my mother's only response. (To my chagrin, I only realized much later that she was worrying about whether I had lost my virginity.)

Suddenly tired, I fell into a deep sleep. When I woke up in the morning, my mother was already dressed. She suggested that the four of us have breakfast together, and for the first time Chōkō formally introduced Morita to my mother. The two men had undoubtedly talked of many things during the night, but of course, I had no way of knowing what they had said. My mother made a special effort to speak kindly to Morita, but instead of answering her,

---

[xviii] Natsume Sōseki (1867–1916), Japan's preeminent modern novelist, was Morita's mentor.

he just sat there utterly dejected, with his head down. I also remained silent. Chōkō, for his part, kept praising my mother. "When something like this happens, no one knows what to do, and it's impossible to even think straight. But your mother—she remains calm and makes all sorts of good suggestions. Really, if it hadn't been for your mother—" Not to be outdone, my mother apologized for putting him to so much trouble.

We all took the same train back to Tokyo. Morita sat by himself across the aisle, but then all of a sudden he burst into tears. I was shocked. Was this man still capable of tears? And why in the world was he crying? I was puzzled because I had never seen him cry before. (When we were together, I was the one who was often moved to tears, while he remained dry-eyed.) A grown man bawling in front of strangers—the unseemly display of emotion was disgraceful. I asked Chōkō to speak to him. I have no idea what he said, but Morita pulled himself together and they spent the rest of the trip talking.

Just as the train was about to arrive in Ōji, my mother announced that she and I were getting off. Taken unawares, I stood up and said good-bye to Morita. "Since things have turned out this way," he said, "we won't see each other again and won't exchange letters." He spoke quickly, as if he were delivering an ultimatum, and did not sound at all like himself. His preemptive tone, his whole manner was extremely annoying. I wanted to get back at him, but under the circumstances, I bit my tongue and followed my mother off the train.

My mother and I spent the night at an inn in Ōji. This, too, she had arranged in advance with Chōkō, who meanwhile had taken Morita to Natsume Sōseki's home to seek his advice. Why should he seek Sōseki's advice? Shouldn't Morita and I settle our affair by ourselves? I was irked, but I could also understand my mother's position. In deference to my father, she had probably decided that she should first determine the true facts of the matter and then figure out a solution before taking me home. Then again, she may have wanted to avoid inquisitive newspapermen. In the event, my father sent a man to take us home early the next morning. I do not know why he did this, but perhaps Chōkō had spoken of the piteous plight of a mother and daughter left at a strange inn.

At home, my father was in bed with an upset stomach, brought on by worry and stress. I bowed deeply and made my apologies. "Please forgive me for causing you so much trouble." He barely concealed his anger as he fixed his eyes on me: "I hope you realize what you've done." My grandmother, however, was overjoyed to see me. "Thank goodness, you're back safely," she said with tears in her eyes. "You don't have to worry. Everything will be all right." I had not cried so far, but at this, the tears came pouring down my cheeks. "Come change into fresh clothes and get a good rest. The bath should be ready soon." My grandmother did her best to console me.

A day or two later, Chōkō came to report to my father that Sōseki had thought of a way to settle the affair. Instead of returning to his home, Morita would stay with Sōseki for the time being. Morita and I were to refrain from doing anything; the matter would be handled by the "grown-ups," that is to say, Sōseki and Baba Kochō, who were in complete agreement. Morita, moreover, would formally apologize to the Hiratsuka family, and at an appropriate time ask for my hand in marriage. My father reacted coldly and said he had no idea what his daughter was thinking. He advised Chōkō to speak to me directly.

Chōkō came to my room with my mother to tell me what had happened. More dumbfounded than angry, I asked myself: What on earth does Morita think about all this? And what kind of a solution is it that ignores the views of the parties involved? If Sōseki and Kochō thought that marriage was the answer to every problem between men and women, they were no different from ordinary people on the street. "It's out of the question," I said. "Marriage is the furthest thing from my mind. I am sure that Morita Sensei thinks the same way." Chōkō raised no objections and simply said, "Very well. Since you're against marriage, I'll speak to Morita and make sure he agrees."

His mission accomplished, Chōkō reverted to his usual chatty self. "I can't tell you what I've been through. Morita had me fooled this time! Up to now, whenever he had a love affair, he'd tell me all about it, but this time he kept everything to himself. And do you know why? It was because you had the upper hand, and I can see why. In any case, I was really shocked. For a while, I couldn't figure out what to do. But your mother is truly admirable. Not only was she never flustered, but she came up with all kinds of good ideas. The expression a 'woman of wisdom' refers, I suppose, to someone like your mother. Well, you really suffered a loss, didn't you, going off like that?"

"A loss?" Again, I was dumbfounded. Words like "loss" or "gain" simply did not exist in my world. Had I even dimly entertained such notions, I would never have done anything so utterly stupid with such ease.[5]

"I think you should stop seeing Morita," Chōkō went on. "But what happens between you and me is another matter—we'll always be friends. You can trust me not to be like him. When it comes to art, I consider myself his equal in understanding and passion, but I have common sense. So after everything's calmed down and you're allowed to go out, come and see me anytime you like." Then he told me that he had been baptized during his university days and delivered a brief sermon touching on his own philosophy of life. "You're strong, but you don't use your strength to serve society. That's why you ended up the way you did. Tolstoy says somewhere that unless you act for the sake of others, you will never appreciate the true meaning of life. From now on, why don't you act for the good of humankind?"

In a few days Chōkō returned with Morita. I sat in the room as Morita apologized to my father and promised not to see me again. He may have been acting on the orders of the two "grown-ups," Sōseki and Kochō, but nothing could have been more ridiculous. I looked on with complete indifference.

Several days later, a letter from Sōseki arrived, addressed to my father and stamped "Confidential." He wrote to say that Morita had lost his job because of the incident, and since the only way he could earn a living was through his writing, would my father be so good as to give Morita permission to write a novel based on it?. He himself would take full responsibility and make sure that Morita did not cause any more trouble or sully the family name in any way. My father flatly refused; not only had the man caused a scandal, he was now proposing to write a novel about it and live off the profits. Furthermore, this matter directly concerned his beloved daughter. He told my mother to go to Sōseki's house to convey his answer. After repeated pleas from Sōseki, however, my father eventually gave his consent. By coincidence, my father and Sōseki had been instructors at the First Higher School at about the same time, but since Sōseki was a known eccentric and seldom spoke to anyone on the staff, they had never exchanged a word.

I myself had never met Sōseki, but had heard about him from Morita, who had been his student in English literature at the First Higher School and Tokyo Imperial University. They were apparently quite close; Morita regarded Sōseki as his mentor, though I imagine he took advantage of the relationship in his immature way. He certainly had no qualms about criticizing Sōseki's books. "They aren't novels in the true sense of the term. They're the products of a scholar, typical of the *Hototogisu* poets with all their airy theorizing about being detached from the world. His kind of novel doesn't appeal to me at all. And do you know what? Sōseki doesn't know a thing about women. He writes novels about them, but the only woman he knows is his wife. His heroines are all in his mind, and not a single character's alive. He listens carefully to the conversations of his students, especially those about women, and then he writes them up in the next installment of his serialized novels. I'm the one who has to tell him how women really talk." Morita also gossiped about such topics as Sōseki's domestic situation and the sort of person his wife was.

The Aftermath of the Affair

The repercussions of the Shiobara Incident, the name given to our affair, were much worse than I had feared. Not only was I reviled by the press, but within ten days of my return, I was expelled from the college alumnae association. The notification was delivered in person by Ideno Ryū, a board member and former classmate. She looked ill at ease and even showed some contempt for me, but I told her exactly what I thought: "I don't believe that I've done anything to dishonor the association, but if that is what the board thinks, I will of course accept its decision."[6]

In fact, even before I had returned, Naruse Jinzō himself had come to our home as soon as the incident was reported in the newspapers. Ostensibly he had come to extend his sympathies, but he had said to my father, "Your daughter always stood out from the crowd, and I had hoped she would make her mark in the world, but now with this—"

To tell the truth, I could not have cared less. Even before graduation I had distanced myself from the school and had little sense of loyalty. All that mattered was that I had graduated, that I had been deeply influenced by Naruse Sensei, and that I would no doubt respect him for as long as I lived.

Yet, in truth, the public outcry and wild speculations were extremely unpleasant. Still more odious was the gall of the reporters who hounded me for interviews. I knew that if I talked to them, they would invariably distort what I said. As a matter of fact, on the one occasion when I tried to explain my actions, I discovered to my horror that they deliberately twisted the facts to suit their own preconceptions. I also received all sorts of strange letters, some jokingly proposing marriage, one even enclosing erotic prints. (I had never seen pictures of this sort, and I must admit I was shocked.) One proposal, well intentioned but amusing, was from a medical student at Tokyo University who was training with Sōkatsu-rōshi at Ryōmō-an. He appeared out of the blue at our front door and demanded to see my parents. I recognized him from sesshin but had never spoken to him. I declined politely. The young man knew I had come under heavy criticism and no doubt felt sorry for me. Perhaps he thought he was doing his bit to "save all sentient beings from deluding passions and lead them to Buddhahood."

At my father's office, too, several people suggested he resign. Because of this and the mounting public criticism, he told me to go away for a while. I was just as anxious to leave, so I asked Kimura Masako to talk to Shūgaku and see whether I could stay in a small house on the grounds of Engakuji. I received permission, moved in, and for the next three months lived in complete isolation, each day and each night, all twenty-four hours, on my very own, or as they say, "heedless of the calendar."

By then, Shaku Sōen had already retired and been succeeded by Miyaji Sōkai-rōshi as chief abbot. Though this may sound impertinent, I could not warm up to him; perhaps we were not fated to be master and student. So instead of training with him, I meditated on my own and burned one incense stick after another. I stayed inside most of the time and only went out for walks, going through the main gate toward Matsugaoka and farther on to

Tōkeiji (the temple that served as a sanctuary for unhappy wives during the Tokugawa period).

The poet Noguchi Yone was also living on the temple grounds. Our paths crossed now and then, but according to the woman who served Noguchi his meals, he was a recluse. His only visitor was his American wife, who came once in a while but never stayed long. The woman also said he was eccentric and irritable, spent the whole day at his desk, and shouted at anyone who made a noise. I read some of his books several years later — On the Poet Bashō, The Poetry of the Man'yōshū, The True Spirit of Japan, and others. I was favorably impressed, but this was perhaps because I knew him, in a way.

My mother came to visit me just once. Otherwise, no one came, not even Masako, who had been drawn unwittingly into the incident. Her father, ever the stern army officer, had been terribly angry. "You knew all along what your close friend was doing and you kept quiet? How am I going to face her parents or the public?" Masako's name was not removed from the alumnae register, but she felt herself under a cloud, and she soon left for the Kansai area to teach home economics at a girls' school. I shall always remember her parting words. "Well," she had said, smiling ruefully, "I won't be mopping up after you anymore, will I?"

◎ ◎ ◎ ◎ ◎

Sometime during the summer Sōkatsu-rōshi returned from the United States. I went to see him, and in the course of the conversation, he said he was leaving again for the United States and asked if I wanted to come along. He mentioned this casually, but I wondered whether he had heard of the incident. I jumped at the offer; I would be able to continue my training with him and also leave my home and country.

I obtained permission from my father and made my preparations. I then heard that Rōshi's longtime attendant, a middle-aged woman (a widow who had received inka), was spreading rumors. She was going around saying that Rōshi had complained about how I had talked him into taking me to the United States. I had not realized that personal relations among his entourage could be so complicated. Disillusioned, I decided not to go. Had I gone with Rōshi to help him with his work, I would have received a thorough grounding in Zen practice. My life, too, would have been completely different. Is life all too often determined in a passing moment? I wonder.

Of the original group of people who had accompanied Rōshi, only Sasaki Shigetsu (a graduate of the Academy of Fine Arts) stayed on in the United States. He taught for many years, and died [in 1945]. [After the war,] I heard that his American wife, Ruth, was studying Zen at a temple in Kyoto and hoped to meet her, but unfortunately she died before I had the chance.[7]

◎ ◎ ◎ ◎ ◎

That same summer, my mother, who was worn down by the worry and stress, became ill, and my father ordered me to go with her to Chigasaki where she could avoid the city heat and recuperate. I am sure that part of her illness was his fault, since he most certainly blamed her for much of what had happened. My mother must have had a hard time mediating between her husband and her daughter, but even when we were alone together in the house we rented, she never complained. She was not the type to show her emotions, and when Morita came to see us at Chigasaki—he was the only visitor—she received him graciously, without so much as a frown.

My mother was the one who told me of the pressure on my father to resign. But he remained in his job, so the pressure probably came from some of his colleagues and was nothing official from his superiors. I was naturally pained to think that I had hurt his honor and good name—matters dear to a government official—but I remained convinced that I had done nothing particularly wrong and suffered no sense of guilt. Nor did I think that I had been egregiously unfilial. What I had done was not my parents' problem but my own. I was not in any way brazenfaced about this, and the damage I had done to my family did tug at my conscience. But I often thought how much easier life would be without family or parents. I desperately wished to be independent, yet I had no choice but to live under their protection, taking advantage of their affection and forbearance. (I continued to receive a generous allowance from my mother and money for special expenses.) True, I was given the greatest conceivable freedom for a young unmarried daughter, but this, too, could be a psychological burden. I wanted to go away. I felt as if I were being crumpled like a piece of paper by the disapproving outside world. Away from Tokyo, I would be able to put my life in order and take stock of things.

I Go to Nagano

In early September [1908], I left for Nagano Prefecture to visit Kobayashi Iku. One of the "Pirates" at Ochanomizu, she had gone on to the Higher Normal School and was now teaching at a girls' high school in Matsumoto. I envied her luck in living so close to the Japanese Alps and had thought of her as soon as I made up my mind to leave Tokyo. My mother, considerate as always, provided me with ample funds.

The train to Matsumoto was delayed, and since I was already late, I satisfied my curiosity by staying at a cheap inn that catered to itinerant merchants. Iku came the next morning and gave me a warm welcome; she had not changed a bit. We spent the night at her school dormitory near Matsumoto Castle and left the next morning for Asama Hot Spring, where we stayed for four or five days. Surrounded by the violet blue peaks of the northern Alps—Norikura, Yarigatake, Yakedake—I felt at peace, as though I had returned to my spiritual home.

Back in Matsumoto, Iku introduced me to a family who were wholesale dealers in silk cocoons. I arranged to rent a room from them and looked forward to settling down in Nagano for a while. But Iku, who was aware of the local tendency to kowtow to government officials, had evidently told the family head about my father's position at the Audit Board. Iku meant well, but the man was a typical example of the ambitious provincial inordinately attracted to power, and he suddenly changed his attitude toward me. His behavior struck me as yet another instance of what I hated about society, and I moved out after a week.

I next arranged to live at a fish farm in Nakayama, a small village several miles southeast of Matsumoto. Far from public transportation, the farm was accessible only by foot, so I sent my luggage ahead with a load of silkworm pupas (used to feed carp) and walked the entire distance. The big fishpond was a natural body of water that looked as if it dated back as far as the surrounding mountains. Overhead, kites hungry for fish circled in the cloudless autumn sky.

My room was in a separate wing of the main building, far removed from the noise of the workplace. Although the place was quiet even during the day, the silence at night was deafening. There was a small artificial pond in the garden in front of my room, and in the dead of night, I would hear the carp leaping to the surface, the sound echoing as if they were plopping inside me. I passed the time reading, sitting in meditation, and walking. I usually walked during the noon hours, gazing at the tiers of mountains and the fathomless, deep blue sky. Not far from the fish farm I discovered a dry riverbed with clusters of yellow cottonweed sprouting from the gray pebbles. I followed the riverbed's course, taking in the widening vista. I rarely saw a human being.

In the evening, after I finished eating the supper brought by the owner's daughter-in-law, I read and meditated. One book I particularly liked—I had brought along several—was a collection of Poe's poems and fables. Sitting by the faint lamplight in the stillness and solitude of the mountains, I imagined myself in a tale from the medieval past and appreciated all the more the fantastic and mystical elements in Poe's writings. I had brought the book with me because Chōkō, who had seen my translation of Turgenev's sketches, had suggested that I try Poe. His stories were relatively easy to follow, unlike "The Raven" and others of his poems, which spoke to me directly but were difficult to comprehend. Far removed from harsh reality, I was fascinated by his strange and febrile imagination. When I put out the journal *Seitō* several years later, I included my translations of the stories I read at that time: "The Shadow," "Silence," "The Power of Words," "The Black Cat," "The Red Masque of Death," "The Dialogue of Eros and Charmian." (Jōdai Tano gave me some help on this project, as did another graduate of Japan Women's College who specialized in English literature.)

I had also brought the copy of *Smoke* that Morita had lent me. I glanced at the opening chapter, but quit after a few pages. When I departed from that area, I threw the book into the riverbed with all my might, certain that in the spring the river, swollen by the melting mountain snow, would carry it to some unknown destination.

Morita, I should mention, was still writing to me, despite his promise to my father. Neither of us felt particularly bound by this, and in fact, just before my departure for Nagano, we had secretly met and agreed to inform each other of our whereabouts. He had left Sōseki's house by then and taken a room at a temple in Ushigome. He had also started writing a novel based on the incident. When the book was eventually published, it attracted wide attention and prompted one newspaper to dub me "Miss Zen Studies."

Morita, incidentally, had never approved of my interest in Zen and seemed to take this as a personal affront. At our last meeting also, he had made all sorts of negative remarks: "I refuse to believe that Zen made you the woman you are. I don't even want to believe it. You were born different, and that's why I found you so attractive." "You have the clarity of vision that Dostoevsky and other epileptics have before an attack." "When I look at you I sometimes think you suffer from a kind of monomania." And so on.

The altered state of consciousness brought about by focusing on a kōan was indeed a kind of obsession, and in that sense, he had observed me correctly. "It isn't just any monomania," I said, just to tease him. "It's 'eromania.'" "Really?" he replied. "If you're telling me the truth, then you're superhuman! Everything you've done up to now is superhuman." He clasped my hand and blurted out, "I'm capable of anything if it's for your sake. I'll follow you to the end of the earth." But the next moment, he started berating me all over again. "Why in the world would you want to do zazen?" To this, I merely replied, "There is no simple explanation." For in truth, there were no whys and wherefores for something so deep-seated and instinctual as a spiritual need. The tears tumbled down my cheeks as my mind flashed back to the time when I had been filled with spiritual anguish, when I had longed for a divine revelation and fought a life-and-death battle to attain kenshō.

Chōkō, too, seemed to disapprove of Zen, or at least my zazen. While he didn't know much about it, he said, he thought Zen was deep but also somewhat narrow. A person as intelligent as Chōkō could make such remarks because Zen was not a system of thought but something prior to cognition, something that had to be experienced with one's own blood and tears. There was no deep or narrow in Zen; looking to the innermost recesses of consciousness made it possible to experience the vast, undifferentiated, all-encompassing oneness of life. So I made a point of avoiding the subject.

Morita wrote in his letters that he would come to Nagano as soon as he finished his novel and that nothing he had written would hurt my reputation; there was no cause for worry. I suppose he wanted to reassure me, especially since my father had strongly opposed his plan to write the novel. Still, I was surprised and irritated by his defensive, apologetic tone. I mainly wanted him to write a good novel, or rather, for him to set aside petty worries and pour his heart and soul into his work, to write in "dead earnest," "as if his life depended upon it." (I was particularly concerned about this, for I had never felt, not even when we went to Shiobara, that Morita did anything in "dead earnest" or "as if his life depended upon it.") Still, I was happy to receive his letters and a copy of Hedda Gabler.

The weather turned cold. The mountains became white with snow, the logs on the hearth of the main building burned brightly, and a wooden rack for a charcoal foot-warmer was set into the floor of my room. Worried that I had no winter clothes, my mother urged me to come home. I knew my stay was only a temporary escape, but even so, I was reluctant to leave; I was happy living all alone, deep in the countryside, far from the distractions of the mundane world. There was one thing that bothered me, however. Although I was in excellent health, I noticed that whenever I sat down to meditate, something opaque, a murkiness at the back of my head, prevented me from entering a state of perfect concentration. It was not a headache but an inability to still my thoughts. I also felt a general lassitude of mind and body. In spiritual terms, I had definitely regressed.

I could only conclude that the incident had exacted a toll, and I was saddened to think that this was the cause of my mental and physical fatigue. (Not that I felt discouraged in the usual sense of the word. I had no worldly ambition and did not care if I was denounced or shunted aside by society. Society operated by its own rules. I had mine. That was that.) I had not talked to a rōshi for a long while. I was anxious to return to my former state of being. I could already see Nantenbō-rōshi's room in my mind's eye.

Morita's Novel

I received a letter from Morita in early December, just as I was thinking of returning to Tokyo. He had finished his novel, and beginning on New Year's

Day [1909], *Black Smoke (Baien)* would be serialized in the *Tokyo Asahi shin-bun*, with an introduction by Natsume Sōseki; advertisements for the series would come out soon. *Black Smoke*—I immediately thought of Turgenev's novel, but I soon found out that it did not even get a single mention. (In Morita's novel the male protagonist lends "Tomoko" a copy of *The Triumph of Death*.)

Morita had repeatedly written that he would come as soon as he finished his book, but I knew that he could not be trusted to keep his word. And since I was reluctant to upset him while he was still writing, I deliberately avoided any mention of a future meeting. But by then he was finished and presumably had resolved the affair in his mind. Or, to put it another way, he had written the novel he had planned from the very beginning (and this had nothing to do with whether he had planned it consciously or not). It was surely time for us to forget the past and start afresh in life. At least, this is what I thought.

"I'll kill you, and afterward live out my days in a lone cell in a snowbound Sakhalin jail, observing the changes in myself." Morita had exaggerated his claims as a writer and artist, and I, in turn, had taken his literary obsession at face value. He had failed to kill me, but presumably had striven to the limits of his power to write a novel based on his own experience. I rejoiced for him, and while I had no clear expectations, I fervently hoped that the book would be worthy of his efforts.

I left Nagano in the middle of December, bidding a fond farewell to the mountains. I stopped in Matsumoto to see Kobayashi Iku, and, as thanks for her help, gave her the dagger I had carried with me ever since I attained kenshō. I hired a rickshaw at Ueno Station and went straight to Morita's lodgings in Ushigome. I wanted to end our relationship before going home, but he was out, and since it was already late, I asked the caretaker to give him a letter I had written beforehand. On purpose I had written succinctly, even bluntly: "Now that you've written your book, let's put an end to this. I shall go my own way."

I spent the night at an inn near his lodgings. The next morning I thought briefly of seeing Morita, but decided against this and headed home. I pictured him reading the cold, heartless letter and recalled his infuriating behavior the time my mother and I were about to get off the train at Ōji. Was I subconsciously trying to pay him back? But I was certain I had done the right thing. There was no reason for us to meet; it was fortunate that he had been out.

My mother and grandmother welcomed me home with smiles. My father was away on an extended trip. I was grateful that I did not have to see his smug face, the Kaiser mustache, and the pince-nez perched on his high-bridged nose. My study was exactly as I had left it—the books on the shelves, the objects on the desk, the scrolls written in Sōkatsu-rōshi's brushwork, the white porcelain incense burner. It was as though the room had been waiting for its master's return.

Soon after I was settled, I went to the Nihon Zengakudō in Kanda Mitoshiro-chō, where Nakahara Nantenbō-rōshi held a monthly sesshin. The Zengakudō was not a temple but an old building that had been converted into a center for Zen studies by Okada Jiteki, a medical doctor who had trained with Nantenbō. It was no surprise then that most of the participants were doctors, with only one or two women. Nantenbō was then the abbot of Kaiseiji in Nishinomiya and already in his seventies. In contrast to Shinjō-rōshi, who was spare and austere, my new teacher was big and muscular, with a ruddy complexion that betrayed a fondness for drinking. In fact, he looked exactly like one of those stiff-necked, stubborn old men frequently found in the countryside. As soon as I entered the room for my first interview, he went into a tirade. "Kamakura Zen—and did you learn anything? Nothing, I'll bet. Coddled by your teacher, too. If you think you've achieved kenshō, you're making a big mistake."

I wondered why he was so critical. He did not name names, but was he referring to the priests trained at Engakuji? If so, why had he sent his own adoptive son, my friend Shūgaku, to train with Shaku Sōen at Engakuji rather than keeping him at Zuiganji, his own temple in Matsushima? Was something wrong with my attitude, and was this his way of telling me to go back and start from the very beginning? I was baffled.

As expected, I was assigned "Jōshū's dog," the first kōan in the Mumonkan.[xix] Like my previous Zen masters, Nantenbō gave no explanation. Instead, he offered a demonstration: "Mu, Mu, Mu, Mu, Mu. Exhale deeply as long as you can and growl from the pit of your stomach." He did this over and over, and then he dismissed me.

I went to the hall to join the other participants. Evidently most of them had been assigned the same kōan, since the hall sounded like a pigsty from all the grunting. Accustomed to sitting in perfect quiet, I found the noise rather disconcerting. All the same, I was grateful to Rōshi. When I started zazen at Ryōmō-an, I had approached the kōan about the "original face" as an intellectual problem. At every interview, I had been scolded for giving a philosophical explanation. I had put tremendous effort and perseverance into understanding it, but now, with Nantenbō's practical advice, I hoped to avoid such a detour and proceed in a straight line.

One of the men who came to the Zengakudō was Nakano Seigō. Clean-cut and good-looking, with the bookish mien of a student, he had recently

---

[xix] Also known as Jōshū's Mu kōan: On being asked by a monk whether a dog has Buddha Nature, Jōshū replies "Mu!" "Mu" is a negative, but in this instance, it does not mean a simple "no."

graduated from Waseda with a degree in political science. I happened to be sitting in the lounge one day when he came in. He had just had an interview, and while lighting up a cigarette, he started muttering to himself. "Who needs Zen. If you've got it, you've got it." He turned to me with a smirk. "Hah, did I tell that Rōshi a thing or two!" I had no idea what had taken place during the interview, but I felt annoyed by his arrogance and competitiveness and I could not stop myself from making a few remarks of my own.

Nakano stopped coming to sesshin. He probably decided it was a waste of time and most likely did not achieve kenshō. I saw him a number of years later when he was a member of the Lower House. When I went to ask for his advice about the New Women's Association, he remembered our dispute and was helpful in many ways.

Another person I saw at the Zengakudō was Takashima Heizaburō. I had attended his lectures on child psychology in college, but dressed as he was in a cotton kimono and hakama, he looked more like an elderly student. "So, how have you been?" he asked with a friendly smile. At school, too, unlike the other professors, he had always smiled as he lectured. Seeing him there, I felt I had discovered the secret of his kindly and gentle ways. Still, when he sat for meditation, he looked so fierce that it was almost painful to watch. Takashima Sensei is widely recognized as Japan's first child psychologist, but I wonder how many know about his Zen practice (or I should say his religion).

◎ ◎ ◎ ◎ ◎

[I would like to skip ahead in my story to say that] I had been working on the "Mu" kōan for almost a year and come no closer to understanding it. So in late [sic] December (1909), I went to Nishinomiya to attend rōhatsu sesshin, the intensive winter session, at Nantenbō-rōshi's temple. About twenty people came from all parts of the country. Aside from me, the divorced daughter of a Kansai merchant and a simple-hearted old woman from the countryside were the only women. With the exception of a couple of middle-aged and elderly men, the rest of the participants were monks still in training. There was not a single student or intellectual present, which made the atmosphere different from what I was used to at the Zengakudō. A local doctor, who was reputed to be Rōshi's most outstanding student, made an occasional appearance in a supervisory capacity. Solidly built, with an imposing presence, he impressed me at once as a man possessing spiritual distinction. He later was ordained and, as Tōin-rōshi, became active in Zen circles.

For the benefit of my readers, I shall describe a rōhatsu sesshin. It begins on the first of December and ends on the eighth, the day Sakyamuni attained

Supreme Enlightenment. We sit all day and all night, wearing the same clothes and never bathing. For meals, we eat a bowl of boiled barley, a cup of miso soup, and some pickled greens three times a day. In spite of the cold, we sit stockingless on a small cushion placed on the bare wooden floor. Needless to say, there is no heat. Because I was unaccustomed to the diet, in particular, the barley, I immediately came down with a severe case of diarrhea and more or less went without food for the duration of the session.

Each time an incense stick burns out—this usually takes about an hour— the presiding monk strikes a wooden clapper, the signal for us to file into the adjoining room for a brief rest. If there are people in a state of perfect stillness and reluctant to get up, they will sit for the entire day. At night, we are permitted to lie down in the adjoining room and practice "sleeping Zen" for a while. This does not mean that we sleep soundly. In fact, we are still meditating; sitting up or lying prone, it is the same thing.

I do not want to sound boastful, but several people, including the young monk in charge of the *keisaku*,[xx] praised my sitting posture. On one occasion when I was meditating by myself, the old woman from the countryside came up to me with clasped hands and addressed me as "Blessed Goddess of Mercy." On the last day of the session, I was told that I had passed the "Mu" kōan, the kōan about the "sound of one hand clapping," and several others. (I had already passed some of the same kōan when I was training with my previous teacher.)

The next morning, we gathered for a ceremony in the main hall. Apparently I had been the only one to achieve kenshō. Rōshi, who could be quite sarcastic, glared at the young monks. "This young miss from Tokyo achieved kenshō and with flying colors, too. So what have you been doing all this time?" I was so embarrassed I wished I could disappear. In front of the image of Buddha, I read the Act of Repentance and chanted the Four Vows. I stood upright, my hands pressed together, but I could feel every inch of my body shivering and shaking. I was then given a short black cotton surplice and the religious name Zenmyō. "Zen" came from Zenchū, Nantenbō's religious title, "myō" was a variant reading of my name, Haru.

I will now describe an escapade I made that very morning. I had eaten very little all week, and to make sure that I was strong enough for the long ceremony, I stole out of the temple just before dawn, took the first train to Kimura Masako's house in Amagasaki, and asked her to cook me a pot of rice gruel. I gulped it

---

xx A paddle used occasionally on those meditating if their posture is wrong, if they doze, or if the monk with the keisaku feels they need it.

down with slices of raw sea bream she had found at that early hour, and returned to the temple in great haste. The ceremony was just about to begin. "Where were you?" asked one of the monks. "We've been looking all over for you. We knew you wouldn't run away on a day like this." I merely smiled.

After the formal closing of the session, Rōshi's attitude changed, as if he had become quite another person. He insisted that I rest for a couple of days before returning to Tokyo, ordered an attendant to set out quilts in the room next to his, and had a foot-warmer put in. He also told the attendant to bring a pot of hot rice gruel, and then, placing a small dish of rock candy beside my bed, said, "Go ahead, take a piece," in the tone of a grandfather speaking to his grandchild. So I stretched out between the soft quilts and spent the time meditating.

On the way back to Tokyo, I stopped to see Masako and stayed up all night talking with her. She had mastered the local dialect and seemed completely at home in her lodgings. She told the elderly owners what she would like for her meals, and they in turn trusted her and treated her as the child they never had. She lived as she wished, "taking the initiative in all things," as the classic phrase goes. I could never hope to emulate her.

When Nantenbō-rōshi turned eighty, despite his students' protests, he announced that he was preparing to go to the next world.[xxi] A solemn ceremony marking his decision was held at his temple in Nishinomiya. He no longer came to Tokyo and refused all requests for interviews, and the Zengakudō was closed. He made this decision because Sakyamuni had died at the age of eighty, but to this day, I find his reasoning beyond understanding.

I shall always remember what Rōshi said after an interview one day. I was about to excuse myself from his room, when he asked out of the blue, "Did you really run away with a man?" I said yes, and after making my prostrations, I stood up to leave. Then, in a voice full of loving kindness, he said, "Now that you're on a big boat, you'll be all right."[xxii] I said nothing, but thought, no, he's wrong. I had done what I had done because I was already on a big boat. How else could a big fool like me do something with no hesitation, fear, or calculation? This conversation took place when Morita's novel was being serialized in the newspaper, and I doubt that Rōshi was reading it; he had probably heard about the incident from someone else.[8]

[xxi] *Senge*, literally, to move from this world to another to teach; refers to the death of a high-ranking priest. Death by choice was not uncommon among Buddhist prelates and usually entailed self-imposed starvation. Nakahara Nantenbō (1839–1927), who was also a distinguished painter and calligrapher, actually died at age 88.

[xxii] From the phrase, "to feel as if one is on a big boat," that is, to feel secure and free from worry.

⊙ ⊙ ⊙ ⊙ ⊙

As advertised, the first installment of Morita's novel appeared on January 1, 1909 in the *Tokyo Asahi*.[xxiii] I had not opposed his writing of this work and was well aware that he had never loved or understood me. While I had no particular hopes or expectations, I was still curious. We subscribed to the paper, so my parents, or at least my mother, must have glanced at what he had written. But no one mentioned the novel, as if the whole subject was taboo, and I read it surreptitiously in my room.

Out of consideration for my parents, who no doubt were going through a difficult time, none of our relatives had said a word about the incident. I also was careful about what I said, but Aunt Ai came to visit one day and in her usual easygoing manner, she told my mother: "My husband's been reading that novel in the *Asahi* and says it's quite interesting." My mother winced, and this was a most uncharacteristic expression for her.

With each installment, I found myself increasingly unhappy and perplexed. The novel was obviously modeled on *The Triumph of Death* and so a certain lack of sincere feeling was perhaps to be expected. But why did Morita have to tell the story according to his own tastes and preferences, and in a most tendentious manner at that? To me at least, another obvious failing was the extensive use of my letters—rewritten though they might be—and the total omission of his own. Yet he had clearly put much effort into writing the novel, and he deserved congratulations for that.[9]

As I recall, I ran into Morita at Suidōbashi Station sometime during the summer, soon after I started taking lessons in *naginata*.[xxiv] I had not seen him since the publication of his novel in the *Tokyo Asahi*, and we agreed to take a walk even though evening was near. It started to rain, but we had much to talk about, so we went into an inn in Misaki-chō. Since the rain was coming down in torrents, the maids closed all the wooden shutters. Shut up in the muggy, airless room, we talked and talked, not realizing that we had missed the last train. We decided to stay for the night and continue our conversation. I also asked one of the maids to send a telegram to my parents informing them of my whereabouts.

Our conversation, naturally, centered on his novel. To clear up any misunderstandings he might have, I brought up the subject of Zen and sexual desire.

---

xxiii *Black Smoke* was serialized from January 1 to May 16. In the novel, Tomoko (Raichō) tells the narrator, Yōkichi (Morita), that she likes to watch the black smoke billowing out of factory chimneys.

xxiv There is a chronological confusion here since Raichō says later that she started taking lessons in naginata (a form of fencing using a long wooden stick) after attending the rōhatsu sesshin in December 1909. Her narrative sometimes goes back and forth.

I said Zen did not deny sexuality, and no one practiced zazen in order to get rid of physical desires. Rather, zazen brought liberation from such desires. Many Zen priests were uncompromisingly celibate, but they had chosen this way of life entirely on their own, and after having first affirmed the reality of sexual desire.

To make my point, I told him about "the old woman burning the hermitage," the famous kōan dealing with the problem of sexual desire.[xxv] Morita, however, refused to believe that zazen liberated a person from sexual desire. To be perfectly honest, I was not qualified to speak on the subject. I had started zazen when I was still innocent of such desire, and even at the time of this meeting with Morita, my information was based only on hearsay or my imagining; unlike hunger or thirst, I had never actually experienced the physical sensation. But I wanted Morita to have a deeper understanding of my innermost being, and since we were talking about sex, I told him about my blunder with a certain young monk. Instead of accepting my account at face value, he misinterpreted this as well.

We argued through the night in the stifling heat, and when the day dawned, Chōkō appeared at the inn, to our great astonishment. How in the world had he found us? My mother had apparently asked him to take me home, and he had come, first thing in the morning. I felt terrible—I should never have stayed at the inn. Morita also looked embarrassed and kept muttering excuses as if he'd been caught in the act. Meekly, I followed Chōkō home.

The Shiobara incident and now this. In one way or another, Morita and I had caused Chōkō a great deal of trouble. He could hardly be blamed for complaining that we had "given him a hard time." His diligence in carrying out my mother's wishes was admirable, too, though I sometimes wondered if there wasn't an element of simple curiosity in his behavior. After all, he was still young, not even thirty.

⊚ ⊚ ⊚ ⊚ ⊚

My feeble attempts to translate Poe had convinced me that I should study English in earnest, and several weeks earlier, in April (1909), I entered the Seisoku English Academy in Kanda. When I first went to register, the person in charge said that no women were allowed, and even after I pointed out that the regulations mentioned nothing about this, he insisted that there was "no

---

[xxv] An old woman gives a hut to a monk and feeds him for twenty years. To test the monk, she tells a young woman to go and embrace him. When the young woman asks how he feels, he replies, "An ancient tree grows on a cold rock in winter. Nowhere is there any warmth." On hearing this, the old woman is enraged, chases the monk from the hut, and burns it down. What should the monk have said?

such precedent." "In which case," I replied, so as not to be thwarted, "please let me enroll and establish a precedent." My persistence paid off.

There were no examinations, and students were free to choose their courses, so I went in the evening as well, wearing my long dark-gray cloak. The wooden building was rundown, the classroom poorly lit, and the students—who were all men—dressed in every attire imaginable and looked generally unwashed. Seated alone in the back row, I talked to no one and no one talked to me.

One of the classes was English grammar, taught by Saitō Hidesaburō. He had great enthusiasm for his specialty, and to emphasize a point, he struck the desk with a folded fan just like a professional storyteller. This, together with his other mannerisms, kept the students entertained. He also lectured on *Nature* and other writings by Emerson, but instead of explaining the ideas, he parsed each sentence clause by clause. Thanks to Saitō Sensei, I finally acquired a firm grasp of English grammar. Another class I enjoyed was on *King Lear*.

Besides studying English, I took lessons in naginata. This was after the rōhatsu sesshin in Nishinomiya. I had passed the "Mu" kōan and was in that state of exaltation in which "mind and body are one." I was confident I would do well. My teacher, Yasawa Isako, was a small elderly woman who had trained in the Bukō school of naginata. She had taught at the college, where naginata was part of the physical education program, but after her recent retirement, she opened her own practice hall in Koishikawa Hara-machi. Thanks to zazen, posture and form posed no difficulty for me, and I was praised from the very beginning. I learned a number of moves, but since I was the only student, I did not participate in any matches and stopped going after mastering several moves. I kept the naginata, and whenever the mood seized me, I took it down from the wall and went through the motions, shouting with each thrust.

Haiku was another new interest. I read all the major poets—Bashō, Buson, Onitsura, Issa—and wrote pallid imitations, which I submitted to Naitō Meisetsu's column in the journal *Japan and the Japanese* (*Nihon oyobi Nihonjin*). One haiku I wrote at the time was: "A flash of lightning / The specter of a cloud / Caught in the dark." Another was "Bonfires here and there / Passions rising / Dancers on the shore." I continued to compose haiku through the years, but made little noticeable progress.

In March 1910 [1909], I went to Kyoto for the first time in my life. My parents gave me 30 yen for the one-week trip. I stayed with Kimura Masako at her home in Amagasaki, and after we toured the sights in Kyoto, we went on to Lake Biwa and stayed the night at an inn in Ishiyama. To my great embarrassment, I kicked over the wooden foot-warmer in my sleep. The quilts caught fire, black smoke filled the room, and we rushed to the public bath downstairs to dampen the quilts. No one noticed, but the next morning I confessed to the proprietor and paid him accordingly.

◎ ◎ ◎ ◎ ◎

The three pillars of my life were zazen, English classes, and reading at the Ueno Library. In my spare time, I visited Chōkō and attended meetings of the Keishū Literary Society, which had broken up after the unfortunate incident with Morita but continued to meet informally at Baba Kochō's house in Ichigaya. Among those who came were Yamakawa Kikue and several other former members, as well as Okamoto (Ōnuki) Kanoko, who was new.

Kochō was then in his early forties. Slender, of medium height, and with aristocratic good looks, he was the very model of the stylish modern intellectual. A born raconteur, he could hold forth on any subject. His talks on literature were far from systematic, however, and ranged from anecdotes about Higuchi Ichiyō and Saitō Ryokuu to gossip about literary coteries, European authors—Turgenev, Björnson, Ibsen, Hauptmann—and even physiology. "When human beings started to walk on two legs," he said, "their internal organs were dislocated and they've been unhealthy ever since. It's better for your health to get down on all fours now and then, and that's why I have my wife mop the floor." His wife, who may have been a bit older, was shy and withdrawn, and seldom joined our conversation.

Okamoto Kanoko was still a student. She wore her maroon hakama tied high up on her waist, and truth to tell, had no sense of style. I was certain I had never seen her before, but as we walked together after a meeting, she said she had seen me at the Ueno Library. She then described what I had been wearing—patent-leather shoes with silver-colored metal ornaments on the toes, a kimono of such and such a design—what I was doing, and so on. She spoke with obvious relish and at such length that I became exhausted just listening to her.

Kanoko was very proud of her older brother Ōnuki Shōsen and said he was presently translating Turgenev's *Smoke*. She had a big, round face and big, dark eyes and was not as heavy as she became later. When she talked, she went on without a pause, fixing her eyes on you tenaciously as if she didn't want to let go. She had the easy assurance of a daughter of a good family, but once something aroused her interest, she bored into the subject relentlessly and examined every detail. Even then, she was clearly not an ordinary person.

◎ ◎ ◎ ◎ ◎

Since the incident, I had become closer to Chōkō and started dropping by his house from time to time. He lived in Hongō Nishisuga-chō, near Nezu

Shrine, in a large mansion he had apparently rented under some kind of special arrangement. Ikuta Shungetsu, who was not a relation, also lived in the house and earned his keep by minding the front door. He was painfully shy, and since I was reluctant to bother him, I usually made my way through the garden in the back and went directly to Chōkō's study. In retrospect, I think it was rude of me to appear unannounced, but Chōkō always welcomed me and invited me in to talk about philosophy, literature, and new books. We went from one topic to the next without a break. He also looked at the translations, travel sketches, essays, and poems I had written in Nagano.

Much as I enjoyed my conversations with Kochō and Chōkō, I was still undecided about my future. I vaguely thought of writing about religion, but for some reason, I had always had a certain aversion to professional writers, particularly women writers. More to the point, I lacked the requisite ambition and confidence. If I thought of the future at all, I thought of living in a place with a view of mountains—a village in Nagano, say, where I would keep bees, meditate, read, and write. I also thought of opening a small tea shop high up on a mountain pass, or in Kamakura in front of Engakuji. For a while, I gave this serious thought, quite confident that I would be able to support myself.

Given my state of mind, I had little interest in social or political issues. Even something so controversial as the Great Treason Incident failed to arouse my interest.[xxvi] Chōkō talked about it, but I only listened halfheartedly, as if it did not concern me. Chōkō had an enthusiasm for politics unusual in a literary person, and he often discussed current topics—he later supported Ozaki Yukio's Movement to Protect Constitutional Government[xxvii]—but I was preoccupied with spiritual matters and paid only the slightest attention.

Nietzsche was also one of his favorite subjects. I had read essays on Nietzsche by Takayama Chogyū and Tobari Chikufū in college and been deeply impressed, so I listened attentively and even purchased the English edition of *Thus Spake Zarathustra*, which Chōkō was translating at the time. But I do not think I was influenced by his opinions of Nietzsche in any way. I would also like to stress that my relationship with Chōkō was never one of student and mentor. There are people who see us in this light, but they have forgotten that he was then in his twenties [and only four years older than I]. Indeed, his influence on my intellectual formation was quite negligible, and at most it was my budding aspirations as a critic that were stirred by our conversations. Be that as it may, I shall always think of Chōkō with gratitude

---

xxvi In August 1910, Kōtoku Shōsui and eleven other radical socialists, among them Kanno Suga, were executed for allegedly plotting to assassinate the emperor.

xxvii Popular movement in 1912–1913 to protest military interference in parliamentary government.

and admiration for remaining true to his motto to be "friendly, courteous, and kind to women."

The future writer Satō Haruo was also living in the house. A student at Keiō University and the son of a doctor in Wakayama, he was the very image of the pampered "young master." I remember Chōkō saying jokingly, "Satō's lucky. His father's a doctor in Shingū, and whenever he sends a manuscript home, his father pays him for it." But Chōkō doted on him, and Satō took advantage of this. More than once, I saw him standing on the lawn and shouting at Chōkō at the top of his lungs in the most impudent and insolent manner.

Satō had been invited to stay because Chōkō had heard that he was looking for lodgings. The house was spacious, the rent consequently expensive, and the extra income no doubt welcome. So perhaps it was to be expected that Satō acted as if he owned the house, and among other things, ignored me whenever I came to visit. I am generally tolerant of people, but I must admit, he made a bad impression. Satō was completely different from Ikuta Shungetsu, who lived under the same roof but was too timid to look anyone in the face. That probably explains in part my reaction to his know-it-all attitude.

Years later, in 1956, Satō asked me for a favor. He was writing a book on Takamura (Naganuma) Chieko and wanted to know if I remembered anything about her. The request was conveyed through my friend Otake Kōkichi, so I agreed to meet him at her house. I had not seen Satō for nearly fifty years. Dressed in an elegant and expensive kimono and hakama, he looked every inch the successful, self-possessed author, with no hint of his youthful self. Then he started to talk. His buckteeth and his loose lips were just as I remembered. He was in failing health, and when it was time to leave, he was unsteady on his feet and had to be helped by Chiyoko, his beautiful and intelligent-looking wife.

Shūgaku

Ever since the incident with Morita, I had refrained from going to Kaizenji or seeing Shūgaku. The temple had been mentioned in the newspapers, but more important, I wished to spare him further pain. According to Kimura Masako, he had been deeply shocked by the incident and begun to drink heavily; if I turned up at the temple, it would only make things worse.

Masako returned to Tokyo for the summer holidays (1910) and went to visit Shūgaku. He told her he was eager to see me, so at her suggestion we decided to go to the temple together. Despite all that had happened, Shūgaku seemed genuinely happy to see me. He took us to a restaurant in Ueno and treated us to a sumptuous meal with abundant helpings of sake.

Our acquaintance renewed, I visited him now and then, sometimes alone and at other times with a friend. But he was no longer the Shūgaku I had known. When I first met him two [four] years earlier, he had been a young monk who had just completed his training at Engakuji. Now, as resident abbot of the newly revived temple, he was a person of authority, robed in a white silk kimono and purple surplice. Only his penchant for puns, acid tongue, and warm hospitality remained the same. The biggest change was his excessive fondness for women and drink. For this, I was partly to blame, for he had apparently begun his pursuit of pleasure soon after that fateful kiss. His life of dissipation was not entirely his fault.

Especially when he was drunk, he often boasted to me about a geisha he knew. So one day I asked him to show me the machiai where he met her. It turned out to be a fancy restaurant near the Yushima Tenjin Shrine, a far cry from the dubious establishment I had gone to with Morita. Anyone who saw us must have been struck by the strange sight of a black-robed priest and a young woman in hakama entering a machiai in broad daylight. Shūgetsu introduced me to the madam of the house. "This young boy is very special," he said. "So please take good care of him." "Oh my, but isn't he handsome!" The woman clearly knew how to handle her customers. She was also graceful and quite attractive.

That day, Shūgaku and I were finally joined together. I was young and unmarried, but I did not consider my behavior immoral. I had come on my own, and what had happened was of my own volition. Still, it would be stretching the truth if I said that I acted out of love for Shūgaku. The Shūgaku I loved was the person I had known four years earlier, the pure and innocent monk, not the worldly, confident priest with position and power. This is not to say that I surrendered my virginity to someone I didn't care about at all. I was still fond of Shūgaku, and he would always have a place in my heart.

I never would have done such a thing had I not been involved with Morita. Soon after the incident, an utter stranger sent me erotic prints, and my curiosity had been piqued, perhaps unconsciously. The vague desire to know more about the act may well have led me to sleep with Shūgaku. For unlike young women today, I had only the dimmest conception of sexual matters. I was physically immature to begin with, and even when I saw cats and dogs in the act, I never related this to human beings.

I remember a biology class in college. The lecture was on fertilization, but instead of talking about human beings, the instructor used the reproduction of sea urchins as an example. Peering into the microscope, I could see a host of spermatozoa advancing toward an egg cell. The instructor said that human sperm were much the same, only shaped somewhat differently. I was puzzled about how sperm met up with an egg in human beings and thought of raising my hand, but I changed my mind at the last minute. When I saw the erotic prints some time later, I was glad I hadn't asked the question.

Shūgaku and I became much closer. He called me "Haru-bō" or "Haru-kō"[xxviii] but never mentioned the possibility of marriage. I took this to mean that he had arrived at a deeper understanding of who I was. Discreet and circumspect, he was never the one to suggest that we go to a machiai. The sexual dimension of our relationship remained much the same, our friendship as tranquil as still waters.

[xxviii] In this context, the suffixes -bō and -kō indicate familiarity and affection, in much the same way that Raichō's father used to call her Haru-kō.

5

Seitō

I have before me an office daybook, its moss green cover worn with age. Stamped on the spine in faded gold letters are the words "Office Daybook for 1911 Printed by Hakubunkan." Inside, on the front page, the big, bold characters read "Seitō Office Daybook." As I look at Yasumochi Yoshiko's handwriting, I can almost feel the joyous expectation that filled our youthful spirits as we were about to embark on a new venture. The next pages are blank. Then, the first entry:

> May 30. Warm and cloudy.
> Hiratsuka Haruko and I went to Kaederyō to mimeograph copies of the statement of purpose and statutes for Seitō. In response to our request, Nakano [Hatsuko] and Kiuchi [Teiko] have written to say that they not only support our plan to publish a journal, but will be happy to join the society and serve on the governing board. Haruko and I are much encouraged and informed them of a meeting of board members to be held the day after tomorrow.

The short entry is written with a pen. When I look at Yoshiko's skillful, though somewhat illegible, writing, I can see, through the mists of memory, the two of us nearly sixty years ago, trudging uphill to the college in Mejiro. We went to Kaederyō [a dormitory for graduates] to use the mimeograph machine. I hesitated at first—officially, I was no longer an alumna—but went at Yoshiko's insistence: "No one's going to mind. In fact, everyone's looking forward to seeing you." The visit, in a sense, marked the first step toward publishing the journal *Seitō*. As to its future fate, I did not have the slightest inkling.

To begin with, I did not make the decision to publish a journal; I agreed only at Chōkō's urging. Though this was my first real job, I had yet to take it seriously. True, I was already twenty-six, but my days were filled with zazen,

English classes, and trips to the library, with little time left to see people, let alone hold down a job. I knew I would have to be independent one day, but I felt no pressing need to be financially self-sufficient. The paramount goal in my life remained unchanged: to plumb the depths of my being and realize my true self. At that stage, the prospect of a job held no appeal. To be truly human, to be a free agent like the True Being of the past, to be godlike and live at the heart of the universe—that was what mattered, not financial independence.

Those were different times, and we looked at the problem of having enough to live on differently. It would be hard for young women today to imagine how generally optimistic we were. In my own case, I had used my shorthand at various times and was confident that I would be able to support myself in a pinch. Or, if need be, I could always take up a pilgrim's staff and survive quite nicely.

Chōkō had spoken to me several times about starting a literary journal expressly for women writers. Perhaps he thought that a journal of this nature would serve as a rallying point and would advance the cause of women writers, who tended to be excluded by their male colleagues. Or, with his kind heart, he may have hoped to pry me loose from my daily routine of zazen and library trips and goad me into doing some serious writing. And then again, he may have been thinking of the collection of writings by the Keishū Literary Society that had never achieved its potential to become a full-fledged journal because of my affair with Morita. Whatever the reason, his suggestion was not surprising when you consider his strong interest in women writers, his pedagogic bent, and his eagerness to foster young talent. He had no doubt singled me out because I was the only woman who was a frequent visitor to his house.

As I said, I was less than enthusiastic. I had no wish to be a professional writer. I had neither the temperament nor the talent, and even if I did, I doubted that writing a good novel would bring me the kind of emotional and intellectual satisfaction I sought. To be sure, young women at the time felt the powerful attraction of literature, to an extent unimaginable today. Aspiring writers sent manuscripts by the hundreds to magazines like *Joshi bundan*.[i] But I had no such inclinations, nor did anyone I knew. At one point I may have vaguely thought of writing about my experiences and ideas, but putting out a literary journal was the furthest thing from my mind, so I had turned a deaf ear to Chōkō's proposal.

He refused to give up. "It should cost this much to print this number of copies. Why don't you ask your mother for the money? I'm sure she'll give it

---

[i] *Joshi bundan* (*Women's Literary Forum*): Magazine started in 1905 by the poet Kawai Suimei.

to you. Gather your friends together and give it a try." He had even calculated the expenses, and having become friends with my mother, he seemed to think that she would be willing to furnish the funds.

I mentioned Chōkō's idea to Yasumochi Yoshiko, a college classmate of my sister's. Diagnosed with tuberculosis, she had spent three years convalescing at the same sanatorium in Chigasaki, and, in need of funds, had done clerical work and even volunteered for clinical experiments (Yoshiko called herself a "guinea pig"). She had graduated this spring and was living with us while she looked for a job. My sister, by then, had left for Kobe, where my adoptive brother had been assigned, so it was up to me to keep Yoshiko company. We shared rooms—fortunately, she was placid and easygoing—and we often talked about literature. Having specialized in Japanese literature, she was knowledgeable about haiku and waka. I, on the other hand, knew more about Naturalism, neo-Romanticism, and other contemporary trends. We had our disagreements: during her long stay at the sanatorium, she had been influenced by Christian teachings,[ii] whereas I lived by the truths of Zen Buddhism. But she was just as much an idealist, an ardent practitioner of the Okada Method of Quiet Sitting, and, like me, dissatisfied with the lot of women and impatient to do something about it.[iii]

Yoshiko leaped at the chance. "Oh, let's do it! We'll do it together!" She had no desire to return to her home in Shikoku; this was just the sort of job she was looking for. She urged me to take it on.

By then, I had more or less made up my mind. But there was still the question of money. Chōkō had talked as if I had merely to ask my mother. I was loath to do this, however, since I had sponged off my parents long enough. In that day and age, a twenty-six-year-old daughter with a higher education did not live at home clinging to her desk because of any encouragement or forbearance on the part of her parents. She was there because she had no alternative if she wished to remain true to herself, even if this risked causing them further grief. At that stage in my life, I could hardly ask my mother to finance the kind of work that was bound to displease my father, who firmly believed that a woman's duty was to be "a good wife and wise mother." She would be caught in the middle and suffer yet again.

Still, no matter how many times I turned this over in my mind, I could not think of a way to raise money. But I also felt that once I made my decision, the money would come from somewhere. Then, as now, I had absolutely no

---

ii The director Takada Kōan was a fervent Christian.

iii *Okada-shiki seizahō*: A method of meditation devised by an agronomist, Okada Torajirō. Said to be effective for a wide range of ailments including loss of weight, tuberculosis, insomnia, and heart disease, it was popular among intellectuals at the time.

financial sense. I had some pocket money, which did not amount to much, though I may have inadvertently hinted to Yoshiko that I had more.

Yoshiko and I agreed to put off the crucial question of expenses and instead started working on a plan for the journal. My mother happened to overhear us and became alarmed that I was up to something outrageous. She asked about what we were discussing, and that is when I told her about the journal. "And have you got the money for it?" she asked. I said no, not at the moment, but we hope to raise some in the future. She was appalled at our lack of common sense, but then said, "Well, I have some money set aside for you. If your project is serious, I'm willing to give you a little. Your father won't approve of this, of course." She promised to give me 100 yen to cover the expenses for the first printing.[1]

The money she mentioned was probably my dowry, which was sitting undisturbed in a bank somewhere. And she was giving the money to me and not to the journal. She may even have been happy to do this; she did not know what kind of journal it was, but her daughter, who refused to listen to any talk of marriage and stayed buried in her books, had finally decided to work. I also asked my mother for money to cover miscellaneous expenses like lunches and transportation for Yoshiko and me. She was not too pleased about this, but she never complained and took out a little at a time without telling my father. Nor did she complain about Yoshiko, who stayed off and on at our home until she moved to the Seitō office in Sugamo in April 1913.

With the money assured, we began working in earnest on the statement of purpose and statutes for the journal. By mutual agreement, I wrote the final draft. As I remember, the wording was more or less as follows:

> This is no longer the time for women to indulge in somnolent indolence. We must rouse ourselves without delay and develop to the full the talents that Heaven has given to us. We hereby launch Seitō, an organization made up exclusively of women and dedicated to the furtherance of women's thought, art, and moral cultivation. We also inaugurate our journal *Seitō* and open it to all nameless women who share our ideas. We hope and moreover, believe, that the journal will give birth to outstanding women writers of genius.[iv]

The statutes were virtually the same as those that appeared in the inaugural issue. I shall cite the first; the others were equally succinct.

> Statute 1: The society aims to awaken women, to enable each one to manifest her unique inborn talent, and to give birth to women writers of genius.[2]

[iv] Hereafter *Seitō* in italics will refer to the journal and Seitō in roman type to the organization.

The wording fails to convey adequately what I wished to say. I was not claiming that the society had been founded in the hope that one or two women of literary genius would emerge from our ranks. Rather, I was trying to say that its purpose was to enable women to give full expression to their inborn talents and to realize their individual genius. Or to put it another way, I was calling out to women to demonstrate their hidden talents through literature and to cast off the shackles of oppression. In short, I was saying that each and every one of us was a genius. I later spelled this out in the essay I wrote for the inaugural issue; the first statute was merely a distillation of my thoughts at the time.

When I drew up the draft, I was not what one could call socially conscious. Also, I did not particularly look forward to working with other women even though I was a woman myself. When I looked at the women around me, they seemed false. They were presumably endowed with extremely admirable qualities, but these remained hidden because of social conditions. They were surely capable of greater things, but their innate strengths were kept in check. The time had come for them to throw off the dead weight of oppression, assert their true selves, give full expression to their individual talents, and articulate their thoughts boldly and honestly. Then, and only then, would they truly be women. I wrote the first statute with these thoughts in mind.

We took the draft to Chōkō as soon as we were finished. [This was on May 29.] I introduced Yoshiko and told him that we were thinking of doing all the work ourselves. Chōkō looked very pleased. Thus far, we had not consulted him and knew that the draft might not necessarily reflect his ideas, but he made only two suggestions. One was to change the phrase in Statute 1 from the society "aims to awaken women" to "aims to promote the development of women's literature." Yoshiko and I demurred, since we preferred our version, but in the end we decided to follow his advice, and that is how it was published.

His other suggestion was to add a sentence [to Statute 5]: "Prominent women writers will be asked to serve as supporting members of the society." Yoshiko and I saw no need to seek the support of established authors, but Chōkō began reeling off the names of writers famous and not so famous: "Let's ask this person, and yes, that person, too." He also suggested that we ask Mrs. Mori Ōgai, Mrs. Oguri Fūyō, and other women married to famous authors to serve as supporting members. Only later did I realize that he was right in saying that if the membership were limited to unknown young women, the journal would end up as just one more cliquish literary magazine.

The discussion then moved on to naming the journal. Yoshiko suggested "Keishū bundan," "Keishū bun'en," "Joryū such-and-such," and other names with "woman" in the title. I thought of "Kokuyō." My father had brought back an obsidian stone from Hokkaido, and for a while, I displayed it proudly in the alcove of my study. Chōkō mentioned several possibilities, but then, he suddenly slapped his thigh and said, "Why don't we call it 'Bluestocking'? It wouldn't be a bad idea to throw out a challenge to the public." I had never heard of the word.

According to Chōkō and an encyclopedia article I read afterward, "Bluestockings" referred to a group of women in the mid-eighteenth century who regularly gathered at the London salon of Elizabeth Montagu to discuss art and science with men. They were called Bluestockings because they wore blue rather than the usual black stockings, and the word had subsequently become a pejorative for women who behaved in a novel or unwomanly manner. Our work was certain to incur public criticism, and by calling our journal "Bluestocking," we would be throwing down the gauntlet, so to speak.

When the term was first introduced to Japan in the 1880s, "Bluestocking" had been awkwardly rendered as the "Party of the Blue Tabi Socks." We decided to translate it as "Seitō" [using the character "sei" for "blue" and a less-known character, "tō" for "stocking"]. Some people are under the impression that Mori Ōgai suggested the name, but this is incorrect.[3]

On June 1 (1911), we held our first meeting. The entry for the day reads as follows:

Meeting [of the five founding members] held from 1:00 p.m. at the Mozume home. Present were Mozume Kazuko, Hiratsuka Haruko, Nakano Hatsuko, Kiuchi Teiko, Yasumochi Yoshiko. Due to her mother's illness, Ida [Mozume] Yoshiko unable to attend. Agreed to mail copies of statement of purpose and statutes to prospective members and supporters along with a letter. Also agreed:

1. Hiratsuka will act as publisher, editor, and representative of *Seitō*; Nakano will serve as legal guarantor.
2. The journal will be published once a month (postage 1 sen 5 rin).
3. Charge 15 yen for a full-page advertisement, 8 yen for a half page.
4. Ask Naganuma Chieko to do the cover for the first issue.
5. Ask Ikuta Chōkō to determine the publisher, printer, and distributor.

The following persons will visit prospective supporting members:

Yasumochi: Kunikida Haruko
Hiratsuka: Koganei Kimiko, Yosano Akiko, Oguri Yasuko [Kazuko]
Mozume: Mori Shige, Hasegawa Shigure, Okada Yachiyo
We will make inquiries at Nikolai Cathedral for Senuma Kayō's address.

The following persons are on the mailing list: Tamura Toshiko, Chino Masako, Yamamoto Ryū, Mizuno Senko, Mizui Ryō, Ojima Kikuko, Nogami Yaeko,

Tahara Yū, Kawada Yoshiko, Nagashiro Michiyo, Hosokawa Toshi, Ōtake Masako, [?] Kikue, Hashimoto Yae, Kawasaki Fumi, Ueda Kimiko, Kobashi Miyo, Tokunaga Hatsuko, Shimizu Kin, Takamatsu [?], Akashi Shizue, Nitobe [?], Inoue Tamiko.

Also: Yosano Akiko, Hasegawa Shigure, Oguri Yasuko [Kazuko], Okada Yachiyo, Kunikida Haruko, Mori Shige, Koganei Kimiko, Senuma Kayō.

(signed Yasumochi)

They were no doubt sent copies of the statement of purpose and statutes.

Most of the women on the list were graduates of Japan Women's College. Of the five founding members, Nakano Hatsuko and Kiuchi Teiko were Yoshiko's classmates and friends of my sister. Hatsuko and Teiko were in the Japanese literature department, so I did not know them personally. They both hoped to become professional writers and had joined Kōda Rohan's literary circle while still in college.

Nakano Hatsuko was the eldest daughter in her family, and since her father's retirement from the publishing business, she had assumed the main responsibility for the family's finances. She worked as a reporter for the *Niroku shinpō* immediately after graduation and at that time was an editor of the journal of the Nurses' Association. Even as a college student, she had been levelheaded and cautious, not at all the type to become a fervid follower of Naruse Sensei. She was more like an intelligent middle-aged matron than a young girl, and wore her hair in an ichōgaeshi, which suited her large, pale face. Because of her literary interests, she readily accepted Yoshiko's request to become a founding member, but never, to the end, submitted a manuscript. As an editor she set impossibly high standards for herself and seemed to put her hopes instead in her close friend Kiuchi Teiko, who was a year or so younger. The two, in fact, were inseparable, so when Hatsuko became a founding member, Teiko naturally followed her lead.

Kiuchi Teiko, too, was the eldest daughter in her family and responsible for finances since her father's retirement from government service. She was determined to qualify for a teaching certificate and was studying French at the upper division of the Futsueiwa Girls' High School. She looked sickly— a shadow of melancholy hung about her—and like her friend, she already seemed middle-aged with nothing of the zest of youth. In contrast to Hatsuko, however, who had the confident air of a professional, she was shy and seemed content to stay under her friend's wing.

Mozume Kazuko became a founding member quite by chance. I had originally thought of asking some of the members of the Keishū Literary Society, but had decided against this since they were all dilettantes and Yamakawa Kikue, the sole exception, was busy with her studies at Tsuda Eigakujuku.

I then saw a picture of Mozume Kazuko and her older sister Yoshiko in the *Asahi*. They were reported to be members of Natsume Sōseki's circle, a rare privilege for women at the time. Yoshiko had been a classmate of mine at Seishi Elementary School and her older sister, who was two classes ahead of me in high school, had taken koto lessons with me. Although I had not seen Yoshiko for at least a decade, I asked her to be a founding member. She said she would be delighted, but when she married a diplomat who was scheduled to go abroad, she suggested her sister Kazuko in her place. (At a time when few women wrote detective stories, Yoshiko later published under the pen name Ōkura Teruko. Her private life, by all accounts, was rather unhappy.)

We needed an office, so I was extremely grateful when Kazuko offered her room at her parents' home in Komagome Hayashi-chō. Actually, I should have volunteered, but I could not bring myself to do so. My father was certainly one reason, but more important, I still regarded the journal as a side job and could not bear the thought of having the center of my life disturbed. Kazuko's father, Dr. Mozume Takami, was then absorbed in his life work, the *Kōbunko Encyclopedia*. The tree-shaded house was large, and since her room was at the far end of a long hall, our presence was barely noticed. We never saw anyone in her family, though now and then, at noon, we would catch a glimpse of the maids and student assistants carrying lunch trays down the hall.

The first meeting went smoothly, with no objections to the statement of purpose and statutes that Yoshiko and I had drawn up. Hatsuko and Teiko may have had some reservations about the prose—I long ago lost the original copy—but neither seemed particularly interested in expressing their opinions. As I recall, Yoshiko and I did all the talking. Everyone agreed that Hatsuko should be the journal's editor and publisher.[v] She was knowledgeable about publishing and experienced in the ways of the world. Naturally, this, too, should have been my responsibility, but I was reluctant to be in the public eye and have my name appear as the publisher. Yoshiko could have taken on the job, I suppose, but she lacked tact. I could easily imagine her getting into an altercation of some kind. Hatsuko, with her self-assured, grown-up manner, was ideal; I am sure I was the first one to urge her. Later, when the journal came under government censure and she had to report to the authorities, she remained unperturbed and uncomplaining.

As noted in the June 1 entry, we asked Naganuma Chieko to do the cover for the inaugural issue. She was my immediate choice. A talented artist, she was studying oil painting at the Taiheiyōgakai in Yanaka. She was a year behind me in college and, as I mentioned, we had been tennis partners but

---

[v] Contradicts June 1 entry.

never had a sustained conversation. After graduation, I had occasionally seen her from a distance at gatherings like the Umehara Ryūsaburō exhibit at the Venus Club in Kanda Misaki-chō or the Rodin exhibit sponsored by *Shirakaba*[vi] at the Sankaidō in Akasaka Tameike. In fact, it would have been hard to miss Chieko—the collar of her kimono was daringly pulled back and the hem was trailing, and her loose hair flopped over her forehead. Stranger still was her languorous walk, at once demure and seductive. Even as a student she had been eccentric, not at all the typical home economics student. I had watched her with friendly fascination, and in choosing an artist for our cover, I thought of her at once. I also hoped she would join the society.

Chieko accepted our request but declined to become a member. She met her future husband Takamura Kōtarō later that year and was no doubt busy, but she came to our New Year's party in 1912. I still have the group photo that appeared in the February 1912 issue.

The entries for June are written by various members.

June 3

Visited Kunikida Haruko at her home in Akasaka Tamachi Nanachōme. She agreed to be a supporting member and send a manuscript each month.... Also said she will make inquiries regarding advertising and printing and visit Hiratsuka on the seventh. (signed Yasumochi)

Kunikida Haruko was Kunikida Doppo's widow. Yoshiko and Doppo had been at the same sanatorium in Chigasaki, where he eventually died. That was where Yoshiko met Doppo's wife, a quiet and unassuming woman of about forty who worked as a supervisor of salesgirls at the Mitsukoshi Department Store. She had published several stories but was not a professional writer.

June 6

Visited Okada Yachiyo in the afternoon. Hasagawa Shigure was also there. Talked to them about the purpose of the journal and obtained their consent to be supporting members.... (signed Mozume)

Visited Koganei Kimiko and Yosano Akiko in the afternoon. Both agreed to be supporting members. Yosano promised to send a manuscript each month. (signed Hiratsuka, Yasumochi)

Sent letter to Chino Masako in Kyoto asking her to be a supporting member and to contribute manuscripts. Also to Mizui [Ryō] wishing her a speedy recovery and requesting an essay on *Hedda Gabler*.

[vi] *Shirakaba* (White Birch): A journal of literature and art founded in April 1910.

We asked Okada Yachiyo because Kazuko's brother was a friend of Yachiyo's brother, [the playwright] Osanai Kaoru. We also asked Hasegawa Shigure[, who was already known for her plays]. Koganei Kimiko was Mori Ōgai's younger sister. Already in her forties, she had not published for some time. I did not know her, but she lived close to my home in Akebono-chō, so I volunteered to visit her. She was very much the upper-class lady, elegant and modest. She expressed interest in our journal and said she would help us as much as possible. As I recall, she sent in one manuscript.

Yosano Akiko

I shall never forget my visit to Akiko at her home in Kōjimachi Nakarokuban-chō, if only because she was so different from the unkempt woman who had given lectures to the Keishū Literary Society four years earlier. She was wearing a light cotton kimono boldly patterned with bush clover, *kikyō*, and other autumn flowers, and had her hair swept up fashionably in an exaggerated pompadour. She looked strange, but dressed with distinct flair. She spoke in just the same way as the last time I saw her, mumbling low in the Kansai dialect and not once looking me in the face.

Although I could barely hear her, she seemed to be saying that women were hopeless, that they were inferior to men, and that she had seen many submissions [to *Myōjō*] from all over Japan, but the good poems were invariably by men. I may have misunderstood her, but was she trying to warn us that our bold talk about publishing a women's journal and producing women writers of genius was arrogant and presumptuous? Or was she saying just the opposite—that because of the dearth of female talent, we must put forth the greatest efforts to succeed? In any event, I asked her to be a supporting member and to write something for the inaugural issue, as well as in the future. When I think of it now, I was really asking more of her than was absolutely proper.

Akiko sent in a manuscript on August 7, well before the deadline and earlier than anyone else. We were overjoyed. She had meant to encourage us, after all. Her contribution, written expressly for our first issue, was a series of ten or so short verses entitled "Rambling Thoughts." I shall quote the first two:

The day the mountains move has come.
Or so I say, though no one will believe me.
The mountains were merely asleep for a while.
But in ages past, they had moved, as if they were on fire.
If you don't believe this, that's fine with me.

All I ask is that you believe this and only this.
That at this very moment, women are awakening from their deep slumber.

If I could but write entirely in the first person,
I, who am a woman.
If I could but write entirely in the first person,
I, I.[4]

Akiko's powerful poems were paeans to women, and nothing could have been more appropriate for the first page of our inaugural issue. We were all thrilled, but I was particularly so since she had been so negative about women that day. I may be wrong in my judgment, but had our heartfelt, if naïve, statement of purpose stirred the poetic imagination of this extraordinarily sensitive woman?

Most of the women we asked to be supporting members gave us their unqualified consent. They included Hasegawa Shigure, Okada Yachiyo, Yosano Akiko, Koganei Kimiko, Senuma Kayō, Oguri Kazuko, Kunikida Haruko, and Mori Shige. They also promised to write for us—a group of complete unknowns—for no remuneration to speak of. It would be unthinkable today, but they were all young, and rather than joining with us to declare themselves publicly, they may simply have seen the journal as an outlet for their writings.

The Inaugural Issue

We hoped to bring out the first issue in September [1911], but of course we were complete novices in editing, printing, advertising, and selling. To quote from entries of the time:

> June 7
>
> Meeting held at Seitō office. Five members present. Decided on the contents for first and second issues. Third issue is to be devoted exclusively to stories by Seitō members. Nakano Hatsuko and Kiuchi Teiko will be in charge of visitors. Agreed to hold discussion meeting on *Hedda Gabler* on July 1. Meeting adjourned at six. Received positive reply from Chino Masako.

Our decision to plan ahead for the second and third issues was undoubtedly based on Chōkō's advice. Chōkō, incidentally, never interfered with the editing, though he took such an interest in women writers that he even went through the manuscripts in the "Reject" pile.

Kazuko's brother also poked his head in from time to time (he knew a great deal about the publishing world). "So, a bunch of inexperienced young ladies is putting out a magazine. You'll be lucky to publish three issues!" He liked teasing us, but also gave us practical advice, like compressing the lines in an advertisement to save space. Kazuko used to look alarmed whenever her brother teased us, but she was efficient in handling the office work. Attractive, with porcelainlike skin and a cool, fresh look on her face, she was not a so-called cloistered young lady but practical and worldly-wise beyond her years. She was more like someone brought up in the hustle and bustle of downtown Tokyo. I sometimes wondered if she wasn't exasperated at having to work with such neophytes.

Yoshiko, in the meantime, was constantly toting up figures on her abacus and going off to solicit advertisements. My mother furnished the initial funds, but Yoshiko and I were determined to be financially independent—the sooner the better. Yoshiko took her work seriously and hoped to make it a full-time job. By contrast, I went to the office only sporadically and spent most of my days attending English classes and the weeklong sesshin under Nantenbō-rōshi's guidance at the Zengakudō whenever he came to Tokyo. I wore, as usual, a hakama—light wool for summer—and clogs.

Letters requesting membership came every day; one applicant even came to the office.

June 18

10 a.m. Sugimoto Masao came with a letter of introduction from Chino Masako in Kyoto. She was with someone named Tsuda Seifū. Masao requested membership as well as letters of introduction to Hiratsuka and Hasegawa Shigure. (signed Yasumochi)

The same day, Masao came to my home accompanied by a young man sporting a flowing Bohemian tie. I assumed he was her husband, but then learned that he was Tsuda Seifū, an artist recently returned from France. I am not sure what their relation was. (Tsuda was then living in Mejiro, near the college, and I heard later that Naganuma Chieko and other students who were interested in art often went to his house.[vii]) About this time Masao apparently went with Tsuda to visit Sōseki and asked him to take a look at something she had written. After this, they were both invited to join Sōseki's circle.[5] Masao was tall and thin, with wide shoulders and an angular body. She dressed simply, without a trace of vanity, and had a masculine air about

---

[vii] Raichō misremembers. Chieko graduated four years earlier, in 1907.

her. She lived in Kyoto. I was not sure what she did, but she became a faithful and prolific contributor—we could hardly keep up with her—writing in a dry, matter-of-fact style that suited her personality.

June 21

Announcement in the *Yomiuri shinbun* about forthcoming publication of *Seitō*. Visited Mori Shige and asked her to be supporting member. Said she would send manuscript by the end of July. Letter to Nagashiro Michiyo returned, address unknown. (signed Mozume)

We sent the announcement to the arts section of the *Yomiuri* and other local newspapers on the advice of Kazuko's brother. (Nagashiro Michiyo was an aspiring writer who served as the model for the woman in *The Quilt*, the novel by Tayama Katai.)

July 1

Hiratsuka, Kiuchi, and Nakano came around two-thirty in the afternoon. Worked on the advertisements for *Seitō* and discussed possibility of exchanging advertisements with other journals. Hiratsuka will open a bank account at the post office. Nakano brought a sign for the office. Sugimoto Masao came. Kiuchi and Nakano left at five-thirty and Hiratsuka about twenty minutes later. (signed Mozume)

Hatsuko, a skilled calligrapher, made the sign. We put it up on the house's back gate, the entry we normally used.

July 2

Visited Mori Shige in the morning. Asked for the title of her story and reminded her to send it in by the 6th. Hiratsuka came. Talked about exchanging advertisements with other journals. Visited offices of *Kokoro no hana* and *Shinchō* to request addresses of their women contributors. Visited Matsubara [Nijūsankaidō] in the afternoon to discuss exchanging advertising with *Jogaku sekai*. He said only for announcing articles. Went to *Hototogisu* office but no one there. Arranged to go again. (signed Mozume)

July 3

Visited Mizuno Senko to talk about her manuscript. Said title will be "A Sense of Relief." Package from Hiratsuka. (signed Mozume)

Nijūsankaidō was a friend of Kazuko's brother and the head editor of *Jogaku sekai*, a woman's journal with the largest circulation at the time. He must have been surprised at our naïveté in asking him to exchange advertisements.

July 6
    Hiratsuka stopped by on the way to the library. (signed Mozume)

All the entries from July are in Mozume Kazuko's handwriting, so Yoshiko must have gone to the sanatorium in Chigasaki, where she periodically helped out.

On the same day, we received a reply from Iwano Kiyoko, who had been recommended by Chōkō: "I've just thought of someone good. She lives in Osaka and she's married to [the writer] Iwano Hōmei. I guarantee you that she'll join. And she's really interesting. She wears her hair in this enormous bun, and whenever I go to see her husband, she joins the conversation and gives her views in a beautiful, clipped Tokyo accent, all the while smoking a pipe and laughing out loud in a high-pitched voice. She's also thinking of writing a novel."

This was not the first time I had heard Iwano Kiyoko's name mentioned. [A year or so earlier,] the newspapers made a big to-do over the fact that she was living with Hōmei and carried sensational articles about whether the "flesh would triumph or the spirit."[viii] I also knew that she was an advocate of women's rights and had participated in the movement to revise Article 5 in the Police Security Regulations. I did not ask her to join, however, because she belonged to an older generation and seemed to be a woman of incomparably greater experience. Then, prompted by Chōkō, I wrote a special invitation with a brush and enclosed a copy of the statement of purpose and statutes.

Kiyoko's answer was most heartening. She wrote in a firm, almost masculine hand to say that she was in complete agreement with our goals and objectives and happy to join the society. She was delighted to learn that young women had banded together to raise the consciousness of women and was pleased to give us her full cooperation. She would be submitting a short story in the near future. Her message was refreshingly terse, with nothing suggesting an older woman. I was cheered, and felt that for the first time in my life, I had found a friend in an older, more experienced woman.

The daybook is virtually blank for several weeks, with only a fragmentary line or two entered almost as an afterthought. In August, the entries suddenly pick up:

August 4
    Communication from *Fujo tsūshin* regarding an article about Seitō.

[viii] Kiyoko (1882–1920) publicly announced that she would not yield physically to Hōmei until she loved him in mind and spirit. Homei was then separated from his wife.

August 5

Went to Seibidō to discuss printing. Rough estimates are as follows:

Incoming	Outgoing
Sales (1 copy 17 sen) 153 yen	Miscellaneous 5 yen
Advertisements 68	Bank Deposit 20
Total: 221 yen	Printing 110
	Advertising 50
	Fee for classification as third-class mail 10
	Postage 1 yen 40 sen
	Total: 196 yen 40 sen

Net profit: 24 yen 60 sen

August 6

Nagumo Noboru of Hakuhōdō came to discuss advertising. Gave estimate for printing 100 circulars announcing contents of first issue. Employee of Seibidō came with estimate. Yoshiko is back in Tokyo. Kunikida Haruko came with suggestions for advertising and printing.

Manuscript (of poems) arrived from Yosano Akiko.

Article in *Yomiuri* about *Seitō*. Hiratsuka and Yasumochi calculate we will break even.

Illustration from Naganuma Chieko for cover. Hiratsuka went to talk to her about cover.

August 8

Manuscript of play from Araki Ikuko. Kiuchi obtains estimates from Seibidō and Sanshūsha for printing journal. Nakano has left for Chiba.

August 9

Asked printers for (…) for advertisements.

Manuscript arrived from Tamura Toshiko.

August 10

Went to Shinbashidō and asked for estimates for printing. Also discussed advertising. Phoned Tōkyōdō about handling sales but told no one was available. Head of Shinbashidō phoned again saying he would like to handle printing. Promised to phone Sanshūsha tomorrow and also ask Morita of Shūitsudō to come to the office. Decided on content of ads in newspapers and journals. Cover arrived from Naganuma.

August 15

Employee of Masamichi Company came in the afternoon and gave estimates for newspaper ads. Said 33 yen 28 sen for 26-line ads in *Asahi*, *Kokumin*, and *Yomiuri* newspapers.

As the entries indicate, activity reached a fever pitch as the September deadline drew near. We had originally hoped that Chōkō would take over the negotiations for printing and sales, but as it turned out, we did everything ourselves, with Yoshiko handling most of the work. Big and solid, she looked like the type of person who would stand her ground in an argument. She did everything in a businesslike way, responding to every remark and query with an emphatic grunt in a manner that lacked even the slightest hint of feminine charm. But everyone was helpful, knowing that we were inexperienced young women eager to put out a magazine.

The estimates for printing were approximately the same, so we settled on Sanshūsha, the Kanda firm that was slightly more expensive but handled journals like *Shirakaba* and *Subaru* and was known for its high standards.

August 23

Uncertain about finances, Hiratsuka and Yasumochi visited Nunami Keion, editor of the haiku journal *Haimi*, to ask for advice. He suggested that we send out 1,000 postcards to potential subscribers. Asked Bunseisha if they are willing to put in an ad. Yasumochi visited Azuma of *Jitsugyō no Nippon* to see if he will put in an ad. Stopped by Maruzen and succeeded in getting ads. Hiratsuka went to Sanshūsha on business. Did some proofreading at night. (signed Hiratsuka)

Following Keion's suggestion, we sent postcards to well-known women, and to save on postage, arranged to have circulars inserted into newspapers. We also put announcements about the journal in the *Asahi, Yomiuri*, and *Kokumin shinbun* newspapers and exchanged advertisements with *Joshi bundan, Subaru, Kokoro no hana, Hototogisu*, and other periodicals.

Yoshiko and I did most of the proofreading, with Hatsuko initially helping out. As I said, we were beginners, but thanks to Hatsuko and the staff at Sanshūsha, we soon became familiar with technical details such as fonts and proofreader's marks. As work progressed, I found myself increasingly caught up in our new venture.

We were now ready to launch *Seitō*. But we needed an opening statement. Yoshiko was the logical choice to write it since she had worked tirelessly, putting her heart and soul into the journal. But she was busy attending to last-minute business, and the copyediting was all but finished. We could not wait a day longer. "You do it," she said to me. Pressed for time, I said yes.

The late August night was hot and sultry. I opened the shutters in my study and meditated. I then sat at my desk, resolving to finish by morning. I had not consulted the other founding members, nor had I talked to Chōkō. With no reference materials at hand, I had to rely on myself. My mind was as blank as the paper before me. I wrote straight through without a break until the first hours of dawn. "In the Beginning, Woman Was the Sun" suffers from an awkward and immature style, but I wrote those words with every fiber of my being, my pent-up thoughts flowing out unchecked. In my wildest dreams I did not imagine how much my opening statement would stir the young women of my generation.

The next day I showed Yoshiko my essay. I could not tell whether she agreed with the contents, but since she raised no objections, I took it to the printers, proofread it, and added the finishing touches. In a room on the second floor of the printers, we perspired in the midsummer heat as we checked the proofs for the last time. The first issue of *Seitō* was ready at last with 134 pages, not counting the advertisements. We were going to print 1,000 copies and charge 25 sen.

Chieko's cover was a stylized, full-length figure of a woman outlined in dark brown against a cream background. The characters "Seitō" were also in dark brown. For its time, the picture was daring and certain to awaken the aspirations of young women.

The contents were as follows: Yosano Akiko's poem sequence "Rambling Thoughts"; "The House of Death," a story by Mori Shige; "Crepe Myrtle" and "The Shore at Noon," poems by Hakuu (Yoshiko's pen name); "Life Blood," a story by Tamura Toshiko; my opening essay, "In the Beginning, Woman Was the Sun"; "The Cat's Fleas," a story by Kunikida Haruko; my translation of "The Shadow" by Poe; "The Frolics of the Sun God," a play by Araki Ikuko; "The Midsummer Festival," a story by Mozume Kazuko; [my] translation of an essay on *Hedda Gabler* by [the Russian poet and critic] Dmitri Merezh-kovski. They were all rather amateurish.[6]

Besides the five founding members, there were eighteen members in all: Iwano Kiyoko, Chino Masako, Ōmura Kayoko, Katō Midori, Tahara Yūko, Ueda Kimiko, Yamamoto Ryū, Araki Ikuko, Mizuno Senko, Tozawa Hatsuko, Ojima Kikuko, Ōtake Masako, Kanzaki Tsuneko, Tamura Toshiko, Nogami Yaeko, Akune Toshiko, Sakuma Tokiko, Sugimoto Masao. Nogami Yaeko is mentioned in the Editors' Notes of the October 1911 issue as having cancelled her membership, but as she recently told me, she had been interested in the journal because of her friendship with Kiuchi Teiko but never joined. She was nevertheless a steady contributor to the end.

The response to *Seitō* exceeded our fondest hopes, despite our having advertised in only three newspapers. There was no question that the journal, "created by women for women," galvanized young women who were disillusioned and dissatisfied with their lot but lacked the courage and strength to throw off the crushing burden of tradition. As enthusiastic letters requesting membership and copies of the journal poured in day after day, we could only look at one another in amazed delight. Akiko's poems and my opening essay, "In the Beginning, Woman Was the Sun," received the strongest responses.

Until then, I had been less than serious about the journal, but once I realized the gravity of my responsibility, I steeled myself to meet it accordingly.

In contrast to the overwhelming outside response to my essay, the founding members and other members remained curiously silent and offered no opinion, positive or negative. I felt let down and wondered whether they thought I had been unduly boastful, only seeking to express my own views. As aspiring writers, Hatsuko and Teiko surely had their opinions, but neither said a word. The essay is quite long, so I shall only set down some of the passages:

In the beginning, woman was truly the sun. An authentic person.

Now she is the moon, a wan and sickly moon, dependent on another, reflecting another's brilliance.

Seitō herewith announces its birth.

Created by the brains and hands of Japanese women today, it raises its cry like a newborn child.

Today, whatever a woman does invites scornful laughter.

I know full well what lurks behind this scornful laughter.

Yet I do not fear in the least.

But then, I ask, what are we to do about the pitiful lot of women who persist in heaping shame and disgrace on themselves?

Is woman so worthless that she brings on only nausea?

No! An authentic person is not.

We have accomplished all that is possible for women today. We have exerted our hearts and minds to the limit and brought forth a child—*Seitō*. The child may be retarded, deformed, or premature, but there is no way to avoid this. For now, we must be satisfied.

Then again, have we really exhausted all our efforts? Who, I ask, who will ever be satisfied?

But I have added yet another grievance against women.

Are women so spineless?

No! An authentic person is not.

Nor shall I ignore the fact that *Seitō*, born amid the scorching summer heat, possesses a passion so intense that it destroys the most extreme heat.

Passion! Passion! We live by this and nothing else.

Passion is the power of prayer. The power of will. The power of Zen meditation. The power of the way of the gods. Passion, in other words, is the power of spiritual concentration.

And spiritual concentration is the one and only gateway to the realm of mystery and wonder....

I shall search for the genius to be found in the very center of this spiritual concentration.

Genius itself is mystical. An authentic person....

...In the beginning, woman was truly the sun. An authentic person.

Now, she is the moon, a wan and sickly moon, dependent on another, reflecting another's brilliance.

The time has come for us to recapture the sun hidden within us.

"Reveal the sun hidden within us, reveal the genius dormant within us!" This is the cry we unceasingly call out to ourselves, the thirst that refuses to be suppressed or quenched, the one instinct that unifies all and sundry instincts and ultimately makes us a complete person.

It is this cry, this thirst, this ultimate instinct that leads us to intense spiritual concentration.

And there, at the zenith of spiritual concentration, genius reigns on high.

Statute 1 in the regulations states that Seitō aims to bring forth women of genius one day.

Each and every woman possesses hidden genius, the potential for genius. And I have no doubt that this potential will soon become a reality. It would be deplorable, indeed, if this tremendous potential were to remain untapped and unfulfilled for lack of spiritual concentration....

...Freedom, liberation! The pleas for women's freedom and liberation have been murmured for years. But what do they mean? Haven't both freedom and liberation been terribly misunderstood? The term "women's liberation" alone covers a multitude of issues. And even supposing that women are liberated from external pressures and constraints, given access to so-called higher education, allowed to work in a wide range of occupations, given the vote, released from the confines of home, the custody of parents and husband, and allowed to lead a so-called independent life, will they achieve freedom and liberation? To be sure, these conditions and opportunities will enable them to achieve true freedom and liberation, but they are no more than expedients, the means, and not the goal. Nor do they constitute the ideal....

...That said, what is this true liberation that I most earnestly desire for women? Needless to say, it is nothing less than the fullest expression of the genius and enormous talents that are hidden within us. And in order to realize this, we must cast aside every obstacle that stands in our way. But when I say obstacle, do I mean external pressures or the lack of knowledge? No, this is not what I mean, though these certainly should not be discounted. What I am saying is that the main obstacle is ourselves—we, the possessors of genius, we, who are each one of us a sacred place in which genius resides.

Only when we cut ourselves loose from the self, will we reveal our genius. For the sake of our hidden genius, we must sacrifice this self....

...Together with all women, I want to believe in women's hidden genius. I want to place my trust in this unique potential of ours and rejoice in our good fortune to be born as women.

Our savior is the genius within us. We no longer seek our savior in temples or churches, in the Buddha or God.

We no longer wait for divine revelation. By our own efforts, we shall lay bare the secrets of nature within us. We shall be our own divine revelation.

We do not seek miracles or yearn for the realm of mystery and wonder in some far-off place. By our own efforts, we shall lay bare the secrets of nature within us. We shall be our own miracles, our own mysteries.

Let us devote ourselves unceasingly to fervent prayer, to spiritual concentration. Let us continue our efforts to the very end, until that day our hidden genius is born, until that day the hidden sun shines forth.

For on that day, the whole world and everything in it will be ours....

...Woman will no longer be the moon. On that day, she will be the sun as she was in the beginning. An authentic person.

Together, we shall build a domed palace of dazzling gold atop the crystal mountain in the east of that land where the sun rises.

Women! When you draw your likeness, do not forget to choose [draw] this golden dome....[7]

Such then was my opening essay. Little did I dream that, in its modest way, those words would influence the women's liberation movement in Japan. First of all, we did not launch the journal to awaken the social consciousness of women or to contribute to the feminist movement. Our only special achievement was creating a literary journal that was solely for women. Also, unlike young women today, we had no theoretical understanding of social issues or of the Woman Question. We were extremely unhappy with women's condition and outmoded moral conventions, but this was no more than an instinctive reaction; we had no idea how to escape our predicament.

In my own case, I began reading Japanese and Western books on women's issues only later, when I awakened to Seitō's new mission. I was dimly aware that such issues had been debated abroad since the nineteenth century, but I never related them to my personal life. This does not mean that I placidly accepted the forces of oppression around me. My resentment against the irrationality and injustice of women's oppression had long rankled in me and had become more intense when I came under public ridicule [at the time of the Morita incident]. So when Chōkō remarked, "Women like Ophelia have their merits, too," I wondered how a man could be attracted to someone like her. In writing my essay, I was not consciously thinking that Seitō would open the way to women's emancipation or that I was making a declaration of women's rights. At the same time, I admit that I was not unprepared to fight, if the need arose.

To reiterate, the basic theme of my essay was that before anything else, women must achieve an understanding of themselves as human beings and as individuals. They also must experience a sweeping, self-liberating spiritual revolution. And in order to do this, they have to cast aside all external and internal pressures, reclaim their true selves, and assert their autonomy as fully developed human beings. This belief and nothing else engendered the idea that came to me without any intellectualizing: my rejection of the present situation and my embrace of the notion that "In the beginning, woman was truly the sun. An authentic person. Now she is the moon, a wan and sickly moon, dependent on another, reflecting another's brilliance."

People doing research on *Seitō* have often asked me how I happened upon the image of woman as originally the sun and now the moon. This certainly was not a result of any historical research on the position of women or of logical reasoning. Rather, the images came in a rush of clarity the moment I fixed my eyes on the blank sheet of paper. Once I knew that I had to write an opening statement for the first issue of a women's journal, everything I had read, heard, thought about, experienced, and stored in my subconscious had emerged and taken shape in those words (and ideas). To be sure, the sun and the moon symbolized the objective realities of women's history—the breakdown of a matrilineal society and the rise of a patriarchal system; the tyranny of men and subjugation of women; the gradual decline of a woman's status as a human being—but I had not consciously planned to use those images beforehand.

Others have pointed out a close resemblance between my metaphorical use of sun and moon and the rhetoric in Nietzsche's *Thus Spake Zarathustra*. In writing the essay, I do not recall consciously thinking of Nietzsche, but if a resemblance exists, this, too, was not thought out beforehand.[ix]

Speaking of Nietzsche, I have already mentioned that I first read about *Zarathustra* in articles by Tobari Chikufū in *Teikoku bungaku* and Takayama

---

[ix] Raichō doubtless refers to the chapter "Of Immaculate Perception" in part 2 of *Zarathustra*, which begins with the line "When the moon rose yesternight, I fancied she would give birth unto a sun, so broad and big she lay on the horizon." Nietzsche expanded the imagery in such phrases as "Look there! Detached and pale she [the moon] stands there before the dawn of the day! There it cometh already, the glowing one,—its love unto earth cometh. All sun-love is innocence and creative desire.... Verily like the sun I love life and all deep seas." Raichō no doubt read the English translation by Alexander Tille, which was published in 1898–1899 (*Thus Spake Zarathustra: A Book for All and None*, 171–175). Though it is widely assumed that in comparing woman to the sun, Raichō was thinking of the Sun Goddess Amaterasu, the mythic progenitor of the Japanese imperial line, she herself never mentions the goddess by name until the late 1930s, and then in connection with the emperor.

Chogyū in *Taiyō* during my third year of college. These were cursory intro-
ductions at best—a complete translation did not appear until several years
later. After college, I struggled through an English translation, and to this day
I remember my excitement and fascination. This was soon after I achieved
kenshō, and Nietzsche's thoughts about life and creativity seemed to have
much in common with the insights gained from zazen. I was particularly fascinated by his negation of all values and by his attack on established religion
and ethics, especially on Christianity and its slave mentality. He advocated the
creation of new values and saw the superficiality of present-day humans not as
their true state but as something to be overcome in order for them to become
"overmen," and in asserting that they were in the process of attaining that
state of being, he recognized the unlimited possibilities of the human future.
What would Nietzsche have written, I often wondered, if he had known about
East Asian thought, that is to say, Zen?

An advertisement for Chōkō's translation of *Zarathustra* (published by
Shinchōsha) appears in the inaugural issue of *Seitō*. I do not remember reading it, yet since the date of publication is August 1911, I may well have owned
a copy. For some reason, I only remember the English translation, a large,
thick book bound in dark blue cloth that sat on a shelf near my desk. Yet if
the phrase I quote from Nietzsche is the same as in Chōkō's translation, I
may possibly have referred to his book.[x] At the risk of being tedious, I will not
categorically deny the allegation that I was influenced by Nietzsche in writing
the essay, but immeasurably more important were the truths I gained from
zazen. Had I not followed the path of Zen, the essay would certainly have
been far different.

The sun, that enormous body of light, has ever been the symbol of the
source of life. Thus, when I said we had to "reveal the hidden sun, the hidden
genius within us," I was calling out to women to reach into their innermost
selves and recover their lives and their creativity. I personally had been drawn
by a chain of circumstances to practice zazen and to arrive at the state of
heightened spiritual awareness called kenshō. But I also believed that one
could reach the Ultimate by other paths, and I had tried not to use the word
Zen so that my essay would not be subjected to narrow interpretations.[8] (This
would not be the only time.)

The greatness of human beings, the greatness that distinguishes them
from animals, lies in their powers of concentration. This tremendous power

---

[x] The phrase is "Surface is woman's mood, a foam driven to and fro on shallow water. But a man's mood
is deep, his stream roareth in underground caves: a man divineth his power, but understandeth it not"
(Ibid., part 2, "Of Little Women and Young," 89). Ikuta Chōkō (1882–1936) translated other works by
Nietzsche, *Triumph of Death*, *Das Kapital*, *Divine Comedy*, and other classics.

of spiritual concentration enables human beings to plumb the source of life, become one with the universe, and draw limitless strength from an immense sense of fulfillment. Yet throughout history, women's power of spiritual concentration had been diminished, if not lost entirely; women had become powerless creatures, without any sense of autonomy. Thus, instead of resigning themselves to their low estate, women had to recover this power by their own efforts and boldly manifest their tremendous hidden potential. In other words, filled with great hopes for the future of women, I was urging them to undergo an inner revolution.

When people think of the movement begun by *Seitō*, they immediately associate it with so-called women's liberation. But I was not advocating women's political or social liberation. Rather, in my belief that women had to awaken to their true selves as human beings, I was calling for a spiritual revolution that aimed at total liberation and was not thinking in terms of women's rights as espoused in the West. Having said that, it would not be amiss to say that my vision for women contained the seeds of what would become a demand for women's political and economic freedom and independence.

In addition to my opening statement, I included my translation of Merezhkovski's essay on *Hedda Gabler*. I have forgotten how I came across the text, but Morita may have enclosed it with the English translation of the play that he sent to me in Nagano. Or I may have heard about it from Chōkō or Baba Kochō. In any case, I did not translate the essay specifically for the inaugural issue, but had been working on it sporadically. I later asked Takeichi Aya (a member), who specialized in English at my college, to check my manuscript for errors. Ibsen was popular among young people at the time, and I had probably decided to include Merezhkovski's essay because I thought *Hedda Gabler* was one of the more interesting of his plays. The October issue [vol. 1, no. 2] carries a joint discussion of the play [by Yasumochi Yoshiko and myself]. If I remember correctly, we read the Japanese translation of *Hedda Gabler* by Chiba Kikkō, a businessman who translated other works by Ibsen. I had the opportunity to meet him once when he had a meeting of the Teiyū Ethical Society at his home.

The Public Response

In putting out a journal that called for the restoration of woman's rights as a human being, a possible confrontation with advocates of "good wife and wise mother-ism" was not totally unexpected. What we did not anticipate was a fight against the forces of extreme conservatism. Before going into this, I shall briefly describe the state of the country at the time.

The year of *Seitō*'s publication, 1911, was exactly six years after Japan's victory over czarist Russia and one year after its annexation of Korea. Recognized as a world power, Japan was poised to enter a turbulent era as a capitalistic nation-state. On the one hand, the ultranational conservatism of the postwar years remained as strong as ever in intellectual and literary circles, while on the other hand, the influx of ideas from the West had led to a veritable flood of translations and adaptations. Broadly speaking, in philosophy, the new ideas were represented by two opposing schools: one that espoused a rigorous scientific positivism, the other a Nietzschean philosophy that stressed the primacy of the self and the idealistic philosophy of Rudolph Eucken. In literature, the Naturalist school vied with groups centered on *Shirakaba*, which stressed the importance of the individual and personal fulfillment. The younger generation avidly read translations: in Russian literature, Tolstoy, Gorky, Turgenev, and Chekhov; in Western European literature, Ibsen, Strindberg, Hauptmann, Zola, Flaubert, Maupassant. At the same time, in the wake of the Great Treason Incident, ominous signs of thought control pointed to a "season of winter" for intellectual freedom.

Against this background of conflicting developments, the most conservative voices were arguably in the field of education. Just this year, a Bill to Revive National Morality had been introduced in the Diet. The morality was based on the principle that loyalty to emperor and loyalty to parents were one and the same. Accordingly, the Ministry of Education summoned ethics teachers in normal schools throughout the country to Tokyo to attend Dr. Hozumi Yatsuka's seminar on the "Fundamental Principles of National Morality."

A Conference of Women Educators was also convened around this time. A set of guidelines were discussed and approved, but the resulting "Ten Precepts for Women" were so negative and reactionary that even the newspapers, normally conservative in matters concerning women, referred to them as the "Ten Thou Shalt Nots for Women."[9] Given the climate of opinion, it is not surprising that Kawata Shirō's *The Woman Question* (*Fujin mondai*), which contained an abridged translation of Mill's *The Subjugation of Women*, was banned on publication the previous year.

Formal education for women fared no better. In the name of higher education, several colleges, a vocational college for medical studies (Joshi Isen), and other professional schools had been established. They were somewhat progressive but inferior to those for men and basically committed to educating good wives and wise mothers. Their expectations for education betrayed, held down by the feudalistic family system, many women found that the only path left open to them was literature. And by expressing themselves through words, they had begun to awaken to their inner selves and to question their lack of self-awareness and individuality and their parasitic dependence on men. Young women today cannot imagine the degree to which young women at that time were drawn to literature. Seitō provided a new venue, and that, I believe, explains its great appeal.

If one were to characterize Seitō at the time of its birth, I would say that it was a rebellion conscious and unconscious, a challenge expressed through literature to feudalistic ideas about women. Indeed, the very fact that women, on their own, had created a journal for women writers was of tremendous significance. I was amazed by the magnitude of the response from young women and could not but feel a renewed sense of the gravity of the work I had begun.

I find it strange that my sister Taka did not become a member, especially since she was fond of literature and a classmate of Yoshiko's. Perhaps I had not invited her. She was living in Kobe with her husband, her tuberculosis had flared up, and much of her time seemed to be taken up with Tenrikyō, to which she had recently converted.[xi] I did not ask my good friend Kimura Masako and high school classmates Ichihara Tsugie and Kobayashi Iku because their interests were not literary. Nevertheless, as a token of their friendship and support, they thoughtfully contributed money.

My mother, the journal's biggest financial supporter, knew of its publication, of course, but she gave no indication of having read it, nor did she say anything critical. My father, I assume, was still unaware of its existence, since both my mother and I were careful not to mention it.

◎ ◎ ◎ ◎ ◎

As announced in the Editors' Notes of the first issue, a meeting for members was held on September 2 at the Seitō office. Besides [four of] the founding members, Ojima Kikuko, Tamura Toshiko, and Akune Toshiko attended. Tamura Toshiko was already famous. After withdrawing from Japan's Women's College [because of illness] — she was in the first graduating class — she had joined Kōda Rohan's circle, married a fellow writer, Tamura Shōgyo, and recently won first prize for her novel Resignation (Akirame) in the Osaka Asahi competition.

Toshiko and her friend Kikuko came to the meeting in separate rickshaws. In fact, it was rumored that Toshiko hired a rickshaw whenever she went out and that her bills exceeded the monthly rent of 7 yen 50 sen for her house in Yanaka. She started complaining the minute she heard that Hatsuko was not coming. "But isn't she a founding member? Really!" At that her friend Kikuko chimed in, "And to think I came here even though there's no one else home to keep watch on the house. Why, a thief's probably in there right now." Then,

---

[xi] An offshoot of Shinto founded by Nakayama Miki in 1838.

when Toshiko heard that the purpose of the meeting was to talk about the journal's future, she sniffed, "Oh, so it's another discussion, is it?" She picked up the September issue of *Chūō kōron* near her and started flipping through its pages. "Ah, here's something by Masamune Hakuchō—'A Glimmer of Light.' There's not much point in reading this kind of stuff, but why don't we discuss it today?" In any event, this is how Kazuko remembers the meeting.

I myself have no memory of her snide remarks, though it is true that Toshiko said whatever was on her mind, regardless of people's feelings. I distinctly remember one remark, and it was, to say the least, insulting. "What makes you think you can put out a magazine? And who, may I ask, is taking ultimate responsibility?" Then, instead of making suggestions, she ridiculed us mercilessly and walked out of the room with a look of scorn on her face.

I shrugged off her remarks, for from the very beginning I had suspected that we could not rely on the established writers we had invited. Kazuko, however, seemed to take the episode as a personal affront and sank into gloomy silence. We heard afterward that Toshiko claimed she had left the meeting because "it was a waste of time talking to a bunch of inexperienced young ladies."

Toshiko's behavior was less unpleasant than bewildering. To me, she seemed to belong to a world apart. Her big body, her heavy makeup, and the exaggerated expressions on her long, thin face reminded me of a Kabuki actor playing the role of a woman. I couldn't quite figure her out. But after seeing her several times, I came to appreciate her. Open and forthright, she was good company. Once, we went together to visit Yoshiko in Chigasaki and, despite the violent wind, took a walk on the beach. "I can't stand windy days," she said. "It messes up my hair. Just look at it!" I paid no attention and walked on. "You won't get me to come here again. How could you bring me to a place like this!" She was furious, but the next time I saw her, she had completely forgotten about it.

By comparison, her friend Ojima Kikuko did not stand out in any way. She took great care of her appearance, with not a wisp of hair out of place in her elaborate coiffure. She looked less like a writer than a person who stayed at home all the time, and not necessarily as the lady of the house. A native of Toyama, she spoke with a regional accent that was hard to understand at times. As yet unmarried, she supported her mother and younger sister by teaching at an elementary school and writing novels.

My Pen Name

I have mentioned that I was reluctant to have my name associated with the journal: other concerns took precedence, and I had yet to give myself wholeheartedly to the work. Also, having begun the journal without my father's permission, I wished to protect his good name and spare my mother further pain. A pen name seemed the wiser course, and so I decided to use "Raichō."

"Raichō", or thunderbird, is ordinarily written with the kanji for thunder and bird. But the image evoked by the kanji for thunder did not suit my character, nor for that matter, the bird, which is actually a snow grouse.[xii] Thus, instead of using kanji, I wrote "Raichō" in the syllabic hiragana, and [in accordance with the old orthography], wrote it *ra-i-te-u*. People often refer to me as Hiratsuka Raichō and write my name with four kanji, but in my writings, I have never used my family name, only my pen name. With the changes in orthography following World War II, my name should properly be written as *ra-i-chi-yo-u*, but for aesthetic reasons I have stuck to the old transcription.

My acquaintance with the thunderbird, or snow grouse, went back to the time I lived near the northern Alps in Nagano. I have described the bird in "Autumn in the High Plains," a longish essay about my stay in Nagano, which appeared in the November and December [vol. 1, no. 3 and no. 4, 1911] issues. Much of my description is imaginary—my only glimpse was of a fledging caught by an employee at the fish farm—and from what I read in Kojima Usui's book on mountains. I was charmed by the picture of the adult bird with its round and sturdy-looking silhouette, its air of calm repose. I was also intrigued by the fact that it lived at an altitude of 3,000 meters, subsisting on alpine vegetation, and turned pure white in the winter. I was further attracted by the fact that the bird had been indigenous to Japan since the Ice Age. So I did not choose the pen name entirely by chance.

I began the essay when I was still at the fish farm. I also began translating Poe at the time. As I remember, I was in the midst of translating "The Black Cat" when a huge black cat with a long tail stalked by my room. I shuddered—to this day I dislike cats—but it did not come in.[xiii]

A Doll's House

In September 1911, the same month we launched *Seitō*, *A Doll's House* was performed to great acclaim by the Literary Arts Association, a theater group founded by Tsubouchi Shōyō, a professor of literature at Waseda University. This was followed by a more lavish production in November at the Teikoku Gekijō, a new theater noted for its Western-style seats and troupe of female performers. Talk of the play was on everyone's lips and Matsui Sumako's por-

---

[xii] The kanji or ideogram for "thunder" is a composite of "rain" and "paddy."
[xiii] Volume I ends here.

trayal of Nora extravagantly praised. The New Theater movement[xiv] had just begun, and the themes posed by Ibsen were bound to generate discussion among the public and in literary circles.

We had published Merezhkovski's essay on *Hedda Gabler* in the inaugural issue and followed it with a joint review of the play in the October issue. For this reason, we next decided to ask members to write on *A Doll's House*. This was not because of its topicality, but because we felt the play called for serious discussion. With this in mind, we presented a reading list in the November issue: critiques by Georg Brandes, George Bernard Shaw, Merezhkovski, and other European writers, as well as works in Japanese, including Shimamura Hōgetsu's translation of the play (*Waseda bungaku*, January 1910) and Takayasu Gekkō's *Ibsen's Social Plays* (January 1901).[10]

Today, members would have undoubtedly attended the play as a group. In our case, we went separately. Unsociable by nature, I went alone and sat in the back row, hoping not to be recognized. The theater was full, the audience for the most part young men, with a scattering of young women here and there. This was not the first time that I attended a New Theater production—I had seen Ichikawa Sadanji at the Jiyū Gekijō—but I was excited nonetheless. In college I had read Kuwaki Gen'yoku's essay on Nora in the *Teikoku rinrikai* journal and been sufficiently intrigued to read the play in translation.

I had never seen Matsui Sumako on the stage, but contrary to what I heard, both her performance and the production proved disappointing. Sumako was said to bring passion and dramatic power to her role, but to the end she failed to engage my sympathy. As the young and innocent Nora, she was convincing enough, but her portrayal of the heroine's inner turmoil as she gradually gained self-awareness lacked emotional depth. She merely became more and more hysterical, leaving me with the impression that the play was about just one more marital squabble. Sumako came from Nagano, and like many born in the region, she no doubt threw herself single-mindedly into everything she did. Judging from her performance, however, I did not think she really understood the play. She was faithful to the script, but her interpretation remained superficial and unconvincing.

Several years later, I happened to become friends with Mrs. Umeda Kiyo, who had been a financial backer for the theater group begun by Shimamura Hōgetsu, Sumako's lover and mentor. She talked about Sumako from time to time, and seemed to think that Sumako did not have natural artistic tal-

---

[xiv] Movement begun by Osanai Kaoru, Shimamura Hōgetsu, and others to modernize drama; the repertoire consisted mainly of European plays.

ent, but had become what she was by sheer diligence, faithfully following everything that Hōgetsu taught her. To this day I regret that I have never met Sumako.

As planned, we published the members' essays on Nora in the supplement of the January 1912 issue [vol. 2, no. 1]. Besides those by Ueno Yōko, Katō Midori, Ueda Kimiko, Yasumochi Yoshiko, and myself, we included translations of criticisms by Shaw and Jeanette Lee, an anonymous article, and an interview with Sumako titled "Some Problems on the Stage." The anonymous author was either Sōma Gyofū or Kawatake Shigetoshi, both of whom had been helpful in putting the supplement together. We also included photographs of Sumako and scenes from the play that we borrowed from the Waseda theater group.

The Nora supplement has an unsigned note that expresses my deep disappointment in the Teigeki production. I may have been unduly influenced by my negative reaction to the production, but my assessment of Nora, written in the form of a letter, was also highly critical. I shall quote a portion:

> Dear Nora,
>
> It would be a different matter if you were a hopelessly impulsive and ignorant girl of fourteen or fifteen, but you are a mother of three children. What you did is beyond comprehension for Japanese women.... Still, you certainly slammed that door with a vengeance. But now that you're one step out the door, I worry about you. It's pitch dark, you can't tell east from west, and your steps are unsteady. I feel I should follow you and make sure you're all right.

In other words, I feared for Nora's future, since her action did not spring from a genuine discovery of the self and her self-awakening was too facile and shallow. I wanted her to look more deeply into herself, for only then would she arrive at true self-knowledge and be able to live freely and independently as a true human being. I was not alone in criticizing Nora. The other contributors, all young and unsympathetic, were equally unsparing in their comments.[11]

◉ ◉ ◉ ◉ ◉

We decided to hold a New Year's party for members in Tokyo, and on January 21 (1912), we gathered at Fujikawa, a restaurant in Ōmori Morigasaki popular with the literati and literature students at Waseda. Araki Ikuko, who was friendly with some of these people, had chosen the restaurant and made all the arrangements. Takeichi Aya, Matsumura Toshi, Koiso Toshi, Hayashi Chitose, Miyagi Fusako, [Naganuma Chieko,] Yasumochi Yoshiko, Ikuko, and I attended. The party was a great success—Ikuko made sure that there was plenty of food and beer—and since I do not remember collecting money, she must have paid all the expenses.

Araki Ikuko was a member from the beginning, but unlike most of the original members, she was not a graduate of Japan Women's College. In fact, she had joined by mere chance. Several years earlier, when Ikuko was managing a boarding house for Waseda students in Mejiro, Yasumochi Yoshiko's mother, who had come from Shikoku to attend her graduation ceremony, had taken a room there. Yoshiko was staying with her mother, and in the course of a conversation with Ikuko, discovered that they had a mutual interest in literature. Then, when Ikuko mentioned that she admired Tomoko in Morita's novel *Black Smoke*, Yoshiko exclaimed, "Why, the model for the heroine is my friend!" and brought her to the office to meet me.

Ikuko's father died, and by the time she joined *Seitō*, she had taken over the family business and was managing an inn in Kanda Misaki-chō called Gyokumeikan. She had beautiful skin and big, dark eyes that sparkled with coquettish charm. Like other people in the innkeeping business, she was affable and outgoing. She was also emotional, especially when she had too much to drink, and would weep copiously as she talked about her current boyfriend. She apparently had a patron, an older man who owned a rubber plantation in the South Pacific. He was rarely around, and in his absence, she had fallen in love with Masuda Atsuo, a Waseda graduate, who, together with fellow graduates Mitomi Kyūyō and Imai Hakuyō, ran a literary magazine. Her knowledge of literature no doubt came from him and other young men with similar interests who frequented the inn.

An eccentric named Miyazaki Tamizō was one of the regulars at the small and dilapidated inn. More like a member of the family than a paying guest, he trusted Ikuko completely and obeyed her like a child. Seedy and permanently disheveled, he looked like a widower who had no one to take care of him. He was also huge, which made him look odder still.

One day, he handed me a book and solemnly urged me to read it. The title was *Equal Distribution of Land: The Prerogative of Humankind* (*Tochi kinkyō: Jinrui no taiken*) and the author was none other than himself. He also gave me a brochure with the aims and regulations of the Society of Comrades to Regain Land, an organization he had founded. The society professed to restore to human beings their rightful claim to equal ownership of land, by which they would secure the means for an independent livelihood. Such rights, furthermore, were due every man and woman upon reaching adulthood. When I read the brochure, I could see why he was so strange.

Miyazaki was not the only social activist who stayed at the Gyokumeikan. Revolutionaries who had fled China also came at the recommendation of his younger brother Tōten.[xv] The inn, in fact, had a motley assortment of guests, and I had the feeling that they were seeking not merely a roof over their heads, but a haven where they would be protected.

Ikuko herself was not particularly progressive in her ideas or outlook. She tended to be guided by her instincts and emotions, so she rarely carried through what she had begun. But she lived boldly and freely, unconstrained by convention, even as she supported her mother and siblings, and in this sense, Ikuko represented a certain type of woman of the period. Among the carefully brought up young ladies who made up the majority of members at the time, she was clearly the exception. Her writings were uninhibited, too, and as I shall relate later, one of her stories caused trouble with the authorities.

Miyagi Fusako, a new member, was also unusual in her own way. She arrived with a dissolute-looking young man who was notorious in literary circles for stirring up controversy. He left right away, but not long after, he applied for membership and sent in a manuscript using the female name F[ujii Natsu]. We reported this disturbing incident in the Editors' Notes of the first anniversary issue [vol. 2, no. 9], and to prevent a repetition, we requested future applicants to enclose a photo with their manuscripts.

The moment Fusako entered the room, Yoshiko and I looked at each other in dismay. We could not imagine how this woman had slipped into our organization. Heavily made up, with her hair looped in momoware style like a young girl, she was draped in a kimono of rippling silk, the collar pulled all the way back to expose the nape of her neck. Yet for all her elegant pretensions, she looked just like a second-grade geisha who hadn't quite sloughed off her peasant origins.

"Oh, please call me Chā-chan," she said as she introduced herself, and then to everyone's further consternation, she proudly announced that Yoshida Goten was her ideal.[xvi] She was petite, with gently sloping shoulders, but there was no mistaking the aura of decadence about her. So when I heard less than a year later, in November, that she had married Mushakōji Saneatsu,[xvii] I was shocked, and wondered if the male of the species had any sense at all. I heard from Otake Kōkichi, who joined later, that she had introduced Fusako to Mushakōji. In any event, it was the first and last time she came to a meeting.

[xv] Miyazaki (Torazō) Tōten (1871–1922): Political activist who befriended the Chinese republican revolutionary Son Zhongshan (Sun Yat-sen) when he was in exile in Japan. Tōten raised funds for Son's cause and later joined him in China.

[xvi] Yoshida Goten, better known as Sen-hime, was the granddaughter of the shogun Tokugawa Ieyasu. Married off as a child and widowed early, she remarried and according to legend seduced many men. "Chā-chan" is probably what Fusako was called as a child.

[xvii] The scion of an aristocratic Kyoto family and a leading figure of the Shirakaba literary group.

On April 18, our special short story issue (vol. 2, no. 4) was placed under official ban.[xviii] "The Letter," Araki Ikuko's story about a married woman writing to her young lover in anticipation of another tryst, had been deemed unfit for public consumption.[12] All the copies had already been sold, so we suffered no financial loss. According to Mozume Kazuko, at about ten on the night of the 18th, she heard a dog's persistent bark at the back gate and went to check. Standing there were a policeman with a lantern and two men in plain clothes. "This is the Seitō office, right?" they said and ordered her to take them to the office, where they confiscated the one remaining copy lying on the chest of drawers. Kazuko said she looked on helplessly, and was informed about the ban only when the men were putting on their shoes to leave.

Her father, luckily, was unaware of what had happened, but since she had her own misgivings, she asked us to move the office elsewhere. So in mid-May, we rented a room at Mannenzan Shōrinji, a Rinzai temple in Hongō Komagome, where the resident abbot had let us hold meetings from time to time through Shūgaku's good offices.

In April, the same month that Seitō was censored, I finally met Iwano Kiyoko. She and her husband, Hōmei, had moved to Tokyo, and we decided to hold a welcome party for them at Tsukubaen, a restaurant in Tabata with a distant view of the cherry blossoms on the banks of the Arakawa. She'd responded promptly to my request in July, and since her letter was succinct and her handwriting firm and bold, I pictured a woman of sturdy build, healthy and full of life. But more recently, I had read "Withered Grass," [her story in the February 1912 issue] describing the desolation of a woman trapped in a loveless marriage. I wondered if she had written about herself, and I pictured someone pale, emaciated, and worn down with misery.

The woman who appeared at the restaurant was not at all what I had imagined. Small and thin, with thick makeup and hair gathered up in a voluminous marumage, she looked like a housewife with a taste for flashy clothes. Even more surprising was her dark green mantle, which clashed with her Japanese-style hairdo. Perhaps I was struck by how exhausted she looked even with a layer of makeup because of the contrast with Hōmei, who exuded health and vigor. Kiyoko put on a brave front, however, making every effort to hide her fatigue and woes. As Chōkō said, she had a beautiful voice, her speech was crisp and clear, and she had a habit of breaking out in high-pitched laughter. And yet, seeing the cigarette tremble in her slender, veined fingers, I could not help thinking of the woman in "Withered Grass." Her relationship with

---

[xviii] Under the Press Law of May 1909, companies had to submit freshly printed copies to the local procurator, the local police, the Home Ministry's Police Bureau, and the district procurator. The home minister alone had the power to impose a ban.

Hōmei had already begun to deteriorate, but of course I had no way of knowing this.

In "The Conflict of Love," a story she published in the autumn of 1915, the narrator writes:

> I shall never complain of my anguish to anyone. I may cry in my heart, but I shall never show my tears. I have cried unceasingly in my heart ever since I started living with my husband, but not once have I complained to anyone, not even to a friend or the one parent I have left.

Again, in her diary (*Ikeda nikki*), which was discovered later, Kiyoko wrote:

> This is my first experience of married life, the first time I have given my body and soul to a man. But my fantasies about marriage have long since vanished. There is the old saying that marriage is the grave of romantic love. I had nonetheless believed in the possibility of a true marriage, the external and internal union of two people joined by mutual love and effort. I thought that a marriage failed because the parties had not worked hard enough. But all this is probably an illusion on my part.

Before living with Hōmei, Kiyoko had been involved in a long platonic relation with a man. (This was when she was a newspaper reporter.) But the man was unhappy with the arrangement, and when he married another woman, Kiyoko tried to drown herself off the coast of Odawara. She had been rescued by a fisherman, who saw her white socks bobbing in the waves. I became close to Kiyoko, but I will touch on our friendship later.

Otake Kōkichi

It was also in April, either before or after the party at Tsukubaen, that Otake Kōkichi came to the house with Kobayashi Katsu. Katsu, who was still a student at the upper division of Futsueiwa High School, joined in October at the suggestion of her friend Kiuchi Teiko. The daughter of the famous artist Kobayashi Kiyochika, she had grown up in Asakusa. With her darkish skin and the alert expression on her thin, sharp-featured face, she looked very much like a girl from the old part of Tokyo. Her stories, too, reflected the tastes and interests of the denizens of that area. The two had met when Kōkichi came from Osaka to Tokyo to stay with her uncle, the artist Otake Chikuha, and they had been corresponding ever since.

Although this was the first time I had met Kōkichi, I felt as if I already knew her. Among the letters we received, serious as well as frivolous, were many from young women with literary interests and some from men, but those from Kōkichi had stood out for their pure idiosyncrasy. I shall quote her first letter:

November 30, 1911 Evening

I've known about Seitō from the time I was in Tokyo. A postcard printed with my aunt's name and address in bold characters came in the morning mail, but when I handed it to her, she looked puzzled. (This was one of many postcards we sent to prospective subscribers.) She read the announcement on the back, and when she noticed that I was peeking over her shoulder, she said, "I'll take out a subscription if you're interested." Seitō seemed like a group of unusual women, so I told her, "Yes, why don't you subscribe? It sounds interesting, doesn't it—" I really appreciated my aunt's offer, and from that day on, I went around acting as if I'd become a member and was actually reading the journal. My aunt never brought up the subject again. I still wanted to read it, but I didn't receive a postcard, so I thought I couldn't subscribe. I didn't want to press my aunt, since she'd been kind enough to let me stay at her home.

I'm now back in Osaka. I live with my parents and two younger sisters. I graduated from a local high school last November and studied traditional art when I was living with my uncle in Tokyo. The day before I left Tokyo, two new friends came to see me. We were talking about this and that when someone mentioned Seitō. The name rang a bell in my dull brain. One of the friends is Kobayashi Katsu. She said she'd joined Seitō and urged me to join, too. I'd almost forgotten about Seitō, so I was delighted to hear about it again. But then, I returned to Osaka without joining, something I truly regretted. To make up for this, I combed the bookstores in Shinsaibashi looking for your journal. But it was already November 29 and all the copies had been sold. I felt like crying.

I made the proprietor of a bookstore promise to send me the next issue as soon as it came out. She was really annoyed because I acted so childishly. So from next month I'll be a part of the group of women who read Seitō. Does this mean I've become a member? Does buying the journal each month make me a member? I don't exactly know what to do because, unfortunately, I haven't read the journal from the first issue.

I can't seem to forget what my friend said about being a member. I want to be a member too. And that's why I've written this long, boring letter. I'm embarrassed that I've said so many foolish things, but that's the sort of person I am—I just can't be dishonest about myself. So I'll just go ahead and send this letter.

I was just about to finish this when guess what! I received a letter from the friend I mentioned. She says anyone who joins the society will be able to write truthfully about herself. I want to write truthfully about myself too, and the sooner the better. Please tell me how I can join.

I was thinking of including the return postage, but then changed my mind. I wouldn't want you to think I was overly eager. Please don't laugh at this self-centered, rude letter.

When I go to Tokyo the year after next, or if I go on the spur of the moment, I'll visit your office and apologize in person in my crude, childish way.

The letter was written with a pen, in neat, printlike script. The prose was peculiarly her own, clumsy and yet not clumsy, innocent and unself-conscious like a child's. I was curious to know what kind of person she was, but had not answered.

A stream of letters followed, and soon enough, "that strange person in Osaka" became a familiar presence in the office. I also learned more about her from Kobayashi Katsu at a December meeting. "From the way she writes, you'd think she was a little girl, but she's really as big as a man and talks without inhibition in a loud voice. She's nineteen and a fan of Kitahara Hakushū's poems. Oh, she's different, all right—I'd say almost frightening."

Kōkichi kept sending letters, heedlessly pouring all her youthful reveries and hopes, all the perturbations of her childish, prideful heart into her writing. She signed with a different name each time, but finally settled on Kōkichi.[xix]

I decided to send her a letter of acceptance and ended it saying, "I understand you are studying painting. Would you be interested in designing a cover for us? Something really stunning? We would be willing to use it instead of the present cover."

And then, the writer of all those letters came to my study. I shall quote from a piece Kōkichi wrote [much later for the February 1935 *Fujin kōron*].

> The moment I arrived at my Uncle Chikuha's house, I sent a special delivery letter to Katsu asking her to arrange a visit with Hiratsuka-san. I counted the minutes waiting for her answer. At long last, the day came for us to visit Hiratsuka-san at her home in Akebono-chō. As we were led to her study, I caught a glimpse of the garden dappled by the gentle April sun.
>
> The study had a big, round window. When I entered, I felt as if I were in a Zen temple deep in the mountains. The faint fragrance of incense hovered in the air. Katsu had told me that Hiratsuka-san practiced zazen early each morning. Doves cooed on the eaves. In a few minutes I heard footsteps approaching. The door slid open, and I quickly lowered my head. I had wanted to meet her

---

[xix] Her real name was Kazue. Kōkichi is a man's name, though the kanji for "kō" means crimson.

for so long that I dared not look at her face. She spoke in a hushed voice that seemed to enfold me. I summoned my courage and raised my head.

She was sitting upright, her shoulders drawn back, her small hands, so like ivory, folded on her lap. She was breathtakingly beautiful, her features even and refined. When my eyes met hers, she smiled, her eyes glowing with the good will she felt toward someone younger than she was. So this is the woman herself, so this is the woman herself. I tensed up, as though I were paying homage to a graven image.

The moment passed, and little by little I began to speak normally. "You must do your best," she said. I had heard my parents say the same thing over and over, but now, I listened in submissiveness and joy. Yes, I will do my best! And I will help Hiratsuka-san as much as possible. As we were about to leave, she gave us several old copies of Seitō. Katsu and I walked to the main street in silence, as if we'd suddenly become dumb. I was afraid that if I opened my mouth, priceless gemstones would come flying out. I trod the ground as gently as possible. No doubt about it—both Katsu and I had been in a daze throughout the meeting.

My first impression of Kōkichi was of a boyish young girl with a nicely rounded face. She wore a serge hakama, a matching kimono, and a haori of dark blue Kurume cotton, a man's outfit that became her tall but well-fleshed figure. She was the first daughter of Otake Etsudō, the eldest of three brothers who were established painters in the Japanese style. After graduating from Yūhigaoka Girls' High School in Osaka, she had come to Tokyo to study at the Women's Fine Arts School in Kikusaka, but had withdrawn and was staying at the home of her Uncle Chikuha when she saw the postcard from Seitō.

After her first visit, Kōkichi often came to see me in my study. She also came to the office to help with the editing and artwork. She looked dashing in her man's kimono and hakama, and sometimes she wore a man's kimono, with a narrow sash tied low on her waist, and a pair of leather-soled woven sandals. Striding into the office, her arms swinging, she would say whatever was on her mind, burst into song, and laugh out loud in her big voice. She was absolutely uninhibited. You would have thought she was born that way, and just watching her was a pleasure. The other members were equally entranced, for there was no hint of the offensive tone that sometimes crept into her letters. And like a guileless, spoiled child, Kōkichi exulted in all the attention. She breezed in and out looking as if she could hardly contain her happiness.

Kōkichi's family moved to Tokyo. She was gregarious by nature and since she, like so many people in the Kansai area, enjoyed showing off, she invited all the members to her home in Nakanegishi. She has described the May 13 meeting in the Editors' Notes for the June 1912 issue [vol. 2, no. 6].

Before writing this column, I should mention that on the night of the meeting, the members partook liberally of sake, beer, and wine. Sad to say, we're
much too honest, timid, and green behind the ears, and lack the courage to
conceal the names of what we drank. Well, I'll just go ahead and say we drank
yellow wine, pink wine, glittery blue wine. We've never been less than true to
ourselves. We're not the kind of women people label as the New Women....
We're quite happy to tell the public how we live and that we do our work with
the utmost seriousness and honesty.

   Thirteen members attended the meeting, and all the people there were the
type who'd get drunk on tap water, cider, lemonade, or tangerine juice. Anyway,
we raised a toast to Kōkichi for her painting *Ceramic* and a toast to Hayashi
Chitose for her debut as Marie. It goes without saying that we raised a toast to
ourselves in the hopes of future blessings and success in our endeavors.

Kōkichi dwells needlessly on the subject of drinking, but Ikuko and I were
the only ones who actually drank. She herself was quite content to gaze at the
bottles lined up in front of her. *Ceramic* was the two-paneled screen for which
she won third place in the Tatsumikai exhibit in April. "Marie" referred to
the role Hayashi Chitose played as Magda's younger sister in the Literary Arts
Association's production of Sudermann's *Homeland*.

   Chitose, whose maiden name was Kōno, was a graduate of the Japanese literature department of Japan Women's College and was married to the playwright
and actor Hayashi Yawara. She was small and beautiful. In fact, she was almost
too beautiful to be effective on the stage. Her portrayal of Marie won her acco-
lades as an actress "second only to Matsui Sumako," but unlike Sumako, she
was an intellectual, and paradoxically, this, too, seemed to work against her acting career. The stories and criticisms she wrote for *Seitō* were quite impressive.

   Kōkichi and I became much closer after the May 13 meeting. I knew she
was friendly with young poets and artists who belonged to the Pan-no-kai
Society and had a number of other male acquaintances, but she did not seem
to be attracted to them as men and instead directed all her feelings toward
me, charging full tilt, as it were. Though we saw each other every day, she
also sent a stream of letters, all written with a brush in her distinctive handwriting on rolls of stationery. I answered her once in a while—about one to
ten—but she kept on writing, so I did my best to discourage her from getting
any closer.[13]

   Still, there is no denying that Kōkichi's youthful presence lit up the office.
Her lively, if sometimes ill-considered comments in the Editors' Notes were
also popular with readers. She was proud of her notes, but before long, her
heedless disclosures led to negative articles about us in the newspapers—"New

Women Drink Five-Colored Liquor," "New Women Dally in Yoshiwara," and so forth. Her notes also brought criticism from other members.

"The New Woman"

The label "New Women" had been conferred on us by journalists from the time we began publishing articles on women in modern European drama: Nora, in the January 1912 supplement; [Mrs. Alving] in Ibsen's *Ghosts* [March issue]; and more recently, following the controversial banning of *Homeland*, Magda, in the June supplement.[xx]

Before *Homeland* opened, [the translator] Shimamura Hōgetsu was interviewed in the *Yomiuri*: "Many of Magda's lines speak directly to people today. Certain basic issues play a part in the script—the rights and wrongs of pursuing a path of one's choosing or of wandering as a way of life; the relationship of art to life; the Nietzschean overman." I was naturally opposed to the ban, but more critical of Magda:

> Magda does not in any way present us with a new problem or any means of solving that problem. When it comes to our homeland, family, and parents, we are all in the same situation as Magda, though we may differ in degree. We have progressed beyond thinking of the problem in intellectual terms. Indeed, I fear we have become inured to the problem and are no longer shocked. But even those who have found an intellectual solution to the conflict between the old and the new are still emotionally involved in the dilemma. These people may be modern in their minds, but they remain surprisingly old in their hearts. And that, precisely, is Magda's problem.

The series of discussions on women in European plays, along with the way we dressed and behaved—Kōkichi's unorthodox appearance in particular—had created a public image of Seitō as a group of New Women. Women who discussed Nora and Magda were ipso facto New Women who admired Nora and took Magda as their ideal. One journalist had even joked that Seitō was the "training school for made-in-Japan Noras." Indeed, since "New Woman"

[xx] The play, which was called *Magda* in its Japanese production, was banned after three performances. It tells the story of Magda, who leaves home to escape a forced marriage to a clergyman. She bears an illegitimate child and supports herself and the child as a singer. She eventually returns home, and in the course of an argument, her father dies of apoplexy. The play was allowed to reopen after Hōgetsu rewrote the ending with Magda saying a few words of contrition.

had become the catchphrase of the day, the *Yomiuri* was eager to exploit this by publishing a series of articles on the New Woman that started on May 5. The series featured Tamura Toshiko, Hayashi Chitose, Naganuma Chieko, Nakano Hatsuko, Senuma Kayō, and others.

As to the phrase "New Woman," I note that Tsubouchi Shōyō used it as the title of a lecture he gave on heroines in modern European drama at the Osaka Education Hall in July 1910. He subsequently wrote a series of articles on the same topic in *Waseda Lectures* (*Waseda kōen*) from September to November. His discussions of Ibsen's plays, Sudermann's *Homeland*, Shaw's *Mrs. Warren's Profession*, and other plays were then published in book form as *The So-Called New Women* (*Iwayuru atarashii onna*) in 1912.

⊚ ⊚ ⊚ ⊚ ⊚

In any event, it was not surprising that the press would seize on what Kōkichi had proudly written in all innocence and blow it up all out of proportion. A case in point is "The So-Called New Woman," a series of articles that ran for four days in the *Kokumin shinbun*, starting on July 11. I shall quote some of the more flagrant examples of the journalistic imagination gone wild.

> The July issue of *Seitō* reports the curious doings of Raichō and the good-looking young boy she has been "wooing" with her left hand.[xxi] In the evening, said young boy, a fresh-faced student of twelve or so, may be seen in the neighborhood of Hakusan, walking hand in hand with Raichō. But there's something else. The other night, Raichō, Otake Kōkichi, and Nakano Hatsuko gathered at Otake Chikuha's house in Nakanegishi and decided to go off to Yoshiwara, of all places. The women were conveyed on three rickshaws to the lusty shouts of the runners and arrived at a teahouse called Matsumoto in Nakano-chō. They asked one of the attendants to conduct them to the geisha house Daimonjirō, and there they tasted the offerings of the pleasure quarters to the full. The next morning, they dashed back to the Matsumoto since they were eager to see the customers taking leave of the geisha. But then, inexplicably, Kōkichi fell to the ground, senseless. She soon recovered, and the women made their way safely home, swaggering along the banks of the Sumida River.
>
> When *Ceramic*, Kōkichi's entry in the Tatsumikai exhibit, sold for 100 yen, she was eager to share her good fortune, so she decided to throw a party and sent invitations to Seitō members. She served her guests a concoction of red, blue—

---

xxi In the Editors' Notes for the June issue, Kōkichi had written: "Raichō is busy doing work with her right hand and making love with her left hand."

in all, liquors of five different colors, pouring the heaviest one into a wineglass first. Brandy and whiskey were included, of course. After admiring the many-hued drink, the guests took turns sipping the fiery liquid, spouting modish non-sense and smacking their lips in a state of blissful intoxication.... Raichō offered the five-colored drink to the aforementioned young boy and gazed transfixed as he sipped noisily through a straw. At this, the mannish Kōkichi made such a commotion that the maid could only look on in astonishment.

The reference to the "good-looking young boy" was based on Kōkichi's comments in the Editors' Notes of the July issue [vol. 2, no. 7]:

All sorts of amusing speculations have been made about the object of Raichō's "left-handed love." According to a private detective, he is a stunningly handsome young boy. Rumors are that the youth downed a drink of five colors at the Bar Kōnosu and has gone again to visit Raichō in her study tonight.

Kōkichi had been writing about herself, but the newspaper had not understood this and made up a story to amuse its readers.

In the same Editors' Notes, Kōkichi writes about an exhibit of paper dolls [made by Tamura Toshiko] and fans [painted by Naganuma Chieko] and again refers to the five-colored cocktail:

[After seeing the exhibit,] I went to the Kōnosu and thought that [Toshiko] could have made at least one paper doll of a man. I then saw the bright red cherry in the cocktail and thought of the fans Chieko painted. Sipping the five-colored cocktail with a blue straw, "I" talked to "I" of such things.

In future issues, Kōnosu and the infamous "five-colored cocktail" appeared frequently in the Editors' Notes. Kōnosu was a restaurant-bar in Nihonbashi Koami-chō which, along with the Cafe Plantain, was patronized by young writers and artists. Knowing that the bar advertised in literary magazines, Kōkichi had gone with an artist friend to solicit an advertisement for Seitō; in fact, an advertisement appears in the July issue. She happened to see the manager making the cocktail—he told her it was the rage in France—and she wrote about it as if she had actually drunk it: "Oh, the indescribable pleasure of drinking the cocktail from a stylish wineglass!" But rather than the drink itself, it was the novelty and exoticism that captured her silly, childish heart.

The story about our "Dalliance in Yoshiwara" was also a pure fabrication. It was true that we had gone, but this was at the invitation of Kōkichi's uncle, Chikuha, who was reputed to be the most talented of the three brothers. He was also a man of the world and a habitué of the pleasure quarters. I once mentioned to him that when I wrote I did not think of myself as a woman but rather set down whatever I wanted and what I felt was true; it did not matter whether the reader was a man or a woman. He nodded vigorously in approval. "Ah, just as I thought. That's how it should be." Because of his niece, he had always been sympathetic to Seitō and had probably extended the invitation in this same spirit.

The invitation had come through Kōkichi [in early July] and at the last minute. Chikuha had already made all the arrangements, though he himself did not plan on coming. We managed to contact Nakano Hatsuko but were unable to get in touch with other members, and so the three of us decided to go.

As instructed, we first went to a teahouse that welcomed and guided the patrons, and then to the Daimonjirō, the geisha house with a fine reputation that was patronized by Chikuha. We were conducted to a room reserved for a geisha named Eizan. A paper doll was displayed in one corner. When we were told that Tamura Toshiko had made the doll, Kōkichi became quite excited and said that it was a pity she hadn't come with us.

In a few minutes, a rather unpleasant middle-aged woman came in. A fixture at geisha houses, she was supposed to make sure that everything was proceeding properly, and in fulfilling her responsibilities, she prattled on and tried to make us feel at home. Eizan eventually appeared, and as we dined on sushi and sake, we talked of various matters. She said she was a graduate of Ochanomizu, but seemed reluctant to tell us anything that might be considered confidential. Her feeling was understandable. She had never entertained women customers and had no way of knowing what kind of women we were, though we were about the same age.

We spent the night in another room and left in the morning. I was kept awake all night by the sound of slippers shuffling up and down the long hall, a sound that remains with me to this day. Chikuha may have been one of the patrons, but he was nowhere to be seen. He had extended the invitation because he thought that women with an interest in the Woman Question ought to look into the condition of their less fortunate sisters who worked in such establishments. We were aware of the evils of prostitution, of course, and the efforts made by the Salvation Army and the Women's Christian Temperance Union to abolish it, but this was not foremost in our minds. We had really gone to satisfy our curiosity and see whatever we could see.

Eizan, incidentally, was rather plain, but she had improved upon her looks with a skillful use of cosmetics, a becoming hairstyle, and elegant kimono. Kōkichi started corresponding with her, but then, in her usual impulsive and trusting way, she talked about the visit to Ono Ken'ichirō, an acquaintance of her father's who worked for the *Tokyo nichi nichi*. "Women Who Clamor to Be New," a series of six articles, appeared in late October. The newspaper, which claimed to have heard about the visit from Kōkichi herself, reported that we had stayed in Yoshiwara for three nights. A man might have stayed this long, but for three women to spend three nights was utterly ridiculous. The articles, together with those in the *Kokumin shinbun*, created a furor—the much-discussed New Women had dared to venture into a man's preserve. But I will touch on these articles later.

I bore the brunt of the public criticism against the "dissolute and profligate" Seitō women. Stones were thrown at the house day and night, and since my study was close to the front gate, I could hear them hitting the wall and shingled roof. A suspicious-looking character turned up and demanded to see me. I also received a written threat: "Come meet us at such and such a place. The Black Shirt Gang." I am sure my parents knew about the newspaper articles, but they never said a word, nor did they complain about the stones thrown against the house. While the public raged with indignation, all was calm at home.

An angry letter came from Yasumochi Yoshiko, who was working temporarily at the sanatorium in Chigasaki:

So, I hear the three of you went off to Yoshiwara. How could you have done something so stupid and thoughtless? I have no way of knowing why you did it, but I feel humiliated and sad. I'm also extremely annoyed.

She continued in the same vein.

I've noticed lately that *Seitō* has taken on a fatuous and pedantic tone. The initial seriousness has been lost, and there's no sign of earnestness or dignity. I can no longer respect it. The journal is like a tomboy who prides herself on defying convention and doing things women never dare to do. I am grieved to think that we've brought up a child who lacks both dignity and refinement.

As I mentioned earlier, during her illness, Yoshiko had been influenced by Dr. Takada, the head of the sanatorium, who was a Christian, so for her, our visit to Yoshiwara was inexcusable. Yet, despite her indignation, she loyally stood up for Seitō in the face of mounting criticism and was an unfailing source of strength. Other members also criticized Kōkichi for her indiscretions, and I knew their criticism was directed against me as well since I tended to defend her. News of the dissension must have leaked out, since the aforementioned article in the *Kokumin shinbun* refers to it in its leading paragraph:

Among the members of Seitō, the society of so-called New Women, there are five or six daughters from good families who write and act in a reckless manner that would make a man blush. Because of the public uproar, Dr. Mozume Takami, Mozume Kazuko's father, has ordered her to cancel her membership lest she ruin her prospects for marriage. Some of the members have called for the removal of the few who make a show of being New Women and engage in loose behavior. For the time being Seitō seems to be suffering from an internal discord that may lead to a breakup in the near future.

The newspaper was exaggerating, of course, but there is no denying that the reports stirred up unrest within the society. Women who had been proud to belong to Seitō shrank from being identified as a New Woman. A number of members living outside of Tokyo requested that their names not be mentioned or withdrew altogether. Fearing for their jobs, several teachers at elementary schools and girls' high schools cancelled their subscriptions. Kazuko did not withdraw, as was reported in the article, but started using the pen name Fujioka Kazue.

In view of the trouble she had caused, Kōkichi offered to resign, but I saw no need for such a step. It did not matter what the public or other members said; I knew her for what she was. For better or for worse, she was a free spirit, restless, irrepressible, and brimming with the vitality of youth. With her keen eyes, she gazed out upon the world around her, but despite this she was shy and innocent. How could I rebuke her for a minor indiscretion?

Driven by some strange compulsion that was either guilt or remorse, Kōkichi slashed her left arm with a knife. When I undid the bandages and saw the gaping wound, I felt as if I had been presented with living proof of the desperate love she bore for me. Since she was surrounded by disapproving colleagues and overly sensitive to begin with, Kōkichi's health visibly deteriorated. I urged her to see a doctor at the Takada Hospital. She was diagnosed with tuberculosis and sent to the sanatorium in Chigasaki.

I went to see her as soon as I finished editing the August issue. I knew the village well; my sister had stayed at the sanatorium and my mother and I had spent a summer at a rented house there. Also, for several years, I had been renting a couple of rooms at a fisherman's house to escape the city heat.

I found Kōkichi in good hands. Yoshiko, or "Auntie," as Kōkichi called her, was still at the sanatorium and making sure that she ate eggs and drank milk. Once Kōkichi was given permission to take walks on the beach, she often came to my lodgings unannounced and acted as if she'd forgotten all about the trouble she had caused. Kimura Masako came from Amagasaki. Then Araki Ikuko came to stay for a while, and since Chōkō and his wife were also spending the summer in the village, it was as if Seitō had temporarily set up office in Chigasaki. A group photograph taken after an outing on the Banyū River appears in the September 1912 anniversary issue.

Okumura Hiroshi

One afternoon in late August, I was told that I had visitors at the sanatorium. Two young men I had never met were waiting in the parlor. One was Nishimura Yōkichi, the owner of Tōundō, a publishing house that specialized in literature and the arts. An amateur poet, Nishimura belonged to a circle of poets and artists whose writings he planned to publish in a journal called *Kokuyō*. He had become friends with Kōkichi through one of her uncle's students and had asked earlier if we were interested in having his firm publish *Seitō* and handle its business. We had accepted the offer with the condition that we do the editing ourselves. He had come all the way from Tokyo to make the final arrangements. (Until now Yoshiko had handled most of the business for a small monthly compensation. We were now breaking even, though once in a while I still had to ask my mother for money to make up a deficit.)

Yoshiko, Kōkichi, and I went over the details and agreed to let his firm handle the printing and all financial matters beginning with the September anniversary issue. *Seitō* would continue to solicit manuscripts, edit, contact members, and hold study meetings. We were pleased with the arrangements: Tōundō was a highly respected firm whose publications included *Zamboa*, the poetry magazine edited by Kitahara Hakushū, and anthologies of well-known poets like Wakayama Bokusui (*Death or Art*), Ishikawa Takuboku (*A Handful of Sand*; *Sad Toys*), Miki Rofū (*The Hunter with White Hands*), and Maeda Yūgure (*Harvest*), as well as Ishikawa Sanshirō's *The Philosopher, Carpenter*. Under Tōundō's management, sales would rise and at one point reach a height of 3,000 copies.

The other young man introduced himself as Okumura Hiroshi. In contrast to Nishimura, a typical city dweller of delicate build, Okumura was big-boned, exceptionally tall, and quite striking with his pale, oval face and long black hair parted in the middle. He was also taciturn. While the rest of us talked, he seemed content to sit back and listen. There was a touch of childish innocence around his puckered upper lip, which looked as if it had been gently pinched. I liked him at once.

I guessed he was an artist. He carried himself with a natural grace, so when I looked at his hands resting on the table, I was surprised to see the thick black hair on his long, tapering fingers. I had no idea why he had come with Nishimura but assumed they were friends. He left before Nishimura, saying he was spending the summer at his family home in Fujisawa but would be back sometime with his paints and brushes. Both Kōkichi and Yoshiko shouted after him. "Be sure to come back. To paint pictures, all right?"

Okumura told me later how he happened to come with Nishimura that day. He was sitting in the waiting room of Fujisawa Station on some errand for his father when he noticed that the young man opposite him was reading the latest issue of *Zamboa*. He himself dabbled in poetry and contributed to *Shiika*, the magazine headed by Maeda Yūgure. Okumura was eager to read *Zamboa*, and so he asked the man if he could take a look. The two started talking, and on a whim, the man said, "I'm going to the sanatorium in Chiga-saki on business. Would you like to come along?" Okumura had fond memories of the pine grove on the shore, the windmill, and the white chalk walls of the sanatorium, so he had agreed at once, little suspecting that he would meet three young women.

Okumura has described our first meeting [in a novel he wrote later], saying he "shuddered the moment his eyes met mine, as if he'd been pierced through the heart, and for the first time in his life experienced an entirely new sensation when he looked at a woman." At the very same moment I also was attracted to this far from ordinary young man—who was innocent and like an overgrown baby—with an intensity I had never before felt for the opposite sex.[14]

That night, or perhaps the next morning, Kōkichi sent a letter to Okumura before we even had a chance to talk about the meeting:

> I have a premonition that something terrible is about to happen. I am in tur-moil, sad, frightened, anxious. Until that something is settled, I will spend my days in misery. And on the day it occurs, I will be reborn. In the meantime, I am lonely, I am in pain.
>
> Raichō wants you to come. And when you come, you must stay overnight. She'll be waiting for you. So do come.

Needless to say, neither Yoshiko nor I knew about the letter. (I did not know about it until I read Okumura's novel some thirty years later, but I was taken aback by the last lines, which were written as though Kōkichi were conveying a message from me. I was also surprised by the speed of her reaction and the acuity of her morbid sensitivity, especially in matters of rivalry in love.)

Several days later, Okumura unexpectedly came to my lodgings. He was on his way home from a sketching trip and stopped by to show me some pictures he had made of a pine grove near the mouth of the Banyū River. I looked at them and asked him to draw the cover for the September anniversary issue.

He returned in two or three days with a draft. It was drawing toward eve-ning, and we decided to ask Kōkichi and Yoshiko to join us for a stroll on the beach. We walked down to the row of sheds set up for patients to breathe in the sea air and talked as we gazed at the sea and the clouds, lit up by the declining sun.

Kōkichi had a suggestion. "Why don't we hire a boat and go out on the river? That way, we'll get a wonderful view of the moon." We hurried back to the sanatorium, quickly ate supper, and invited Ono [Higashi], a patient who was Yoshiko's friend, to join us. He offered to row, and though the boat threatened to be swept away once or twice, the view, as Kōkichi predicted, was indeed beautiful.

The hours passed. When Okumura missed the last train for Fujisawa, he said he would walk home, but Yoshiko insisted that he stay in her cottage, an old thatched hut in a pine grove near the sanatorium. She could always find a spare bed. We bid each other good night and went our separate ways.

I had no sooner settled down to sleep when I heard the roar of distant thunder. Within minutes, it rumbled over the house as bolts of lightning streaked across the night sky. I usually have no trouble sleeping, but sleep would not come. I was worried about Okumura. He was alone in a hut, within a stone's throw of the mortuary. Frightened by the thunder and lightning, he was probably cowering under his covers. I got up and asked the landlord's wife to go with me to check. She brought a lantern with her, and making our way through the pine grove, we headed for the hut. In hindsight, I realize that I should not have asked her, for I not only inconvenienced her but probably aroused her suspicions about my ulterior motives. But at the time I could only think of Okumura's safety. Had I known of Kōkichi's letter, I most certainly would have had second thoughts.

Okumura was safe and sound. Our behavior was irreproachable as we headed for the sanatorium under the guidance of the landlord's wife. But just as we neared the back gate, the thunder came crashing down over our heads. I cried out, and the next minute, I found myself in Okumura's arms. The landlord's wife shouted, "It just missed us!" and started running across the field toward her house. We followed in the pelting rain, stepping over the sweet potato plants.

That night, Okumura and I slept side by side under a big, green mosquito net. We had borrowed some sleepwear—a matching set of striped cotton kimono worn by fishermen to celebrate a good harvest—but with his arms and legs sticking out of the sleeves and hem, he looked just like a little boy. I am sure he was uncomfortable about sharing a room with a woman, but he showed no sign of embarrassment and acted like his usual natural self.

The thunder gradually receded. Lying there in the dark, I was unable to stop myself from reaching out and touching his warm, throbbing skin. The summer night was humid. I slept fitfully. By morning, I knew that my feelings for Okumura had changed from ordinary interest to something stronger.

We rose with the first rays of dawn and walked down to the sea with our fingers entwined. The beach was deserted, the sand swept clean by the thunderstorm. My heart, overflowing with the joy of being alive, seemed to expand beyond all bounds as far as the horizon.

We had no way of knowing it, but Kōkichi had apparently come to reconnoiter before daybreak. She saw our sandals side by side on the steps outside our room, and her worst fears were confirmed—Okumura and I had spent the night together. Determined to have me all to herself, she was deeply shocked. She jumped to conclusions and talked to Chōkō, as well as to Yoshiko, hinting that Okumura and I had had sexual relations. She even sent a letter to Okumura: "I promise you. I'll get my revenge." "I'm in love with Raichō." Okumura had no idea what she was talking about and was completely nonplussed.[15]

There is no denying that Kōkichi was infatuated with me at the time. A third party who called this homosexual love may well have been correct. On my part, it is true that I was very fond of Kōkichi—she had practically thrown herself at me—but my affection had no sexual dimension. I was attracted by her emotional openness, her freshness, and her finely honed sensibility. Something about her stirred my sense of play. Kōkichi meant a great deal to me, but my deepening feelings for Okumura surely prove that my feelings for her were not homosexual.

Knowing how she felt about me, I had tried to keep my distance, if only to save myself. Still, I had let her do as she pleased, even indulged her, as others no doubt thought. In an attempt to present Kōkichi as she really was and to dispel any misunderstanding about her, I wrote two essays. The first, "To Chigasaki, to Chigasaki," was published in the August issue [vol. 2, no. 8], and the second, "One Year," in the February and March 1913 issues [vol. 3, no. 2 and no. 3]. Reading them again, I see that I wrote to please myself, setting down my thoughts as they came to me, with no thought about the public's reaction. Seitō was meant to be a venue for unfettered self-expression, and as it was, no one at the office raised any objections. I hoped to continue "One Year," but for some reason abandoned it midway through.[16]

I returned to Tokyo in September. Soon after, I received a letter from Yoshiko saying that Kōkichi was "sharpening her knife, vowing to kill Okumura." Yoshiko sounded as if she was at her wits' end, but then Kōkichi was pronounced recovered and allowed to go home.

◎ ◎ ◎ ◎ ◎

In the meantime, Emperor Meiji passed away on July 30, and a state funeral was held on September 13. The same day, General Nogi Maresuke and his wife Shizuko committed suicide.[xxii] Their deaths were widely reported in newspapers and journals across the country, but with the exception of several poems by Harada Kotoko in the October issue, neither the September nor the October issue of *Seitō* makes any mention of this or the outpouring of public grief. We were as yet unconcerned about issues like the emperor system or social conditions. The September anniversary issue, with the cover by Okumura, is no different from the other issues, only more evocative of the sea air at Chigasaki.

I have mentioned the group photograph in the September issue, but looking at it now, I recall a remark that Yoshiko made after the outing. "I think Ikuta Sensei is seriously ill." We knew Chōkō went away once a month and came back with a small bandage on his face. We also noticed he moved his fingers stiffly, but he had dismissed this as a "slight case of rheumatism." We chided Yoshiko. "Really, you can't mean it." But she was convinced she was right. "Haven't you seen the way he lights his match? Take a good look next time."

Back in Tokyo, I hoped to see Okumura, but he had gone on a sketching trip to the island of Jōgashima. While there, he received an unexpected visit from Niizuma Kan, a fellow contributor to *Shiika* magazine who said he had come to seek poetic inspiration. After inviting himself to stay, he noticed the letters and packages from me, and this made him curious to know more about our relationship. He even showed some signs of jealousy when he tried to pry information from the closemouthed Okumura. The two had never been very friendly, but under Niizuma's persistent questioning, Okumura felt he had to say something. Next Niizuma started criticizing Seitō, made references to my past, and said, "You're still young. You'd be smart to break with a woman like that." Until then, Okumura had been alone amid the beauty of the island and thought of me with longing. But the warning from the seemingly experienced Niizuma, together with Kōkichi's jealous outbursts and threats, left him thoroughly confused. He thought things over and decided to end our relationship. He sent me a letter to that effect.

Of course, I knew nothing of what had happened and was puzzled by his letter, especially his elaborate conceit about birds: two water birds were enjoying each other's company in a pond until a young swallow came along and muddied the water. The swallow, alarmed about causing a disturbance, will

---

[xxii] Nogi's suicide was seen as an act of atonement for the mistakes of his military career, in particular, the enormous casualties of the Battle of Port Arthur during the Russo-Japanese War (more than 70,000 were killed or wounded; his two sons were killed). His death was also idealized by many as the highest expression of traditional morality.

fly away to restore peace. Mixed in were other conceits, equally mannered and pretentious, which were utterly at odds with the Okumura I knew.

I sent a reply by way of a note on the flyleaf of *Light and Shadow*, the latest book of poems by Maeda Yūgure: "With the coming of spring, the swallow will surely return." The "young swallow" disappeared, but as Okumura told me later, his letter had been drafted by Niizuma. Insisting that the letter was for Okumura's own good, Niizuma had made him copy it in his own hand. I will touch upon this incident again, but from that time on, the phrase "young swallow" became a popular word for a younger male lover.[xxiii]

The Seitō Study Group

With the business side entrusted to Tōundō, we could now focus exclusively on the journal. We also decided to revive the study group, which had been suspended. I have neglected to mention this, but the group had been formed in April [1912] and met regularly on Tuesdays and Fridays to listen to Chō-kō's lectures on Maupassant's short stories and Abe Jirō's lectures on Dante's *Divine Comedy*. Abe was already famous for his essays called *Santarō's Diary*; I myself would read them with great interest when they were published as a book by Tōundō in 1914. The epitome of the serious gentleman scholar, he was about twenty-six or -seven, good-looking, and with a small but perfectly proportioned body. It was his idea to lecture on the *Divine Comedy*.

When we originally formed the group, we had invited nonmembers as well, and to prevent curiosity seekers from wandering in, we had included a warning [in the May 1912 issue]: "Persons attending the lectures must be strongly motivated. The meetings are not for the entertainment and amuse-ment of young ladies. We ask you to bear this in mind." We scheduled the meeting [for the first Wednesday] in October and set up a blackboard in a ten-mat room behind the main hall of the Mannenzan temple. A sizeable num-ber expressed interest, but the actual turnout was disappointingly small, ten at the most. It was a pity, since Abe's talks, while as demanding as a classroom lecture, were rich in content and delivered with great enthusiasm.

Chōkō's talks were of a more practical nature. A longtime admirer of the short stories of Maupassant, especially the prose in "At the Water's Edge," he had urged us to read them at the Seibi English Academy. At these talks

---

[xxiii] According to Okumura's novel, Teruko (Raichō) showed the letter to Shigeri (Kōkichi), who then talked about it to her friends (*Chance Encounter*, 105). Kōkichi also referred to a "young swallow" (*wakai tsubame*) in the Editors' Notes of the October 1912 (vol. 2, no. 10) issue in such a way that the readers would have easily guessed who it was.

also, he analyzed each story, pointing out the passages that might help us in writing fiction. He told us that in writing a short story, what was left out of a potentially longer narrative often made all the difference. Chōkō had a habit of wandering off the subject, but we found his discussions useful. I attended regularly, as did Kōkichi, Kobayashi Katsu, Saiga Kotoko, Koiso Toshiko, Ishii Mitsuko, and later, Iwano Kiyoko.

Besides lecture meetings, we also held parties like the one for Ueno Yōko in September. A graduate of the Japanese literature division of the Tokyo Higher Normal School, she was my age and said that she had joined as soon as she read the first issue of *Seitō* when she was teaching at the Fukui Prefectural Girls' High School. According to Oku Mumeo and Ifukube Takako, who were her students at the time, she spoke enthusiastically about Seitō in her classes. She was married to a naval officer and was at that time teaching at a school in Sasebo.

Among Yōko's contributions were "Pain and Art" [vol. 1, no. 4], "A *Doll's House* and the Woman Question" [vol. 2, no. 1], and "Men and Women as Seen from the Theory of Evolution" [vol. 2, no. 10]. Her essays were of a high caliber, if somewhat ponderous, and I expected someone mature and terribly correct. Far from it: she was pretty, with well-defined features, and though she wore her kimono tucked short at the waist and had the prim air of the typical normal school graduate, she was cheerful, articulate, and obviously very bright. Certainly, her decision to join Seitō distinguished her from the common run of normal school graduates who thought alike and were unsympathetic to our cause. To give an idea of her unconventional thinking and her courage in speaking out as a working teacher, I shall quote the following passage from an article she wrote before joining Seitō:

> Does the policy of the Education Ministry meet the needs of the times? I must answer in the negative.... What does the ministry hope to accomplish by its recent decision to endorse a practical curriculum [in girls' high schools]? Instead of extending the years of study to raise intellectual standards, it proposes to allot precious hours to more classes in cooking, crafts, and sewing....
>
> ...Another problem is the ministry's passive, play-it-safe attitude. This is particularly pronounced in the classes on moral education. The level of teaching is also low, the teachers inert and apathetic. When a student shows any sign of independence in her opinions or resistance to authority, she is invariably given a D in deportment. The spirit of initiative is simply not tolerated. ("The Woman Question and the Ministry of Education," *Collected Works of Ueno Yōko*, vol. 1)[17]

Yōko also contributed fiction and an excerpt from her modern-day translation of the *Pillow Book*. She continued to teach and write even after she had a child, and in 1921, won honorable mention in a competition for novels sponsored by the *Osaka Asahi*. She had almost superhuman energy, but even with all her vigor, determination, and the support of an understanding husband, she found herself caught between work and family. She died early at age forty-two; I have no doubt that the cause was exhaustion. Her husband later published all her writings.

Another party was on October 17, a full year after the launching of *Seitō*. The experience had been daunting in many ways, but we had survived and felt like celebrating. On Otake Chikuha's recommendation, we gathered at Ikaho, a restaurant in Uguisudani that was popular with the literati. He must have put in a good word, since the proprietor refused to take any payment. Chikuha knew that we were under attack from all quarters, and this was probably his way of showing his continuing support.

I have only a dim memory of the members who came, but I do remember meeting Kamichika Ichiko, Senuma Kayō, and Nishizaki Hanayo for the first time. The party was very lively, and afterward, a smaller group sat down for a more intimate meal. We kept pouring sake for each other, I had too much to drink, and in a tipsy haze, I came back from the toilet still wearing the toilet slippers. This was the first and only time I was consciously drunk.

Kamichika Ichiko had requested membership and sent in a manuscript in July. "A Certain Letter," which was written in epistolary form, was a bold and forceful portrayal of a love affair. The story suggested a writer who was spirited and intelligent, so I was not only pleased that she applied but also looking forward to meeting her.

Ichiko arrived late but made up for this by talking nonstop. She was voluble, but not garrulous or gossipy as so many women are. Her conversation, like her writing, was informed with passion and intelligence. Her face, too, made a vivid impression, with its stern, almost mannish features and large eyes. Her eyes glistened as if they were filled with tears and emitted a strange, provocative light, at once disquieting and hinting at something dangerous. She had probably joined because she hoped to be a writer, but she may also have been attracted to our ideals in reaction to her school and church.[xxiv]

She looked extremely happy that day, as if she had finally found a place where she could be free. She drank cup after cup of sake, but then suddenly turned pale and fainted. When she came to, she apologized profusely. "Oh, how awful! What have I done? Please don't tell anyone." She kept repeating this, and I was somewhat disillusioned since her behavior seemed out of character.[18]

[xxiv] Kamichika Ichiko (1888–1981) was then a student at Tsuda Eigakujuku. She was baptized while she was attending a missionary school in Nagasaki.

After her first contribution, Ichiko wrote for us under the pen name Sakaki Ei, but then withdrew the following spring, less than a year after she joined. To skip ahead in my narrative, Tsuda Umeko, the principal of her school, had apparently been informed of the scuffle at our first public lecture [on February 15, 1913,] and called a meeting to issue a stern warning: Seitō was an organization that spread subversive ideas, it was the devil incarnate, and under no circumstances were the students to succumb to the temptation to join. She then bid the students to join her in prayer. Ichiko hoped to avoid any misunderstanding or trouble. With graduation approaching, she could ill afford to alienate the principal and jeopardize her chances for employment, so she had withdrawn. I did not blame her, though to be truthful, from the first time we met, I had been disappointed by her excessive concern for what people thought.

Despite her precaution, Ichiko was assigned to a girls' high school in Hirosaki, Aomori Prefecture, in virtual exile at the northern end of Honshū. She was dismissed after one term when the school authorities saw a photograph of Seitō members in *The Inside Story of the New Women*, a potboiler by Higuchi Raiyō. The photograph was the one that appeared in the September anniversary issue, but the author had misidentified Kimura Masako, who happened to join us, as Kamichika Ichiko. In retrospect, it was probably all to the good, since Ichiko eventually joined the *Tokyo nichi nichi* and had a distinguished career as a reporter.

Senuma Kayō belonged to Ozaki Kōyō's literary group, but was a specialist in Russian literature. Married to Senuma Kakusaburō, a priest at Nicolai Cathedral, and the mother of six children, she had twice traveled to Russia and was said to be fluent in the language. Unlike most Japanese translators who relied on English versions—Noboru Shomu was the exception—she worked directly from the original. A petite and dainty middle-aged woman, she wore a white dress and bonnet, an outfit unusual for the time. We warmed to her immediately. She began with the first installment of her translation of Chekhov's *Uncle Vanya* [for the February issue, vol. 2, no. 2] and sent translations of *The Cherry Orchard*, *Ivanov*, and [Aleksei Nikolaevich] Budishchev's *Northeast Wind*. This was the first and only time we saw her in person. To our regret, she died young, [at age thirty-nine,] from complications following the birth of her seventh child. Kobayashi Katsu, who went to Kayō's house in Kashiwagi to pick up a manuscript, told us that the house was surrounded by a field of sunflowers, and that she was invited to stay for a supper of roasted sunflower seeds and Russian-style stew.

Nishizaki Hanayo was from Tokushima in Shikoku. She liked to talk about herself and told us that she had already published under the pen name Chōsokabe Kikuko in *Joshi bundan*. She had come to Tokyo with her parents' permission in the hope of becoming a professional writer. To support herself, she had at one time worked as a secretary for the writer Mizuno Yōshū and as a substitute teacher at an elementary school in Ōji. She was presently a reporter for a magazine called *Living* (*Seikatsu*). All this was related in great detail, in a thick Tokushima drawl.

Hanayo was tiny, and though she was probably about twenty-four or -five, her plain hairstyle and subdued kimono made her look much older. An air of gloom clung to her also, as if she came from the less fortunate fringes of society, but once she started speaking, her passionate nature became clear. When she got carried away, she had a habit of edging closer, and Kōkichi, jealous of anyone who tried to come near me, promptly nicknamed her "Little Badger." Of all the women who had joined Seitō up to then, Hanayo was the first one who literally had to fight to survive, and in this respect, her writings from 1912 to 1913 were of particular significance.

In this connection, I should mention that the graduates of Japan Women's College who joined Seitō at its inception had started to drift away without making much of a contribution, whereas the newer members, who joined out of strong personal conviction, remained true to their original impulse. Did this mean that the earlier members who received a so-called higher education found it difficult to break loose of social restraints and express themselves freely? If so, their inability to forge ahead on their own certainly attests to the sorry state of women's higher education at the time. It is also interesting that the high school graduates—and not the college graduates—were the ones who lived for the most part in accordance with Seitō's ideals of emotional and intellectual freedom, personal autonomy, and respect for the individual.

Itō Noe

The October 1912 issue [vol. 3, no. 10] lists Itō Noe as a new member, but in a sense you could say that I had already met her in late spring, when I received a letter. The return address on the thick envelope was written in a simple but firm hand: Itō Noe, Imashuku Village, Itoshima County, Fukuoka Prefecture. We received many letters from young women seeking advice—in fact, too many to answer—but this one was clearly different. I was deeply moved because the writer seemed to fling all her troubles at me with physical force.

Noe described her upbringing, personal character, present situation, and in particular, the marriage forced upon her by her family. The letter literally churned with her inchoate resentment of outmoded morality and convention. Unable to bear the pain a minute longer, she intended to defy her family with the last ounce of her strength and live according to her convictions. In order to achieve this goal, she was coming to Tokyo and hoped to meet us. The tone of the long letter, crammed with her tiny writing, was arrogant and full of her own assumptions, but there was no question that Noe's letter made a more distinct impression than the hundreds of others that came to the office.

Not long after I had received the letter, the maid came to my room to announce a visitor. "She says her name is Itō Noe." Failing to make the connection, I said, "Oh, really—what kind of person is she?" "I'd say about fifteen or sixteen. She looks just like a nursemaid." Noe did indeed look like a nursemaid, even younger than Kōkichi or Katsu, and scarcely old enough to have written that letter. She was small and compact, and with her half-width red sash tied behind in a young girl's shell-shaped style, she did not look as if she had finished high school. Her full, round face radiated health; her large, clear eyes hinted at a stubborn, competitive streak and glowed not so much with knowledge or intelligence as with the raw energy of a wild animal. When she talked, her nostrils flared, her thin wide lips twisted and curled. Everything about her exuded an untamed life force. This may have been the first time we met, but she spoke about what was on her mind in a passionate, logical, and unself-conscious manner. She was not at all like Kōkichi but fascinating in her own way.

Noe gave me further details about her life. An uncle, who acted as her guardian, had secretly arranged to have her marry a young man who lived in the United States but owned land in Kyushu and had returned briefly to find a bride. She was furious—the man was a complete stranger—but under pressure from her relatives, she went through the ceremony. As the situation became increasingly intolerable, she reached the breaking point, fled from her husband, and came to Tokyo, where she was now living at the home of Tsuji Jun, an English teacher at the Ueno Girls' High School.

I listened to her, incredulous that this childlike girl was actually "married." I admired her courage and decided that Seitō would have to help her in some way. After declaring that she was returning to Kyushu to settle the matter once and for all, Noe left. She said she would be coming back to Tokyo.

In a letter that arrived about a month later, she sounded desperate. She was being persecuted by her relatives constantly, and since she could envision no solution, she often thought of killing herself. Totally worn out, she was in poor health, and all she could do was to walk down to the shore and cry and cry. She had made up her mind to run away again, but she was penniless. Would I please send some money?

I knew I had to do something quickly, and as a first step, I went to see Tsuji Jun, the teacher who had taken her in. Noe had said that he lived in Somei, so I went from door to door and finally found his house. I was told he had moved to Takinogawa, and I went there straightaway, but he was out. I left a message and my calling card with someone in the house.

Tsuji came to the house the next day. He assured me that he would assume responsibility for Noe when she returned to Tokyo, so, much relieved, I sent some of my pocket money to Noe. I knew nothing of Tsuji's relationship to her, nor did I have any sense that this merited serious thought. She looked no older than a child and had presumably told me everything about herself; I had no reason to think she would hold anything back, much less that the two were lovers. In talking about Noe, Tsuji had said, "She's a smart little girl," as if she were one of his students. I learned later that he had lost his job because of Noe, but being as obtuse as ever about such matters, I did not discover the true nature of their relationship until she became pregnant. (Noe always referred to Tsuji as Sensei, but after the birth of the child, she started calling him Tsuji.)

Noe returned to Tokyo in September and began working for us the next month. Ebullient and full of energy, she made a lively trio with Kōkichi and Katsu. Whenever the three got together, they burst out into gales of laughter, as Kōkichi slapped the other two on the back with her big hands. We gave Noe a monthly allowance of 10 yen, the most we could spare. I once asked Yoshiko to increase the amount, but she flatly refused. As office manager, she had to watch every penny.

[At eighteen,] Noe was the youngest, but she proved to be efficient, practical, and reliable, quite unlike Kōkichi. She was also less complicated and easier to understand. I had great hopes for her. Her first piece, a poem called "The Eastern Shore," was published in the November issue [vol. 2, no. 11]. The poem, sentimental and typical of a girl her age, depicted herself standing on the seashore, weeping in despair. The precocious and talented Noe would submit many articles in the years to come.

The same issue carried two pieces by Kōkichi: a poem, "A Cold Monster," and a sketch, "Mingling with the Crowd." They were her farewell to Seitō.[19] On the surface she was much the same, but she had no doubt arrived at some kind of decision. For Kōkichi, the final blow may have been the articles in the *Tokyo nichi nichi*, the first of which appeared on October 25, under the heading "Women Who Clamor to Be New." I shall quote from the opening paragraph.

Nora, Magda, and their ilk are the topics of the day. New Woman, Awakened Woman, Self-Aware Woman, Woman of a New Era—the names are legion for a certain type of woman. Of these, no group draws more attention than the young ladies at Seitō, not least because of the rumors surrounding their outrageous behavior—drinking five-colored cocktails, going off to Yoshiwara to consort with geisha, roaming the streets near the Twelve-Story Building in Asakusa to strike up friendships with prostitutes. As a result, sales of their journal have soared, but at the same time, the daughters of respectable families have been forbidden to open its pages. The name Seitō may conjure up the image of women who waste their time drinking and declaiming impertinent nonsense, but if one looks at the society's statement of purpose, one finds that it is extremely serious. To wit: "The society aims to promote the development of women's literature, to enable each member to manifest her unique inborn talent, and to give birth to woman writers of genius." Inasmuch as the journal's influence on young women grows by the day, we propose to examine the nature of the organization and the lives of its members.

The articles were not as far-fetched as those in the *Kokumin shinbun*, but based as they were on Kōkichi's incautious remarks to the staff reporter Ono Ken'ichirō, they contained a great deal of nonsense, and quite naturally, the people at the office, including myself, had taken her to task.

Kōkichi sent a letter of protest to Ono, and this, too, was published in the paper:

> I admit I entirely forgot myself and talked too much. But I find it especially painful that everyone thinks I have nothing good to say about Hiratsuka-san. When I think that I have dragged her into this, I can't help feeling sorry for myself, for being so pathetically stupid like a baby.

Half apologetic, half defensive, poor Kōkichi once again blurted out what she thought on the spur of the moment, only to regret it later.

Members were critical, but no one had come right out and said that she should leave. Yoshiko alone hinted strongly that something had to be done. She had long disapproved of Kōkichi's irresponsible behavior—I took this as an indirect criticism of my lack of oversight—and the mad outburst at the sanatorium had been the last straw. Kōkichi herself had said that she was leaving "to make amends," but we did not know how serious she was; nor, in all likelihood, did she. Thus, each time she announced her "withdrawal," we had said nothing and wondered whether she really meant it. I saw no particular reason to dissuade her. Even if she left, our personal relationship would remain the same. She herself may not have realized how much her thoughtless behavior had disrupted Seitō, but I had come to think she should leave for the good of the society. Also, I had become even more strongly convinced that she should go back to painting, which was her true calling. Before going to the sanatorium, she had been eagerly talking about her next project, a six-paneled screen for the autumn exhibit sponsored by the Ministry of Education. Not only did her family of artists expect much of her, she owed it to herself to develop her talents.

Kōkichi left on the last day of October, saying everyone should come and see the screen when it was finished. None of us could quite believe that she had really gone, and sure enough, on the pretext of helping out, she came by the office and my house almost every day, and was more often a hindrance than not.

◎ ◎ ◎ ◎ ◎

In the meantime, I had not heard a word from Okumura since the letter about the "young swallow." A young man had slipped into this emotional void — Nishimura Yōkichi, the head of the firm that handled our business. Kōkichi had apparently berated him for bringing Okumura to the sanatorium, and to apologize for his part in the unfortunate affair, he sent me a letter. The letter, together with the fact that he published Seitō, had gradually led to a more personal relationship.

Nishimura was about a year older [younger] than Okumura but much more mature. His boyish smile belied a discernment beyond his years. He was quiet and circumspect, never given to idle gossip, and highly intelligent, with the delicate sensibilities of the true city dweller. He was also an experienced businessman and no doubt regarded our work at Seitō as child's play.

In addition to being practical and business-minded, he was interested in literature and contributed poems and sketches to Kokuyō and Life and Art (Seikatsu to geijutsu), both published by his firm. He addressed me as "Honorable Elder Sister" in his letters, which tended to be sentimental and invariably ended with a lament that he was too busy to pursue his own literary interests. He seemed to be frequently at odds with his adoptive father, who was nominally retired but still had a hand in the business and criticized him for publishing so many works of "pure literature." As an adoptive son, he was expected to marry the daughter of the family.

Nishimura was also close to Kobayashi Katsu. Having grown up in the same downtown area, they had much in common and often took long walks together, but since Nishimura was already betrothed, the relationship was not what Kōkichi imagined. I went for walks with Nishimura, too, and learned a great deal about downtown Tokyo. One time, we even peeked into the Tai-yōkaku, a rather disreputable establishment in Asakusa that served fare more typical of country spas. On occasion we held hands, but he never overstepped the boundaries of propriety; I would always be his "Honorable Elder Sister." When Okumura reappeared on the scene, he discreetly withdrew.

◎ ◎ ◎ ◎ ◎

As a result of the public outcry, we lost some members toward the end of 1912, but our roster of writers remained strong. Among these were Katō Midori,

Ogasawara Sadako, Mizuno Senko, and Yasuda Satsuki in fiction and Mika-jima Yoshiko, Chino Masako, Saiga Kotoko, Okamoto Kanoko, and Hara Asao in poetry.

Katō Midori, who was married to the writer Katō Asadori, had joined on Iwano Kiyoko's recommendation. Originally from Osaka, she was on the staff of the *Tokyo nichi nichi*. She was so determined to achieve her goals as a reporter and writer that for a while she had sent one of her children out to nurse.[xxv] Energetic and efficient, she struck me as more an active person than a writer. Predictably, most of her stories dealt with the conflict between fam-ily and independence, the competing demands pulling at a woman who was simultaneously a wife, mother, and reporter. I regret to say that she died quite young [at age thirty-three].[20]

Ogasawara Sadako, like Nishizaki Hanayo, started out writing for *Joshi bundan*, and the two were in fact good friends. A talented artist, she made a woodblock print for the cover of *Seitō Fiction*, volume 2 in the *Seitō Book Series* (Tōundō; February 1913). One of her stories ["Guests"] appeared in the book. She rarely came to meetings, and my memory of her is rather hazy, but she was a pale, slender beauty, with a modest demeanor that was then consid-ered ideal. She also died young.[21]

I regret to say that I never met Mizuno Senko, who was a member from the beginning. As I recall, she was a disciple of the writer Tayama Katai and showed great promise but died young [at age thirty].

I notice that Okamoto Kanoko is listed as a new member in the December 1911 issue [vol. 1, no. 4]. I have already mentioned meeting her when she was still Ōnuki Kanoko and a member of the Keishū Literary Society. Her pushy and persistent manner left a strong impression, and I had probably asked her to join soon after starting the journal. Married to the artist Okamoto Ippei, she had recently given birth to a baby boy called Tarō.

Of the poets who wrote for us, Kanoko was the youngest [twenty-three], but she had already published in *Myōjō* and *Subaru*. Her first contribution, a series of waka poems called "My Door," appeared in the March 1912 issue [vol. 2, no. 3]. Though they were somewhat immature, these poems spoke from the heart of the hurts and anguish of a sensuous young bride. A collection of her poems, *A Twinge of Jealousy* (*Karoki netami*), was published in December by Tōundō as volume 1 in the *Seitō Book Series*. Bound in the Japanese style, the book had a mauve cover with a hemp leaf design that had been created by her husband, Okamoto Ippei. The poems were hand-blocked on rice paper with illustrations by Wada Eisaku.

[xxv] The practice was not uncommon, especially when there were too many children or the mother was in poor health. The child unfortunately died.

By the time she joined Seitō, Kanoko had become a shadow of her former self. Thinner and looking careworn, she was apparently in poor health. She came to see me once and talked about her troubles at home. She had her same old habit of fixing her large eyes on you, but her eyes seemed even larger and gleamed with a strange light. Ever since I first met her at Baba Kochō's house, I thought there was something unbalanced about her, but afraid of saying the wrong thing, I held my tongue. I learned later that Kanoko was going through an extremely difficult time. Her beloved brother Ōnuki Shōsen had unexpectedly died and her mother died soon after. Then, while she was enduring these sorrows, her husband had reverted to his dissolute ways.

Despite this, Kanoko's creative urge remained as strong as ever. From January to November 1913 alone—with the exception of May—she contributed about twenty poems a month. But after sending in "A Lament" for the November issue [vol. 3, no. 11], she abruptly stopped. The Editors' Notes in the December issue touches briefly on Kanoko:

> Okamoto Kanoko has had a nervous breakdown and is now at the Okada Hospital. To our deep regret, we shall not be reading her gentle and sensitive poems for a while. We hope and pray for her swift recovery. We have received a short communication from her: "When I think that I can no longer write poetry, I feel there is no point in living. I am too young to waste away like this. I grieve and suffer with every drop of blood in my youthful body. I am miserable. This is all I can write for now."

Slow to recover from the birth of her second child in August, she had become temporarily deranged from distress about the breakdown of her marriage. She spent two years in the hospital.

In 1915, Kanoko sent a long manuscript personally addressed to the editor. "Shedding My Hospital Robes" was published in the September 1915 issue [vol. 5, no. 8].[xxvi] One of the poems describes her ordeal: "Was it a sea of fire? A mountain of ice? Three years have I wandered, whimpering in pain." But she then immersed herself in books on Buddhism and Zen practice, reached a deeper level of consciousness, and emerged as a writer of capacious heart and imagination. I shall never forget her.

Mikajima Yoshiko, a substitute teacher at an elementary school in Nishitama and a member of Yosano Tekkan's New Poetry Society, was perhaps the most prolific of the Seitō poets. Her poems in Subaru were highly regarded by both Yosano Tekkan and Akiko. After joining Seitō and submitting her first poems in March 1912 [vol. 2, no. 3], she continued to submit poems until the

---

xxvi There was no August issue.

very last issue in February 1916 [vol. 6, no. 2]. Sometimes, she sent as many as a hundred at a time.

Her poems took on a darker tone after she switched to the Araragi group, but when she wrote for us, her works were flowery and romantic, filled with the imaginings and longings of young love. Her exquisite depiction of the subtle psychological shifts within a woman in love spoke to young readers with a heart-stopping immediacy. Yoshiko, for instance, would snatch her manuscripts as soon as they arrived and sigh over lines like "A nameless bird flew by and sang / reminding me of the lover I have yet to meet." "Like the solitary plum still unfurled / I wait in anguish under the March sky."

She married her lover, Kurakata Kan'ichi, in 1914. They had a baby girl, but Yoshiko had contracted tuberculosis in her youth, and as this worsened, she was increasingly confined to her bed. Eventually Kurakata abandoned her for another woman.[22] The first time I met her was in 1919, at a gathering of former Seitō members at my sister's home (she was then thirty-four). She was still in relatively good health and living with her husband, but I could not believe that the wan and emaciated, prematurely old woman was the author of those flowery and passionate poems. She was gentle and unassuming, and her goodness spoke for itself. Ten or so years later, when her friend Hara Asao was involved in a notorious scandal with Ishihara Atsushi, Yoshiko wrote an article in her defense in the May 1921 *Fujin kōron*.[xxvii] Yoshiko's mentor, Shimaki Akahiko, was incensed, and she left the Araragi group to join the circle led by Koizumi Chikashi. She died in 1927, at age forty-two.

Hara Asao's first submission was a set of twenty-nine poems called "Sweet Bondage" [January 1913; vol. 3, no. 1]. Included with her application was a picture of Asao holding a baby boy. The father, a married man, had been her instructor at the Women's Fine Arts Academy in Tokyo. "Tears," in the September 1913 issue, reflects her pain at the time: "My black hair shorn / But sadder still to receive no word from you." "What am I to do with myself / Too weak to acknowledge that I have been truly abandoned."

An only daughter, she subsequently married a painter of Western art, and they had a child, but for some reason, he left and never returned. Her poems in the October 1915 issue [vol. 5, no. 9] are understandably filled with the pathos of a broken heart: "Tired from waiting for your letter / In sadness I let the days slip by." "Let the child strike me with his little hand / His foolish mother's cheek, wet with tears." In matters of the heart, Asao seems to have been most unfortunate.

[xxvii] Ishihara Atsushi was a professor at Tōhoku University who was married and had children. After he was forced to resign, he and Asao lived together for several years but eventually separated.

Many years later her daughter-in-law Hara Momoko showed me a letter I had written to Asao. The letter, dated February 7, 1913, is written on pale brown Seitō stationery and addressed to her home in Miyagi Prefecture: "Thank you for your letter. It is our policy not to return manuscripts. We cannot print all of your poems at once, but we hope to include them in a future issue...." Asao must have submitted "Tears," the poems we published in September.

Chino Masako was a college classmate of Yoshiko's and a member from the very beginning. Besides poems—she belonged to the New Poetry Society—she also contributed short stories. She lived in Kobe with her husband, [the German scholar] Chino Shōshō, and was unable to attend meetings, but I remember her as a classical beauty, quiet and retiring, just like her poems.

Harada Kotoko also belonged to the New Poetry Society and was close to Mikajima Yoshiko. She contributed many poems, but she lived in Nagoya, and so I never had the chance to meet her. Takeyama Hideko, the younger sister of the poet Kaneko Kun'en, also sent poems but never attended a meeting.

6

A New Direction for Seitō

The following announcement appears in the Editors' Notes for the December 1912 issue:

> We are not sure when or where the term "New Woman" first became popular, but it seems to have caught the fancy of a number of newspapers and magazines. We even wonder whether the journalists themselves didn't invent the phrase and set it afloat like a toy balloon. Happily enough, we at Seitō have been likened to this toy balloon and lifted hither and yon. So here at the editors' office, we have been thinking of publishing our own thoughts and opinions on this much-publicized New Woman in the January issue. It's the New Year—why not have some fun? No—we take that back. We plan to pursue a completely different approach from journalists and will be serious, very serious, as we look into the so-called New Woman to see what the truly New Woman is.

Seitō had finally awakened to the need to explore women's issues, and as announced, the January 1913 issue [vol. 3, no. 1] carried a special supplement entitled "The New Woman and Other Issues Related to Women." We were determined to respond forcefully to public criticism of the New Woman, and at the same time we wanted to clarify our own thoughts about how we, as members of Seitō, ought to live. As a result of the scandal surrounding the "five-colored cocktail" and "a dalliance in Yoshiwara," too many members were backing away from the organization. The contents of the supplement, I believe, give a clear indication of our new resolve: Raichō, "Love and Marriage"; Itō Noe, "The Path of a New Woman"; Iwano Kiyoko, "Men and Women Are Equal as Members of the Human Race"; Katō Midori, "Concerning the New Woman"; Chōsokabe Kikuko (Nishizaki Hanayo), "Explaining the New

Woman"; Ueno Yōko, "Transcending the Popular View"; Miyazaki Mitsu, "A Request to Readers"; Hori Yasuko, "I Am an Old-fashioned Woman."

Chōkō approved of our new direction. He also urged us to hold public lectures, saying he would be happy to speak and would ask Baba Kochō and other friends to do the same. I was disinclined to do this. Nothing would be gained by rushing ahead, especially since none of the members was a skilled public speaker, and relying on men somehow went against our principles.

As I explain in the preface to my translation, I originally planned to write an essay on the New Woman, but in the course of reading various books on women's issues, I came across Ellen Key's *Love and Marriage* and decided to introduce her ideas instead.

I first came across Ellen Key's name in "Genjitsukyō," an article by Kaneko Chikusui in the September 1911 issue of *Taiyō*.[i] I was fascinated by Key's ideas and jotted down some of them in my diary. A day or two later, I received a visit from Kawai Suimei, the editor-in-chief of *Joshi bundan*. He said he was planning to publish several prominent people's views on romantic love and asked me to write something. Since I am hesitant by nature, I declined, but I asked if he had seen the current issue of *Taiyō*. "There's a very interesting article about Ellen Key," I told him. "No, I haven't," he replied, "but I was just talking to Mori Ōgai about it. She seems to be quite an unusual woman." I next asked whether he knew the titles of any of her books. He did not, and with that, I more or less put her out of my mind.

I then happened to read "On the Freedom to Divorce," an article by Ishizaka Yōhei in the December issue of *Teikoku bungaku*. In this article, he introduced Key's ideas and referred specifically to chapter 8 in her *Love and Marriage*. Since I was collecting materials to write my essay on the New Woman, I hastened to Maruzen to buy a copy.... Key's book raised a broad range of issues. While I was mulling over her ideas, I decided to spend the coming year focusing on women's issues. Also, rather than write an essay based on my shallow and uninformed ideas on the New Woman, I decided to present a translation of Key's book. To the best of my abilities, I have tried to be faithful to the original.[1]

Until that time, I had read very little on women's issues. I was simply not interested, or to put it another way, I did not think of myself as a woman. My first priority was to heed the dictates of my inner self. But circumstances had changed. The public had branded our members as the New Women and as

---

[i] Kaneko Chikusui (1870–1937) believed that religion and a philosophy of life had to be based on life as it was actually lived, and introduced Key's ideas in his article, including her views on love and marriage.

this became more of a problem, I concluded that the subject deserved serious study. I started to read, albeit indiscriminately, English-language books on women's issues and women's movements.

Then, around this time, Takita Choin, the editor of *Chūō kōron*, asked me to write a short essay for the New Year's issue. I said no, but he was not easily turned down and came to see me again. He planted his big body in my study and said, "We've already announced it. You've got to write something right away." I found myself unable to refuse, so I wrote an essay the very same day called "I Am a New Woman." (I deliberately identified myself as a New Woman, not for the public so much as for the fainthearted members who feared being labeled in the same way.) I shall quote from the essay:

I am a New Woman.
At least, I hope and strive each day to be truly a New Woman.
The sun alone is truly and forever new.
I am the sun.
At least, I hope and strive each day to be the sun.

"The sun is new each day, verily, does it renew itself each day, again and again." So reads the inscription on the washbasin of a ruler of ancient China. Glorious indeed is the virtue, the celestial virtue of the ever-renewing sun.

The New Woman rejects "yesterday."[ii]
No longer will she tread in submissive silence the path taken by oppressed women of the past.
No longer will she be kept in ignorance, enslaved, or reduced to a lump of flesh by man's egotism.
The New Woman is determined to destroy the old morality and laws established by men for their own convenience.

But the myriad ghosts that haunted the women of the past relentlessly pursue the New Woman.
When "today" is idle, "yesterday" rushes in.
The New Woman does battle with the ghosts each day.
The moment she lets her guard down, the "New Woman" reverts to her former self.
I am a New Woman. I am the sun. I am myself and myself alone. At least, I hope and strive each day.

[ii] The version in *HRC* (1:257) says "The New Woman curses (*norou*) yesterday."

The New Woman will not only destroy the old morality and laws built on man's egotism, but by virtue of the forever renewing sun, she will establish within her soul a new kingdom with a new religion, a new morality, a new set of laws.

Therein lies her inborn mission. But what is this new kingdom whereof I speak? This new religion? The New Woman has yet to know the answers to this.

But in order to know the unknown, she studies, she cultivates the self, strives, and struggles.

For now, she desires only power, the power to persevere so that she may fulfill her ordained mission, so that she may prevail in her studies, self-cultivation, efforts, and struggles to know the unknown.

The New Woman does not seek Beauty. Nor does she seek Goodness. What she cries out for is the power to establish the new and unknown kingdom, the power to fulfill her sacred ordained mission.

I was still groping to articulate my ideas, but I believe my declaration states unequivocally the goals I had set for myself as a New Woman. I was pleased to see an English translation, together with a kind introductory note by the translator, Hanazono Sadamu, in the January 11 issue of the *Japan Times*.

The principle followed in the education of women at one time in Japan was to make them good housewives. To-day, however, the economic conditions have altered, and have accordingly changed the object of education given, which now aims at fitting young women to gain their own living. In consequence, they are becoming professors, doctors, writers, musicians, officials, journalists, shop assistants, nurses, etc. They are not allowed to and do not live idle lives, but the tendency is for them to engage in outside professions, because they prefer independence and economic freedom to everything else. These young women are hampered in no way in living their own lives as they see fit. They have become their own moral mentors. They make their own personal living codes.[iii]

"I am a New Woman" was published in the January 1913 issue of *Chūō kōron* as part of "Fifteen Famous Women: One Woman, One Topic." Others, selected no doubt by Takita Choin, were Hatoyama Haruko, "Issues Related to the Female Suffrage Movement"; Tamura Toshiko, "Homosexual Love"; Shimoda Utako, "An Answer to the Question Concerning the Influence of Mrs. Nogi Maresuke's Suicide on Women's Education"; Yosano Akiko, "Parisian Women Loved by Men"; Kunikida Haruko, "A Widow's Life"; Kagetsu

---

[iii] This is the original English introduction by Hanazono.

Okami, "Japanese Women as Seen by One Who Has Seen European Women"; Hasegawa Shigure, "Noh Dances and Other Traditional Dances"; Hinata Kimu, "Appraising Flowers"; Toyotake Roshō, "Tokyo and Osaka as Seen from the Stage"; Tanahashi Ayako, "High School Girls Then and Now"; Otake Kōkichi, "A Gathering of Geisha"; Mori Ritsuko, "My Life Before Becoming an Actress"; Ikeda Shōen, "A Day in the Recent Past"; Egi Kingin, "How to Have a Peaceful and Harmonious Home." My essay came last. The selection of topics and authors gives a fair indication of the temper of the times.

I was extremely busy from January to February. Besides editing the February supplement on women's issues, I had to make arrangements for the first public lecture scheduled for February 15, 1913. Initially, most of the staff was lukewarm about Chōkō's proposal to hold a series of lectures, but after his repeated assurances that he would line up as many speakers as we wanted, we agreed. Chōkō, I should add, was something of a busybody and also liked being the center of attention. He had confidence as a public speaker, his ability to inflect his voice being a point of pride. He doubtless assumed that he would be giving the opening lecture. Other speakers were Baba Kochō and Abe Jirō; Iwano Kiyoko and her husband, Hōmei, volunteered. Kiyoko had honed her skills when she campaigned for the revision of Article 5 a decade or so earlier with Fukuda Hideko, Nishikawa Fumiko, Imai Utako, and other socialist women. She also seemed to enjoy speaking in public.

Kōkichi came to help with the preparations and took charge of the handbills, posters, and tickets. Although officially no longer a member, she continued to visit the office and my study and for that matter had made the cover for the New Year's issue [vol. 3, no. 1], a striking woodblock print of Adam and Eve [standing under the Tree of Knowledge]. (I read later in a biography of her Uncle Chikuha that her future husband, the artist Tomimoto Kenkichi, actually drew the draft version of the cover.)

She was working on a six-paneled screen of loquats for the forthcoming Tatsumikai exhibit and had recently rented a big room in Chōkō's house in Hongō Nishisuga-chō. I do not know why she did this—I was not consulted— but she may have moved out of her home temporarily because a fortuneteller had predicted that the oldest daughter of the Otake family would die of some sickness, and she had just recovered from tuberculosis.

Kōkichi was given the best room in the house—Chōkō's study—which overlooked the broad lawn and the trees at Nezu Shrine. He was fond of her and amused by her eccentric behavior. "Kōkichi's a character, isn't she," he said. "She goes around showing a frame without any picture in it." One might have expected her to have had some scruples about living under the same roof with Chōkō, who was still young, but no one, not even his wife, seems to have thought twice, since nothing about Kōkichi suggested a nubile young woman.

Satō Haruo was still living in Chōkō's house, and he immediately fell in love with Kōkichi's younger sister Fukumi, who frequently came by to deliver messages from the family. Just as her name suggests, Fukumi was big but sweet-tempered and feminine.[iv] Unlike her sister, she was a classic Kansai beauty. Satō sent love letters through Kōkichi and wrote poems lamenting his unrequited love: "My love conveyed through another / my hopes more fragile than a thread. Unable to fathom a maiden's heart / I shed tears that never cease," and so on. He apparently wrote about Fukumi in one of his stories ("Enkō"), but I have not read it.

Fukuda Hideko

We published the February (1913) issue, together with a supplement that contained four articles: Fukuda Hideko, "The Solution to the Woman Question"; Iwano Hōmei, "A Cruel View of Love and the Woman Question"; Abe Jirō, "In Lieu of a Conversation"; and the first installment of my translation of Key's Love and Marriage. On the eighth, the issue was judged "injurious to public order" and banned. No single article was specified, but I guessed that the cause of the ban was either Noe's "Recent Thoughts," an essay in the main part of the issue that condemned the traditional view of marriage, or Hideko's essay outlining the socialist position on the Woman Question. I shall quote a passage from Hideko's essay:

> Under what conditions, then, will we be liberated? No matter what others may
> say or argue, I believe a complete and satisfactory liberation will not take place
> until a thoroughgoing communist system is firmly established. This holds true
> for men as well as women. On the day a communist system is implemented, as a
> matter of course, love and marriage will also be free.

Her essay was a theoretical proposal for solving the Woman Question and for raising women's position in a future society. It contained nothing radical, so it was probably not the contents per se but Hideko's name and her association with the socialist Heiminsha[v] that offended the authorities.[2]

I do not remember how I happened to ask Hideko to write for us, but I may have thought that a socialist viewpoint should be represented in the journal. I knew she had participated in the Freedom and People's Rights movement

---

[iv] "Fukumi" is made up of the characters for "happiness" and "beauty."

[v] Heiminsha (Commoners' Association): Socialist organization founded by Kōtoku Shūsui, Uchimura Kanzō, and Sakai Toshihiko in 1903.

and been involved in the Osaka Incident; there was good cause for her being called the "Joan of Arc of Japan."[vi] Then, through Ishikawa Sanshirō, she had established ties with the Heiminsha, and in 1907, started *Women of the World* (*Sekai fujin*), Japan's first socialist magazine for women.[3] I wrote to her out of the blue, without a proper introduction, and awaited her essay with keen anticipation.

I read the manuscript as soon as it arrived. It was written in a firm, masculine hand and the argument, cogent and straightforward, was clearly the work of a practiced writer. I was impressed, and the possibility of a ban never crossed my mind.

The government censorship led to an even wider rift between my father and me. He read about the censorship in the newspapers and was particularly alarmed that the essay in question was by a socialist woman associated with the Heiminsha. Until that time, he had said nothing about the groundless attacks on Seitō, but this was too serious to ignore. At a time when the Great Treason Incident was still fresh in public memory, my father, a loyal servant of the state, was horrified to find that his own daughter was consorting with an unregenerate socialist and had possibly invited her to the house. Not that he necessarily knew what socialism stood for, but as a supporter of the absolutist emperor system, he had probably dismissed it outright as subversive and dangerous.

I was summoned to his study. He was furious. I saw no need to apologize, since I had done nothing reprehensible. To allay his fears, however, I said that I had not published the article because I was particularly friendly with Hideko, and that moreover, I had no personal contact with socialists. My father, as always, remained in perfect control of himself, his voice calm and words carefully chosen. But his face was flushed, the cigar in his hand shaking, and I was pained to think that once again, my mother would have to suffer the consequences.

He then started to lecture me on the function and meaning of the family system and the nation-state. In no mood to argue, I said, "Father, I understand what you are saying, and I realize I have caused you a great deal of worry, but if I may be excused—" "Very well," he said. "If you feel you have to publish articles by socialists, you'll have to give up the journal. And if you think you're unable to do this, you can leave the house and do it." His parting words struck deep into my heart.

[vi] The Osaka Incident (1885) was a plot led by the radical liberal Ōi Kentarō to assassinate the leaders of the conservative faction in control of the Korean government and further the reformist cause both in Korea and in Japan. Hideko (1865–1927), who was Ōi's lover, was given a four-year prison sentence for her part in the abortive plot. She married Fukuda Yūsaku in 1892.

To be truthful, my father and I had stopped having private conversations since the affair with Morita. I consciously avoided him, and aside from the customary exchange of greetings and desultory mealtime chitchat, I barely spoke to him. We lived in two completely separate worlds. In my mother's case, too, I responded to her queries if she was worried about something, but apart from our discussions on journal finances, we never talked about my personal affairs. At those rare moments when she criticized me, she usually objected to the way I looked: "It's all right to part your hair in the middle and tie it in a ponytail when you're home, but when you go out, couldn't you at least arrange it properly?" I rather doubt my father knew about the money she gave to Seitō, but had he known, I am sure he would have vented his full fury on her.

Such were the unforeseen personal and official repercussions of Hideko's essay. I admired its breadth of vision and lucid exposition, but I did not think I had learned anything new. I had already read about the socialist position on women in Sakai Toshihiko's *The Woman Question* (*Fujin mondai*) and in a translation of Carpenter's book, which theorized about a free society.[vii]

In April—this was after we moved the office to Sugamo—Hideko came to the office for the first time. As I remember, she came with an introduction from Itō Noe and Tsuji Jun, whom she met through Watanabe Masatarō, [a socialist] associated with the Heiminsha. She had been living with Ishikawa Sanshirō in Yokohama, but following his departure [for Europe], she moved to Komagomebashi and was selling fresh eggs to support herself; she later peddled yard goods and secondhand clothes.

To be honest, my first impression of Hideko was not pleasant. In fact, I was quite taken aback. She was a big woman well past middle age, with yellowish, bulging, bloodshot eyes and a forbidding expression on her parched orange-tinted face—she may have been suffering from a chronic heart condition. Her entire appearance told of long years of unrelieved hardship. Yet, for all that, she bore herself with the air of the seasoned political activist, without a trace of gloom or melancholy. When she talked about the past, her eyes lit up as she described her heady youth as a fighter for the People's Rights movement. But when she talked about her former male comrades, who had bent their principles to make their way in the world of politics, she practically sputtered with indignation and contempt.

After her first visit, Hideko dropped by the office from time to time. We heard from a member, Sakamoto (Takada) Makoto, that Ishikawa had actually

---

vii Sakai Toshihiko (1870–1933), one of the founders of the Heiminsha, was sympathetic to women's issues. Raichō probably refers to Sakai's partial translation of Edward Carpenter's *Love's Coming-of-Age* (1896).

written the essay. Educated at a missionary school, she worked as a typist for a foreign firm in Yokohama and had known Ishikawa and Hideko when they lived near her house. Whatever the truth actually was, the staff soon accepted Makoto's assertion.

Speaking of Ishikawa, I remember seeing him at Bunshōdō, the printers for Tōundō. This was around October or November 1912, when Kōkichi still came to the room on the second floor where we did the proofreading. Ishikawa was putting the final touches on his magnum opus, *The History of Social Movements in the West* (*Seiyō shakai undō-shi*), but as if to avoid people, he shut himself up in a dark, dank room and worked in total silence, while we laughed and chattered in our large, sunlit room. The only time I saw him was in the hallway, and though we recognized each other, we had not been formally introduced, so we merely exchanged friendly nods. Small and bone-thin, with the pallor of a prisoner, he was shy and almost feminine in manner. His book, thick and with a bright red cover, was published after he left the country and immediately banned. Years later, I saw him again, when he was living in the countryside near Seijō. He had become a recluse, raising goats and vegetables with the help of a cheerful young girl called Mochizuki Yuriko, who affectionately called him "Papa."

Needless to say, Ishikawa left Japan because of constant police harassment, but I think he was fleeing from Hideko, too. According to Sakamoto Makoto, Hideko was fiercely attached to him, and having been betrayed by several men in the past, she was suspicious of his every move. Her jealousy was only part of the story, I am sure, but I can see why he might have wanted to put an end to their relationship.

Since I am writing about Hideko, I will skip ahead several years to 1918. She was still peddling yard goods from door to door, and because I was too poor to buy anything, I appealed to my sister, who was interested in clothes and had money to spare. Her husband was by then a section head at the Ministry of Communications and had the use of a big government house in Kobiki-chō. My sister made a purchase each time Hideko dropped by, but said to me one day, "Fukuda-san's the limit. She comes with her mind already made up—she says this kimono is just right for you, so please buy it!"

The two nonetheless became good friends, and Hideko often stayed for a meal. My sister enjoyed Hideko's stories, and Hideko, in turn, did favors for her, like finding a maid or a tutor for the children. By coincidence, one of the tutors, an impoverished student at Tokyo University, was the nephew of Miyazaki Tōten's wife. Hideko made herself at home in my sister's living room and whenever I went there, she would be seated next to the hibachi, gossiping about her turbulent past and the people she had known. Even now, I can see her pale, worn face, so at odds with her big, sturdy frame.

The biggest blow in Hideko's old age was the death of her youngest son, her pride and joy, who had been ill with tuberculosis. She wept when she told my sister. My sister, too, had suffered from the same illness, but she had been sustained by her abiding faith in Tenrikyō. She grieved for her friend. "The poor woman. She's strong-minded and keeps up a brave face, but at heart, she's a mother just like the rest of us."

On May 2, 1927, as Hideko lay on her deathbed, she asked for my sister, saying she wanted to thank her. My sister rushed to her house in Minami Shinagawa but was too late. She went to the room on the second floor to pay her respects and gently lifted the white cloth covering Hideko's face. As she told me afterward, the look of utter despair on the woman's face turned her soul to ice. "I've seen the faces of a lot of dead people, but never one so terrifying. Her afterlife isn't going to be easy. I feel sorry for her, but I think she's gone straight to hell." My deeply religious sister pitied Hideko from the bottom of her heart.

In the years to come, I learned more about Hideko and was reminded of what my sister had said about her face. I pitied her in my own way, for in truth, from beginning to end, for sixty-one years, she had fought and struggled as a woman and mother. In 1965, on the centenary of her birth, a group of men and women in her birthplace, Okayama, decided to set up a memorial in Kasaiyama Park and asked me to write the epitaph. I chose a line from her autobiography, A Half-Life (Warawa no hanseigai, 1904): "My life has been one adversity upon another. But I always fought back. Not once, not even once, did I flinch from adversity."[4]

◎ ◎ ◎ ◎ ◎

On February 15, we held our first public lecture at the YMCA in Kanda Mitoshiro-chō. The hall was full, the audience no doubt curious to know more about the "New Woman." The program was as follows: The Founding Spirit of Seitō, Its Work and Future Goals (Yasumochi Yoshiko); Recent Thoughts (Itō Noe); On the New Women (Ikuta Chōkō); What Men Require (Iwano Hōmei); On Behalf of Women (Baba Kochō); On Intellectual and Economic Independence (Iwano Kiyoko).

In order to prevent an onslaught of male hecklers, we announced beforehand that any man attending had to be accompanied by a woman. Despite this, well over two thirds of the thousand or so in the audience were men. Fortunately, the audience was well behaved, but halfway through the program, something surprising occurred. I shall quote from the February 16 Yomiuri:

Tempers Flare: The Prophet and Hōmei Come to Blows
at Lecture on the New Woman

On opening the door gently, one is assailed at once by a seductive aroma. On the stage is Mr. Ikuta Chōkō, and behind him, a bevy of dazzling young ladies, including Miss Yasumochi Yoshiko, a woman of ample girth comfortably ensconced in a chair. To her left, grouped around a stove, are the Misses Raichō, Kōkichi, and [Araki] Ikuko. As one might expect from a gathering of this sort, women make up half of the audience, the majority with their hair arranged in *hisashigami* style, others in a matronly marumage or maidenly Shimada, and a solitary figure in a girlish momoware. More conspicuous are a silver-haired woman and a mother with a baby strapped to her back.

Mr. Ikuta had just begun his lecture. He spoke with polish and ease, first defining what the term "New Woman" meant. "This may be my own opinion, but to me a New Woman is a woman who is dissatisfied with outmoded ideas and customs, in other words, a woman who is unhappy with her traditional place in society and seeks equality, or at least, approximately equal rights with men."

The next speaker, introduced by Miss Yasumochi, was Mr. Iwano Hōmei. His choice of topic, "What Men Require," was signally apt. He started off with an anecdote about a friend who had divorced his wife because she was always taking naps. But just as he was warming to his subject, the self-proclaimed "prophet," Mr. Miyazaki Toranosuke leaped up onto the stage, his whiskers bristling with anger. "Iwano!" he bellowed. "I hear you've changed wives several times over. I'd like an explanation." Short-tempered to begin with, Iwano shouted back, "Shut up, you fool!" The two men started scuffling like a pair of gamecocks—not that they were trying to display their masculine powers in front of the assembled ladies, but the strange spectacle of the two men grappling, one a true believer in the supremacy of the spirit, the other a proponent of mystical semianimalism,[viii] seemed to symbolize the present state of the world of thought. Bedlam broke out, with the audience booing and cheering one man or the other. Mr. Spirit was finally pushed off the stage, and, urged by the other speakers and their ladyships, returned to his seat.

Hōmei resumed his lecture in a quavering voice and expounded on his theory of man's inherent bestiality. In conclusion he said, "I divorced my first wife because I could not stand living in the same house with a woman totally devoid of self-awareness. I was, so to speak, a male Nora."

Mr. Baba Kochō spoke next. He said that women were oppressed by men

---

[viii] In his book *Mystical Semianimalism (Shinpiteki hanjū-shugi*, 1906) Iwano Hōmei (1873–1920) stressed the nonrational, or "animal" side of humans and claimed that existence was purposeless from a moral viewpoint. The book was misinterpreted by many as espousing unfettered eroticism, and Hōmei was dismissed from his teaching post at a commercial school.

because "organized power had triumphed over unorganized power" and thus women must "sweep away old customs and live in a state of self awareness." He then said, "In view of the changing times, I think birth control is necessary." At this, once again, Miyazaki stood up and shouted "Fool!" He immediately sat down, but before leaving the stage, Mr. Baba assured his audience that he was "only speaking for himself and not for Seitō."

The last speaker, Mrs. Iwano Kiyoko, was the only woman on the program. Dressed in a silk crepe kimono and satin obi, her hair piled up in a towering marumage, she was greeted with enthusiastic applause as she mounted the stage. She began her talk about women's independence with an anecdote that illustrated the changes in women's thinking. When she had been a newspaper reporter seven or eight years ago, she had joined a group to petition the Diet to revise Article 5 in the Police Security Regulations, which forbade women from attending political meetings. She solicited the opinion of several upper-class women about the proposed revision, but they had all given the same answer: "I'll have to talk it over with my husband." Later, when she asked them again, they told her that their husbands were against it. "Pitiful, isn't it, that women can't make up their minds without consulting their husbands." But, she went on to say, the influence of Naturalism had brought about sweeping changes in the world of ideas, leading to the creation of organizations such as Seitō. Mrs. Iwano ended her lecture with a warning: "Even if you are intellectually awakened, if you do not have financial independence, you will eventually lose your intellectual freedom and be doomed to live unhappily with a husband who lacks understanding. I became an actress because of my love for the art, of course, but also because I did not wish to be dependent on my husband." Her ideas were clearly reasoned and delivered with great aplomb. By the time Raichō closed the meeting in a barely audible whisper, it had already become dark.[5]

The meeting was all in all a success, but neither Yoshiko nor I was inclined to hold another one. Although it was ostensibly sponsored by Seitō, none of the members except Kiyoko had volunteered, and even Yoshiko had probably spoken out of a sense of duty. I was grateful to the men, but since we were capable of putting out a journal on our own, I felt chagrined to think that we had to depend on their services. I learned afterward that Fukuda Hideko attended the lecture with Ishikawa Sanshirō and Sakamoto Makoto.

The Real New Women's Association

One unexpected result of the lecture meeting was the formation [in March] of the Real New Women's Association (Shin Shinfujinkai) composed of a group of women who had set themselves in opposition to us as the "truly New Women." The newspapers gleefully pounced on this, and did their best to foment rivalry between the two organizations with articles like "Two New Women's Societies" and "The New Women's New Enemy."

The founders of the society were Miyazaki Mitsuko (Toranosuke's wife), Kimura Komako, and Nishikawa Fumiko, all of whom had evidently been disturbed by Iwano Hōmei's talk, or more to the point, by the scuffle between Hōmei and Toranosuke. As Nishikawa Fumiko explained in a newspaper interview:

> We have no choice but to oppose a speech that insults women and encourages divorce and adultery. We thus propose to form a woman's association with genuinely new ideas, hold monthly lecture meetings, and publish a journal.

A public lecture was duly announced for March 16, to be held at the Wakyōgakudō Hall in Kandabashi. I went out of curiosity, without telling anyone on the staff. Compared to our February meeting, the audience was decidedly rowdy. The men hooted and jeered. The main speakers were the three founding members, but with each one going on a different tangent, it was obvious that the meeting had been put together at the last minute. They had no agenda to speak of, and the only reason they had joined forces was to criticize Seitō, or to put it more bluntly, to make a name for themselves by exploiting the public antipathy toward the New Women. The meeting was painfully embarrassing.

At least, Nishikawa Fumiko, a typical housewife, limited her talk to a common-sense discussion of women's issues. Miyazaki Mitsuko, who spoke with the zeal of a practiced soapbox orator, spouted nonsense about the supremacy of the spirit and derided Seitō as a bunch of fallen women. Kimura Komako was an altogether different type. Her liberal use of cosmetics, huge marumage, and theatrical gestures on the stage contributed to the impression that everything about her was boorish and exaggerated. I could not but wonder how three women so disparate in personality, ideas, and background could have gotten together. I wished them well, but I doubted the society would last long.

I headed for the door without waiting for the meeting to end, but someone apparently recognized me, and in a few minutes, Nishikawa Fumiko approached. She was all smiles as she urged me to "stay for a cup of tea." Reluctant to give the impression that I was trying to escape, I followed her to the waiting room. There I found none other than Miyazaki Toranosuke installed on a chair, his whiskered face looking as sallow and undernourished as ever. Just as I suspected, he had masterminded the meeting.

The moment he saw me, he started attacking Hōmei. "Why do you want to associate with someone like him? And tell me, what made you ask him to give a lecture?" He seethed with hatred for the man, so I pressed him: "You seem to detest his philosophy of mystical semianimalism and momentarism,[ix] but have you actually read his book?" He said, "I don't need to read such rubbish." "Well, I find his philosophy highly original, with deep insights drawn from his own experience—it isn't just empty speculation. I read the book with great pleasure, but since you keep saying that you don't have to read it, I see no point in continuing this conversation." And with that, I left the room.

Sakai Toshihiko's wife, Tameko, and Hori Yasuko, Ōsugi Sakae's [common law] wife, were also in the room. They had probably come because they were married to socialists and knew Fumiko and her husband [Nishikawa Kōjirō], who had long been involved with the socialist movement. I knew Yasuko by name—she had recently contributed an essay—but I had never met her. She was a shy, typical Japanese wife, so I wondered what had induced her to marry [a radical socialist like] Ōsugi. But more about those two later.

As I expected, the Real New Women's Association quickly fell upon hard times. To quote the December 15, 1913 *Kokumin shinpō*:

> The society has encountered financial difficulties. As of this report, Nishikawa Fumiko, hitherto in charge of advertisements, acts as she pleases, in total disregard of the other founders. For now, the society is in no condition to challenge Seitō.

Kimura Komako and Miyazaki Mitsuko eventually left the organization, but Fumiko, the only one with a modicum of sense and experience, continued to publish the journal with the help of her husband. The society lasted until the late 1920s, endorsing studies on women's issues, the temperance movement, female suffrage, and whatever else in vogue happened to catch its interest. Noe and I each wrote a review of Fumiko's book, *On the Emancipation of Women*, in the May 1914 issue of *Seitō* [vol. 4, no. 5].[6]

◎ ◎ ◎ ◎ ◎

In March, as a sequel to Okamoto Kanoko's *A Twinge of Jealousy*, volume 2 in the *Seitō Book Series* was published by Tōundō. The book, with a lovely woodblock print by Ogasawara Sadako on the cover, had eighteen

---

[ix] Momentarism (*setsuna shugi*): Hōmei claimed that one should not think about the past or future but live in the fullness of each moment.

authors, virtually the entire roster of our writers: Nogami Yaeko, Ogasawara Sadako, Mizuno Senko, Koganei Kimiko, Araki Ikuko, Ojima Kikuko, Katō Kazuko, Hitomi Naoko, Katō Midori, Iwano Kiyoko, Okada Yachiyo, Kanzaki Tsuneko, Kamichika Ichiko, Mori Shige, Hayashi Chitose, Chino Masako, Fujioka Kazue (Mozume Kazuko), Kiuchi Teiko. A third volume, with my translations of Poe's prose poems, was announced, but was cancelled when, in the face of public criticism, the society shifted its focus to women's issues.

The change in focus did not mean that *Seitō* had deliberately abandoned its original purpose as a forum for women writers. On the contrary, we saw it as a fresh start. At that time we were under constant criticism, and banding together, asserting ourselves, and nurturing our inner resources were even more important. With this in mind, we decided to open the literary study group to a wider audience and hold a series of public lectures, making transcripts available for members living outside of Tokyo.

The announcement on the opening page of the April 1913 issue [vol. 3, no. 4] reads:

An Invitation to Join the Seitō Literary Study Group

History of Philosophy, History of Civilization, History of Fine Arts (Abe Jirō); Sociology, Aesthetics, Literary Criticism (Ikuta Chōkō); History of Modern Thought (Abe Yoshishige); Philosophy of Momentarism (Iwano Hōmei); Modern Drama (Iba Takashi); Changes in Women's Issues (Shimamura Hōgetsu); Modern Continental Literature (Baba Kochō); Theory of Art: Poetry, Fine Arts, Music (Ishii Hakutei and Takamura Kōtarō); Study of Foreign Languages, Emerson (Iwano Hōmei); Dante (Abe Jirō); Modern English Literature (Baba Kochō). The first of the lecture series will be held on April 7 at the Giin Club in Kōjimachi Uchisaiwai-chō. The membership fee is 1 yen a month (1 yen for admission to lecture is separate).

We were certainly ambitious. In order to work exclusively on the new undertaking, Yoshiko gave up her part-time job at the sanatorium and moved back to Tokyo. Lining up the lecturers was easy enough, but finding a hall was a different matter. Yoshiko trudged around for hours looking for a place, only to be turned away; any association with Seitō or the New Women was to be avoided at all cost. She persuaded the people at the YMCA—we had rented the hall in Kanda once before—but they changed their minds: "We realize you're serious and appreciate the work you do, but you know how the public is—" Some of the excuses were laughable. At one place, a church, she had been refused on the ground that "Seitō women indulged in drink and amused themselves in Yoshiwara." At another, "All right, but on the condition that you don't use our premises for assignations." She often came back to the office close to tears, but after wasting nearly a month, she finally succeeded. Her experience drove home to us the magnitude of the public hostility generated by irresponsible journalists.

We were disappointed by the response to the study group. Many expressed interest but said they were worried about what people might think. Others signed up but cancelled their membership. Short of the numbers we had counted on, we reluctantly suspended the series.

It had also come to our attention that Chōkō had begun to distance himself from Seitō. He had been extremely helpful in the beginning, but now he seemed to have developed cold feet, as if he wanted no part of the criticism directed against us. He did not say as much, but we detected a certain evasiveness, and to spare him further embarrassment, we included the following remark [in the Editors' Notes of the May 1913 issue]:

> There seems to be the general impression that Ikuta Chōkō has had a particularly close relation with Seitō. We fear this may cause people to look at him in a false light, and so we would like to make clear that we, the members of Seitō, are solely responsible for matters connected with our organization.

The wording is needlessly cryptic, but this was because we could think of no specific reason for publishing these words. Of course, we may have perceived the situation incorrectly, especially since most of what we knew about Chōkō was filtered through Kōkichi, who was still living at his house. But the coolness in our relationship was not only his doing. In the past, we had consulted him at every turn, but increasingly we had come to rely on our own judgment. Athough he had given us advice about the new study group, we had invited speakers like Ishii Hakutei, Takamura Kōtarō, and Iba Takashi on our own. To compound matters, we had neglected to publish Chōkō's February 15 lecture.[x] Had he been too preoccupied to send back the corrected transcript? Or had he already begun to dissociate himself from Seitō? To this day, I am puzzled.

In any case, his preference had always been for "women like Ophelia." He was sympathetic to women, but when faced with the virulent attacks on Seitō, he may have had mixed feelings. Intellectually, he accepted the New Woman, but emotionally, he preferred the kind of woman who stayed at home quietly attending to her sewing. [In 1921,] Chōkō published a book, *Liberation from Women's Liberation (Fujin kaihō yori no kaihō)*, in which he extolled the virtues of the traditional family, and I responded with an article in the January 1927

---

[x] The lectures by Baba Kochō, Iwano Kiyoko, and Hōmei were published in the March 1913 supplement.

Fujin kōron called "A Rejoinder to Ikuta Chōkō's Argument Against Women's Liberation." Perhaps, from the very beginning, we never saw eye to eye.

Chōkō was also in bad health, and the symptoms of his illness were all too evident on April 14 when Kōkichi held a party at his house to celebrate the acceptance of her screen, *Loquats*, by the Tatsumikai.[xi] Soon after, Kōkichi's parents ordered her home. To the end Chōkō never spoke of his illness. Even after his skin showed undeniable symptoms, he continued to attend meetings and give lectures as if he were unaware of the danger he posed. Much as I felt sorry for him, I sometimes wondered whether he did this out of malice.

Several years later, when I had a baby girl, he came to see me. The child was then two or three, but I remember looking on in horror as he patted her head and said what lovely black hair she had. He seemed reluctant to leave, so I prepared a bowl of noodles and set the tray on the tatami. "My rheumatism's been bothering me lately," he said. "Could you put the bowl on a table?" He handled the chopsticks awkwardly, complaining all the while about his "rheumatism." As soon as he left, I scoured the room with disinfectant, more sad than angry. This was the last time I saw him[; he died in 1935].

After moving out of Chōkō's house, Kōkichi started a magazine with money furnished by her Uncle Chikuha. The first issue of *Saffron* was published by Tōundō in March 1914. Predictably, the magazine was lavishly illustrated, with a cover by Tomimoto Kenkichi, and reflected Kōkichi's exquisite aesthetic sensibilities. The format faintly resembled *Seitō* and in addition, the writers included Kobayashi Katsu and Kamichika Ichiko, as well as nonmembers like Matsui Sumako, Hara Nobuko, and Yagi Sawako.

By this time Kōkichi had stopped coming to the office or to my house. In starting the magazine, she had not asked for my opinion; nor did she send a complimentary copy. Her feelings were no doubt confused and complicated. Despite its splashy debut, the magazine folded within months. Then, in November 1914, without any warning, she married Tomimoto. I was aghast when I saw her wedding picture. She was dressed in a formal long-sleeved kimono and had her hair arranged in the traditional bridal coiffure, just like an ordinary bride who had sacrificed herself on the altar of social convention. My disappointment was especially keen because I had once had such high hopes for her.[7]

⊚ ⊚ ⊚ ⊚ ⊚

Our plans for a larger literary study group had come to naught and circumstances had compelled us to turn to women's issues. We were bound to clash

---

[xi] Chōkō is believed to have suffered from Hansen's disease (leprosy).

with reactionary forces sooner or later, but even so, I regret that it came so soon. The journal had enabled a number of women writers to develop their talents, but had yet to make a significant contribution to literature as a whole. In two or three years, I am certain we would have accomplished much more.

In April [1913], we moved once again, from the room at Mannenzan to a small rented house in Sugamo-chō. Now, for the first time, we had a place to ourselves. Our reasons for moving were threefold: first, Yoshiko had quit her work at the sanatorium and was looking for living quarters; second, even the good-natured abbot had had his fill of reporters descending upon the temple and gently suggested that we leave; third, thanks to Tōundō, we were now assured of a regular monthly income.

The house, near the present Sugamo Station on the National Railway, was newly built and enclosed by a hedge. It became our bastion against the raging fury of the public. Nakano Hatsuko, Kobayashi Katsu, Itō Noe, Yasumochi Yoshiko, and I were responsible for the monthly colloquium and weekly open house; Yoshiko was live-in caretaker. By then, Kōkichi had disappeared from the scene. The memory of my father's anger over the banning of the February issue still rankled, so I asked my friends to visit me at the office. I also wished to spare my mother, for in her usual unobtrusive way, she had always seen to the visitors' comfort. Iwano Kiyoko and Hōmei, who had also moved to the area, often stopped by on their walks.

We had all but settled in when we received a summons from the Censorship Office of the Metropolitan Police Bureau. Hatsuko and Yoshiko reported to the office at ten in the morning on April 25 and were told that a substantial number of passages in the April issue had been deemed "harmful to the time-honored virtues of Japanese women." The men said they were willing to let us off with an oral reprimand this time, but would be less lenient in the future. We were advised to take every precaution not to publish anything that threatened public morals. They did not specify the article, but I knew they must have singled out my essay, "To the Women of the World." I had voiced my doubts about the concept of "good wife and wise mother," objected to the way women were inextricably bound by the institution of marriage, and taken a stand against the irrationality of the present marriage system, especially as defined by the Family Law in the Civil Code.[8] Thus, I was not surprised when *From My Study*, a collection of my essays, was banned upon publication by Tōundō on May 1. The book, my first, included the essay and was judged "destructive to the family system and disruptive of social mores." I removed the essay, changed the cover, revised the title to *At the Locked Window* (*Tozashi aru mado nite*), and had the book published again [the next month].

Seitō was not the only publication to run afoul of the authorities. That same year, *Jogaku sekai* and *Joshi bundan* were banned in May; *Shirakaba*,

Shin shōsetsu, Sunday, and *Ukiyo* in June; *Shūsai bundan, Sunday,* and *Dai-kokumin* in July, all on the charge that they had "disturbed public peace and order." On April 20, the Ministry of Education announced its policy on those women's magazines that espoused ideas inimical to the idea of good wives, wise mothers. To quote from the April 21 *Osaka jiji shinbun*:

> To prevent the minds and morals of men and women students from being corrupted by the subversive ideas and salacious writings of the women who declare themselves New Women, the Ministry of Education has decided to impose certain controls. Upon consultation with the Home Ministry, the Ministry of Education will take appropriate measures in the near future.

Almost certainly, *Seitō* was the primary target. On April 26, the *Yomiuri* published the following statement by Oka, the Home Ministry's chief of public security.

> I am hard put to ascertain whether the proliferation of newspaper articles on the New Woman is a reflection of the changing times or the consequence of Japanese women being unduly swayed by distorted Western ideas about women. I am also at a loss as to whether the assertions are justified or not, though I myself find, to my extreme regret, that some of the articles and novels by these women are indecent and often brazenly employ the most offensive language. I also find regrettable their criticism of women's deference to men and their call for the destruction of traditional morality. Japanese women have always taken pride in their virtuous ways, but if these ideas are disseminated, who is to say what immeasurable harm they will wreak on family and society?

The next day, the same newspaper carried an article criticizing the government policy on women's magazines.

> It has long been my hope that the regulation of speech and thought would be based on a correct understanding and thorough assessment of a given situation, but rarely has this been the case. I find it deeply regrettable that in comparison to the number of warnings issued to those who are one step ahead of the times, only a negligible number of warnings has been issued to those who are one, ten, or even a hundred steps behind the times.

The country in the meantime was going through a series of political upheavals. The second Saionji cabinet had fallen the previous December when the army refused to name a replacement for General Uehara Yūsaku, who resigned after his request for two additional regiments was denied.

General Yamagata Aritomo, the leader of the so-called Chōshū clique, was known to have been behind this. Public opposition to army influence had just gathered strength when General Katsura Tarō, the new prime minister [who belonged to the same clique], invoked an imperial rescript to form the next cabinet. In protest, the Association to Protect Constitutional Government, formed in December by journalists and the Seiyūkai and Kokumintō parties, held nationwide rallies. [To counter this, Katsura announced he would form his own party, and used another rescript to prorogue the Diet.] The Diet reconvened on February 5; Ozaki Yukio (Seiyūkai) delivered his famous speech demanding that Katsura be impeached: "The man barricades himself behind the throne and uses imperial rescripts as bullets to attack his political enemies." His speech led to an adjournment, and when the Diet reconvened five days later, thousands of demonstrators surrounded the building and clashed with the police while others stormed the office of the pro-government *Kokumin shinbun* newspaper and set fire to police boxes. Katsura resigned, and on the 20th, Yamamoto Gonnohyōe was named to form a new cabinet.

The so-called Taishō Political Crisis energized the forces of political democracy and ushered in a new age, but nothing seemed to change as far as the public attitude toward the New Women was concerned. The newspapers continued to make outrageous charges, and among the most ridiculous was an article in the January 15 *Niroku shinpō* called "Sorting Women Writers."

Beginning with Hiratsuka Haruko, the seventy-odd members of Seitō—including Nakano Hatsuko, Araki Ikuko, Kanzaki Tsuneko, Sakuma Tokiko, Iwano Kiyoko, Sugimoto Masao, Kitahara Sueko, Ogasawara Sadako, Inoue Tamiko, Kobayashi Katsu, Otake Kazue (Kōkichi), and Kiuchi Teiko—are all women who have failed to find husbands, who have been driven to despair by men, or who aspire to be immoral women like Yūran.[xii] They claim that they can do everything that men can, and, as is well known, they dine at restaurants and houses of ill repute, ensnare men with their charms, and then ruthlessly shove them away. They think nothing of having physical contact with the opposite sex, and if by chance they marry and get bored, they say they can always marry someone else. Some even coolly profess in public that the second marriage is better than the first. Not that Hiratsuka or Otake would in any case ever contemplate marriage.

---

xii Honjō Yūran was a graduate of the Meiji Girls' School who was known for her wit and checkered career. In turn an actress, owner of a café, *rakugo* raconteur, and would-be prostitute in Yoshiwara (none of the houses would hire her on the ground that she was too educated), she claimed to have seduced more than 90 men and eventually hoped to reach 100.

The article in the January 31 *San'yō shinpō* ("Raichō and Kōkichi: Recent News About the New Women") was even more preposterous:

Miss Raichō resides in Nishikata-machi in Hongō, Tokyo, under the vigilant gaze of her strict father, a decidedly old-fashioned type. She sits in her study waiting for a visitor. She is not communing with the muse of poetry but resigned to meditating according to the Okada Method of Quiet Sitting. With one eye closed, she is rapt in contemplation, but suddenly opens both eyes and shouts "Kwatsu!" What does she see but a man, a phantasm of her basest instincts. Of late Miss Raichō has been taking lessons in judo, that most unladylike of sports, and she is reputed to be able to trounce a man with the utmost ease. Having done her part at a meeting of the Movement to Protect Constitutional Government, she now agitates for women's rights. Who knows but she may knock down the first person who dares to oppose her.

Leaders in the field of women's education joined the chorus of criticism. Some of the most strident were Shimoda Utako, Hatoyama Haruko, Kaetsu Takako, and Tsuda Umeko, all of whom, I daresay, had never looked at a copy of *Seitō*. Even Naruse Jinzō, the president of my alma mater, saw fit to criticize us in "New Trends in Women's Education Abroad," an article he wrote for the April *Chūō kōron* soon after his return from an inspection tour of women's schools in Europe and the United States:

I cannot pretend to know the fundamental principles nor the future direction of that newly emerging phenomenon in Japan called the New Woman, especially since I have been out of the country for a while. But from what I hear, their ways are akin to a pathological mania. Unacquainted as I am with the particulars of the situation, I shall refrain from making any meddlesome remarks, but I can say this much: some of the women are quite intelligent, but lack common sense. Their only concern is for themselves, and they have no consideration for their parents or family. Indeed, I am of the opinion that they are physiologically defective.

Naruse's remarks in an interview with the *Otaru shinbun* also made me wonder if this was the same man who had once been such a passionate advocate of women's higher education:

I understand that in Japan there are a number of self-proclaimed New Women who publish their writings in magazines, hold public lectures, and buy the favors of prostitutes. This sort of behavior can be seen in a small segment of Western women, but Western women are in general well behaved and would never interrupt a family member who is conversing with a guest. In the United

States, a woman might flatter a guest but would never act in the unladylike manner favored by the New Women in Japan.... In short, women's education abroad is rote and mechanical. The situation is far better in our country, where a woman's education is based squarely on the ideology of good wives and wise mothers and the goal of developing moral character. ("President Naruse of Japan Women's College Speaks on the New Woman," March 10)

My essay "To the Women of Today" was in one sense a challenge to these utterly misinformed educators, and in fact I referred to Naruse's interview.

I have read only one of his articles in an unreliable newspaper and have not seen President Naruse for a while, so I may be speaking too rashly of my feeling when I confess that I was deeply disappointed to hear these words from an educator I have long respected. Has President Naruse, once so zealous and ahead of his time, possibly grown senile? It saddens me to think that the elderly feel they have to cater to the lowest level of public opinion.

The absurd and malicious slurs on the New Women reached their peak from the end of 1912 to the middle of 1913, just before we put out our second anniversary issue. But there was one sympathetic voice—Sugimura Sojinkan, a writer on the *Asahi* staff. I shall quote from "In Defense of the New Women," his article in the April *Chūō kōron*.

Among the weak and downtrodden in present-day Japan, there are none so oppressed as women, and of these, none are as oppressed as the New Women. When I say "oppressed," I mean bullied and belittled without rhyme or reason, just as a daughter-in-law might be hounded by a spiteful mother-in-law. I can understand criticizing a person face to face or dealing a lethal blow to someone who doesn't deserve to exist. But what I cannot abide is the kind of niggardly criticism that derides a person with jeers and innuendoes. I would like to ask my esteemed readers: What is so wrong with being a New Woman?

The author goes on to express his sympathy for actresses, musicians, members of Seitō, and others labeled New Women. He then admonishes his fellow journalists for their bad taste, but says nothing about the actual hardships experienced by the New Women.

I was also surprised to receive a warm and humorous letter of encouragement from Tanimoto Tomeri (Rian), a philosopher and educator in the Kansai area. I had never met him, but was cheered by his sympathetic remarks about the New Woman. I have mentioned receiving threats, but I cannot resist quoting the one sent to the office by the "White Caps."

To Iwano Kiyoko, Hayashi Chitose, Itō Noe, Araki Ikuko: By spreading narrow-minded and "hysterical" ideas, you seek to oppose and destroy society.... The past and present were built by strong people, that is to say, by men.... You constantly demand rights for women, but you fail to perform your duties. This only proves that you are "lower than the lowest human being," a trait common to women and children alike. Even though you try to outdo men by guzzling cheap wine and indulging in luxuries, you have no firm ideas or vision to speak of. What you have is merely a vain desire to attract public attention with your eccentric words and behavior. You sate your lower appetites by espousing Iwano Hōmei's mystical semianimalism.... You are to society what fleas and mosquitoes are to human beings. The harm you inflict is negligible but harmful nevertheless. Therefore, resorting to the following methods, we shall start by killing the four of you.

Rambling and riddled with misspellings, the threat caused more merriment than alarm. I could understand Kiyoko, Noe, and Ikuko, but why Chitose? And why not me, the arch villain?[9]

In June, *Taiyō* and *Chūō kōron* each brought out special issues on women: "Recent Issues Concerning Women" and "Government Controls on New Ideas Circulating Among Women." The next month, *Chūō kōron* published another special issue called "The Woman Question." The issue included thumbnail sketches about me by Satō Haruo, Nishimura Yōkichi, Baba Kochō, Yosano Akiko, Iwano Hōmei, and others.[10]

The educated public had finally begun to treat women's issues as a subject of serious inquiry, but at Seitō, most of the members who aspired to be professional writers remained indifferent, or at least, seemed to think that the subject had no direct bearing on their private lives. Perhaps this was to be expected, given the original impetus of the journal. No less disappointing was the lack of response to my various writings. "I Am a New Woman," "To the Women of the World," *At the Locked Window*, the preface to my translation of Key's *Love and Marriage*—all these had attracted public attention but elicited barely a murmur from the members. I felt a nagging sense of isolation and futility, as though I were wrestling with myself. So, whenever I felt a need to reflect and replenish my inner self, I spent the morning reading about women's issues at the Ueno Library and then headed straight for Kaizenji. The place was deserted except for the times when Shaku Sōen-rōshi came from Kamakura to give the monthly sesshin for Hitotsubashi students. I claimed the room overlooking the lotus pond, and after I had finished meditating, I worked on a manuscript using a sutra stand as a desk.

My friend Shūgaku was still resident abbot. I saw him from time to time, but he never referred to what had happened between us and remained calm and detached, as befitted a man of his training and discipline. We did not talk about Seitō, and even when the society came under intense attack, neither he nor I brought up the subject. As a Zen monk, he probably had no interest in women's magazines. When Kōkichi or Yoshiko occasionally came to see me at the temple, he greeted them warmly and told a younger monk to order some food from a neighborhood restaurant. He was fond of drink, and happily flushed, he regaled us with stories that were more entertaining than those at second-rate yose halls. Before we knew it, it would be too late to catch the last trolley, and when that happened, we spent the night at the temple. Shūgaku liked having people around him, and seemed to enjoy my friends' company.

I See Okumura Again

[I shall now go back several months in my narrative.] The days and weeks slipped by, but time had not dimmed the memory of Okumura, who vanished after sending his farewell note. What I felt was not a hopeless attachment so much as a lingering sense of puzzlement. His note about the swallow—did it reflect his true feelings? I had no way of finding out, but I wanted to know. Even though he had been the one to end the relationship, I did not think that everything was over, and deep in my heart, I cherished a faint hope.

Fate smiled on us, and I saw him again. By an ironic turn of chance, Kōkichi was the one to lead me to him. She went with Itō Noe to visit the actor Kamiyama Sōjin and heard that Okumura was in the Modern Theater Company's production of *Faust*, which was due to open at the Imperial Theater on March 27 [1913] and would continue until the end of the month. She came to see me immediately, her face glowing with pride and pleasure, as if she had completely forgotten that her repeated threats had been partly responsible for his departure. As contradictory as ever, she said, "Oh, why don't you go and see him?" I could hardly take offense.

The news about Okumura sent my heart swirling. Barely able to contain my excitement, I went on the opening night—I had already been given a ticket. The cast of the production, the first in Japan, featured Kamiyama Sōjin as Faust, Iba Takashi as Mephistopheles, Kinugawa Kujaku as Gretchen, and the singers Harada Jun, Shimizu Kintarō, and Nanbu Kunihiko. Okumura was one of the students singing in the scene at Auerbach's Cellar.

The four-tiered theater, with the attendance said to be the largest since its founding, was filled to capacity. Okumura threw himself into his role, and just watching him made me happy. I took a small bouquet of red roses backstage during intermission to let him know I had come, but I left without seeing him.

As Okumura told me later, his decision to be in the play had been fortuitous and quite typical of him. Soon after writing the farewell letter the previous fall, he had gone to see Shaw's *Twentieth Century* at the Yūrakuza and during intermission noticed a handsome young man walking toward him in the lobby. Unusually tall and muscular, with a wide forehead, prominent nose, and chiseled features, the man looked more like a foreigner than a Japanese. Since Okumura kept staring at him, the young man asked, "Why are you staring at me?" and they had become friends.

Harada Jun was a professional singer, the son of a court physician, and about ten years older than Okumura. Like so many who grew up in downtown Tokyo, he was openhearted and sociable, a born conversationalist. Okumura was shy, but the two got along from the start, and in late November, Harada suggested they take a trip to the southern Chiba coast. They stayed at a fishing village, and Okumura sketched and painted while Harada went down to the rocky beach and faced the crashing waves, practicing the tenor parts for *Rigoletto* and *La Traviata*. The villagers, with whom Harada quickly made friends, kept the two supplied with fresh fish and vegetables.

When they were enjoying this idyllic existence, a telegram arrived, announcing that rehearsals for *Faust* were about to begin and Harada was to return to Tokyo immediately. Harada asked Okumura if he was interested in the theater. He said yes—he also needed money—took a test, and was hired.

The play was a great success, and on May 1, the company left for Osaka to perform at the Kitahama Teikokuza for ten days. Okumura, who happened to read in the arts column of the *Osaka Asahi* that I was ill, sent a postcard. I was overjoyed, for I had been half hoping that he would send a note acknowledging the bouquet of flowers. Eager to send a reply, I went to the offices of the Modern Theater Company and the poetry magazine *Shiika* to get his address. I was given Niizuma Kan's address in Ōtsuka, and assuming that Okumura lived with him, I sent a letter in care of Niizuma, together with a copy of my book, *At the Locked Window*.

When Okumura returned to Tokyo in early June, he came to the house, but instead of coming inside, he left a letter in the mailbox. The "young swallow" had returned in "due season," but not because of my letter, for, as I found out later, Niizuma had deliberately withheld it from him.

I was indescribably happy but also disappointed that Okumura had made no attempt to see me. I dashed off a note: "For you, the gates of the house are always open." I also asked him to send my apologies to Niizuma, who for some reason had come to see me earlier, but had not been invited in, since we had never been formally introduced.

Okumura came to the house again. Unfortunately, I was out, but two or three days later, we were finally able to meet again. It was an evening after the rainy season had begun, and the clouds were hanging low in the darkening sky. We sat facing each other in my study. He looked at me shyly, his gaze more eloquent than words could convey, and I, in turn, looked into his eyes—pure and earnest, yet with a tinge of melancholy—and embraced him in my heart with all my being. Any bitterness or doubt about the letter vanished in that moment. There was no need to speak, for we were now bound by a force beyond our control.

As it happened, that very morning I had received the strangest letter from Niizuma: "I have read the letter you sent to Okumura.... I regard him as my cherished younger brother.... I was the one who wrote the letter about the young swallow. Okumura merely wrote the fair copy.... When you asked for his address at the *Shiika* office, I was hoping you would write to me instead and told them to give my address." The letter, scrawled on cheap, tasteless stationery, left me thoroughly disgusted. I decided to ignore it, and of course did not mention it to Okumura that evening.

In his letter Niizuma had also hinted at a homosexual relationship with Okumura. Some time later, when I asked Okumura about this, he said there had been nothing of the sort, but apparently, as soon as Niizuma learned about our relationship, he once made an overture of that nature. The man probably resented having a good friend taken away, but more than that, I am certain he was hoping to drive a wedge between us and claim me for himself. As I will relate later, he stooped to something even more odious.

Late in June, soon after our reunion, I asked Okumura to join me on a trip to Mount Akagi [in Gunma Prefecture]. I had wanted to go ever since I heard about it from Naganuma Chieko and had just received the royalties from my book. The two of us went alone.

The mountain, a verdant green and cloaked with wild azaleas, seemed to be welcoming us with a graceful, feminine charm. The brilliant sun and cloudless sky, the birdsong, the sweet scent of flowers and trees, the soaring heights, the mirrorlike lake—surrounded by nature's infinite grandeur, we felt no need for a ceremony to formalize our union. We rowed out to a small island in the middle of the lake, and there, on a thick carpet of ancient moss and ferns, we vowed our undying love for each other.

Okumura, who had brought his paints and brushes, sketched the azalea-covered slopes, white birch forest, and herd of grazing cows. He left for Tokyo first to attend rehearsals for Shaw's *Arms and the Man*, and I stayed behind at an inn to finish a manuscript. The next day, I received a postcard with two poems he had written while waiting for the train. "Of the sorrow of parting even for a moment / A cuckoo cries deep in the mountains." "I looked back and saw a patch of sky blue / Were they forget-me-nots to remind me of you all alone?"

Two days later, I unexpectedly received a letter from Niizuma. Forwarded from Tokyo, it was marked "Urgent, Personal" in bright red. "If you are determined to ignore me," he wrote, "I shall have to make public everything I know about you and Okumura, including the letters you sent him." I knew the man was too stupid to realize that I was not the sort to be intimidated by threats of exposure, but even so I was outraged. He was despicable, beyond contempt. I could not bear to think that someone so vile considered himself Okumura's friend. Until then, I had tried to deflect my anger by ignoring him, but the letter was so combative and offensive that I was ready to explode. Never, before or since, have I been so infuriated.

I immediately took up my pen and wrote a long letter. I told him that on no account was he to interfere with our love, and that come what may, Okumura and I were determined to overcome all obstacles. I wrote the letter with the full intention of making it public and as soon as I was finished, I sent it to the Seitō office. "Excerpts from a Letter" was published in the September issue [vol. 3, no. 9]. I took this step not only to avoid answering Niizuma directly but also to speak for the countless numbers of young men and women who were held down by outmoded morality and family pressure. I wanted to urge them to rise up and affirm their right and freedom to love.[11]

Back in Tokyo, I showed Okumura the letter from Niizuma. He was dumbfounded, especially since he had considered him his friend. He went to Niizuma's house, retrieved the letters and books I had sent him, collected his personal belongings, and never spoke to him again.

I Move Out of My House

Okumura had taken complete possession of my heart. When I asked him to accompany me on the trip, my feelings had not been that intense, but since our stay on the mountain, I had become convinced that we belonged to each other and were destined to share life's journey. For the first time in my life, I had fallen passionately in love, and with a man who was big and tall but like a child in his innocence and purity of heart. Part of my love sprang from a maternal instinct, for whenever I saw him, I worried and wondered whether he was capable of making his way in the world. For, in truth, Okumura was naïve, one might say even feckless, and like a sister looking after a younger brother, I felt I had to protect him. As it was, I had already taken the lead, and indeed found that I had no other choice.

Okumura moved to Harada Jun's lodgings in Tsukiji Minami Odawara-chō. We arranged to meet at my study or some other place and also exchanged letters. But we could not stand being apart for more than two or three days, so to be closer, he moved to Koishikawa Hara-machi. Each time he came, he brought a picture he had just finished and left it with me until he had painted another one.

I do not know what my mother made of Okumura's visits, but she kept her thoughts to herself and never objected. The timing presented a problem, however. He invariably came in the evening, just when the family was eating together in the dining room, and when I asked the maid to show him to my study, I sensed everyone stiffening in disapproval. The maid always answered the door, so my mother never actually saw Okumura, but as his visits grew more frequent, her vigilance became obvious.

To make matters worse, Okumura was the sort of person who never knew when to leave. He stayed in my study well into the night, and since we were happy just being together, whether we were talking or not, we would lose track of the time. My mother had good reason to be worried. She had long been entrusted with the children's upbringing, and now her grown-up daughter was staying up late with a male visitor in her room. One night, I was quite sure someone was standing in the hall outside my room. She did not say a word, but I knew what she was feeling, and so I wondered if the time had come for me to tell my parents everything about us and move out of the house.

From summer into autumn, Okumura and I walked the entire day, going wherever our fancy took us. In contrast to the situation today, at that time there were secluded spots all over Tokyo: Dōkanyama, Nippori, Tabata, Asu-kayama, the Koishikawa Botanical Garden. We stopped at a shop now and then for a bowl of sweet azuki bean soup or rice cakes, and to my amazement, Okumura kept asking for seconds like a child. I imagine we made an odd couple—a tall, long-haired youth walking hand in hand with a tiny woman dressed like a student in kimono and hakama—but we were too happy in each other's company to care.

One afternoon in September, on a sudden impulse, I decided to take Okumura to Kaizenji. I had never mentioned the temple to him, but the place was like a second home to me, and I wanted him to see it and meet my friend Shūgaku.

The visit was a big mistake. I initially thought of dropping a casual remark like, "He was my first lover, you know," but when I saw the expression on Okumura's face, I quickly changed my mind. In fact, he became irritated the moment I told him that we were going to Kaizenji. He had never associated me with a Buddhist temple, and once we arrived, I could see that he felt completely out of place. By contrast, Shūgaku, who had probably guessed our relationship, was very friendly, ordering food and sake and doing his best to make Okumura feel at home. But Okumura was a painter and artist, not like the college students Shūgaku usually saw. He was offended by Shūgaku's eagerness to please, his endless puns and witticisms, his self-satisfied manner. And worse, Shūgaku and I drank and bantered like old friends.

Okumura later described Shūgaku in his novel *Chance Encounter*:

> As far as Hiroshi [the protagonist] was concerned, the priest, at least ten years older, lived in another world. Dark-skinned and coarse looking, he was obviously a country bumpkin, someone who'd worked his way up from a lowly attendant. His one distinguishing feature, a big, lumpy pug nose, made him look coarser still. He had a jovial laugh, but his eyes were like a shrike's, shifty and contemptuous. Hiroshi disliked him at first sight. There was nothing about the man that appealed to him.

I can see why Okumura was repelled. Shūgaku was undeniably ugly, but that was his charm. Okumura watched us in sullen silence, and before we realized it, he had left the room. I thought he would enjoy the visit; instead, I had hurt his feelings and made him sad and angry.

Yet Shūgaku and I were very fond of each other. But ours was no ordinary relationship. There were no conditions attached, and we asked nothing of each other. By its very nature and substance, my love for Shūgaku was totally different from the love I bore for Okumura. To me, there was no contradiction in loving two men at the same time, but I also knew that Okumura would never understand or accept this. Explanations would not do any good; he would suffer no matter what.

After the visit, I gradually withdrew from the temple. I wish things had turned out differently, but I could not bear to see Okumura suffer. I had to choose one or the other, and he had first claim. (I stopped seeing Shūgaku but continued to hear about him from Kimura Masako until he died in middle age.)[12]

⊚ ⊚ ⊚ ⊚ ⊚

By now, I had more or less made up my mind to move out of the house. I also felt I should meet Okumura's mother, if only because she seemed unnaturally cold and unfeeling toward her son. She had not sent money for several months, and Okumura not only had given up his classes but also was using the same canvas over and over. Also, despite repeated requests, she did not send one word of motherly sympathy or encouragement. Nor did the problem seem to be merely a matter of money. A visit would also give me the chance to explain my feelings for her son and reach some kind of understanding.

I went to Fujisawa in late autumn. Although I knew the family lived near the Yugyōji temple, I did not want to go unannounced and take his father by surprise—he was in his eighties and blind—so I sent a message from the inn near the station and asked his mother to come over.

She struck me at once as the typical goodhearted countrywoman. She was small and spare—I wondered how she could be the mother of such a big son—but her thick, glossy black hair, which was twisted casually in a sokuhatsu much too large for her age, was just like her son's. The pucker on her upper lip also was exactly the same. She had a direct, if brusque manner, and though we were meeting for the first time, she seemed quite willing to talk candidly about the family. "So you see, we really can't do anything for our son. We thought that if worse came to worst, he could always come home. I'm embarrassed to say this, but I am completely preoccupied with taking care of my blind husband. We would be grateful if you looked after our son."

She kept saying this, as if she assumed I would take complete responsibility for her son. I was wearing a somber kimono and hakama, so she may have thought I was much older. Also, while I had not mentioned marriage—I had yet to decide whether I would live with Okumura—the simple and honest woman may have sensed how much I loved her childlike son and wanted to care for him like a mother or older sister.

As she was about to leave, she suddenly started praising her son with a look of relief and satisfaction on her face. "Oh, he was such a good little boy. When he was a baby, people would say he was just like a jewel." Smiling for the first time, she repeated, "Yes, just like a jewel."

Not long after my visit, a large wicker traveling case arrived at Okumura's lodgings. Inside was a miscellaneous collection of antiques and curios, among them a Bunchō landscape, a painting of plum blossoms by Ganku, a couple of scrolls, and old woodblock prints. Okumura remembered seeing the objects in the storeroom, and though there was no accompanying note, he knew that these things were all his parents could offer and were meant to be sold.

Okumura told me later that he came from a samurai family. His grandfather had been in service to the daimyo of Kaga, but on losing his stipend at the time of the Meiji Restoration, he went to Hokkaido to work for the Bureau of Land Development. His son Ichitarō, who had built a sizeable fortune (family documents indicate that he traded in lumber and clothes), decided to retire to a warmer place when he turned forty, about the time of Okumura's older sister's birth. He moved to Fujisawa, his second wife's home, and was already in his early sixties when Okumura was born twenty years later.

The father was apparently good-natured to a fault. He agreed to cosign a relative's loan and suffered a great loss, but nonetheless continued to lend money to friends and relatives and was rarely repaid. Long afflicted with an eye disease, he lost his sight when Okumura was in second grade. From that early period, Okumura stood for his father, writing letters, meeting with relatives and neighbors, and attending to other domestic affairs.

Okumura had always wanted to be an artist, but his father, an ardent devotee of the Hokke sect of Buddhism, hoped his son would enter the priesthood. The conflict between father and son went on for several years, and finally, in the spring of his nineteenth year, Okumura left for Tokyo without his father's permission and enrolled at the studio of Ōshita Tōjirō, a well-regarded watercolor artist. His father eventually adopted a child and made sure that he became a priest.

I had yet to move out. Okumura still came to the house, and I began visiting him at his lodgings. In late autumn, his landlady suddenly asked him to leave. A refined and elderly widow who rented out rooms to supplement her income, she had no doubt read about us in the newspapers and decided that a controversial "New Woman" frequenting her house could only cause trouble. She had to think of her relative—a young girl staying with her to help out. We were caught in a bind: Okumura's visits were causing tension at home, and if I continued my visits, he would have to move elsewhere.

The time had come for me to leave home. I had been thinking about such a change ever since I finished college and kept procrastinating, but I was finally ready. My love for Okumura gave me the courage to make the break, though I also knew it would not be easy. My home had been a virtual prison, albeit an intangible one, but also a haven of repose and comfort. Not only that: I had no clear idea what it would be like to live with Okumura. I tired easily, and I treasured my privacy. Would I be able to bear the strain? Would I be able to handle both my work and domestic duties? I was not at all confident.

More crucial, I was not thinking of marriage in the conventional sense since I was opposed to the institution of marriage based on the present family system. Our life together would be an adventure, a leap into the unknown; our way of thinking and our living arrangements could well change in the future. For the time being, we had to be steadfast in our love for each other and see where life led us.

There remained one last worry, and that was Okumura himself. Diffident and self-effacing, he lacked the kind of ambition usually sought in a man. Again, I may have been asking too much of someone his age; he was incapable of asserting his opinions and in this sense was not someone I could always rely on.[xiii]

I decided to draw up a list of about eight questions and ask him to go over them carefully before giving me his answers. This took considerable courage

---

[xiii] By Japanese count, Okumura (b. October 4, 1891) was 23 and Raicho 28.

on my part, for I knew he would not like the tone. He would feel that I was throwing cold water on his dreams. But I felt it was for our own good; we had to make things absolutely clear. The questions were more or less as follows:

One: No matter how many hardships we face, are you prepared to stay by my side and persevere? No matter how much society denounces us, jeers at us, and puts pressure on us, are you confident that you won't run away?

Two: What would you do if I were to refuse to marry you, that is, reject the kind of relationship between man and woman defined by the present marriage system?

Three: How would you respond if I said I won't marry you but am willing to live with you?

Four: How would you react if I said that for the sake of our love and in order to maintain our freedom to work as we desire, we should live apart?

Five: What would you do if I said I loved you and felt physical desire for you but did not want children? (I wrote this knowing that Okumura was fond of children.)

Six: Have you given any thought to our financial prospects?

Okumura's answers were typical of him—natural, accepting, unmindful of convention. These qualities, I knew, were his greatest strengths. The matter settled, I prepared to move out.[13]

On New Year's Eve, we shared a meal at Maison Kōnosu, our favorite haunt.[xiv] Beyond the glass windows, the lamps cast a shimmering light on the dark river, adding to the poignancy of the occasion. With the coming of the New Year [1914], I would be leaving home. What the future held, neither of us knew. We were about to embark on a journey; the winds would surely bless our love and take us safely to whatever destination lay ahead. Sweet, happy thoughts, but sobering, too.

◎ ◎ ◎ ◎ ◎

At the same time that my love for Okumura was intensifying, I was translating Key's *Love and Marriage*. The work had taken on a greater urgency beyond my original intention, which was to introduce her ideas. It was a period when I myself was coming to grips with the meaning of love and marriage, and so her ideas shed a beacon of light on an unexplored world. Indeed, her thoughts were like a revelation from on high. Because of my love for Okumura, I was personally experiencing what she wrote about love, and I was achieving a

---

[xiv] The chronology leaps ahead three months.

deeper understanding of her insights. For me, her book was a treasure trove, a peerless primer on love. There was first of all the acuity of her observations about love and the breadth of her knowledge. She was widely read in literature; her prose style was dazzling. Tracing the course of love in all its permutations, she described the ways in which women differed from men in their sexual feelings. Since I was ignorant to begin with, there was no limit to what Key could teach me about love.

I had hitherto thought of love and marriage as two separate entities. I recognized the value of love, but I had always either had negative feelings about marriage or dismissed it categorically. Key, on the other hand, claimed that love and marriage existed in perfect harmony, that perfect love united the spiritual and emotive elements of love with the corporeal and sensual. In other words, she presented a monistic view that "betrayed neither the spirit nor the senses." She believed that love enhanced a person's private life by satisfying the quest for happiness and by encouraging the reproduction of the species, which in turn contributed to the species' improvement. In short, love served humankind. Love between man and woman bound together egotism and altruism, acted as the nexus for the present and the future, and ultimately transcended the individual.

Key then claimed that giving birth to a child and raising it to be healthy and intelligent was a sacred act of creation that surpassed the making of ordinary objects. Reproduction was sacred, and motherhood was to be respected and revered. Thus, women were entitled to special rights, wholly apart from equal rights with men. She criticized Mill's *The Subjugation of Women* for merely advocating the rights of women as citizens. He had neglected their right to love and motherhood—surely a vital component of their emancipation—and their need for freedom from religious and social oppression. I agreed with her completely.

Key, a Swedish woman who came of age during the late 1800s, never married or had children. This greatly puzzled me, since she wrote with such sensitivity about love and motherhood. In my own case, without reading Key, I doubt that I would have lived with a man, let alone had children, even if I had been in love. I would have chosen to remain single all my life and my love for Okumura would have made no difference. In this respect, my encounter with Key had a profound impact. The effect was not as fundamentally transforming as kenshō, but was profound nevertheless. Later, after I began living with Okumura and became a mother, I was even more appreciative of her plea for the protection of motherhood and recognition of the social significance of bearing and educating children.

On the eve of World War I, Key's life-affirming ideas on the importance of bearing children and raising a healthier younger generation were welcomed enthusiastically by intellectuals in Germany. She was consequently seen as militaristic and reactionary, but this is a complete misinterpretation of her ideas. It is clear from reading her books—*Love and Marriage; The Century of the Child; The Renaissance of Motherhood; Women's Movements; War, Peace, and the Future*—that she was a pacifist opposed to war and far from reactionary in her ideas about women's emancipation. At the core of her thought is the belief that women will not be truly liberated until mother-hood is honored by society and the rights of mothers are given full recogni-tion. To be sure, due to certain historical exigencies, some of her ideas have become dated and irrelevant, but even so, I believe that she deserves a fresh and impartial evaluation.

The supplement of the May 1913 issue carried a translation of one of the chapters in *Love and Marriage*. It appeared under Noe's name but was trans-lated by Tsuji. The first installment of "The Shadow of an Echo," another piece under her name in the same issue, was also translated by Tsuji.[14]

Itō Noe

Since joining Seitō, Noe had made herself indispensable. She still looked like a pert country girl, with her petite figure and her bright red half-obi neatly tied, but she was quick to learn. Although Tsuji may have helped her, her book reviews were unfailingly to the point. While cheerful and good-humored, she was the first person to lose her temper if anyone attacked Seitō. For that mat-ter, I have never met anyone who could work herself up to such a pitch of indignation. Unable to ignore the criticism, she would slam the offending publication on the table, grab her pen, and dash off a letter to the publisher. Or, she would tuck the half-read magazine under her arm and march out of the office saying, "I'm going home to write something. I'll give them a piece of my mind!" I used to caution her about not writing in haste, since I knew her emotions could get the better of her and prevent her from thinking things through. She wrote quickly, often on the spot, but if anyone challenged her logic, she was at a loss to explain her ideas. For Noe, emotion and action were one, giving rise to an explosive energy that I could only envy.

Kōkichi had never shown the same kind of violent reaction to criticism about Seitō nor Noe's feisty determination to fight to the bitter end. In con-trast, Kōkichi was curiously old-fashioned in some of her ideas and apt to be querulous and on the defensive. Of the three teenaged girls at the office, Kobayashi Katsu was the most mature, sensible, and calm. When everyone else was in a flurry of excitement, she looked on indulgently with a bemused smile, thinking no doubt about her next story about the vanishing downtown district. Each girl was different in her own way, but I pinned my highest hopes on the untamed, passionate, and focused Noe.

To everyone's surprise, Noe, the youngest looking, became pregnant. Obtuse as ever about these matters, I only realized the true nature of her relationship with Tsuji when I saw her swelling abdomen. She never talked about him, and I had somehow assumed that theirs was a simple friendship. Noe may have confided in someone else, but to me, she had not once mentioned that they were lovers.

I was not the only one who was under the impression that Noe was still an innocent young girl. Earlier in the summer, Kimura Sōta, a young man who wrote for a magazine called *Fuyūzan (Fusain)*, had fallen in love with her, and since he thought she was single—they met only once—he bombarded her with at least four or five letters in the space of ten days. Already pregnant, Noe was deeply disturbed, and wrote about her conflicted feelings in the August issue ("Turmoil," vol. 3, no. 8; my review of the article appears in the November issue).[15]

In September, Noe gave birth to a boy. She came back to the office soon after, bringing the baby with her. She worked with the baby sleeping by her side, but once in while, it would let out a piercing cry. The baby, named Makoto, was very sweet, with big, round eyes, and became a favorite in the all-female office. Still, the distraction was annoying.

Noe seemed not to notice this, and in other ways was just as insensitive. The baby, for instance, began to crawl and had accidents on the tatami, but she merely gave a perfunctory swipe with a diaper. Or she went to the verandah and let the baby empty its bowels right into the garden. She never bothered to clean up, and so Yoshiko, grumbling and complaining, had to attend to the mess.

At her home, Noe was just as oblivious of filth or dirt. Later, [when Okumura and I lived near her,] I often saw her sweep the trash into the garden, which already resembled a garbage heap. I suppose there was a kind of virtue in being able to go about one's business undisturbed by petty concerns, and in this respect, Tsuji was well trained and in complete accord with Noe. When she was writing, too, even with the baby fussing and squalling beside her, she worked at top speed, using the wooden hibachi cover as a pad. Her energy and capacity to remain unfazed were nothing short of amazing.

Tsuji's mother, sister, and brother-in-law were living with them at the time. He and Noe had a tiny two-mat room [and although he had been fired from his teaching job,] he made no attempt to find work. They were desperately poor, barely able to pay the midwife and other expenses for the baby. But Noe was radiantly happy, exulting in Tsuji's love. Her shabby appearance was the least of her worries; her fair complexion and jet black hair more than made up for it.

In 1913, in addition to Key's *Love and Marriage*, we published [partial] translations of works by Western feminists: Emma Goldman's "On the Tragedy of

Women's Emancipation" [vol. 3, no. 9] and "Minority and Majority" [vol. 3, no. 11]; Olive Schreiner's "Dreams" [vol. 3, no. 11] and "God's Gifts to Men" [vol. 3, no. 12]. The translations of Goldman's essays appear under Noe's name, but were actually done by Tsuji, who was interested in women's issues. To educate Noe, he was also translating other works by Goldman and a biography about her. Noe's encounter with the intrepid Russian-born anarchist turned out to be as momentous as my encounter with Key.

Yamada Waka

The South African writer Olive Schreiner (1855–1920) was relatively unknown in Japan, and I came across her writings quite by chance. In late September or early October, I received a package from Ōsugi Sakae.[xv] He was then the editor of *Modern Thought* (*Kindai shisō*), and though we had never met, we regularly exchanged complimentary copies. Enclosed in the package were Ōsugi's letter of introduction and a translation of Schreiner's "Dreams" by a woman called Yamada Waka.

The manuscript was written in a childish, unformed hand, but the translation read smoothly and seemed to be accurate. Schreiner's allegorical story was about a woman who travels across the hot African plain and has three dreams as she rests under a tree. In each dream, the woman seeks to be free. In the first one, she is a beast of burden too weak to stand up, but with the invention of machines, she is finally able to travel to the land of freedom. The need for women's liberation was simply and imaginatively explained, much like a story for little children. I was delighted to receive the manuscript, and though the translation was by a complete unknown, I published it straightaway in the November issue.

Not long after, Yamada Waka and her husband, Kakichi, came to the office on the day set aside for visitors. I am not sure what I expected, but both Waka and her husband were tall and powerfully built. Kakichi looked considerably older, close to fifty, and wore a fierce, intense expression, which was unusual in a Japanese. He also liked to talk. He spoke with great animation, occasional peculiarities of speech, and lapses in grammar (he had lived in the United States for many years) about how they had met in the United States and fallen in love, about their life since returning to Japan, and his future hopes for his wife. In effect, he was asking me to take his wife on as a writer for the journal.

[xv] Ōsugi Sakae (1885–1923): Leading figure in the anarchist movement.

Waka, who was listening quietly with a happy smile, finally spoke up. "I'm afraid I have no education to speak of. I had to mind babies when I was a child and attended only a couple of years of elementary school. I learned how to read and write in middle age after I married my husband, so I'm not sure if I can keep up with the rest of you—" She had a deep, sonorous voice and spoke in a thoughtful, measured tone that inspired trust. I was strangely drawn to this older woman who looked the soul of goodness. As big as an elephant, she dressed plainly, with no heed to fashion. I knew I had found a friend. Waka became a member, and over the years, she sent in a steady stream of translations of works by Schreiner, Lester Ward, and Key. Her handwriting remained childish, but her translations were uniformly simple and clear. According to Kakichi, Ōsugi was studying French at a school he had opened to teach English, German, and Spanish as well as French.

I became quite close to the couple, especially after learning that Kakichi not only knew a great deal about sociology but also was interested in women's issues and was reading *Love and Marriage* with Waka. He had many books on the subject, and though I disliked visiting people as a rule, I frequently dropped by and finally moved next door to their house in Yotsuya Minami Iga-chō. Possibly because of their own hardships in the past, Waka and her husband were very kind, in fact, almost too solicitous, but I appreciated their advice since I had led a sheltered life and was hopelessly impractical. This was several years into the future, so for now, I shall relate what Waka told me about her background.

She was born into a farming family in Miura County, Kanagawa Prefecture. With many mouths to feed, the family was desperately poor. Waka was determined to help her struggling parents, so she left for the United States to work as a common laborer on the West Coast. Unable to save money, she drifted from job to job and ended up in a brothel. Kakichi, who was putting himself thorough school working at various jobs (he said he'd been seriously injured while working as a ranch hand), happened to meet her at the brothel, and struck by her good character, he rescued her from her surroundings.[16]

Kakichi had judged correctly; Waka was more than worthy of his zealous efforts to educate her. She was amiable and hardworking, with a generous spirit and a strong sense of justice. Nothing about her suggested her unfortunate past. Waka was in every way an extraordinarily admirable woman.

⊚ ⊚ ⊚ ⊚ ⊚

I shall now say a word about Yasumochi Yoshiko, or "Auntie," as we called her. From the start, she had worked unstintingly, taking care of the office work, and though she had no strong literary ambitions, she regularly submitted her haiku and waka poems under the pen name "Hakuu." Most of her waka were about love, a preference seemingly at variance with her outward appearance and no-nonsense personality, but she had fallen in love, not once but twice.

Her first love was K, a pharmacist at the sanatorium in Chigasaki. They were engaged, but K, an overcautious type who "thumped a stone bridge before crossing," never brought up the subject of a wedding. On the pretext that marriage between co-workers would be too disruptive, he took a position at a hospital in Tokyo and told her to wait until he had enough money to open his own pharmacy. Her patience tried, she quarreled with K whenever she saw him, and the two finally broke off their engagement.

Distraught, Yoshiko was on the brink of a nervous breakdown when Ono Higashi, who was a patient at the sanatorium, heard her story and offered his sympathy. Sympathy developed into something stronger, leading to another heartache, for Ono was married. Waiting at home and attending to his parents was his beautiful young bride.

Yoshiko agonized over her love affair with a married man, but she and Ono surmounted a number of difficulties and eventually married [in 1914]. Ono, a graduate of Tokyo Commercial College, worked at the Maruzen Bookstore and apparently gave her professional advice from time to time. This was, I suspect, not from any sympathy for our cause but from his interest in *Seitō* as a commercial enterprise. It was Ono, in fact, who persuaded Maruzen to advertise in our journal.

◎ ◎ ◎ ◎ ◎

In September, on the occasion of our second anniversary, we decided to revise the statutes and regulations of the society. In view of our new interests, we eliminated all references to "women's literature," changing Statute 1, for instance, from "This society aims to promote the development of women's literature" to "This society aims to stimulate the awakening of women." We also took out Statute 5 ("We open membership, regardless of race, to all women writers who agree with our objectives, women who aspire to be professional writers, and women who are fond of literature"). We cancelled all previous memberships and asked our readers to reapply with a firm resolve and commitment to Seitō's new direction. We made a fresh departure; as I had hoped for some time, *Seitō* would no longer be a narrowly literary journal.

We published the revised statutes and regulations in the Editors' Notes of the October issue [vol. 3, no. 10] and explained the changes more or less as follows:

> In a certain sense, the membership will be more selective and our individual responsibilities even greater. Membership will no longer be a matter of being

fond of literature and paying one's dues or signing up lightheartedly and quitting as soon as public opinion turns against us. At the very least, members must be women who find life's purpose and meaning in Seitō's goals and activities, and, together with the society, seek to fulfill their potential.

It was important to spell out our new position, especially since public attacks on Seitō had led to a divergence of opinion about the nature of the journal. There were the older members who wished to remain faithful to Seitō's original purpose of fostering literary talent, and the younger ones who wished to fight against outmoded morality and focus on women's issues. By asking members to apply anew, I hoped to rid the society of those in the former group who were inexplicably cold or indifferent to our new goals.

We also needed to shore up our finances. We were not desperate, but we had counted on the income from the lecture series to pay for Yasumochi Yoshiko's living expenses. On Yoshiko's suggestion, supported by her friend Ono Higashi and Iwano Kiyoko and Hōmei, we set up the Seitō Supporters Association, a separate entity that would contribute much-needed funds. We invited members and nonmembers alike to join the association, but in an age when women had little economic power, not as many outsiders responded as we hoped. We were also aware that some of the serious and capable members could not afford the monthly dues, so we decided to waive dues for all regular members. Fortunately, this was offset by the higher dues paid by the majority of Seitō members who joined the Supporters Association.[xvi]

The journal itself was selling well. Since entrusting Tōundō with the publishing and distribution work, sales had risen from 2,000 to the highest level of 3,000. Our editing fees remained the same, however, and Yoshiko, who thought Tōundō was hoarding the profits, said we should ask Nishimura for a raise. I disagreed. Sales had increased because of the firm's business acumen, and the profits were rightfully theirs.

Nishimura, I should mention, had heard about my relationship with Okumura, and he avoided personal contact with me with the characteristic tact of a sophisticated urbanite. Even so, he poked his head into the copyediting room every once in a while, less to talk about business than for the camaraderie. He was young, he enjoyed the company of women, and as a poet, he must have felt he was among kindred spirits. Reciprocating his friendly feelings, we admired not only his interest in literature but also his broad grasp of social problems and women's issues. He was in every sense a staunch supporter of the journal.

[xvi] Those in Category A of the Supporters Association paid 1 yen a month, and those in Category B paid 50 sen (*Seitō jinbutsu jiten*, 221).

Despite my objections, Yoshiko went ahead and asked for an increase in our fees. She was refused point-blank. Nishimura's adoptive father, who was nominally retired but still had a firm grip on the business, was unwilling to negotiate. Yoshiko, never the soul of charm or tact, had no doubt approached the matter in her usual blunt way. She may also have secretly hoped for a rejection, which she would use as an excuse to wrest back control of the business side. With sales reaching 3,000, she probably felt the future was assured.

Nishimura's father was not merely angered, he declared the firm would no longer handle our affairs. And so, with the October 1913 issue, all ties with Tōundō were severed. Araki Ikuko, one of the few members with business sense, introduced us to Shōbundō, a bookstore in Kanda Minami Jinbō-chō. The firm agreed to handle the sales, but the figures plummeted, leaving us with an alarming number of remaindered copies. As we soon discovered, they had neglected to distribute copies outside Tokyo.

The following spring (1914), again through Ikuko's good offices, we decided to approach Iwanami Shoten. The owner, Iwanami Shigeo, lived in a house on a back street in Kanda that Ikuko either owned or managed. The store itself faced the main street on the same block as Shōbundō and a cluster of second-hand book dealers. I went with Ikuko to meet Iwanami. He was young, perhaps a couple of years past thirty, but at first glance he reminded me of a humorless and old-fashioned village schoolmaster. He turned out to be friendly, and said he had resigned from his job as vice-principal of the Kanda Girls' High School to open a bookstore and was thinking of going into the publishing business in the near future. He was sympathetic to our journal and said he would be happy to take on the publishing and sales responsibilities. He would do this not as a business venture but as a gesture of good will. I felt a certain resistance to the way he kept repeating "gesture of good will," but he seemed like a trustworthy man of high principles and presumably knew the journal made little money.

A few days later, accompanied by Yoshiko, I went to see him again. We discussed business, agreed on the terms, and promised to send the manuscripts for the next issue. The galley proofs were ready and all seemed to be in good order when something unexpected happened. To work on the final editing, Yoshiko and Noe had gone to a room on the second floor of the store, but when Mrs. Iwanami came in with the proofs, Yoshiko had acknowledged her with a grunt and failed to thank her properly. Mrs. Iwanami was outraged since she had intended to say a word of welcome and instead had been treated rudely.

The unfortunate incident was described in great detail in her husband's special delivery letter, which arrived the next day and was addressed to me personally. He ended the letter apologizing in the politest terms that he would have to decline all future dealings with us. His wife, heavy with child (he mentioned how many months), had made a special effort to climb the stairs, only to be greeted with a grunt. She was terribly upset and insisted that he cancel the agreement. Had the work been a temporary job, he might have gone against her wishes, but since this was not the case, he had no choice but to back out with his deepest regret.

I suspect that his wife had frowned on the arrangement from the very beginning. The thought of her husband dealing with "New Women" must have made her uneasy, and then, this corpulent, sloppily dressed woman had insulted her. She was pregnant and overly sensitive, so perhaps one could not blame her. (Yoshiko herself was probably unaware that the woman was Mrs. Iwanami and of course hadn't meant to insult her; she was behaving in her usual abrupt manner, which was why everyone fondly called her "Auntie.")

As I read the letter, I could picture the little domestic drama: the serious young husband sitting at his desk, writing in great haste to appease his indignant, pregnant wife. It was mean of me, but I found the whole episode so funny that I nearly burst out laughing. Still, I regretted having to break off relations with the bookstore and reproached myself for not having been more conscientious. We had just reached an agreement, and at the very least, I should have gone with Yoshiko and Noe to help edit the proofs.

"To My Parents on Becoming Independent"

I moved out of the house on January 13, 1914. On that day, I finally became independent. Several years earlier, when I ran off with Morita, I had acted on impulse and required no preparation; I only had to put my room in order. This time, I was not rushing headlong to meet death; I was leaving home to embrace life. In the previous case also, I only had to focus my whole being on the single issue at hand. There had been no need to think or plan ahead. Indeed, I had experienced an element of lighthearted anticipation. But this time, I had to attend to a myriad of details.

First of all, there was the question of money, and second, a place to live. Luckily, we found a small two-story house in Sugamo, near the Seitō office. The house was behind the Togenuki Jizō Shrine and close to a hospital for invalid soldiers. In the middle of a large garden that belonged to a nursery, the place was mercifully quiet. Okumura was ready to move in anytime. I still had to tell my parents.

To be truthful, I did not look forward to the prospect. As mentioned, my father and I had long ceased to have conversations of any significance. On top of this, I was not particularly articulate. If I wished to convey my thoughts adequately, I would have to write my parents a letter. This took me several days. There were many things I wanted and needed to say. As I wrote, tears welled up, but I finally finished and gave it to my mother. She had tears in her eyes and most certainly guessed what was inside.

I addressed the thick envelope to "My Esteemed Parents," so I am sure she handed it to my father right away. He said nothing. My mother, too, did not appear particularly fretful or agitated. She had long suspected that something like this might happen and occasionally had to lie down to rest her nerves, but at that time, despite my formal declaration of my intention to leave, she remained outwardly calm. Brought up in a samurai household and trained not to show her emotions, she might shed a tear or two, but would never allow herself to break down in front of others.

My father, for his part, was probably resigned. However enraged or opposed he might be, there was little he could do. I had not sought his opinion or advice but merely stated the facts: the stirrings of my heart that had led to my decision, the kind of person Okumura was, the arrangements we had made to live together. My letter was more like a report. As in the past, he may have vented his fury on my mother. After I ran away with Morita, he had been so hard on her that she had lost weight. In his own way, he could be quite devious, preferring to work off his displeasure on my mother rather than confronting me face to face. And she, too, never came right out and spoke her mind but evaded the issue saying, "Well, that's what Father thinks, so—"

Perhaps it was just as well that my parents looked the other way. I went ahead with the packing—my desk, bookcase, books, clothes, personal articles, a set of quilts. I asked Tomo—a young relative who was staying with us to learn domestic skills—for some help. Since one of her duties was to answer the door, she was the only person in the house who had actually met Okumura. My mother would have welcomed the chance, but she never would have gone against my father. She was aware that I was packing, but she did not look in or offer to help. I knew what she must have been feeling and could not accuse her of being coldhearted. With everything packed, I called for the rickshaw man we usually hired.

I have no memory of what I said to my grandmother. In her eighties, she had begun to show signs of senility, and since I rarely talked to her, I probably said something like "I'm leaving—I'll be back soon." My sister was living in Osaka with her husband. I never said a word to her about my decision.

I decided to publish the letter in the February issue [vol. 4, no. 2] under the title, "To My Parents on Becoming Independent." I originally intended to keep the letter confidential, but while writing it, I came to believe that the public, particularly young women caught in the same situation, should be informed about why I was taking this step and the meaning of such a move.

To be precise, I was doing it because I was opposed to the feudalistic marriage system, but at the same time had fallen in love and let this love develop
in the natural manner. Because I hoped to establish a new concept of sexual
morality by freely choosing to live with my lover, I was certain my action
had a direct bearing on the problems of many women. This conviction—the
same spirit that had led me to publish my letter to Niizuma—impelled me
to go ahead.[17]

◎ ◎ ◎ ◎ ◎

Okumura moved into the house first and I, a day later. The house had an eight-
mat room on the first floor and a six-mat room on the second. Okumura took
the larger one for his atelier, and the smaller one was my study. We mailed
postcards to our friends informing them of the new address and our decision
to live together. Okumura made a nameplate for the front door—a small
board decorated in bright colors with our names side by side. It was promptly
stolen. He made another one, but this too, was stolen, as were several others.
We wondered whether the thief had done it out of curiosity, mischief, or spite.
Was someone who disapproved of our living arrangement trying to punish us
for flouting the traditional family system and all that was "morally beautiful
and true"? Whatever the motive, we never caught the culprit.

As I had fully expected, my published letter provoked a renewed attack on
the New Woman. The public outcry centered on three points: first, Okumura
was five years younger; second, living together outside marriage was immoral
and no different from fornication; third, by refusing to register our union, we
had violated the law and were, in short, not legally married.

Let people say what they wanted, we loved each other and only that was
important. We were not husband and wife as defined by the marriage statutes in the Civil Code, nor did we wish to be. It would have gone against
our principles to have our union recognized and validated by a law we found
unacceptable. Registering our "marriage" would have been tantamount to
assenting to the prevailing system. In that day and age, the only way to show
our opposition was by refusing to legalize our union. And it was precisely for
this reason that I deliberately avoided using the word "marriage," with all its
age-old connotations, and instead used the phrase "living together."[xvii] Furthermore, I had finally extricated myself from my family and saw no reason to
rush into forming a new one. Nor did I see any reason to change my name. I

[xvii] Raichō uses the word *kyōdō seikatsu* (cohabitation), though she later uses *kekkon* (marriage) and *otto*
(husband) from time to time.

had always resisted the notion that women had to take their husbands' name and wondered why anyone would do so with no hesitation or regret.

I did not expect anyone to bless our union. But out of the blue, I received a letter from Sasaki Shigetsu, the young layman with whom I had practiced zazen at Ryōmō-an. A graduate of the Academy of Fine Arts, he had trained with Sōkatsu-rōshi, received certification as a teacher, and gone with Rōshi to the United States to proselytize. He was still there, but had somehow heard about us and written to offer his congratulations. I was also pleased that he referred to Okumura as "Hiroshi-san," as though they were good friends. I hoped to see him again, but he remained in the United States until he died [in 1945].

We now faced the problem of money. Incredible though this may seem, I left home with nothing more than my pocket money, and Okumura was just as impractical. Between us, we had only the money from the art exhibition that friends and Seitō members had organized for us two months previously, plus the little I earned from my writings. At most, we could count on 30 or 40 yen a month. Six or 7 yen went for rent and some more for Okumura's painting supplies. In no time we found ourselves commuting to a pawnshop in Ushigome. This was Okumura's job. He was used to it, for, unable to resist an antique or curio, he would buy something and then have to pawn it. His friend Harada Jun had introduced him to the shop. Harada, in fact, was an inveterate spender, and though he was a professional musician, he had pawned his piano once.

People started addressing me as "Oku-san."[xviii] This was to be expected, I suppose, but I was terribly annoyed each time. I kept thinking they were calling out to someone else and did not answer. Still dressed in kimono and hakama, I must have been a very peculiar-looking "Oku-san."

We took turns cooking, depending on who happened to be free, and sometimes we cooked together. Okumura, who had cooked his meals in the past, was surprisingly skilled, and for someone poor, had several pieces of fancy cookware, including a small French oil stove. I was hopeless, in spite of three years of cooking classes at college. I was simply not interested, and often became so engrossed in my work that the food burned. I remember the time Okumura came home proudly bearing an expensive enameled pan. To his dismay, I ruined it completely the moment I put it on the fire.

Noe heard about my fiascos in the kitchen and invited us to eat at their house. She said cooking for four was no more work than cooking for two, and we would just have to reimburse her for our expenses. Overjoyed at the pros-

---

xviii Mrs. or "lady of the house." *Oku* means "interior space."

pect of being released from the kitchen, I looked for a house nearer to Noe and found one [in June] in front of the Myōgi Shrine in Kamikomagome for a monthly rent of 10 yen.

By then Tsuji's mother and sister and brother-in-law had moved out, and he and Noe were living alone with the baby. Every time we went over, he was working on a translation in his tiny study, with a framed lithograph of Spinoza displayed on the wall above his desk. When he got tired, he took out his bamboo flute and practiced for a while.

Tsuji was [thirty,] a year older than I, but the long, deep lines going from the sides of his nose to his mouth (which students of physiognomy called *hōrei*) made him appear much older. The lines gave him an introverted, melancholy look that suggested experience and a maturity of judgment. His face was not handsome but interesting, austere and without a trace of worldliness. The lower half of his body was spindly, and from the back, he looked not like a man in his prime but weak and defeated, as if foreshadowing his last, dark days. He had a habit of not looking people in the eye, and would raise his eyes to steal a glance now and then. I found this very unpleasant. But he had been the one who first told Noe about Seitō, and with his deep understanding of women's issues, he was making a special effort to guide and educate her. Partly to help with their finances, I persuaded Tōundō to bring out "Love and Morality," Tsuji's translation of a chapter from Key's *Love and Marriage*, and Goldman's "Tragedy of Women's Emancipation." This volume, which included a preface I had written and biographical sketches of Key and Goldman, was published under Noe's name in March [1914].

As to Noe's cooking, I do not know how we stood it. She had no equipment to speak of—Tsuji's mother had probably taken everything—and used a metal basin for a skillet and the back of a mirror for a cutting board. To serve the food, she piled everything onto one big plate. She wasn't a bad cook, only uninterested. Often enough, we could not figure out what we were eating as we consumed some stewlike substance with bits of meat ladled over rice. She was certainly quick, but cleanliness and flavor were the least of her concerns.

Noe's meals were almost inedible, but the conversation afterward was always lively. Cultivated and urbane, Tsuji talked about literature, philosophy, art, and music. A talented artist and musician as well, he and Okumura had much in common. Harada Jun, who had recently married an actress and moved to Sugamo, dropped by now and then. As he regaled us with stories, Noe nursed the baby, her ample breasts in full view, either laughing in her loud voice or fuming in indignation.

Nogami Yaeko, one of our contributors, lived next door. She and her husband were away in their hometown in Ōita Prefecture, and Noe, who had been asked to keep an eye on the house, occasionally prepared the meals in their larger kitchen. I knew Noe was friendly with Yaeko, but I was disturbed to see her use the kitchen utensils and the clean quilts for the baby as if she owned the house.

We were poor, but our lack of money was nothing compared to what Noe and Tsuji endured. They could not even afford lamp oil, and when Tsuji's mother was still living with them—she was from a family of once prosperous rice dealers and was accomplished in the arts—she practiced her samisen in the dark. Creditors periodically appeared at the Seitō office, no doubt told by a desperate Noe that she would pay them as soon as she received her wages. They came to our house also, but of course we were in no position to help pay her bills.

We did not mind skipping a meal or two, but the mosquitoes that first summer were more than we could bear. Too poor to buy a mosquito net, we were wondering how we were going to survive when a big, white mosquito net arrived from the Mitsukoshi Department Store, purchased in my name. I knew at once that my mother had bought it for me—her wayward daughter—and certainly without telling my father. I felt a pang pierce my heart, and I wept.

The eating arrangement with Noe lasted at most a month. Okumura disliked meat and was extremely picky, although I could not blame him in this case. We decided to take our meals at the Kawachiya, a rather fancy restaurant near Komagomebashi, in order to have more time for work. We sat on the tatami at the kind of long table used for marking kimono cloth. I am sure we were the only married couple who ate there regularly. The restaurant used seasonal ingredients, and one day it would be tofu grilled with miso and shiso leaf, another day, broiled eggplant or miso soup made with sake lees. The day's menu was listed on a sheet of rice paper, and much to our regret later on, we often yielded to temptation and exceeded our budget.

Iwano Kiyoko and Hōmei

Kiyoko and Hōmei lived in our neighborhood, so I saw them more often and could not help noticing that Kiyoko looked physically and mentally exhausted. They both acted as if nothing was wrong, but they seem to have been incompatible from the very beginning. In fact, when I first met Kiyoko in April 1912, she already showed the strain. As I mentioned earlier, their decision to live together [in 1909] had created a stir, and one newspaper had speculated about whether "the flesh or spirit would triumph." They were legally married [in February 1913], but Kiyoko soon became disillusioned and started writing fictionalized accounts of a neglected wife's loneliness. (It was Hōmei, in fact, who first encouraged her to write.) I have already quoted from "Conflict of Love"; here I shall quote from "Fortune-telling," a story she published in the September 1913 issue [vol. 3, no. 9].

> If that's what he intends to do, I'll just go ahead and do what I want. I'll forget about our life at home and make my own world. I'll think of myself as single and the man in the next room not as a husband but as a boarder, a complete stranger with whom I have no physical or spiritual ties. As long as I think of him that way, what he does is none of my affair. Even if he doesn't speak to me for a year, my feelings won't be hurt. Well, I think I'll go somewhere tomorrow and have some fun. I hear the flowers are in full bloom—I'll ask a friend or someone else to go with me.

As it happened, earlier that year, Kiyoko had suddenly invited Noe and me to see the irises in Ayase. She always dressed very well on such outings, and that day, too, she put on a bright pink haori that contrasted cruelly with the ravaged skin under her thick makeup. Kiyoko's broad, flat face was not beautiful, but when she smiled, her face would suddenly brighten with a vivacious charm. Her voice, as I said, was beautiful.

We took a small motorboat to Ayase and spent the day walking around the area. Noe laughed and chattered in high spirits and Kiyoko joined in happily. She thanked us at the end of the day, saying how much she enjoyed our company, but then, as if she were talking to herself, she mumbled, "Iwano and I haven't spoken to each other for a week." I was not living with Okumura at the time, but her words, which hinted at the complexities of married life, stayed with me for a while.

Kiyoko was honest and uncomplicated, and came straight to the point in her judgments. There was nothing vague or evasive about her. But she could also do puzzling things. I noticed that some of the furniture in her house had tags marked "Property of Kiyoko." By marking which spouse owned which item, I suppose Kiyoko, a by-the-book feminist, was asserting her property rights. Or she may have done this to prevent Hōmei from pawning her possessions. Still, I found this odd.

She could also be quite cold, rigid, and exacting, but this was more than offset by a sentimental streak and a genuine concern for others. For instance, she looked after Noe and Tsuji and asked him to make a draft translation of Plutarch's *Parallel Lives* for Hōmei. Once, the two men were drinking when I went to see Kiyoko, and Hōmei, who had evidently had too much, was berating Tsuji for his spinelessness and lack of ambition. Not one to mince words, Hōmei often lectured me also: "You're wasting your time translating. Go ahead and write something on your own." I could never tell whether he was giving me advice or trying to cheer me up.

One time when Okumura and I attended a meeting of the Tōkakai, an informal literary group, Hōmei insisted on taking me out on a boat in the pond of the restaurant garden. He rowed recklessly; I begged him to let me off, and just as I was about to step ashore, I fell in and got soaking wet. Instead of asking me how I was, he kept apologizing about the soiled kimono, as though the only thing that mattered to a woman was her kimono. Of course, as Okumura said afterward, I should have known better than to get in a boat with Hōmei.

In appearance, in temperament, in every respect, Kiyoko and Hōmei were opposites. It was, as they say, bad karma; the marriage was doomed to failure. I shall touch on their breakup later, but I will mention one thing that surely exasperated Hōmei. Kiyoko was a stickler for cleanliness and kept a clean white rag outside her room for people to wipe their feet on before going in. The rag was always as spotless as a fresh napkin.

◎ ◎ ◎ ◎ ◎

Yasumochi Yoshiko was also having her share of troubles. Her love affair with Ono had run up against some obstacles, and, looking gloomy and dejected, she forgot things and neglected her work. Her younger sister then unexpectedly came to Tokyo and moved in with her at the office in Sugamo. This irritated Yoshiko, who scolded her in front of us and made the rest of the staff feel awkward. Yoshiko herself realized that, despite good intentions, her lack of tact had led to a rupture with Tōundō and later with Iwanami. To add to this, I was worried about my own household finances and could not offer her financial or managerial assistance. Increasingly depressed, she seemed to be on the edge of a nervous collapse. We persuaded her to return to her family home in Shikoku for a rest, and in late April, Ono, Okumura, and I saw her off at the train station.

With Yoshiko gone, we closed down the office in Sugamo and moved the papers and furniture to our house in Kamikomagome.[xix] Like it or not, I became responsible for management, as well as for all other matters. Noe and I took charge of the editing, while Kiyoko and I handled the Supporters Association and miscellaneous paperwork. By then, Kobayashi Katsu, who was engaged to one of Chikuha's students, was spending most of her time helping Kōkichi with her magazine *Saffron*.

It was more than three months since Okumura and I had moved in together. I was mentally and physically exhausted and longed to get away, so during the loquat season in early summer, we decided to go to a hot spring in Toi, a village on the Izu Peninsula famous for that fruit. I have forgotten how we paid

---

[xix] Raichō and Okumura moved to Kamikomagome in June.

for the trip. I asked Noe to take over—she agreed with a big smile—handed her the house keys, and promised to be back in a week. We took the train as far as Numazu, where we continued by steamboat. Out on Heta Bay, the boat rocked violently and for the first time in my life I became seasick.

I have two photos from the trip. In one, we are sitting on a rock wearing matching kimono of striped cotton that were furnished by the inn. In the other, we are again sitting close together on a rock with a couple of loquats on our laps. The photos were taken by a professional photographer in the village—we did not own a camera—and while these are not particularly good, they are, so to speak, our honeymoon pictures. I have written about the trip in the July *Seitō* ["A Seven-Day Trip," vol. 4, no. 7].

⊚ ⊚ ⊚ ⊚ ⊚

We returned to Tokyo refreshed. About a month later, in midsummer, a young woman called Chihara Yoshi turned up at our door. Many of our readers, including young girls, married women, and even schoolteachers, wrote to us asking for advice, and some, who had run away from home, even came to the office saying they were willing to do any kind of work. Yoshi, too, had escaped from an unhappy marriage and begged us to let her stay.[xx] I was extremely reluctant. I was unsociable by nature, Okumura and I had just started living together, we were poor and cramped for space. But after hearing her story—I have forgotten the details—I relented. Yoshi was well built and good-looking with a beautiful complexion. She also had literary talent, and wrote for us in the months to come.

We asked Yoshi to take on the cooking—we were still eating out—and since the summer heat was at its peak, we asked her to share our mosquito net. To my great dismay, she tossed about in her sleep, kicking off the covers and sprawling out in a most unseemly fashion. She stayed one month, two months, three months, until she finally found a job. To this day, I am amazed at how happy-go-lucky we were—Yoshi, for imposing on "newlyweds" for three months, and the "newlyweds" for tolerating this. I do not know how Okumura felt about the arrangement. I am sure there were unpleasant moments, but he never complained or looked aggrieved.

⊚ ⊚ ⊚ ⊚ ⊚

During that same summer I had the pleasure of meeting Itō Shōshin and his wife, Asako. This was at Kiyoko's house, where a *Yomiuri* reporter named

---

[xx] Chihara Yoshi was not married at the time.

Shibuya Umanokami taught French two evenings a week. I had heard about [Shōshin's commune] Mugaen when I was in college and read his essay "Conviction" in the inaugural issue of his journal *Selfless Love* (*Muga-ai*). I was then in the midst of my search for the meaning of existence (this was before I attained kenshō), and though I only half understood his account of experiencing "selfless love," I had nevertheless been moved. I also knew that he had been expelled from Shinshū University and stripped of his priesthood and that Kawakami Hajime had resigned from his teaching position [at Tokyo University] to join the commune.[xxi]

Nearly ten years had passed since I read his essay, but I was delighted to meet him, and so unexpectedly at that. Even more surprising was his appearance. Small and thin, he looked just like an old country peasant. He was a man of few words, but his smile, in fact his whole being, radiated warmth, serenity, and goodness. His wife was much the same. Having suffered from a severe skin disease as a child, she was completely bald, but she had feminine grace and by all indications was a woman of passionate convictions and abundant sensibilities.

My acquaintance with the couple was limited to the classes we attended together. They soon moved to Kyoto, where Shōshin worked for a Buddhist newspaper called *Chūgai nippō*. On returning to Tokyo in 1919, Asako joined the New Women's Association, and then after World War II, she and Shōshin participated in the movement for world government. Far from being a so-called professional Buddhist, Shōshin was a staunch believer in religious freedom and late in life promoted ecumenism. I believe both he and his wife deserve to be studied and given wider recognition.

The Debate on Chastity

The so-called "debate on women and chastity" occupied center stage at Seitō from the end of 1914 into 1915. The debate was sparked by "On Eating and Chastity," an essay by Nishizaki Hanayo in the September issue of *Echo* (*Hankyō*), a journal begun by Ikuta Chōkō [in 1914]. Before going further, I shall say something about Hanayo.

As I remember, she came to see me on a bitterly cold day toward the end of 1913, just before I moved out of my parents' house. I had not seen her for some time but found her sadly altered. Her straggly hair was arranged in an ichō-

---

[xxi] Itō Shōshin (1876–1963) was deeply influenced by Tolstoy and espoused a humanism based on "selfless love" (*muga no ai*). Kawakami Hajime (1879–1946) left his family and renounced all his possessions, but stayed at the commune for only two months.

gaeshi, her skin lifeless from malnutrition, her hands painfully chapped—everything about her bespoke a life of hardship. She said she was working at Kotobukitei, a yose entertainment hall in downtown Tokyo. Her job was minding the shoes and clogs left in the entryway by the customers. When I'd last seen Hanayo, she was working as a reporter for a magazine and wore her hair in proper uptown fashion; I now understood why she had adopted the downtown hairstyle.

Her work was evidently exhausting, but, as she told me proudly, she had observed life in its manifold aspects, taken notes assiduously like a student, and filled several notebooks. Her wages, unfortunately, were not enough to pay the monthly dues. What should she do? I told her we would waive the dues in exchange for her writings. I will quote from one of her sketches ["The Way I Live," vol. 4, no. 2]:

It's been twenty-five days since I began working at the Kotobukitei, but I feel my heart lighten when I think that I've written a story about my experience. I had all but given up hope, but then I realized that I had to overcome death and live my life anew. Coming here at a grave turning point in my life was my salvation. On the surface my behavior may look the same, but at least I have not merely changed my clothes to engage in something underhanded, like some people.[xxii]

I've filled three notebooks with my observations about the good-natured owner and his shrew of a wife; the flirtatious maid Omoto with her loose ways; lovely Osome in love; the child Okimi, abused like an animal but fiercely determined to survive; the geisha T, with her job in Mukōjima, always on the outs with her stepmother; T's older sister Sanpei, a geisha in Yanagibashi; the dashing handyman Tome and his wife Oasa; Gen, the fellow attendant who lusts after me. They're all in my notebook, each one a character in a story set in a downtown yose hall. When I think of what I've been through to take these notes, I can hardly hold back the tears.

Even after I leave this place, I'll do whatever is required of me. I'll work as a maid, but in a different segment of society and in a more intelligent way. My heart churns whenever I ride a trolley car and see a sign that says EMPLOYMENT AGENCY FOR MEN AND WOMEN. Beyond the blue curtains hanging at the doorway of the agency are human beings, all with their life stories. Beyond the blue curtains are men and women, each one alive. Beckoning me from beyond the threshold of that doorway is a "crucible of life" teeming with human beings.

[xxii] Hanayo is referring to Shimoyama Kyōko, a newspaper reporter who worked at the same entertainment hall in order to write an exposé.

Reading Hanayo's sketches, I was filled with awe and admiration. She knew exactly what she wanted from life and was determined to fight for it. Hidden within her small, frail body was a powerful life force, a thirst and passion for life and literature. In this regard, Hanayo's writings from the end of 1913 to the middle of 1914 were of inestimable value. They may not have been intellectually profound, innovative, well argued, or polished, but they were a naked record of her life, unique and intensely lived. Each word and each phrase was written with her flesh and blood. I cannot think of any other contributor who wrote with such searing ferocity.

I shall quote from another piece in which she described the contradictions, pressures, and anguish of a woman's desire for a man's love, the need to earn a livelihood, and the wish to fulfill awakening aspirations ["Face to Face with Romantic Love and the Difficulty of Making a Living," vol. 4, no. 1]:

> I looked at myself and saw a woman stained in blood, a woman smeared with mud. But this frail woman had persevered. She had endured and survived. And what a life it was, piteous and painful. The woman had fought tooth and nail, but in the end, her fight, which had been fraught with peril, had brought forth a life-giving flower. To bring forth yet another flower, she will probably be stained with blood all over again. Her present joy will lead her to the next round of suffering. Abandoning God, she will become a demon. So let her be a demon! (So long as this follows a natural course.)

The young poet Ikuta Shungetsu read Hanayo's essay and fell in love with her sight unseen. He arranged to meet her at the home of his mentor, Kawai Suimei, and he and Hanayo were married soon after, in either March or April. I had seen Shungetsu from time to time when he was living in Chōkō's house, but since he was so terribly shy, I was astonished to hear that he had proposed to Hanayo.

To return to Hanayo's essay in *Hankyō*, "On Eating and Chastity" was a critique of the traditional view of female chastity. Briefly put, she argued that a woman may be forgiven if she gives up her last precious possession as a last resort; this is particularly so when it is not a question of her alone, but also of her dependent siblings. The duty to obtain food comes first and takes precedence over a woman's duty to preserve her chastity. The age-old emphasis on defending virginity does not come from beliefs about sin, but from the idea that virginity is an advantageous condition for marriage. As long as a woman is aware of this, she should have the freedom to give up her chastity for food.[xxiii]

[xxiii] Hanayo, who was single, was raped by a superior at her workplace but stayed on because she needed to support her younger brother.

Yasuda Satsuki was outraged by Hanayo's views. She felt that Hanayo was demeaning not only herself, but all women. Satsuki was appalled that a woman who considered herself awakened would advance such an argument. As she wrote in the December *Seitō*:

> How can one possibly live without thinking of "one's own chastity"? Is it so nec-
> essary to eat? … Chastity should concern every aspect of a person, or at least, of
> a woman. Chastity is never something that can be detached, a prized possession
> that can be separated from the whole person. It is impossible to say that chastity
> stops here and that anything beyond is not chastity. Chastity should concern the
> whole person. Under no circumstances should it be considered as something
> that can be broken into pieces. ["On Living and Chastity," vol. 4, no. 11]

Satsuki considered inexcusable the very thought of bartering one's chastity for bread. Her language is extreme, and she neglects to explain why chastity is so important in the first place. Clearly, her views do not reflect the traditional view of chastity as a female virtue. For "chastity," she could just as well have said "the self" or "love." She continues:

> I live in order to find fulfillment for myself. For this, and this alone. I was moved
> to write this essay because I was so utterly confounded by what Ikuta [Nishizaki]
> Hanayo wrote. The fact that no one criticized her September essay leaves me
> with the unpleasant feeling that readers just shrugged their shoulders and said,
> "Women—what can you expect, when they've got to eat." Human beings must go
> forward toward their goal in a straight line. Ultimately, I am myself and no other.

The concluding lines vividly express Satsuki's spirit, character, and sense of pride. Satsuki was very much in love at the time, so Hanayo's argument must have been all the more unacceptable. Her lover was none other than Okumura's friend, Harada Jun, whose actress wife had died during pregnancy. Inconsolable, Harada had given up his job at the theater, wandered from place to place, and in early summer settled in a village on the Chiba coast. He would sing with all his might while looking out at the ocean, bury himself in the sand up to his neck, sneak into a farmer's house to sleep on the straw, and otherwise behave so strangely that he soon came to the attention of the local residents. Satsuki and her parents happened to be living in the same village. She took pity on Harada, cared for him, and the two fell in love.

Emboldened by her love affair, Satsuki broke with her parents and opened a small fruit shop called Satsuki in Koishikawa Hakusan. She worked extremely hard and went herself to do the negotiating with the wholesale dealers in Kanda Tamachi. With her small frame and thin face, Satsuki looked delicate, but she was forthright and capable, even bossy. Whenever I stopped by, she was dressed in a worker's jacket and apron, her hair pulled back and secured with a big comb, and briskly issuing orders to the young male help.

Harada often came to see her at the store. He had always been candid about his feelings and given to exaggeration, but unable to contain his happiness, he went around telling his friends, "I'm so in love with Satsuki, I don't know what to do. I feel like eating her up." I had known Satsuki from the time she joined Seitō, but now, because of her relationship with Harada, Okumura and I became quite close to them. We were delighted when they were married in January (1915).

Their marriage, sad to say, was far from happy. Harada was invited by Kobayashi Ichizō to help form the Takarazuka Girls' Opera Troupe and moved to Osaka with Satsuki [in 1916]. He was successful and popular, he and Satsuki had two boys, and they seemed to lack for nothing. But Harada was a habitual womanizer, and the second son was left brain-damaged after a severe case of dysentery. The two of them, unable to agree on how to bring up the child, gradually grew apart. Satsuki soldiered on, but she left her husband after twenty [seventeen] years and took the older son with her. Left ill and exhausted by the need to earn money, she despaired of getting better and died by her own hand. When I look back, her essay on chastity now seems prescient about her life: she walked in a straight line, and her end point was suicide.

Hanayo's marriage was unhappy, too. Shungetsu [suffered from a nervous disorder and] committed suicide [at age thirty-eight]. During the transitional years from the Meiji to the Taishō era, both she and Satsuki remained true to their principles and suffered as women, but their approach to life could not have been more different. I remember a remark that Harada made at the time of the divorce. "I admire Satsuki, all right, but you know what they say about fish staying away from clear water."[xxiv]

The third person to enter the debate was Noe, who wrote a short essay called "Miscellaneous Thoughts on Chastity" in the February issue of Seitō [vol. 5, no. 2].[18] With a view to putting an end to the debate, I wrote an essay called "The True Value of Virginity." I shall quote some of the passages to present the gist of my argument.

Virginity must be honored and respected; purity is precious and not to be abandoned lightly. This, at least, is what people believe, as though it were an abso-

---

lute truth. But why is it immoral to give up one's virginity? And why do people categorically condemn single women who lose their virginity outside of marriage? Ikuta (Nishizaki) Hanayo, Harada (Yasuda) Satsuki, and Itō Noe have presented their differing views on the value of virginity, but no one has examined the intrinsic value of virginity itself.

I do not think that generalizations can be made about whether virginity is precious or not. One can only say that a woman must cherish her virginity until the most appropriate moment comes. Or to put it another way, clinging to one's virginity at an inappropriate moment is as bad as giving it up at an inappropriate moment.

I then explain what I mean by "the most appropriate moment":

I believe the most appropriate moment comes when the spiritual longing for the loved one and the physical desire engendered by this is fused within a person. (I do not think a virgin can have physical desire for a person of the opposite sex without an element of romantic attraction. If that does occur, the case is an exception.) To be more realistic, the woman herself ultimately knows when the appropriate moment has come to surrender her virginity.

Seen in this light, what actual situation do women face? Under what conditions do they lose their virginity? And how many do so at the most appropriate moment? The majority, I fear, lose their virginity in the manner decreed by custom, that is to say, under the pressure of external circumstances, and give up what is rightfully theirs for the sake of others. Furthermore, they can do nothing to prevent this. In my opinion, marriage, as recognized by society and approved by public morality as the legitimate place to lose one's virginity, is for the most part a sordid and criminal custom. Those unfortunate women who forfeit their virginity for reasons of poverty or from a misguided sense of morality (selling themselves to help their parents or siblings, for instance), are not to be censured any more than the carefully brought up young ladies who marry without love and surrender their virginity without a murmur.

I therefore fervently hope that marriage devoid of love is speedily abolished and replaced with a true marriage in which a woman's virginity is given up at the appropriate moment. [July 1915 *Shinkōron*; HRC 2:56–60]

My essay drew unexpected praise from an acquaintance, the critic Tanaka Ōdō.[xxv] I had reviewed *The Beliefs of a Philosopher* (*Tetsujin shugi*), his two-

---

[xxv] Tanaka Ōdō (1867–1932): A professor at Waseda who studied with John Dewey at the University of Chicago.

volume collection of philosophical essays, in the July 1912 issue of *Seitō*, and he then wrote a generous review of my book *At a Locked Window* in *Chūō kōron*. We met quite by chance at Iwano Kiyoko's house. Already in his sixties [late forties], he was the "perfect gentleman," quiet and somewhat effeminate in manner. He was a frequent visitor to Kiyoko's house, seemed to be very fond of her, and took her out for walks. I often found Ōdō and Hōmei arguing about some point or other. Ōdō, who was a philosopher by training and presumably stronger in theory, invariably had to concede to Hōmei, whose arguments looked at things from all angles and who spoke more forcefully, in a loud voice. Total opposites in personality and intellectual approach, the two men were like yin and yang.

Ōdō was single and no doubt lonely. He also started coming to our house, but he sometimes stayed for hours, and for want of a topic, went on muttering in numbing detail about the advertisements for his forthcoming book or the outline of the book he was presently writing. During one visit, Okumura, who was resting in the next room with a fever, lost his patience and shouted, "I've got a fever. I'm not feeling well, so would you just leave!" Ōdō also sent letters. In his big, sprawling handwriting he addressed me as "My Dear Esteemed Friend Hiratsuka Raichō" and invited me to his lectures. He would inform me about his topic, remind me to sit in the front row, and so forth. But for some reason, he never conveyed his good wishes to Okumura, as if he had completely forgotten about his existence.

⊚ ⊚ ⊚ ⊚ ⊚

Another acquaintance I made about this time was Ogura Seizaburō, the only man we specifically asked to write for *Seitō*. He was a classmate of Tsuji's at the Seisoku English Academy and had come to the office to see if we would mention *Sōtai (Reciprocity)*, a journal he had started to publish for the scientific study of sexual problems. I shall quote from the Editors' Notes by Noe in the February 1913 issue.

> We are pleased to announce the publication of a new journal called *Sōtai*. It is small but extremely serious and quite unlike other journals. The founder Ogura Seizaburō, who does all the research single-handedly, has assembled a wealth of materials. We find the birth of a journal of this nature far more gratifying than the birth of ten worthless literary magazines. Among the titles listed in the table of contents are "Sexual Experience and Interpersonal Trust;" "Erotic Feelings, Erotic Sensations;" and "Premature Ejaculation Due to Anxiety."

Ogura was then a graduate student at Tokyo University. When he came to the office, he was wearing a soiled black cotton haori, and with a dull, stolid expression on his face, he looked the picture of gloom. When he spoke, too, he had an annoying habit of closing his eyes and mumbling as if he were thinking out loud. We became friends nonetheless, and at our house one day, he began talking about Noe's essay, "Turmoil," from the viewpoint of a sexologist. I found his analysis intriguing, and as I had recently written a critique of her essay, I asked him to write up his thoughts. His essay was published in the January issue as "Female Characteristics as Seen in Noe's 'Turmoil'" [vol. 4, no. 1].[19] The other articles he contributed were "Sexuality and Women's Issues" [vol. 4, no. 12] and "The Fruit of the Tree of Knowledge" [vol. 5, no. 1].

A devout, churchgoing Christian, Ogura said he decided to embark on a scientific study of sex because of the guilt he had felt upon discovering that he was having adulterous thoughts even while listening to sermons. To gather materials, he formed a society called Sōtaikai and asked the members— mainly writers, artists, photographers, newspapermen, and doctors—to meet once a month and talk or read reports about their sexual experiences. His wife thought this rather excessive and began to suspect that he had married her for the sole purpose of studying her as well. The marriage was strained for a time, but she eventually understood the true nature of his research and became his invaluable assistant.

I was fascinated by Ogura's writings, especially since my recent reading of Key had opened my eyes to the intersection of physical and spiritual love and the importance of female sexuality. As I wrote in the May 1914 issue ["Recent Readings and Miscellaneous Thought," vol. 4, no. 5]:

> I am still a child in every respect, and particularly when it comes to human sexuality. In fact, I was so ignorant that I was not even aware that I was ignorant.
>
> Obviously this is the first time I have lived with a man. The experience has made me realize even more acutely my ignorance about the sensual aspects of love, which, perhaps, is a sign that I have, in one respect, made great progress in my life as a sexual being.
>
> From time to time, I hope to write about the development of the sexual aspects of my life. I began to write something for this issue, but was unfortunately detained by pressing business.

Ogura was also the one to tell me about Havelock Ellis's seven-volume *Studies in the Psychology of Sex.* I was particularly interested in reading about homosexual love, for I had been baffled and disturbed by Kōkichi's abnormal love and violent outbursts of jealousy, and I thought Ellis's writings might help me understand her. I took the volume dealing with homosexual love along when I went with Okumura to Mount Akagi, and while I did not find the book especially enlightening, I asked Sakamoto Makoto to translate the chapter dealing with homosexual love between women. This translation was published in the April 1914 issue under her pen name, Nomo.[20]

Ogura also hit upon the idea of forming a nudist club. If people got used to seeing one another naked, he said, they would not be unnecessarily aroused. We often talked about the club, but nothing came of it.[21]

Being a Woman, Wife, and Mother

The office was now at my home, and the responsibility for putting out the journal rested entirely on my shoulders. I also had to attend to my own writing and worry not only about journal finances but about my personal finances as well. I managed to bring out the May, June, July, and August issues, but sales, which reached their peak under Tōundō's management, continued to decline. Naturally, I was in no position to ask my mother to make up the deficit.

I was desperate. I needed my own time for quiet reflection, for undisturbed reading and writing. If I kept up this hectic pace, I would no longer have an inner life of my own. The thought was terrifying. I was bone tired, my head throbbed, my chronic headaches came back. It was all I could do to handle the daily mail. Unable to finish the third anniversary issue on time, I was barely able to publish an issue worthy of the occasion in October. Drained of will and energy, I longed to be released from my responsibilities and go away on a trip. But with no money in sight, this was out of the question.

I talked to our publisher, Nichigetsusha, and arranged to have my recent essays published as a book under the title *Modern Times and Women's Lives* (*Gendai to fujin no seikatsu*). The journal owed money to the printers, so I paid them with some of my advance money and used the rest for a trip.

On October 12, Okumura and I left for Onjuku, a village on the Chiba coast that Harada said was beautiful. I felt as though I were running away. Before leaving, I asked Noe to be responsible for the November and December issues. I knew I was asking a great deal, but there was really no one else. All the capable members were wrapped up in their private lives—Iwano Kiyoko had given birth to a baby boy in February, Yasumochi Yoshiko had returned to Tokyo in July but was busy preparing for her marriage with Ono, Kobayashi Katsu had married and left Tokyo. Noe had her hands full with the baby, but I felt close to her and knew I could depend on her. I had really given her no choice, but with a smile on a face full of youthful promise, she said, "Leave everything to me. I'll have Tsuji help me."

We planned to stay in Onjuku until the end of the year, so after spending a few days at the only inn in the village, we rented a big room in a fisherman's house, borrowed basic necessities, and did our own cooking. We went down to the beach each morning to buy fish that had just been netted—pike, horse mackerel, sardines. As a rule Okumura avoided fish, but now, he ate one big helping after another.

The beach was much larger than we had expected. Dune upon dune rippled into the distance, an occasional cloud casting a long purple shadow on the glistening surface. As we sat on the sand between one dune and the next, we could easily imagine that we were the only living creatures in a vast desert, the illusion broken only by the tiny flowers at our feet, their thick petals shimmering like gold in the bright sun, and farther off a herd of cows grazing peacefully.

Okumura, who had brought his painting supplies, spent his time sketching the dunes and the cows. He was bursting with creative energy, for he had just held his first one-man show, and his painting of the Mera coast had been accepted by the prestigious Nikakai for its annual exhibit. Okumura's show had been at the Hibiya Fine Arts Hall from the twenty-third of September to the twenty-seventh. One of the visitors was Sōma Kokkō, the proprietor of the Nakamuraya Bakery in Shinjuku. She had come with Yasumochi Yoshiko, who attended the daily sessions of the Okada Method of Quiet Sitting at the store.

This was the first time I met Kokkō. I took an immediate liking to this refined and unassuming woman. After looking at all the art, she said, "Have you sold some of the pictures? I don't see any red dots." I told her the truth. "No, nothing as yet." "But that's not the way to do business," she said. "You're supposed to put dots on the paintings you want to keep to give the sales a boost." She then purchased a painting of a Tokyo street scene and told Yoshiko to put on a dot right away. Innocents that we were, we appreciated her shrewd counsel. The first meeting with Kokkō led to others. In the future, I went to her store in Shinjuku with one of Okumura's paintings whenever we needed money. The kind woman always obliged.

While Okumura painted, I made a concerted effort to recover my mental equilibrium and physical health. In good weather I went down to the beach, stripped to the waist, and basked in the sun. I also did breathing exercises, walking on the water's edge and breathing deeply in and out to the rhythm of the breaking waves. After I walked as much as I could, I sat on the warm sand and took a nap or read a book. Plovers skittered nearby, leaving delicate three-pronged markings on the mirrorlike surface of the sand. I did a minimum of work, checking the galley proofs of *Modern Times and Women's Lives*, which had been sent from Tokyo, and going over my translation of Key's *Love and Marriage*. This was in the evening. The noon hours were strictly for regaining my physical and mental health.

Half a month passed, and on a particularly fine day, we took a side trip to see Osenkorogashi, the cliffs on the eastern coast of the Bōsō peninsula. From there, we went on to Nabuto, spent a sleepless night listening to the roar of the surf, and returned to Onjuku. Waiting for me was the November issue and a letter from Noe. Inconsistent, at times incoherent, the letter was obviously dashed off in a frenzy of excitement.

> I've done such a poor job with the November issue that I'm thoroughly fed up with myself. If at all possible, I'd liked to be excused from doing the December issue. I never imagined it was so much work. I'm afraid I was overconfident. It's no wonder you were always pressed for time.

Noe then contradicted herself.

> Of course, once I get used to it, I suppose I'll be able to do it—but not as your stand-in. If you're willing to hand over the editing, the business side, everything, Tsuji and I are prepared to take over the journal and do our very best.

But then she reversed herself again.

> At this point, I think you should go ahead and make *Seitō* into your personal magazine. This way, you'll be able to coordinate your life and work and make a fresh start.

The letter ended on an inconclusive note.

> If this is what the work is like, I was better off the way things were before. In any case, I'll be waiting for your considered judgment on the matter. Who knows, though, I could change my mind in the meantime.

I wrote back immediately, saying I would hold her responsible for the December issue; I understood her predicament, but she had given me her promise. As to the future, I would have to think about it; for now she was to wait.

The time had come to rethink the future of the journal. I had left Tokyo without the slightest intention of abandoning *Seitō*, much less relinquishing it to Noe. But in fact, the work encroached on my new life with Okumura and had become a burden. If I were to devote myself wholly to the journal, I would be living a lie, for I was unwilling to squander my life and my energy on the burdensome business of putting it out. Unsociable by nature, I also begrudged the time and effort spent on members and readers who had run away from home. I had in a way sown the seeds of their predicament and real-

ized that I had to bear the consequences, but even so, putting them up, finding jobs for them, and giving them advice had become increasingly onerous.

Financially, too, I could no longer afford to give my all to *Seitō*. To earn
money, I had to write for other publications. If I were forced to make a decision and were allowed to follow the promptings of my heart, I would, without
a moment's hesitation, choose to live quietly alone with Okumura and spend
my time reading and writing. But to do that, I would have to discontinue the
journal once and for all.

But then again, I was unwilling to let go completely. I had started the journal and put a great deal of time and effort into its success; I was loath to finish
it off with my own hand. I could turn *Seitō* over to Noe and Tsuji, but because
of their way of life, I doubted it would last long.

I decided to have a talk with Noe, and five days after receiving her letter,
I left for Tokyo. In the meantime, she had sent another letter saying she had
made up her mind to assume all aspects of the journal and hoped that I would
give my consent. Noe was her usual irrepressible self. "Oh, please let Tsuji
and me do it," she exclaimed as soon as she saw me. "We promise to do our
best. You won't have to do a thing—just write something for us each month.
We'll have to ask you to be the official publisher, but we'll take all the responsibility. We promise not to cause you any trouble. Please don't worry. Tsuji
will take care of all the editing." She spoke as if the matter had already been
settled between them. I was heartened by their determination, but also bothered by the way they took everything for granted. Their optimism also seemed
unwarranted. Up to that time, they had been onlookers and probably had not
given much thought to the practical side of publishing a magazine. I pointed
this out, but again, Noe assured me that once they took over, they would sim-
plify the operation and cut everything down to the bare essentials. In fact, they
were even thinking of changing their living arrangement.

I was unconvinced. I knew that neither Noe nor Tsuji was the type to work
in a businesslike manner or to carry things through to the end. But Noe seemed
determined to have her way, so I finally relented. I told her that I would hand
over the journal and write an occasional piece, but would decline having
my name listed as the official publisher. I also told her that before coming to
see her, I had 80 percent made up my mind to discontinue the journal. She
refused even to consider the idea. We would seem to have lost the good fight
and the public would interpret our actions as a defeat. That, she said, would
be unbearable. No matter how small the journal might be, she wanted it to
continue. Perhaps I was less sensitive, but I did not feel the same degree of
attachment. For by then, I was already thinking of starting a new journal at
an opportune time, not one made up of women writers, supporting members,
and the like, but something more clearly defined, an intellectual journal that

focused exclusively on women's issues. As a final precaution before leaving, I asked Noe to spend the next day thinking over her decision and to come to the house in Kamikomagome the day after.

Noe came two days later; she had not changed her mind in any way. I asked her take everything in the office to her house in Koishikawa Takebaya-chō—the books, bookcases, desks, journals, English and Japanese dictionaries, register of members, the stationery.[22] As of January 1915, in name and fact, Noe would be responsible for Seitō. To explain the change in leadership, we each wrote an essay in the January issue.[23] The same day, I cleaned out the house in Kamikomagome and sent our belongings to my parents' house in Akebono-chō. I joined Okumura in Onjuku, and together, we quietly welcomed the New Year.

⊙ ⊙ ⊙ ⊙ ⊙

We reluctantly returned to Tokyo in February (1915) and moved into a run-down house with only two rooms on a narrow alley in Koishikawa Nishihara-machi, an area cluttered with dingy shops. The neighborhood was a slum by any definition, but the house had an open veranda and a rather large yard, and cost only 5 yen a month.

Okumura resumed the classes he had started at the Athénée Française and commuted each day to the Koishikawa Botanical Garden with his canvas, paints, and brushes. I went to Yamada Kakichi's house to learn more about Lester Ward's theories on sociology. At the request of a reporter at the *Jiji shinpō* newspaper, I also started writing a novel. The reporter had originally come to Onjuku to confirm a rumor that I had left Tokyo because I was pregnant. He quizzed the maid at the inn where we stayed temporarily, came to see me, and having concluded the rumor was false, returned to Tokyo. Then he sent a letter asking me to write a novel based on the incident with Morita Sōhei. I myself was thinking about doing the very same thing but kept putting it off. If I did not take the offer, I might never write the book. We also needed the money, so I agreed, even though I realized that the project might involve some risks.

I called my novel *The Mountain Pass* (*Tōge*); the first installment appeared [on April 1, 1915]. I continued to work on it, but one day, I was overcome by nausea and suddenly lost my appetite. As the symptoms grew worse, I became sicker than ever before in my life. It was morning sickness. But worse than my physical discomfort was Okumura's behavior. He had been sulking ever since I began working on the novel, retreating into himself and looking morose, as though the book had cast a pall on him. Busy with writing and sick to my

stomach, I would ask him to do some errands, but he only answered halfheartedly and made no move to leave. In the past he had cheerfully offered to do
the cooking, but now he refused to lift a finger.

I knew he was trying to punish me for writing the novel, but I was still terribly annoyed. I had heard of people being irritated and constantly "on edge,"
but for the first time in my life, I was feeling exactly that. Okumura, who was
abnormally sensitive to filth of any kind, or should I say, anything unsightly,
looked away in disgust whenever I vomited. At barely twenty-four [twenty-
five], he was perhaps too young to accept the fact that he was about to become
a father or to have the generosity of heart to sympathize with his pregnant
lover, especially when he was torn by jealousy.

I reluctantly gave up the novel midway through. Years afterward, Tokutomi
Roka's widow told me that her husband had followed the series with interest
and that she found the cuttings from the newspaper among his possessions. I
myself have quite forgotten how the novel began or ended.[24]

My morning sickness was unusually severe. This was my first pregnancy,
and, underweight to begin with, I had no idea of a proper diet and ate poorly.
Thankfully, the morning sickness did not last long.

The Debate on Abortion

I was pregnant. I thought about my new condition, but my heart did not leap
for joy, and not solely because of morning sickness. I had always believed that
becoming a mother should be a free act based on a conscious personal choice.
Thus, even as I affirmed my love for Okumura, I had avoided becoming a
mother. If a woman did not want children, she should exercise self-control.
Yet, in practice, I had been less than consistent in trying to avoid conception,
and as a result, I was about to become a mother even though I was unqualified. I felt sad to think that I could not welcome the creature born of our deep
love with unbounded joy.

I spent each day assailed by doubts. Would we be able to bring up the child
in our poverty-stricken condition? Would we be able to continue our work
and care for the child at the same time? Would I be able to reconcile my life
as a mother and my life as an individual who aspired to personal development
and fulfillment? To be absolutely truthful, I dreaded the thought of becoming
a mother.

Beset by these dark thoughts, I read a story by Harada Satsuki in the June
1915 issue of Seitō [vol. 5, no. 6]. She, too, was pregnant, and suffering from the
same doubts. Her story in defense of abortion, "To My Lover from a Woman

in Prison," was based on one of her dreams and was written in the form of a
letter by a woman who has been imprisoned for having an abortion.[xxvi]

> Month after month, a woman's body releases an egg cell. Just because I hap-
> pened to conceive, I did not actually feel that a life or a person had come into
> existence, let alone feel an instinctive love for the fertilized egg. I just thought
> of this as an appendage to my body, and who has ever heard of anyone being
> punished for cutting off her own arm?
>   ...People go on having children without even pausing to think that they're
> bringing those who will succeed them into this world. At least, this was true in
> my case. And of course, children don't ask to be born. Can there be anything
> more terrifying than bringing a precious life out of nothingness into existence,
> without any forethought or preparation, or worse, knowing that you aren't ready
> to bear the responsibility?...It's the law, not me, that says abortion is a crime.[25]

In sum, Satsuki was saying that people should not become parents unless
they are qualified for the task. Otherwise, abortion was the answer, even
though this might violate the law. People have to be true to their convictions.
The argument was typical of her—bold and decisive. Given my own doubts,
her story fairly took my breath away.

Noe, who read the manuscript, presented a counterargument in the same
issue. In the form of a personal letter to her friend Nogami Yaeko, she wrote:

> Satsuki seems to think that as long as [the child] is inside her womb, it's part of
> her body. I disagree. Even when the child is inside me, it properly has a "life" of
> its own, its own existence no matter how faint or incomplete.

She also addressed the problem of poverty.

> The child is born with its own unique fate. Being poor is by no means a misfor-
> tune. If a child is born into an environment such as ours, this, too, is fate. And
> who knows, if the child is destined to be born into wealth, we may well escape
> from poverty by the time it is born.

Noe had written from her own experience as a mother, but her argument skirted the issue entirely and expressed her characteristic optimism.

[xxvi] Under the Anti-Abortion Law of 1907, a woman who procured an abortion was liable to a prison
sentence of up to one year and the person performing it risked imprisonment of up to five years. The
law was not guided by a concern for the pregnant mother or fetus but by the government's desire to
increase the population and build up the nation's military power.

(Because Satsuki's article challenged the law against abortion, the June issue was banned.)

In the September issue [vol. 5, no. 8], Yamada Waka presented her views on abortion. Since she was fully committed to Key's ideas about the sacredness of motherhood, she attacked Satsuki head on:

> I believe that both abortion and contraception are heinous sins. They are immoral acts that destroy individual happiness and national prosperity. Marriage is a free act, a right bestowed by Heaven, and to shirk the duties that come as the natural consequences of this right is the height of cowardice.... . A nation that claims to protect life and property can never condone an act that not only destroys a life created by a power beyond human beings but also endangers the mother's life.

Yamada Waka's opposition to contraception sprang from her instinctual love for children. Leaving aside the question of whether she was right or wrong, her argument was consistent and characteristic of her. Unable to bear children, she had adopted three, all about the same age. Two were orphaned relatives, the third, a child of a close friend who had died in the United States. She was not their natural mother, but she was more loving than any other mother I knew. Her unconditional opposition to abortion and contraception thus had a strong emotional element.

As an expectant mother, I found the question of abortion of utmost pertinence. I wrote an article on abortion, contraception, and other related matters for the same issue, drawing on my experience of living with Okumura and my unforeseen pregnancy. "On the Conflict Between Life as an Individual and Life as a Sexual Being" is written in the form of a letter to Noe. It is twenty pages long, so I shall present the gist of what I said.

> When I first realized that I was pregnant, my biggest fear and concern was whether the child would interfere with my life as an individual and with my work. Like you—and Satsuki—I also worried about being poor. But a more troubling question was whether I would be able to reconcile my life as an "individual self" and as a "sexual being." For a while, I was tempted to have an abortion, though I differed from you in having no "moral compunctions" about it. Rather, what deterred me was the question of whether rejecting the child was the right and wise thing to do, not only for the present but for the future as well. Would we not regret it one day? Supposing there were a woman who, after careful thought, had an abortion for the sake of her art, research, or work, and by extension, for the good of society and civilization, would I accuse her of committing an unforgivable act?

In other words, I was telling my readers that I acknowledged the signifi-cance and value of motherhood. At the same time, I also believed that the inevitable conflict between being an autonomous individual and a child-bearing member of the human species was not just a personal problem, but one that concerned all Japanese women who were independent or hoped to be liberated. In our present age when abortion is so easily accessible, I sometimes wonder what people make of all the heated arguments set off by Satsuki's story.

Contraception was no less problematic. I accepted it as a practical and realistic proposition, but I also felt a certain resistance. Nowadays it is taken for granted as a natural right, but back then, contraception was beyond the purview of most people and not even raised as a social issue. Only after Mar-garet Sanger's visit to Japan in 1922 was it openly discussed. Information about preventive methods was virtually impossible to obtain (I heard about some-thing called "Your Friend" but did not look into it). In our own case, Oku-mura and I considered contraception unnatural, something that somehow sullied our love. When faced with the prospect of using contraception, we chose abstinence as the lesser evil.[26]

To my surprise, my essay elicited a long letter from the writer Arishima Takeo.[xxvii] He had read the essay in his wife's copy of *Seitō* and written to say that he was "deeply moved and wished to send his compliments." I had never met him, but was pleased to know that a man had given serious atten-tion to a topic concerning women. The letter, written throughout in elegant and forceful brushstrokes, suggested a person of unusual character. We later became friends.

⊚ ⊚ ⊚ ⊚ ⊚

One night, we were suddenly awakened by someone pounding and shouting "Hiratsuka-san! Raichō! Okumura!" It was Takebayashi Musōan, a member of the Tōkakai. He had come with a friend and was obviously very drunk. We pretended not to hear, but he kept on pounding so hard that we were afraid he might break down the thin wooden door. We wondered what the neighbors were thinking, but he finally gave up and left still shouting, "Hey, open the door. What's the matter?"

I have mentioned that Okumura and I belonged to the Tōkakai. That orga-nization, which was founded by Iwano Hōmei, was like a social club for peo-

---

[xxvii] Arishima Takeo (1878–1923): Novelist sympathetic to socialism and women's rights; best known for his novel about a headstrong and self-centered woman who defies social and moral convention (*A Certain Woman*, 1919).

ple with literary interests. Members met once a month on the tenth—hence
its name—at a restaurant called Mikado in Manseibashi. On special occasions, the club went to a restaurant in Ōmori, and it was there that I fell into
the pond. Besides literary types like Musōan, Iwano Hōmei and Kiyoko, Katō
Asadori and Midori, composers and artists like Yamada Kōsaku and Arishima
Ikuma also came. One of the members, Tanaka Kōshi, wrote about me in *Life
and Expression (Jinsei to hyōgen)*, a journal of opinion he edited. I met him
only twice, but for some reason he left a deep impression.

◎ ◎ ◎ ◎ ◎

I was no longer bothered by morning sickness, and in early July (1915), we
moved to a house near Waka's home in Yotsuya Minami Iga-chō. This was
purely for convenience. As I mentioned earlier, I was commuting to their
house to study with Kakichi, and in my condition I wanted to be closer. Okumura also began studying French with Kakichi. The house, which belonged
to Kakichi's brother, had previously been rented by the lawyer Yamazaki Ke-
saya, a friend from their time in the United States.

Once I started living closer to Waka and Kakichi, the first thing I noticed
was how they organized their lives rationally and with a minimum of waste.
They spared no expense for purchases of foreign books from Maruzen, but
for everyday expenditures, they were very careful with their money. Like my
father, Kakichi was fond of cigars and was never without one, but he always
bought the cheapest brand available. When Waka needed fish, she waited
until late in the day and bought only presliced fish that was within a certain
price range. Naturally, our manner of living did not go unnoticed by them. If
I happened to leave the light on, Waka would shout from her window, "You're
wasting electricity!" And Kakichi, who was even more eager to give us advice,
often came into our kitchen to teach us how to cook such things as curry paste
with admirable expertise.

We read Key's *Century of the Child* in the morning, and spent the afternoons reading Lester Ward's writings on sociology. Kakichi believed that a
study of sociology was essential to finding a solution to the Woman Question.
An emotional approach led nowhere, he said, and conclusions drawn from
an exclusively female perspective were just as useless; it was necessary to see
things in a broader sociological context.

Lester Ward (1841–1913) was an eminent American sociologist. He was the
first scholar to systematize the new academic discipline, and his name was virtually synonymous with the field. We read both his *Pure Sociology* (1903) and
Dynamic Sociology (1883), but spent most of the time on the second book,
which presented his views on women's issues.

Kakichi had opinions on every conceivable subject, and rather than read-ing the book page by page, he picked out an idea and digressed into an expo-sition of his own theories. Again, instead of giving us a literal translation, he quickly paraphrased whole passages, so that Waka and I had to study on our own just to keep up. Waka's translations of three chapters from *Dynamic Soci-ology* appear in *Seitō* as "Women's Education" [vol. 5, no. 3], "Science and Women's Issues" [vol. 5, no. 4], and "Female Intuition" [vol. 5, no. 5]. My partial translation of "Maternal Love" in *Pure Sociology* appears in the Octo-ber [November; vol. 5, no. 10] issue. Waka later published a collection of her essays in 1921. She called it *The Social Significance of Romantic Love* and dedicated it to Kakichi, "who taught her everything she knew, beginning with letters, which are indispensable to a civilized life."[27]

In *Dynamic Sociology*, Ward examined contemporary women's issues from biological, physiological, and psychological standpoints. His views were advanced, but as they were derived from a purely scientific perspective, I was not too impressed. I was fascinated, however, by his chapter on "female-cen-trism" in *Pure Sociology* and drew on it in developing my own ideas about feminism. Sakai Toshihiko's translation of the chapter was published in December 1915 [as *Josei chūshin-setsu*]. Instead of explaining Ward's theory, I shall quote from Sakai's preface to his translation.

> I have no doubt that in the near future Ward's theory of female-centrism will foment heated discussion among biologists and feminists and eventually reach the general public. Indeed, as the author himself predicts, the theory will bring about the downfall of male-centrism in the same way that Copernican helio-centrism swept away superstitious geocentrism and Darwin's theory of evolution overturned anthropocentrism.
>
> …The theory posits woman as the primal source of human beings and man as an appendage that appeared later. An even more extreme version of the theory has man as originally a testicle that extricated itself from the wom-an's body and only later developed into an independent entity. Thus, man is no more than the product of woman's whim. This idea will naturally be seen as offensive to a man's dignity and will arouse strong opposition. But this, too, will subside in much the way the vehement opposition to evolution eventu-ally disappeared.[xxviii]

[xxviii] In the chapter "The Phylogenetic Forces," Ward set forth his "gynaecocentric" (as opposed to "an-drocentric") theory, according to which life began as female, man having originally been a "sac filled with spermatozoa in a liquid or gelatinous medium," "at first parasitic and then complemental to the primary organism [the female]" (*Pure Sociology* 373–374).

Saiga Kotoko and Okada Yuki, members who were studying English with Kakichi, joined our morning reading group. Yoshiya Nobuko also joined us briefly and later wrote for *Seitō*. Kotoko was from a merchant family in Chiba Prefecture. A graduate of Japan Women's College, she was five or six years younger than I. She was quiet and demure, but had a will of her own: forced to marry her dead sister's husband, who had been adopted to continue the family line, she had run away and was then living at the home of Miyata Osamu, the principal of Seijo Girls' High School, her alma mater. She told me that she had transferred to Miyata's school because he had praised me in *Jogaku sekai*, saying I was an "outstanding graduate of Japan Women's College" just when I was under attack for my affair with Morita. She also said that her mother had begged her to withdraw from Seitō after policemen made inquiries about her. (Police harassment of Seitō members was unheard of in Tokyo.)

Kotoko contributed fiction, poems, and translations to *Seitō* and deserves special mention for "The Wages of War," the only piece in the journal that even tangentially referred to World War I [vol. 5, no. 10]. Based on a tragedy that befell a soldier's family in Kotoko's village during the Russo-Japanese War, the story contains an oblique criticism of war and an earnest plea for peace.[28] I shall quote from her introduction.

> It has been over a year since the so-called advanced nations took up arms, but as yet there is no prospect of peace. When I think of the cruelties of war, the enormous direct and indirect losses, I cannot but wonder what we mean by "the blessings of civilization" or "the contributions of science." War is truly horrific. Not only does war kill untold numbers of men, leaving their bones to bleach in the wind and rain, it inflicts unbearable pain on those left at home. Victor or vanquished, both sides suffer. Why, I ask, why do human beings waste vast amounts of money, time, and knowledge to engage in senseless murder!
>
> Who was it who said that if women were sent to the battlefield, fighting would cease? Or that they would never tolerate the horrors of war? I agree completely. Compassion and love are the life and soul of women. How could they kill another human being? How could the mothers of children endure the sight of blood in the trenches?

Kotoko put out a collection of her poems, *Sazanami*, when she turned seventy. In her afterword, she set down thoughts that were reminiscent of her *Seitō* story.

> I happened to see a band of musicians advertising a store. As they walked by the house, I stared at them and thought I would like to walk around like that from

one end of the city to another. But instead of advertising a store, I would carry a sign saying I opposed war. Unfortunately, my legs are too feeble. I wonder if there is someone who will take my place.

Noe also joined the reading group and brought the baby Makoto with her, but she quit after two or three classes. Kakichi had little patience with the fussing baby and Noe may have also sensed that he and Waka harbored a vague antipathy toward her. She couldn't very well leave the baby behind, but its presence was still an imposition, and Kakichi, who could be difficult and demanding and had his likes and dislikes, probably took this as one more instance of her careless ways.

Kakichi was also critical of Noe's writings, calling them excessively emotional. She was living with Tsuji at the time, but later, when she ran off with Ōsugi Sakae, he and Waka were indignant. They could not understand how a mother could be so irresponsible as to abandon her own child. Their sympathy for Ōsugi's wife, Hori Yasuko, played no small part in their views, but if I may venture a guess, their condemnation of Noe stemmed more from their general hatred of "egotistical socialists."

Another point Kakichi repeatedly stressed was the irrationality of what he considered self-centered feminist arguments. A sound theory called for a broad vision that encompassed the relations between women and children, women and men, women and society. Any solution that wrested the child from the mother spelled disaster for women, society, and humanity. He also said that when women demanded rights just because they participated in the labor force like men, they not only threw away their self-respect but also surrendered to men.

I regret that more women did not take advantage of Kakichi's broad knowledge to arrive at a deeper theoretical understanding of women's issues. When we began publishing articles on the subject, large numbers of women came to talk about their domestic problems—the office often resembled a counseling center—but not one expressed an interest in thinking about her personal situation in the broader context of women's issues. Among the members, too, only Ueno Yōko, Itō Noe, Iwano Kiyoko, Katō Midori, and Yamada Waka supported the journal's new emphasis. The rest seemed content to stick with literature.

◎ ◎ ◎ ◎ ◎

We were still living in Minami Iga-chō when a woman called Eguchi Ayako suddenly appeared at our house. She told us that she was from Yanagawa in Kyushu, and that her husband's philandering had driven her to commit suicide, but unable to die, she had fled her home. Showing us a picture of herself in a formal white kimono, she said she had tried to starve to death by only drinking "blood red wine." What she did not tell us—and this I heard later from Nishizaki Hanayo—was that she herself had been involved with a local middle school teacher.

After staying with us for a while, Ayako moved to Yamada Waka's house to help out in the kitchen. This didn't work out, and after returning to our house briefly, she went to live with Hanayo and her husband Ikuta Shungetsu. In the course of her wanderings, she met the poet Kitahara Hakushū, who was also from Yanagawa. He had just separated from his wife; Ayako was beautiful, with literary sensibilities; and they were married in 1916. Apparently Hakushū's younger brother detested Ayako, who was impractical and lazy, completely wrapped up in her poetic thoughts. Once, when she saw me holding Akemi in my arms, she sighed, "Oh, just like Mary and the Christ child!"

Hakushū's reputation rose, and his income accordingly, but then four years later, Ayako fell in love with one of his students and left him. The young man went off to the United States, and next she started living with a Zen monk, the abbot of a subtemple at Daitokuji in Kyoto. The monk furnished the money for Ayako to publish her poems—I received a copy—and they seemed to be quite happy, although, according to Hanayo, he lost his chance to become head abbot of Daitokuji when he was criticized mercilessly by the local newspapers.

Three years later a younger monk appeared on the scene. Ayako went to live with him at a temple in Shikoku. (A photo she sent at the time shows her dressed like a pilgrim.) But in time she left him, too, and after staying at a Buddhist home for the elderly in Kyoto, she ended her days with relatives in Kyushu. She was in her forties and childless. Hanayo, who was also child-less, once said, "Yes, I suppose you could say that Ayako was someone who made love her profession." I have told her story because she represented one type of woman who in her own way defied the feudalistic family system of that period.

⊙ ⊙ ⊙ ⊙ ⊙

[In 1915] Kiyoko finally decided to break with Hōmei. The immediate reason was Hōmei's affair with Kanbara Fusae, but needless to say, the basic reason was their inability to get along with each other. Kanbara Fusae had been a Seitō member from the time she taught at an elementary school in Niigata Prefecture. Angered by her male colleagues' lack of sympathy for Seitō, she had left her job and come to Tokyo. Like other members who sought help, she needed a job, and Kiyoko arranged for her to work as a secretary for Hōmei, who, as I mentioned, was translating Plutarch's *Parallel Lives*. A grateful Fusae attended to her duties conscientiously, but in a moment of weakness she yielded to Hōmei's overtures; the result was a classic case of the eternal triangle. True to his philosophy of momentarism, Hōmei had been involved with women before, but since living with Kiyoko, he had been faithful. Kiyoko had her complaints, but on this score she had felt that she could trust him. She was shocked, especially since she had gone out of her way to befriend the woman. She felt betrayed, as if she had been "forced to drink boiling water." After giving the matter much thought, she decided not to divorce him but to get a legal separation.

Kiyoko came to the house to talk about her decision. She looked haggard, but she had not been in such good spirits for a long time. "I'll be just as I was before I married him," she said, smiling. "I'll handle everything myself—my daily affairs, the affairs of my heart. Please don't worry. I've gotten over it. I'm determined to make my way alone and I feel much better."

I told her that I supported her decision to a certain point. She would certainly be happier without Hōmei, but why wasn't she seeking a divorce? She assured me that her decision was not based on any residual affection between them, or some vague hope that he might return to her one day. Nor was she willing, like so many wives, to condone an adulterous spouse for financial reasons or for the sake of the children. Rather, she had made her decision because she wished to protect her "legal position as a wife." She was asserting her rights as a wife not just for herself, but for all unfortunate wives, indeed, for all women.

Kiyoko was not concerned with love or alienation of affection, but with defending her position and rights as a wife within the framework of the Civil Code. Though I admired her courage, I felt she had taken a hopeless stance because the position of the female spouse as defined by the code was humiliating, meaningless, and certainly not worth defending. I also thought she was being inconsistent. She had repeatedly talked about the centrality of love in marriage and said that she and Hōmei had agreed at the time of their marriage that they would terminate it if Hōmei's attention even briefly wandered to another woman.

Hōmei moved out of the house in August and began living with Fusae, while the two children stayed with Kiyoko. The younger child had been born the previous February, and the older child was Hōmei's by his first wife; already in elementary school, the child had asked to stay with Kiyoko. Hōmei neglected to send the money to support the children—about 25 yen a month—and Kiyoko, who was of a legalistic turn of mind, went to court and sued him for failing to live with his legal spouse. When Hōmei countersued for divorce, his petition was dismissed, and he was ordered to "live with Kiyoko in compliance with her appeal." All this took place in December. Since both

Kiyoko and Hōmei were headstrong and hated to lose, their marriage came to an ugly end.

When I heard about the legal proceedings, I felt that Kiyoko and I lived in two different worlds. I was particularly distressed to hear that Hōmei's search for a pretext for divorce had dragged Tanaka Ōdō into the proceedings. Hōmei insinuated that the lonely scholar's friendship with Kiyoko was actually a romantic affair involving sexual intimacies. This was an unfair accusation, sneaky, shameless, and utterly contemptible. Having lived with Kiyoko for five years, Hōmei should have known that she held herself to the strictest standards and would never venture beyond the boundaries of propriety, especially since she wanted to maintain her legal position as a wife. It is no surprise that his brazen petition was rejected.

Kiyoko seemed satisfied with the verdict; her victory was not just for herself but for all women in the same situation. Then she reversed herself when she petitioned for a legal divorce, a move some people called utter nonsense. Fukushima Shirō, the head of the *Fujo shinbun*, wrote: "Kiyoko may have won on paper, but in fact she lost. Hōmei may have lost on paper, but in fact he won. Was there ever such a ridiculous legal proceeding?"[29]

The divorce went through; Kiyoko returned to using her maiden name, Endō, and entered her child as an adopted son in the Endō family register. Hōmei was placed under court order to pay for the child's education, but of course, no one expected him to live up to his obligations. The older child was sent to live with Hōmei. For some reason, whenever I think of Kiyoko, I think of Yasuda Satsuki. As natives of downtown Tokyo—Kiyoko was particularly proud that she was born in Kanda—both were stubborn and assertive, yet surprisingly fragile.

Soon after we moved to the house in Minami Iga-chō in midsummer [1915], Okumura came down with a persistent cough, which at first did not particularly worry us. He was studying French with Kakichi and sketching daily in the Koishikawa Botanical Garden. Then his cough worsened and he also developed a slight fever. He got some medicine from the doctor, since he thought he might be suffering from the aftereffects of a cold he had caught before our move. He did not improve. He gave up painting and his French lessons and spent most of the day lying down. Pale to begin with, his skin took on a greenish tinge and he visibly began to lose weight.

Alarmed, I urged him to see Dr. Takada, the specialist who had treated Kōkichi several years earlier. Okumura had an aversion to doctors, but I finally persuaded him to go. The doctor diagnosed his illness as the preliminary stage of tuberculosis and told him to go to the sanatorium in Chigasaki as soon as his fever abated. Okumura had never been sick in his life and took the diagnosis in stride. But I was deeply concerned, although I kept this to myself.

Unlike today, tuberculosis often carried a sentence of death. When would he recover? What if he died? How would we pay the hospital bills, with the child due at the end of the year? It was all we could do to pay our daily expenses, and in my condition I could not possibly take on more work.

In desperation, I made the round of publishing houses, borrowed as much as I could, and committed myself to several assignments. I also sold what I could of Okumura's paintings and borrowed money from Waka to tide us over. "The Year of Bad Luck," a fictional account about this difficult period in our lives, was one of the commitments I took on the following year.[xxix] It was published along with Tamura Toshiko's "Snake" in the December 1916 *Chūō kōron*.

Okumura's fever dropped to about normal for five or six days, and in September, he received permission to go to the sanatorium in Chigasaki. The place was full of memories, for we had first met there in the reception room, so despite the unhappy circumstances, we boarded the train with a tingle of anticipation. When the time came to say good-bye, Okumura tried to cheer me up. "When the baby's due, I'll be there by your side. I'll be better by then, I promise." But in our hearts, we knew this was too much to hope for.

I returned to Tokyo. With the exception of trips to the sanatorium, I stayed at home, immersed in work, and waited for the baby. Although he had occasional setbacks, Okumura seemed to be improving until I received a letter saying he had to be operated on for an anal fistula. Fortunately, he recovered quickly after only one operation. His natural optimism most certainly helped.

⊚ ⊚ ⊚ ⊚ ⊚

It was December, the baby due any day. At the first sign of labor, I gathered together my personal belongings and a set of baby clothes and took a rickshaw to the Shinoda Hospital in Hongō Higashikata-machi. The director, a female physician, had taken care of my family for years. In deference to my father, my mother never came to the house, but she had made all the arrangements. Everyone on the staff was solicitous, in fact, too solicitous for comfort.

The doctor had warned me that the delivery might be difficult: I was old to be giving birth to a first child, I was not particularly strong, and my pelvis was narrow. The labor pains were worse than I imagined, the contractions weak and prolonged. I spent the night in agony, gasping for breath. In the early hours of the morning, the baby was finally born, feet first, half dead, with the

---

[xxix] In Japan certain ages are considered unlucky: for men, 25, 42 and 60; for women, 19 and 33. In 1915, Okumura was 25 by Japanese count.

placenta wrapped around its jaws. The doctor said that my frequent train trips to Chigasaki had caused the complications. Prepared for the worst, the doctor apparently phoned my mother, who came right away but left once she saw that both mother and child were out of danger.

I had brought a new life into the world. Overjoyed and immensely relieved, I asked the hospital to send a telegram to Okumura. I could hardly wait to see the baby girl, but for some reason no one brought her in. I wondered if something was wrong, but then I learned that this was hospital policy for mothers weakened by protracted labor.

The hospital thoughtfully posted a sign declining visitors, but news of the baby's birth leaked out. Reporters ignored the sign and barged into my room to pester me with questions: "What are your thoughts?" "How do you feel?" Mass communication had not developed to today's level, or perhaps the lack of development made the public always hungry for news. A woman who advocated the freedom of romantic love and a new sexual morality, a woman who opposed traditional marriage and refused to legalize her union—this woman had given birth to an illegitimate child. What could be more titillating?

Noe came to see me. She was furious. "Those stupid reporters! Haven't they got any sense? If they show up while I'm here, I'll tell them a thing or two!" Tanaka Ōdō came with a pot of flowers, but when a reporter tried to slip in, Ōdō merely put on a gentle smile and ushered the man out of the room.

By law, a newborn child had to be registered at the local ward office. This had been weighing on my mind ever since I learned I was pregnant. I myself had no qualms about having a so-called illegitimate child and didn't care what people said, but I was reluctant to cause my father further trouble. He had his social position to consider, and I had embarrassed him enough. So I decided to set up a branch family and designate myself as its legal head. Although this was no more than a formality, I felt I owed this to my parents. There was no doubt that the child was Okumura's and mine, but since we were not married in the eyes of the law and had no family register with our names, I decided to create a new register in my name and enter the child. [In accordance with the existing law,] I wrote to my parents for permission to establish a branch family and sent my mother the documents requiring my father's registered seal.

The child was born, and I had yet to hear from my father, though the deadline for notification was fast approaching. I was deeply worried, but the documents came back just in time. I could now set up a branch family and register the baby as a child recognized by the father. I sent someone to the local ward office to act in my place and do the necessary paperwork. At first, the official in charge refused my request and insisted that an illegitimate child acknowledged by the father had to be entered in the father's register, but he eventually agreed.

I kept Okumura informed about this step I was taking and obtained his consent. But he was not interested in such legal formalities as setting up a branch family or registering the child's birth. So I actually settled everything myself. Sometime later, I discovered that Akemi—so named because she was born at dawn—was entered in the register as "illegitimate." The child was the fruit of our love, its paternity established beyond a doubt, but on paper Akemi was illegitimate and fatherless. Such was the law in Japan at the time.[xxx]

Several days before New Year's, I was allowed to go home. Waka, who visited regularly, came to pick me up. Carrying the baby, she got in one rickshaw while I took another. Together we made our way through the windswept streets, which were crowded with people going about their year-end errands.

At home alone with the baby, I could only marvel at the change wrought by the presence of a tiny new being. Everything about the house was different; I was different. My heart fairly burst with tenderness at the sight of little Akemi sleeping in her red kimono on a little quilt. I could not believe that I had thought of rejecting her for even one moment. In my mind, there was an immense gap between the child in the womb and the child I held in my arms, the child I could touch and feel. When I had first seen Akemi at the hospital, I had gazed speechless at the red face of the small human being swaddled in thick clothes, unmoved by the usual sentiments—"Oh, how sweet!" or "My very own baby!" I could have been a dispassionate observer. But now, my maternal instincts had suddenly burst forth. No one could take the child away from me.

Yet I also have to admit that I was harried by the endless round of tasks, the importunate cries of the baby, the lack of sleep. I had no time for myself; the books on the desk remained untouched. Unable to attend to my own needs, I felt frustrated and anxious. I was too tired to write, and I wondered how we were going to pay the bills. Worried and exhausted, I felt myself dangerously close to losing my mental equilibrium. And all the while, I felt guilty for thinking of my own needs and not giving myself to the child with unalloyed joy.[30]

I made up my mind to close down the house and move to Chigasaki. I knew Okumura's recovery depended on the doctors and medicine, but I was also convinced that his health ultimately rested in my hands. I did not have the dimmest notion how I was going to do this, but I was determined to bring father, mother, and child together. I left on February 11, 1916, the day after I turned thirty [by Western count].

[xxx] The law made a distinction between a child who was born out of wedlock but acknowledged by the father and entered into the father's registry (*shoshi*) and a child who was not legally recognized (*shiseiji*). Had Okumura set up his own family register (*koseki*), the child would have been entered as his child and suffered little social opprobrium. Raichō's two children took the name Hiratsuka.

I rented a room at the house where I had previously stayed. Each day, I carried the baby on my back and took Okumura his meals. A confirmed vegetarian, he was heartily sick of the hospital diet, which was rich in animal protein. He particularly disliked the dishes made with eggs and milk, so I set myself to the task of cooking nutritious vegetarian dishes more to his taste.

Okumura miraculously rallied, as though he had been waiting for us to come. He was permitted to go down to the sheds on the beach for recovering patients. We took our meals there in a festive picnic mood, gazing at the view, which, according to Dr. Takada, was the loveliest in Japan. In the evening, clouds edged with gold hovered on the horizon, luminous in the deepening madder-red sky. Once in a while, a multitude of crows descended on the beach and painted the sand a solid black as they feasted raucously on the pickings.

By the end of the summer Okumura's health had improved enough for him to be allowed to convalesce at home. We rented rooms in the wing of a public bathhouse near the hospital. As I was faced with the triple task of attending to Okumura, the baby, and my writing, I hired a young girl to help me.

The doctor told us to take every precaution to protect the baby, so we disinfected everything. Nursing the baby was even more time-consuming. Akemi had become used to the bottle during her long stay at the hospital and shunned my breast and screamed as if she had been "set on fire." Finally the baby refused to nurse altogether—I did not have much milk to begin with—and I then had to prepare a formula. The baby cried while I was fixing it, and cried whenever I set her down because she was used to being carried by the nurses. In order not to disturb Okumura, who was sleeping in the next room, I walked up and down the hall of the main building all night, jiggling the baby to keep her quiet. At times I felt like crying myself. A mother's life was indeed a succession of never-ending chores. I was frazzled and irritated. Working on a manuscript several nights in a row was nothing compared to this. What had become of my life, my identity as an independent being? I grieved to think of what I had lost.

On top of this, I worried that the baby would become infected despite all my precautions. I thought of sending her out to nurse and made inquiries about a suitable family. None could be found, but this was just as well, since little Akemi had begun to recognize me and smile.

Being a full-time mother and housewife was arduous and painful, but not without its compensations. More important, Okumura was now strong enough to go out and sketch, and when Dr. Takada kindly offered to take a painting in lieu of payment, he started working on a landscape of the hospital grounds. We shall never forget the doctor's generous gesture at this difficult time in our lives. Dr. Takada also asked me to brush a few words in his album. I wrote

"Life, death, equally beautiful." To my delight, he apparently told Yasumochi Yoshiko that my calligraphy was quite the finest he had ever seen.

We kept to ourselves in Chigasaki, though we occasionally saw Shiraki Shizuko and her husband, the painter Uenoyama Seikō. Shizuko, who was known for her sensitive stories, was small and frail looking, and wore her hair in a simple ichōgaeshi. She was living in Chigasaki because she also suffered from tuberculosis, but she seemed to have no concept of the nature of the disease and nursed her baby even when she had a high fever. Alarmed, I finally spoke to her husband about it. "I can't tell her to stop," he said. "It's one of the biggest joys in her life." Shizuko had lost a leg in an operation and hobbled about on a cane trying to write and do the housework. The poor woman died in 1918, at age twenty-four. Her husband took care of the baby, and when I saw him many years later at a Nikakai exhibit, where he had a painting, I was happy to hear that the baby had grown into a healthy adult.[31]

As the family gradually settled into a daily routine, I began translating Key's *Renaissance of Motherhood*. We rarely had visitors, but Katō Asadori, Midori's husband, came to see us one day. In contrast to Midori, who was nervous and tense, he was like a child of nature, roly-poly, with rounded shoulders and a smile of cherubic innocence on his ruddy face. A writer by profession, he complained about his poverty whenever he saw us, but his innate sense of humor soon got the better of him, and he always looked as if he were enjoying life, with dejection far away. As usual, he was in need of money and had come to ask whether there was anything on the Woman Question that he might translate. Since he sounded desperate, I suggested the book by Key that I had just begun to work on. His translation was published, despite my objections, under my name by Shinchōsha in May 1919.

Asadori was gifted and productive but too high-minded to follow the lead of others. Isolated from cliquish literary circles, he remained poor all his life. Some years later, he received an award from the Polish government for introducing Polish literature to Japan and was nominated to the Polish Academy of the Arts.[32] Toward the end of his life, he started a magazine called *Echo* (*Hankyō*), but it was not successful.[xxxi] Araki Ikuko was friendly with Asadori and Midori and helped them out from time to time. She criticized Midori for not being more supportive of her husband, but Midori was a practical person and must have felt frustrated being married to a man with the romantic sensibilities of a poet. As it was, Midori wore herself out working as a writer, reporter, and mother of two small children, and died [at age thirty-four] in 1922.

[xxxi] Not to be confused with Ikuta Chōkō's journal of opinion.

⊚ ⊚ ⊚ ⊚ ⊚

If I may backtrack a month or so, Okumura was still at the sanatorium when he began corresponding with Arishima Yasuko. She was hospitalized with the same illness, and her husband Takeo asked his friends and acquaintances to write to her to cheer her up. Okumura and I received a letter from Arishima and I forwarded it to the sanatorium. "Misery loves company": Okumura wrote to her immediately, and a lively correspondence ensued. Yasuko was unable to see her children and sympathized with Okumura, who had yet to see Akemi. In one letter, she enclosed a photo of herself as if she had a premonition of impending death. She was beautiful, with the sweet, innocent look of a young girl. That was the last letter she sent to Okumura.

Yasuko died in August. The moment he heard of her death, Okumura stole away from the stern gaze of the nurses, found a bouquet of white chrysanthemums in town, and took the train to the hospital in Hiratsuka. Arishima, who was looking in vain for flowers, put them inside the coffin. The cremation took place on the seashore nearby. In the deepening twilight, Okumura stood watching until the last embers died down. He must have found this experience terribly painful, since he talked about that day many times afterward.

Noe and Ōsugi Sakae

Since moving to Chigasaki, I had not heard from Noe. There were rumors that she had left Tsuji in April [1916] to be with Ōsugi Sakae. I was naturally concerned. She had complained about tensions at home but not once mentioned Ōsugi. I also thought of Ōsugi's wife, Hori Yasuko, who had shared years of hardship with him and was now in poor health. To complicate matters further, Kamichika Ichiko, a member of Ōsugi's French-language study group, was also said to be romantically involved with him. Where would this all end?

One day, I received an unexpected letter from Noe. She had left Tsuji. Knowing I would either oppose her or rebuke her, she had probably waited to write until she made the final break. The letter was short and succinct: she fully realized that people would criticize her, but she had no other choice. There was no mention of Ōsugi. I was shocked yet at the same time resigned, since what she did seemed inevitable. Still, I worried about the children.

I was aware that her life with Tsuji was not easy, especially when they were living with his parents, sister, and brother-in-law. Noe, who was caught in a tangle of emotions, no doubt felt like an intruder. Also, even after the birth of the first child, Tsuji made no attempt to look for a regular job. Nor was he a particularly loving or attentive father. His mother, too, unlike most grandmothers, never offered to help with the baby or share household chores. Whenever I went to the house in Takebaya-chō, Noe was the one scrubbing and cooking and cleaning. Although she had no time to study or think, much less do her work, her steely determination somehow enabled her to write with the baby on her lap.

Sometime around the summer of 1914, I noticed that Noe had begun to lose the bloom of youth, the raw vitality that suggested a flower in the wilderness. She looked pale and tired, her narrow forehead marked with worry lines, her eyes dark with despair. She was thinner, irritable, almost hysterical.[33] As I watched her suffer, I felt like scolding Tsuji for being so cold and indifferent. Irresponsible, self-centered, and lazy, he represented a certain type of thoughtless idealist who was oblivious to the world around him. Once, when I went to see Noe when she was still living in Somei, her eyes were swollen red, and with tears welling up, she said, "I'm thinking of going back to Kyushu with the baby, but I won't be able to unless someone comes with me part way." She was still attached to Tsuji and stayed.

From around the fall of 1915 [1914], her ideas made it increasingly clear that Noe was going through what she called "a change of heart." As she wrote in her essay "On Taking Over *Seitō*" in the January 1915 issue [vol. 5, no. 1]:

> Until now I have thought that an immense distance separated me from society and that I would be denying my selfhood if I concerned myself with social issues. No longer do I feel there is a contradiction between the two. After thinking about this many times over, I realize that I have never thought the matter through. I became dissatisfied with my previous attitude, which I assumed was for the best. Now, I can throw myself into a social movement without feeling any contradiction or twinge of conscience. But all this is still in my head and I have yet to work myself up to the proper pitch of passion.

In the Editors' Notes of the November and December 1914 issues, she had already expressed her admiration and support for Ōsugi and Arahata Kanson, whose socialist newspaper *Heimin shinbun* was repeatedly banned. She also criticized the indifference of their wives and the lack of cooperation from their spineless fellow socialists.[34] Under the influence of Watanabe Masatarō and other socialist friends of Tsuji's, her social conscience had been awakened, and the vague and confused emotions she herself had yet to understand would soon lead her to embrace socialism.

There was also a personal reason for Noe's "change of heart"—her growing, albeit complicated, feelings for Ōsugi, who had everything that Tsuji lacked (the capacity for action, for instance).[xxxii] Then, while Noe was going through her "change of heart," Tsuji fell in love with her cousin Kimi. Noe felt as if she had been stabbed in the back, and, pregnant with her second child, she was plunged into despair. I was at a loss for words of comfort.

Tsuji's affair was short-lived and not as serious as Noe feared, but the damage had been done; her feelings for Tsuji were never the same again. She wrote about the affair in an essay called "Random Thoughts" in the July 1915 issue [vol. 5, no. 7].[35] Then, in mid-July, she suddenly announced that she was returning to her family home in Kyushu to have her baby. She planned to stay for three months; Tsuji and the child were accompanying her. She asked Nishizaki Hanayo to take over the editing and Andō Kosan, at the Nichigetsusha, to look after the business for the next three months.

The following message from Noe appears in the Editors' Notes of the September 1915 issue [vol. 5, no. 8].

> Many readers must be alarmed by the gossip surrounding our journal. But rest assured, I have no intention of discontinuing Seitō … I hope to do my share of the work when I return to Tokyo. Being here in my hometown after an absence of many months, I find much that is interesting and amusing. I was hoping to write about my impressions for this issue, but I am afraid I will have to save that for the next issue. Please forgive me.

Noe gives no explanation for returning to Kyushu with her husband and child, nor why she chose to stay at her family home where she was surely not welcome. She was in good health, and three or four months seemed a long time to be away from the office. Many readers must have been mystified. In the October issue a brief note from the publisher says that Noe has written to say she will not return in late September, as planned, nor will she send in a manuscript. "Literary Fragments," a nine-page essay by Noe, appears in the November issue [vol. 5, no. 10], but it is about her impressions of her home village and not about herself. A note by the editor on the back page informs the readers that Noe plans to return "on or about November 20 and is looking forward to putting out the New Year's issue." But again, there is no mention of why she went to Kyushu.

This may be pure conjecture, but I think the trip to Kyushu, though ostensibly to have the baby, was really to save the marriage.[xxxiii] Their relationship had reached an impasse, and her work for Seitō kept getting in the way. Away

---

[xxxii] Noe first met Ōsugi in September 1914. Ōsugi admired her writings, but they did not become romantically involved until February 1916. Stanley, Ōsugi Sakae, Anarchist in Taishō Japan, 94.
[xxxiii] Noe and Tsuji formally registered their marriage in July 1915.

from Tokyo, they might be able to heal the wounds and even rekindle their love. For Noe, at least, the trip was probably a last-ditch effort. As much as she resented Tsuji, she still loved him. She also wanted to continue the journal with his help and guidance, and as she told me later, she had planned to leave the newborn child with a family in Kyushu. (I firmly believe that Tsuji himself never wavered in his love for Noe.)

Noe gave birth to a baby boy in August, and in late November, she returned to Tokyo with Tsuji and the two children. The New Year's edition came out as scheduled. As announced, the journal was drastically changed—the regulations rewritten, the format and layout simplified. If viewed in a favorable light, the issue was a condensed version of the old *Seitō*. The February issue [1916] also was published.

Then, in April, Noe left Tsuji, the older child, *Seitō*, everything, to be with Ōsugi. She took only the baby with her. Just as her love for Tsuji had impelled her to escape from her first predicament, so her new love for Ōsugi impelled her to abandon a hopeless marriage. *Seitō* was suspended indefinitely. In Noe's hands, it had lasted a year and two months.[36]

The Hikage Inn Incident

We were still living in Chigasaki when Noe and Ōsugi appeared unannounced at our door sometime past noon on November 6. They were on their way to Hayama and stopped by to inquire about Okumura's health. I took one look at Noe and could not believe my eyes. Was this the Noe I once knew—the young girl with the wild, untamed beauty who never cared about her appearance? I looked at her in the slanting rays of the late autumn sun and felt myself close to uttering a reproach. In the past, she had occasionally arranged her hair in the traditional style, but that day, she had combed it in the simple style of a middle-aged downtown woman. The collar of her striped silk kimono was pulled back revealingly, and for a change, she wore a proper obi instead of her half-width obi. But she looked less like a chic geisha than a waitress in a tea shop. "My, you've changed. You really have." I could not stop repeating myself. Noe replied with only an enigmatic smile.

Ōsugi—this would be the first and last time we met—was wearing a silk kasuri kimono. Thin but sturdy looking, he had dark skin and stern features. What immediately caught my attention were his enormous round eyes. He did not have a pleasant face, but once he started talking, he was quite likable—cheerful and relaxed, ready to talk about this and that, as though we were old friends.

Noe remained quiet. Up close, she looked thinner in the face, tired, even hard, without a trace of the rounded softness or effervescence of youth. When I asked if she was living with Ōsugi, she mumbled something noncommittal, no doubt hoping to fend off any criticism.

Ōsugi seemed to be fond of children, and with a big smile—he had a wispy goatee—he picked up Akemi and dandled her on his lap, saying, "Children are nice, aren't they—really cute." I took the opportunity to ask Noe about her baby, but her only answer was an expressionless "Well—." The baby, as I learned later, had been farmed out to a fisherman's family in Onjuku, where she had gone [with Ōsugi] after leaving Tsuji.

I am sure that Noe most dreaded being questioned about the journal. Since she had protested vehemently when I said we should give it up and assured me that she could manage on her own, an admission of defeat would have galled her. I could understand how she felt, so I said, "When you do the work yourself, it's much harder than you think, don't you agree? Far different from being on the outside looking in. Well, you mustn't strain yourself—." She said that once everything was settled, she intended to bring the journal out on a smaller scale. She was putting up a brave front, but she sounded doubtful. Actually, the February issue was the last.

I also suspected that Noe had not been the one to suggest coming to see us. She had probably mentioned to Ōsugi that we were living in Chigasaki, and he had suggested the visit on an impulse. Incidentally, they seem to have been shadowed by the police. The neighbors told us afterward that they had noticed two policemen standing guard in front of the bathhouse. They assumed that a thief had escaped inside and had peered through the fence, hoping to catch a glimpse of the culprit.

Noe and Ōsugi left just as the sun was about to set. We went outside to see them off. Ōsugi strode ahead, and Noe, much smaller, followed behind, scurrying along to keep up. If you didn't know better, you would have thought that they were a patron and a teahouse maid out on an evening stroll. As I watched them disappear into the fading light, I felt a pang of sadness and disappointment. Their affair had caused much heartbreak to those close to them. For their sake, at least, I hoped and prayed that the strength of their love would take them forward. From what I saw of the two of them that day, I was not at all hopeful.

◎ ◎ ◎ ◎ ◎

The so-called Hikage Teahouse Incident took place two [three] days later. To quote the headlines in the November 10 *Tokyo Asahi*:

Ōsugi Sakae Stabbed by Mistress. Victim Well Known Socialist. Assailant Female Journalist Kamichika Ichiko. Scene of Tragedy Hikage Teahouse in Hayama Kanagawa Prefecture.

The incident was reported as the inevitable consequence of free love carried to the extreme.

Since I had just seen Noe and Ōsugi, I was stunned. I had heard that Ichiko was close to Ōsugi, but did not know that their relationship was so deep that she would be driven to stab him in a jealous frenzy. I was saddened, too, for had it not been for Noe, she would not have been compelled to do something so desperate. I also thought back to the time I first met Ichiko and noticed that her large, jittery, bloodshot eyes glittered with a strange, ominous light. I do not know what a student of physiognomy would have said, but I, for one, had been quite unnerved. Perhaps, even then, she was the kind of person who was prone to extreme behavior, but then again, maybe stabbing her lover was Ichiko's only choice, given the circumstances. I did not think she was entirely to blame. Even so, I feared the larger reverberations of this three-sided affair of free love gone wrong. It could only hurt the cause of those who opposed feudalistic morality and called for a new sexual morality.

The incident, together with the Iwano divorce proceedings, gave rise to a rash of articles on love and chastity. "Love triangle," "multiparty relationships," and other neologisms filled the air. I felt I had to address these issues, and wrote an article called "So-Called Free Love and Its Limits" [for the *Osaka Mainichi* newspaper]. The following is an excerpt.

Inasmuch as the task of establishing a new sexual morality entails difficult and complex problems, there will inevitably be all manner of unforeseen mistakes and confusion.... Thus, even if an unfortunate incident or two occurs in our midst, I cannot agree with the small number of so-called moralists who prematurely take a gloomy view and say we should turn the boat back, so to speak, to our original point of departure. I believe the wisest course is to remain silent and regard such occurrences with sympathy and forbearance.

This is not to say that I shall remain silent if people commit an act that is immoral or amoral by the standards of even the most advanced morality of our age. Particularly so, if the people involved refuse to reflect on their action, or worse, flaunt and justify it as if it were part of the new morality.

A case in point is the recent incident involving Ōsugi and others. Free love, as the parties seem to think, is not polygamy (or polyandry or a combination of the two). To be more specific, it is not a sexual relationship in which a man and a woman love each other but live apart independently and engage at will in liaisons with whomever happens to catch their fancy. Nor is free love a relationship in which the partners separate arbitrarily once love dims, with no regard to the children. A sexual relationship that is irresponsible and devoid of self-restraint, that is to say, a relationship lacking any desire or will to live in a permanent union, is nothing but an egregious abuse of free love.

…And yet, one of the so-called New Women has completely lost sight of the fact that free love in its true sense must be accompanied by a desire to live permanently with one's partner and a desire to take responsibility for the children of that union. She has accepted her lover's misconceived notions of free love without a murmur of criticism and without any reflection upon her own responsibilities. By putting her lover's notions into practice, she has provoked a murderous act of vengeance. I find this truly regrettable.[37]

Under existing law, Kamichika Ichiko was sentenced to [four years in] prison. Ōsugi, who was at least partly responsible, was not even ordered to appear in court and continued to live with Noe. Hori Yasuko cut off all ties with her husband—they had no children—and moved to the house near Yamada Waka and Kakichi that we had once rented. The couple looked after Yasuko, who suffered from ill health. She died about six months after Ōsugi's and Noe's tragic death [in 1923].[xxxiv] Tsuji, who loved Noe to the end, took care of the older child, Makoto, and periodically left the boy with friends. He spent his last years wandering from place to place, his bamboo flute and flask of sake always at his side.[38]

⊚ ⊚ ⊚ ⊚ ⊚

Ignored and dismissed, women had long been treated as merely "female" and less than human.[xxxv] Thus, in asserting our womanhood, we also asserted ourselves as human beings. We gave voice to our demands—our need for self-fulfillment, our quest to fashion our own lives, all those requirements that originated in the self—and along the way we experienced love, eventually expanding our sense of selfhood to include lover, husband, and children. But we were also confronted by reality, the hard facts of everyday existence. As we then struggled with life's contradictions, sorrows, and disappointments, we had to emerge from our small, individuated selves and our preoccupation with self-transformation to turn our gaze toward society's larger issues. Con-

---

xxxiv On September 16, 1923, fifteen days after the Great Kantō Earthquake, Ōsugi and Noe were murdered by a military officer. See Translator's Afterword, 304–305.

xxxv Here, Raichō distinguishes between "onna," a traditional word that can have negative connotations, depending on the context, and "josei," a more neutral modern word.

fronting us was a multitude of seemingly insolvable problems that called for the strength of more than one individual. A veritable wall towered before us.

The women at Seitō had changed. The journal was no more. For better or for worse, the Hikage Teahouse Incident served as its elegy. My own youth, too, had come to an end.

Translator's Afterword

In the summer of 1917, two and a half years after withdrawing from *Seitō*, Raichō returned from Chigasaki to Tokyo. Okumura had recovered from his illness and she was pregnant again. A son, Yoshibumi, was born in September. Early the next year, her parents unexpectedly gave Raichō the money left over from her dowry to buy a house; the birth of two grandchildren had brought about a reconciliation. The new house, in Tabata, had an atelier for Okumura. A small room on the second floor would be her study. As Raichō wrote:

> Relieved of the care of an ailing husband and settled in our own house, I felt a modicum of inner peace restored. In many respects the year 1918 was a time when I began to reclaim my selfhood. It was also a time when I gave more thought to women's issues, for my experience as a mother and impoverished housewife had convinced me that social problems relating to women, mothers, and children could never be solved by individuals alone.[i]

Larger events also stirred her social conscience. That year, in August, housewives in Toyama Prefecture took to the streets to protest the soaring price of rice. Across the country, the angry populace broke into rice shops and set fire to the houses of the rich. Troops had to be mobilized, and thousands were arrested. The riots, and the Russian revolution one year earlier, spurred the labor and socialist movements. The movement for universal manhood suffrage gained support. There were discussions about such women's issues as equal political rights and the condition of female textile workers.

---

[i] *The Path I Took (Watakushi no aruita michi)* (hereafter *Path*), 190.

Raichō was nevertheless content to stay at home taking care of her young children. She returned briefly to the public eye when she took part in what came to be known as the "Debate on the Protection of Motherhood."

The debate began in March 1918, when Yosano Akiko wrote in her monthly column in *Fujin kōron* that she was opposed to Western feminists who called for state financial aid to young mothers. In her view, this fostered dependence and was no different from state support of the disabled and elderly.[ii] Raichō could not remain silent. In fact, their difference of opinion on the subject had already become apparent two years earlier, when she rebuked Yosano for claiming that Ellen Key asserted the "absolute centrality of motherhood."[iii] Writing in *Bunshō sekai*, Raichō had accused Yosano of misunderstanding Key, for whom motherhood was not an imperative but a free choice.[iv] Now, once again, she felt compelled to respond to Yosano.

> Mothers are the source of life, and by becoming mothers women emerge from their individuated selves and become integral members of the state and society. Thus, the protection of mothers is not only necessary for the good of the individual woman, but since children are involved, necessary for the good of society and all humankind. Given the far-reaching social significance of mothers' work, nothing could be more mistaken than to equate the demand for state protection of women during their childbearing years with "the providing of poorhouses for the elderly and disabled."[v]

The two argued back and forth, each reiterating her position. In September, Raichō's old friend, Yamada Waka, joined the debate. She supported Raichō's position since she was also a firm believer in the sanctity of motherhood.[vi] The same month, Yamakawa Kikue added her voice. Addressing her article to both Raichō and Yosano, she wrote in *Fujin kōron* that while their views were not incompatible, the only way to settle the issue was by "taking an axe to the present economic system, which is the root of all evil." Otherwise, women

---

[ii] "Women's Complete Independence," *Fujin kōron*, March 1918. *Fujin kōron* (*Women's Review*) was a progressive journal founded in January 1918 as the women's counterpart to *Chūō kōron*.

[iii] "I Reject the Overemphasis on Motherhood," *Taiyō*, February 1916. Yosano also wrote that young men and women should not get married until they were financially secure. By then her husband Tekkan's career was on the decline and Yosano, the mother of nine children (she eventually had eleven), was in effect the breadwinner in the family.

[iv] "To Yosano Akiko Regarding Her Ideas on Motherhood," *Bunshō sekai*, May 1916 (HRC 2:146–147).

[v] "Is the Demand for Protection of Motherhood a Kind of Parasitism?" *Fujin kōron*, May 1918 (HRC 2:353).

[vi] "The Protection of Motherhood and Economic Independence: In Reference to the Debate Between Yosano and Hiratsuka," *Taiyō*, September 1918.

would only be supplying cheap labor to capitalists.[vii] The debate continued into the spring of 1919. Raichō's final word on the subject was in January. After describing her own travails as a young mother, she wrote:

> Why is it that the majority of housewives cannot be economically independent? Why must they live off men, despite their never-ending work at home? Why are they not recognized as social and economic entities except through their husbands? Why do they alone receive nothing in a society that compensates every other kind of labor?…The time has come for all housewives to awaken to the enormity of the disadvantages they suffer and the extent to which society ignores, mistreats, and exploits them.… I fully agree with Western women who demand that the state guarantee the livelihood of mothers, or to be more specific, give financial compensation to mothers who must stay at home to take care of their children. For the sake of women and children, I fervently hope that housewives in Japan will similarly awaken to the economic value of their work and demand their legitimate rights from society.[viii]

Raichō's grandmother Yae died in July 1919. As she wrote in her autobiography, her grandmother had exerted a strong influence on her formative years. Yae's last years had been difficult, with her hearing and memory gone. Raichō was moved to write about her death in a short story called "Dying of Old Age."[1]

The next month, Raichō was invited to give a talk at a conference on women's issues sponsored by the *Nagoya shinbun*. Since she had been asked by the *Kokumin shinbun* to write on female labor, she stayed on to make a tour of the textile mills in the Nagoya area. Ichikawa Fusae, who was a mediator at the conference, volunteered to be her guide. She came from the area and was herself interested in labor problems.[2] What Raichō saw was a "veritable hell."

> Fluffs of cotton dust flew in the air, settled on the floor, machines, and rows of columns, covered the girls' heads like bridal veils, clung to their eyebrows and eyelashes, to their perspiring foreheads and cheeks.… More horrifying still, most of the girls were thirteen or fourteen, or at most, a year or two older.… Of an

---

[vii] " The Protection of Motherhood and Economic Independence: To Yosano and Hiratsuka," *Fujin kōron*, September 1918. Yamakawa was married to the socialist theoretician Yamakawa Hitoshi and the mother of one child at the time.

[viii] "The Dilemma of Housewives Today," *Fujin kōron*, January 1919 (*HRC* 3:33–34). For a detailed account of the debate see Hiroko Tomida, *Hiratsuka Raichō and Early Japanese Feminism*, 221–261. Also, Laurel Rasplica Rodd, "Yosano Akiko and the Taishō Debate Over the 'New Woman'" in Gail Lee Bernstein, ed., *Recreating Japanese Women, 1600–1945*.

age when they should have been playing, the girls were slaving in ninety-degree heat, assaulted by deafening noise, shackled body and soul to their machines for twelve hours.... Their eyes were bloodshot, or worse, suppurating, and devoid of the wonder and innocence of children. I shuddered to think of the damage done to their internal organs, particularly their lungs. Seeing their pale, dull, and expressionless faces…I cried out in my heart, "Poor children, I shall speak out for you. I shall defend your rights as children!"[ix]

Returning to Tokyo, she poured out her anger in the newspaper. By autumn, she had a general idea of what she wanted to do: She would form a women's organization whose chief objective was social reform. She drew up a list of goals:

1. Demand women's suffrage as the first step toward social reform. Demand the abolition or revision of feudalistic laws disadvantageous to women. Demand state support of motherhood. Take immediate action to launch a campaign.
2. Form ties with women's organizations throughout Japan and establish a large-scale women's alliance.
3. Hold public lectures in various locales on social issues related to women, labor, and everyday life.
4. Publish a journal about organization activities.
5. Found a school that will serve as an educational institute for working women and publish a working women's newspaper to establish the foundation of a sound and effective women's labor organization.
6. Build a Women's Hall with various facilities.[x]

On Yamada Waka's recommendation, Raichō asked Ichikawa Fusae to help. Ichikawa, then twenty-six, was looking for a job. Also, during their tour of the factories, Raichō had noticed that Ichikawa was extremely efficient and practical.[xi] They named their organization the New Women's Association (Shinfujin Kyōkai) and the journal, *Women's League* (*Josei dōmei*).

Then, in late November, Raichō was asked by the *Osaka Asahi shinbun* to give a talk at a meeting of the Kansai Federation of Women's Organizations. Since the meeting would give her the chance to announce her plans for the new organization, she quickly wrote a declaration and had copies printed to take with her. The declaration read:

[ix] Raichō's essays were published in the *Kokumin shinbun* from September 8. "The Lives of Women Factory Workers in the Nagoya Area," *HRC* 3:93–95.

[x] *Path* 192.

[xi] Ibid. 191–192.

Now is the time for women to unite if they are to fulfill their duties and pursue their rights. If they are to raise their position in society and attain the rights due them as women, now is the time for women not only to broaden their education and reaffirm their sense of themselves but also to unite as one and cooperate with men in the postwar movement for social reform. If they do not seize the opportunity now, the society of the future will exclude women and be even more centered on men....

We do not believe that Japanese women will remain ignorant and incompetent forever.... There are many individuals who bear comparison with Western women. Despite this, why have Japanese women not become an effective social force? Is it not because they remain isolated and make no effort to come together to achieve their common goals, or again, because they have no organization to make this possible?...To remedy this situation...we have decided to form an organization called the New Women's Association. The association will make every effort to encourage women to take collective action, protect women and improve their condition, advance their interests, and secure their due rights.[xii]

Raichō's speech, "A Call for Women to Unite," contained the same message. Unlike Seitō, the new organization would appeal to women from different social backgrounds and aim for political and social goals.

Back in Tokyo, Raichō and Ichikawa compiled a list of friends, acquaintances, and men and women in various fields who might lend their support to the association. They sent out requests, along with copies of the declaration. Approximately 200 positive replies came in, from both liberals and socialists.[xiii]

Normally, the next order of business would have been an inaugural meeting, but they decided to postpone this and draw up a draft for two petitions to present to the Diet. One petition was for the revision of Article 5 of the Police Security Regulations. The other petition was for a law to prevent men with venereal disease from marrying. The first was directly related to female suffrage, the second, to the protection of motherhood. In the aftermath of the rice riots, the Terauchi cabinet had resigned and Hara Takashi, the head of the Seiyūkai party, had become prime minister. The movement for universal manhood suffrage was gaining momentum and rallies were being held nationwide, despite frequent clashes with the police. The forty-second session of the Diet was due to open on December 26, and a bill was certain to be introduced. It seemed the ideal time for the association to present the petitions.

[xii] The complete text may be found in *Nihon fujin mondai shiryō shusei* (hereafter *Nihon fujin mondai*) 2:152–153.
[xiii] *Path* 197.

Pressed for time, Raichō and Ichikawa asked Oku Mumeo to help them. Raichō had met Oku earlier and been impressed by her "open and self-possessed manner."[xiv] Oku had also been a reporter for a pro-labor magazine and worked briefly in a textile mill in order to write about the condition of female workers. They finished the draft and in January 1920 invited about fifteen woman supporters to discuss the petitions.[xv] Aside from some minor rewording, all present approved of the drafts.

Petition to Revise Article 5 of the Police Security Regulations

For the following reasons we humbly request the elimination of "women" from Clause 1 and Clause 2 in Article 5 of the Police Security Regulations.[xvi]

1. Denying women the freedom to join political organizations or attend or initiate meetings of a political nature is in violation of the basic principles of social justice.
2. Denying women the freedom to obtain information about political matters or to participate in political activities can only hinder the development of a sound civilization.
3. If women are to join men in the great enterprise of [social] renewal and give expression to their uniquely feminine ideas in their homes and society, they must be allowed to participate in politics.
4. It is hopelessly outdated to think that giving women access to political information harms traditional female virtue and disturbs domestic peace. Families in our present age require a politically informed wife and mother who can discuss matters with her husband and educate her children wisely....
5. In today's world, women must not only manage family and home, but live as active members of society and, in some cases, hold outside jobs.... The number of such women will undoubtedly increase. For

---

[xiv] Ibid. 198. Oku Mumeo (1895–1997) was a graduate of the home economics department at Japan Women's College.

[xv] Ichikawa wrote in her autobiography that Raichō drew up the drafts and asked the legal scholar Hozumi Shigetō and a lawyer, Hirayama Rokunosuke, to look them over (*Jiden* 55). Ichikawa, who was unmarried, was not enthusiastic about the second petition and admitted that she was not sure what venereal disease was (53). She also thought that the emphasis on the protection of mothers and children was too suggestive of "good wife, wise mother-ism" (68).

[xvi] Clause 1 of Article 5 in the 1900 Police Security Regulations prohibited military men, police, Buddhist and Shinto priests, school teachers, students, women, minors, and people stripped of civil rights from joining political organizations. Clause 2 prohibited women and minors from attending or organizing political meetings.

them, political information is a practical necessity and the lack of political rights a serious disadvantage.

6. As a result of the recent war, a woman's right to vote has been recognized throughout the world. In Japan, too, people are demanding suffrage for men and women alike. To retain the prohibition contained in the existing law goes against the trend of the times.

7. Recently, our government saw fit to include a woman advisor in the delegation to the International Labor Organization Conference, and women presently attend or hold quasi-political meetings. This is irrefutable proof that the prohibition is fast becoming meaningless....

8. It is a profound contradiction to allow women to read political articles in newspapers and magazines and attend Diet sessions, yet deny them access to political meetings and other opportunities for political education, on the principle that they are still politically ignorant.

Petition for the Legal Proscription of Marriage for Men with Venereal Disease

We humbly request the enactment of the following provisions regarding men with venereal disease.

1. Men with venereal disease must not be allowed to marry.

2. A man contemplating marriage must show his intended spouse a medical certificate that proves he is free of the disease.

3. Said certificate must be submitted to the pertinent official at the time the marriage is entered into the family register.

4. In the event the husband is discovered to have concealed his disease, the marriage may be annulled.

5. In the event the husband contracts the disease after marriage or transmits it to his wife, she may file for divorce.

6. Even after the divorce, a wife who has contracted the disease from her husband is entitled to monetary compensation for medical and living expenses, plus a suitable amount to compensate for psychological hardship until she is fully recovered.[xvii]

Four reasons were cited for the second petition: the need for legislation to check the spread of venereal disease; women, who are the main victims, have no means of legal redress; statistically, men are the chief carriers; and

---

[xvii] For the entire text of the petitions see *Nihon fujin mondai* 2:154–156.

"in order to improve the quality of the nation's people and enable men and women to fulfill their common duty to the human race."[3]

Copies of the petitions and the declaration were mailed to supporting members and various women's organizations along with a request to return the papers stamped and signed. By early February, most of the women had sent back their replies. Of these, 2,057 were for the revision of Article 5 and 2,148 for placing restrictions on men with venereal disease. Several women later reneged, saying they'd been "scolded by their husbands."[xviii]

Innocent of political procedures, Raichō and Ichikawa sought the advice of Tomita Kōjirō, a member of the Lower House who belonged to the Kenseikai party. He said that a petition had to be submitted by a Diet member to a House petition committee and advised them to persuade someone to do this. He also said that in the case of Article 5,which was a part of an existing law, they should try to persuade Diet members to present a joint bill as an amendment.

Raichō and Ichikawa identified a number of progressive politicians and visited them at their homes or at the Diet. At a time when the postwar democratic movement was at its peak, very few opposed the revision of Article 5, though several men were of the opinion that women's participation in politics would "ruin the country." No one volunteered to submit a petition, however, and some begged off with such lame excuses as "If I came out openly for women, I'd be laughed at," or "I'd hate to have people think I was soft on women."[xix]

To enlist broader support, the association held a public lecture—"a strictly academic affair"—on February 21 at the Kanda YMCA. Attendance was larger than expected. The speakers were Ichikawa, Yamada Waka, and Iwano Kiyoko, as well as male supporters like Ōba Kakō, Ōyama Ikuo, and Uehara Etsujirō. Kiyoko, who was suffering from a gallstone infection, looked frail and tired but spoke forcefully about a similar petition campaign in the past. It was her last public appearance. Her infection proved fatal and she died in December.[xx]

Prospects brightened when Kodama Yūji, an Independent, offered to submit the petition on revising Article 5. But then, on February 26, the Diet was abruptly dissolved. Saitō Takao of the Kenseikai had delivered a speech in favor of universal manhood suffrage, and the Seiyūkai had voiced its opposition. Without waiting for others to speak or to take a vote, Prime Minister Hara suddenly announced that he would "appeal to the fair and impartial

---

xviii   Ichikawa, *Jiden*, 56–57.
xix   *Path* 201.
xx   Ibid. 203.

judgment of the nation's people" and closed the session. The two petitions were rejected by the committees of both houses and forwarded to the government for "future documentary reference."

The public reaction to the second petition was generally negative. The men, in particular, protested loudly, saying that imposing restrictions solely on men was unfair and went against the principle of the equality of the sexes. Women, too, objected. The arguments against the petition seemed to boil down to three points: Why only venereal disease and not other communicable diseases? Why only men? And weren't the restrictions inconsistent with demands for the freedom to marry for love? Yosano Akiko's article in the February *Taiyō* took up all three points. In an attempt to correct the public misperceptions, Raichō wrote an essay addressed to Yosano in the April *Chūō kōron*.[xxi]

On March 28, the long-deferred inaugural meeting of the New Women's Association was held at the Seiyōken in Ueno. Seventy members came, including twenty men. Among them were Takano Jūzō, Sakai Toshihiko, Shimonaka Yasaburō, Akita Ujaku, and Ōyama Ikuo. The majority of women were former members of Seitō, not only confirmed feminists like Yamada Waka, Iwano Kiyoko, and Sakamoto Makoto but also novelists and poets like Okamoto Kanoko, Araki Ikuko, and Katō Midori. Others who attended were Miyagawa Shizue of the JWCTU, Itō Asako, and a number of newspaperwomen, teachers, secretaries, and housewives.[xxii]

Ichikawa, who was voted chairperson, asked the members to comment on the draft of the guiding principles and statutes. Approved with minimal change, the text read as follows:

Guiding Principles

1. To enable women to realize their potential without restrictions, we shall advocate equal opportunities for women and men.
2. We shall proceed on the premise that women and men are of equal value and shall seek the cooperation of men, while acknowledging the differences between us.
3. We shall affirm the social significance of the family.

[xxi] Raichō explained that the association had focused on venereal disease because unlike tuberculosis, epilepsy, or other diseases, sexually transmitted diseases could be controlled by legislation. Yosano also criticized the association for limiting its campaign to the revision of Article 5 and not pushing for the right to vote. To this Raichō countered that Yosano was being unrealistic and that they had to take things one at a time. "In Reply to Yosano Akiko Regarding the Petition Campaign by the New Women's Association," *Chūō kōron*, April 1920 (*HRC* 3:134–151).

[xxii] *Path* 205.

4. We shall defend the rights of women, mothers, and children, promote their interests, and eliminate all obstacles that stand in their way.

Several objectives were listed in the statutes. One was to launch a movement for more institutions for women's higher education, equal education from elementary school through university, female suffrage, revision or abolition of all laws disadvantageous to women, and state protection of motherhood. Another was to establish contact with other influential women's groups in the country and form an All Japan Women's League. Members were classified as regular members (with monthly dues of 50 sen); supporting members, divided into categories A (with monthly dues of 1 yen) and B (without dues but with a contribution of labor); and sustaining members (both men and women, yearly dues 10 yen). Raichō's house would serve as temporary headquarters.[xxiii]

For Raichō, the day was made more memorable still because of two gifts. One was a painting of a *raichō*, a snow grouse, from Tanaka Jūzō. The painting depicted the bird "perched on a rock jutting out of a mountain stream, looking defiantly at the sky, its breast thrown back and beak wide open in full-throated cry." Tanaka, a businessman, was sympathetic to women's issues (he published a partial translation of Olive Schreiner's *Women and Labour* in 1914) and a generous contributor. The other gift was from Sakai Toshihiko—a copy of his book, *The Woman Question*, which had belonged to Kanno Suga. She had read it in prison while awaiting execution. The book, "its pages well worn, was a poignant keepsake of her brief and tragic life."[xxiv]

A general election was held on May 10. The results were an overwhelming majority for the Seiyūkai party, just as Prime Minister Hara hoped; within days he formed a cabinet. Tomita Kōjirō and Kodama Yūji were defeated, but fortunately, progressive politicians like Nakano Seigō, Uehara Etsujirō, and Nagai Ryūtarō were newly elected.

The forty-third special session opened on July 1. Aware that the special session would be short, Raichō and Ichikawa decided to focus on the revision of Article 5 and ask men from different parties to introduce a joint bill.[xxv] On the advice of Nakano—who remembered the altercation he had had with Raichō when they were training at the Zengakudō ten years earlier—they hurriedly paid calls on senior members of the Seiyūkai party.[xxvi]

[xxiii] See *Nihon fujin mondai* 2:160–162 for complete text.

[xxiv] *Path* 208. Kanno Suga (1881–1911) was implicated in the Great Treason Incident and the only woman sentenced to death.

[xxv] The petition on men with venereal disease was rejected by the committee appointed at the previous session.

[xxvi] *Path* 213–214.

The Seiyūkai declined, saying it would defer until the next session, but Diet members from other parties agreed to introduce one. On July 19, the bill was introduced at long last. Filling the women's gallery were a hundred women from the association. The overflow sat in the space behind the House Speaker, which had been specially opened for the day.[xxvii] Tabuchi Toyokichi, an Independent, gave the speech. He spoke for forty minutes. The hall remained hushed throughout, with only occasional laughter and, in violation of the rules, bursts of applause from the women's gallery.[4]

The bill was referred to the appropriate committee. It was shelved, though the head of the Metropolitan Police Bureau apparently said that the times had changed and the clause prohibiting women from attending political meetings ought to be revised at the next Diet session.[xxviii]

Raichō had never liked meeting strangers, and lobbying politicians left her exhausted. She was thin as a rail. Ichikawa, too, looked gaunt, and possibly because of stress, she started smoking. Wearing a kimono and obi in the summer heat was uncomfortable, and they both switched to Western dress and wore matching suits of navy blue serge.[xxix]

The association's finances were precarious. Expenses for the first five months came to 1,200 yen. Of this, 1,000 was covered by donations, mainly from men like Fukuzawa Momosuke, Arishima Takeo, Kagawa Toyohiko, Takano Jūzō, Katō Tokijirō, and Ōyama Ikuo.[xxx] Nevertheless, the inaugural issue of *Women's League* came out in October. To pay the security fee required by the Newspaper Laws, a benefactor donated 1,000 yen. Someone else donated the printing paper. Okumura designed the cover, a rather drab affair with the journal name printed in black against a gray background. About 2,000 copies were printed and sold, initially for 25 sen and later for 30 sen. Sales were disappointing.[xxxi]

The declaration on the first page was followed by "Women's Mission to Reform Society," a nine-page essay by Raichō. She claimed that "as a candid and spontaneous outpouring of her thoughts, the essay bore comparison with 'In the Beginning, Woman Was the Sun,'" but in truth, it had none of the vivid imagery or incantatory power of her *Seitō* manifesto.[xxxii]

We have now advanced from self-awareness as human beings to self-awareness as women. The feminist position that centers on the self in the narrowly indi-

---

[xxvii] Ibid. 216–217.

[xxviii] Ichikawa, *Jiden*, 76.

[xxix] *Path* 218–219.

[xxx] Ichikawa, *Jiden*, 69.

[xxxi] Ibid. 78–79. There were 331 members of all three categories at the time.

[xxxii] *Path* 221.

vidualist sense is already out of date.... The focus of feminist thought has shifted from equality of the sexes, equal rights, and opportunity, to issues that concern both men and women (that is to say, love and marriage), motherhood, and children. In other words, feminism has shifted from the individual to the group, from self-interest to altruism.

...The procreation of children, in other words, a woman's work of love as a mother in the home has been hitherto dismissed by men and by women themselves. Now this work has once again acquired a sacred and valuable social and moral significance in the hearts of women. The heaven-ordained role of women is to be mothers. And the work of mothers is not merely to bear and raise children, but to bear good children and raise them intelligently.... For the sake of humanity, they must go beyond reproducing the species to improving its quality. Therein lies the social significance of women and mothers. The ultimate goal of the most advanced women's movement is to demand a woman's right to love and to have children so that she may improve humankind (radically restructure society) through love and marriage and through bearing and educating children.

...In the past, we called for the end of sexual discrimination and demanded equal rights as human beings.... Now, as women, we call for rights that enable us to fulfill our rights and obligations as mothers. At the inception of the women's movement, we tended to see female suffrage as an end in itself and as a way to bring about political equality. Now we see it as a right that can be effectively exercised for a certain purpose, namely, reforming society so that women, as women, may carry out their work of love.[xxxiii]

The forty-fourth session opened on December 27. This time, the association submitted three petitions. The third one asked that women be given the right to vote. Drawn up by Raichō, it was the first such petition to be presented by a national organization of Japanese women.[xxxiv] The text had already been published in the November *Women's League* and copies sent out to collect signatures.[xxxv]

Petition to the Lower House for Revising the Electoral Laws

We humbly request the following:
One: Eliminate "male" from Item 1 in Article 8 of the Electoral Laws for the Lower House.

[xxxiii] The entire text may be found in *HRC* 3:159–171. The quotation is on 164–165; 169.
[xxxiv] The association set up branches in Nagoya, Osaka, Kobe, Nara, Hiroshima, and other cities.
[xxxv] Ichikawa, *Jiden*, 88. A total of 2,355 responded (957 men, 1,398 women).

Two: Eliminate Item 3 in Article 8.[xxxvi]

Among the fifteen reasons listed for the petition were:

> To correct the inequities in the present legal and social system that discriminate against women.
> To enable a woman to fulfill her right and duty to love a man of her choosing and to become a mother.
> To uphold the dignity of human sexuality.
> To ameliorate economic conditions that force a woman to work outside her home.
> To raise the status of working women.
> To protect expectant and nursing mothers.[xxxvii]

On February 5, 1921, women turned out in full force in anticipation of the introduction of the bill to revise Article 5 of the Police Security Regulations.[xxxviii] The newspapers aptly called this the "Women's Day at the Diet." The association had hoped the bill would be presented jointly by the parties, but the parties were unable to agree and decided to present three separate bills. The Seiyūkai bill covered only Clause 2, which prohibited women from attending or initiating political meetings.

The bills were introduced respectively by Ichinomiya Fusajirō (Seiyūkai), Koyama Shōju (Kenseikai), and Matsumoto Kunpei (Independent). When Matsumoto said the creation of the bill was a result of the efforts of the New Women's Association and attested to their brilliant political talents, someone in the Kenseikai section shouted, "Hey, Matsumoto, you're not the only ladies' man here!" and brought down the house.[xxxix]

All three bills were referred to a committee, but only the Seiyūkai bill was approved. The Seiyūkai bill was presented to the plenary session of the Lower House, unanimously adopted, and forwarded to the Upper House. On March 1, the bill went before the Upper House and was referred to a committee. The committee approved the bill on March 25, just one day before the closing date of the session. All signs augured well.

[xxxvi] Article 8: The following are eligible to vote in national elections: Item 1. Male subjects of Imperial Japan who are 25 or older. Item 3. The above who have paid 3 yen or more in national taxes for at least a full year before the closing date for voter registration. In the case of individuals who have succeeded to the family headship and inherited the estate, the taxes paid by the deceased family head shall be considered payment by the heir.

[xxxvii] The entire text may be found in *Nihon fujin mondai* 2:178.

[xxxviii] The petition for women's suffrage was rejected, as was the petition on venereal disease, despite rewording to include women.

[xxxix] *Path* 227–228.

On March 26, a number of important bills were under discussion, and by the time the bill on Article 5 was introduced, it was six in the evening. Baron Shimizu Motoharu (Kōseikai) spoke first. In his opinion, if women were allowed to attend political meetings, they would be the first to suffer. "When they should be putting powder on their faces, they may end up using the ashes from the kitchen stove, or worse, start painting their faces with the soot on the bottom of pots."[xl]

Kamada Eikichi (Kōyū Club) spoke next, and after giving a thoughtful speech in favor of the bill, he asked what the government thought. Kobashi Kazuta, the vice-minister of the Home Ministry, stated that the government approved of the bill. But no sooner had he said this than Baron Fujimura Yoshirō (Kōseikai) called out "Chairman!" and stood up to speak. He claimed that women participating in politics went against the laws of nature and cited instances of women in the past who engaged in politics to no good end: Taira [Hōjō] Masako (the widow of Minamoto Yoritomo and so-called "Nun Shogun"), Empress Wu of Tang China (who murdered her rivals to ascend the throne), and Queen Elizabeth of England.

To my mind, the way the members of a peculiar organization call themselves New Women and try to engage in political activities is extremely objectionable. I believe that the approval of the bill by the Upper House would violate the national polity. I am absolutely opposed.[xli]

As Raichō recalled:

The women in the gallery were not the only ones struck dumb. Diet members, too, exhausted after hours of debate, sat in stunned silence, with not a man standing up to speak in defense of the bill. The chairman (Prince Tokugawa Iesato) considered the discussion closed and motioned for those in favor to stand. I looked around. Only a handful had risen from their seats. "I consider this a minority. The bill is rejected." The chairman's expressionless voice echoed in the immense room.[xlii]

Mentally and physically worn out by the relentless pace of the past months, Raichō became severely ill.[xliii] She suffered from pounding head-

---

[xl] Ibid. 230.

[xli] Ichikawa, *Jiden*, 93–94. "National polity" is the standard translation for *kokutai*, itself a vague term for Japan's supposedly unique political structure with the emperor at the apex.

[xlii] *Path* 231.

[xliii] Raichō used the term *jika chūdoku*, which is used loosely to describe an imbalance in the autonomic nervous system. Judging from the symptoms, Dr. Irie Kenji speculates that Raichō's illness may have been psychosomatic. Personal communication.

aches, nausea, and diarrhea. Barely able to eat, she could not even bring herself to leave the house at times. According to Raichō, Ichikawa was also exhausted. "She became increasingly difficult and short-tempered...her thin face set in a permanent scowl." Worried that Ichikawa was on the verge of a nervous collapse, Raichō urged her go to a hot spring to rest. Ichikawa rejected the offer, resigned in June, and left to join her brother in the United States.[xliv]

In July, Raichō also left, to convalesce at a coastal village in Chiba Prefecture. She went without warning, leaving everyone at a loss. Fortunately, association members were able to rent a room on the second floor of a garage in front of the Diet building.[xlv]

The forty-fifth session was due to open on December 26. Once again, led by Oku Mumeo and Sakamoto Makoto (a board member), the association submitted the three petitions to both houses. As before, the members decided to focus their campaign on the revision of Article 5. On February 1 (1922), the parties submitted four separate bills to the Lower House. Only the Seiyūkai bill covering Clause 2 was approved. On March 16, the bill was submitted to the Upper House. Members of the association visited the men on the Upper House committee.[xlvi] The committee unanimously approved.

On March 25, the last day of the session, the bill was finally introduced. Sakamoto Makoto left an account of the event.

> Early in the morning of the twenty-fifth, we hastened to the reception room of the Upper House. We went around the room talking to the members and handing them our calling cards, on which we had written our request to vote for the amendment.
>
> ...It was nine o'clock at night—only three hours left before the closing of the forty-fifth session. The Upper House was still arguing about the [budget for] elevating the five vocational schools [to university status] and [the committee report on] the feasibility of a jury system. An indescribable tension filled the hall....In one last attempt to remind the men to vote for the bill, we

---

[xliv] *Path* 232–234. Ichikawa wrote that when she resigned, she felt as if she were "leaving a child she had brought up" (*Jiden* 96). She went to the United States as a special correspondent for the *Yomiuri* newspaper, enrolled in third grade at an elementary school in Seattle, where her brother was living, and then embarked on a systematic study of the women's movement in the United States. For her account of the New Women's Association, see pages 50–101 of her autobiography.

[xlv] Oku Mumeo, *Nobi aka aka to*, 61–63. In her memoirs Oku also mentions friction between Raichō and Ichikawa, but attributed it to financial difficulties.

[xlvi] Mumeo went to visit Baron Fujimura carrying her baby on her back. Fujimura and his wife, who were childless, were apparently impressed when she changed the baby's diaper in their presence. Ibid. 66–67.

rushed to the waiting room, and addressing each one by name, hastily wrote a request on more than 300 calling cards. We asked the guards to distribute the cards.... From high up in the gallery, we could see white specks dotting the seats.

The women's gallery gradually emptied until there were only three of us— Kodama Shinko, Moroki Yasuko, and myself.... Eleven o'clock. The minutes ticked away.... The men were still debating the bill on the jury system when at ten minutes past eleven, Count Yanagisawa asked the chairman to postpone the debate and attend to the bills already approved by the various Lower House committees. His motion immediately lifted our spirits.

...Eleven-forty. Hattori Ichizō, the vice-chairman of the Upper House committee, gave his report and delivered a short but effective speech explaining its decision. The chairman asked those voting in favor to stand. We leaned forward to hear, the blood rushing to our heads.... The chairman looked across the hall. "We have a majority. The bill is approved." His voice rang as sweetly as a golden bell. The men looked up at us, their faces wreathed with smiles. We looked back, our hearts filled with gratitude. At eleven-fifty, Matsumoto Kunpei came up to congratulate us, and after thanking him for all his efforts, we left the building at five minutes before midnight.[xlvii]

The amendment went into effect on May 10, 1922. On the same day, the Kobe branch of the association held a political speech meeting at the local YMCA. More than 1,500 attended. The titles of some of the speeches were "We Anticipate a Shake-up in the Cabinet," "Mothers and Female Suffrage," "Inadequacies in the Nation's Legal System," and "My Vision of Ideal Politics." Other branches followed suit.[xlviii]

The association's petition campaigns were not without its critics. Perhaps the most caustic was Yamakawa Kikue, who had helped found the socialist Red Wave Society (Sekirankai).[xlix]

We are convinced that alleviating the sufferings of women workers under the capitalist system is absolutely impossible. We also believe that since the [word censored] of capitalism is the only way to rescue these women, it is criminally wasteful to use them, powerless as they are, for ineffective Diet petitions and

---

[xlvii] The entire text of Sakamoto's account may be found in *Nihon fujin mondai* 2:191–196.
[xlviii] *Path* 243.
[xlix] The society was founded in April 1921 by Sakai Toshihiko's daughter, Sakai Magara, and other women socialists. Yamakawa Kikue and Itō Noe served as consultants. Figures for membership range from 42 to 50. In the wake of government suppression of radical groups, the society disbanded in March 1922 and regrouped as the Eight Day Society (Yōkakai), so named because March 8 was International Women's Day.

campaigns. Yet since the ladies and gentlemen of the bourgeoisie are incapable of imagining or placing their trust in a society that goes beyond capitalism, they put all their efforts into ameliorative measures that are shortsighted and ineffectual. Even someone like Hiratsuka Raichō, the acknowledged leader of Japanese women, has been unable to cast off the shackles of bourgeois thinking.... Her recent ideas are no more than a mishmash of the ludic instincts left over from her Seitō days and the self-deluding do-goodism of a bourgeois woman who has been startled from slumber by the warning bell of the coming revolution....

In contrast, the goals of the Red Wave Society... are absolutely clear. Unlike bourgeois feminists, we have no wish to spout empty, flowery words or indulge in cheap sentimentalism. To the end, we will fight resolutely for our ideal—the liberation of the proletariat.[1]

Oku Mumeo wrote a rebuttal in the August issue of the same journal.

It is not as if I do not understand why [Yamakawa's] single-minded commitment to socialism makes her dismiss out of hand everything that is not socialist. Even supposing that socialism is the one and only path to a perfect society, her contention that everything and anything must be socialist is exclusionary and narrow-minded, a fundamental flaw that will work against the building of the next generation.

...I do not think the association's petition campaigns were to no avail.... Nor should we be criticized for alerting women to the existence of a law that put them at a disadvantage.... If we are to raise their awareness as human beings, we must prepare a healthy seedbed. We must set aside the question of whether we are bourgeois or not bourgeois and in the name of women, awaken and act as one. Are we not all oppressed by male tyranny?[li]

Yamakawa quickly responded with an article in the October *Taiyō*.

We, the women of the proletariat, have nothing in common with bourgeois women, who, together with bourgeois men, constitute the ruling class. Cooperation among women in disregard of class distinctions is like the wolf lying down with the sheep.... By the time the New Women's Association gets around to organizing working women, there is not the remotest chance that Japanese society

---

[1] "The New Women's Association and the Red Wave Society," *Taiyō*, July 1921 (*Nihon fujin mondai* 2:202–203). Yamakawa thought more highly of Ichikawa: "I have no way of knowing why she is going to the United States, but the general opinion is that unlike Raichō, she is serious and realistic. I sincerely hope that as soon as she returns, she will join the proletarian liberation movement not only on behalf of bourgeois women but as an ally of all those who are oppressed" (203).

[li] "On Reading Yamakawa Kikue's 'The New Women's Association and the Red Wave Society,'" *Taiyō*, August 1921 (*Nihon fujin mondai* 2:205, 207).

will exist in its present form, and so I shall desist from engaging in polemics with Oku Mumeo. The society to come will prove which of our assertions is realistic and which mere fancy.[lii]

With the principal figures gone, it is not surprising that the association lost its original impetus. Finances deteriorated, several issues of the journal were cancelled, and members quarreled. In December 1922, Raichō, still in the countryside, disbanded the association. She sent a letter saying she had taken the action because of "increasing doubts about the ability of Japanese women to work as a group. At a time when collective action was critical, they regrettably lacked the inner resources to unite." She hoped, nonetheless, to work in the future for the women's movement "as one who is not bound by constraints and in an appropriate role."[5]

The remaining members reorganized into two groups: the Women's Alliance (Fujin Renmei), headed by Oku Mumeo and Yagibashi Kii, and the Women's Suffrage League (Fujin Sansei Dōmei), headed by Sakamoto Makoto and Kodama Shinko. In December 1924, under Kubushiro Ochimi's leadership, the two organizations, as well as others, merged into the League for Securing Woman Suffrage (Fujin Sanseiken Kakutoku Kisei Dōmei). Among those on the founding committee were Ichikawa Fusae, Oku Mumeo, Yosano Akiko, Yamakawa Kikue, and Sakamoto Makoto.[liii]

◎ ◎ ◎ ◎ ◎

After an absence of almost two years, Raichō and her family returned to Tokyo in April 1923. They rented a house in Sendagaya; the house in Tabata had already been sold to pay association expenses and their own.[liv] On September 1, just before noon, a severe earthquake struck Tokyo. Seventy-three percent of the city was destroyed, and more than 106,000 people killed or reported missing. Martial law was declared. As rumors flew that Koreans were setting fires and looting, vigilante groups killed thousands (figures vary) of innocent Koreans. Labor and socialist leaders were rounded up. On the 16th, Raichō received shocking news: Itō Noe, Ōsugi Sakae, and Ōsugi's six-year-old

---

[lii] "From the Viewpoint of Proletarian Women," *Taiyō*, October 1921 (*Nihon fujin mondai* 2:213). Fifty-eight years later, a mellower Yamakawa had kinder words for Raichō and Seitō. "The movement begun by Seitō is historically significant in that it awakened women to their self-worth and challenged the old morality" (*Nihon fujin-undō shōshi* 102).

[liii] *Nihon fujin mondai* 2:237. For a detailed and comprehensive account of the New Women's Association, see Tomida, *Hiratsuka Raichō and Early Japanese Feminism*, 263–330. Tomida also makes interesting comparisons with the women's movement in England.

[liv] *Path* 265.

nephew were ordered to report to the Tokyo Military Police and then were strangled to death by an officer in their cells.[lv] Noe was twenty-eight.

At the request of *Fujin kōron*, Raichō wrote of Noe:

> She was a person of deep contradictions. On one hand she was like a sweet young girl—honest, pure, natural, innocent—and on the other hand arrogant, stubborn, self-centered, irresponsible, brazen, and spiteful....She gave full rein to her emotions, but to the end there was no originality in her thinking.... Incapable of quiet thought, study, or self-examination, she understood with unusual sensitivity and lucidity only the things and people that she was fond of. She grew and nurtured herself by understanding, sympathizing with, and assimilating the thoughts of whomever she loved at the moment,... Noe was a type rare in Japan, a true daughter of nature, who went through life, flaunting the best and the worst in women.[lvi]

Raichō settled into domesticity. When a newspaper asked about her plans for social reform, she was taken aback: "The very thought of a so-called women's social movement made me shudder, for I had yet to recover from the mental, physical, and financial blows of the previous year."[lvii] Even so, women's suffrage was never far from her mind. Heartened by the passage of the Universal Manhood Suffrage Act in May 1925 and the formation of proletarian parties in 1926, she expressed her hope that women would lend their support to the new parties, which were "all concerned with women's issues, in particular female suffrage, and took positions radically different from those of the established parties."[lviii] By this time, like her erstwhile adversary Yamakawa Kikue, she had come to believe that under the capitalist economic system, working women would continue to be "exploited like slaves."[lix] To attain the goals of the women's movement, the "oppressed and dispossessed" had to "join forces with proletarian men."[lx] In anticipation of the first general election under the new manhood suffrage law in February 1928, she once again urged women's organizations to cooperate with the proletarian parties.[lxi]

[lv] Their bodies were wrapped in a blanket and thrown into an abandoned well. The officer was sentenced to a ten-year sentence by a military court but released after three years. Noe had five children by Ōsugi (one child was name Emma after Emma Goldman). The orphaned children were looked after by her relatives.

[lvi] "Itō Noe, Daughter of Nature," *Fujin kōron*, November and December combined issue, 1923 (*HRC* 3:347–348).

[lvii] "From Karasuyama," *Fujo shinbun*, September 20, 1925 (*HRC* 4: 131–132).

[lviii] "Japan's Female Suffrage Movement at a Turning Point," *Fujin no tomo*, April 1927 (*HRC* 4:280).

[lix] "Regarding the Working Women's League," original publication unknown, 1928 (*HRC* 4:248–249).

[lx] "My Expectations for New Women's Organizations," original publication unknown, 1927 (*HRC* 4:335).

[lxi] "To Women's Organizations in Japan: Support the Proletarian Parties Which Espouse Female Suffrage," *Tokyo nichi nichi*, February 6, 1928 (*HRC* 5:20–27).

Apart from occasional pieces on female suffrage, Raichō mainly wrote about nature and family life in women's publications such as *Fujin kōron* and *Fujin no tomo*. Watching her children grow gave her a deep sense of fulfillment:

> The two children were nothing less than gifts from heaven that made me complete as a woman.... I was at a loss when people remarked, "Think of all the work you could be doing if you didn't have to be at home looking after your children." No doubt I probably could ... but unlike in the past, I no longer despaired of being unable to work because of the children. How could I, when I knew the true worth of work, of life itself, was not measured by the amount of work one did or the outward appearance of one's activities?[lxii]

In 1925, Okumura was appointed an art instructor at Seijō Gakuen, a progressive school where the two children were students. Two years later, the family moved to a new house in Kinuta Village on land owned by the school. Surrounded by stands of red pines and open fields, the newly developed area was scenic, but daily necessities such as rice, soy sauce, and miso were difficult to obtain and expensive. In 1928, Raichō was introduced to an employee of Tokyo Kyōdōsha, a consumer cooperative formed by workers at the Koishikawa Arsenal; the young man had come to the village to solicit new members. Raichō, who had recently read about the cooperative movement, joined the following year.

Much of her interest in the cooperative movement derived from her recent reading of Kropotkin's *Mutual Aid*.[lxiii] She was particularly drawn to his view that in all living things, the instinct for mutual aid was of far more vital importance to the well-being and evolution of the species than the laws of competition and survival of the fittest. Since human beings were intrinsically altruistic, he contended, the ideal society should be based on the ethic of cooperativism and consist of voluntary associations formed by the people themselves, that is to say, cooperative unions. For Raichō, who had become disenchanted with the endless factionalism of proletarian parties, the cooperative movement was at once "a peaceful, realistic, and effective way to undermine the capitalist system and build a new self-governing society based on mutual support."[lxiv]

[lxii] "A Mother's Gratitude," original publication unknown (*HRC* 4:241–242).
[lxiii] *Mutual Aid* (1901): Written by the Russian revolutionary Peter Kropotkin, the book was considered the "Bible of the anarchist movement." The English translation was widely read by Japanese intellectuals and a complete Japanese translation was made by Ōsugi Sakae in 1917. By 1921, it had been reprinted eight times.
[lxiv] "On the Development of the Spirit of Cooperation as an Instinct," original publication unknown (*HRC* 5:232–234).

It had the added advantage of being easily accessible to housewives; indeed, without women, the movement could not exist.[lxv] After a period of inactivity, Raichō turned to this new cause.

With funds furnished by the main office, a branch of the cooperative was set up in 1930. A large sign read OUR HOUSE. After a policy disagreement, the Seijō branch broke away and Raichō became the head. Most of the members—about a hundred—were educated middle-class housewives. Children pitched in during the holidays, tagging goods, printing, and distributing fly-ers.[lxvi] The cooperative encountered financial difficulties, and with the outbreak of the China War in 1937 and the imposition of government controls on human and material resources under the National Mobilization Act, it merged with another cooperative in 1938.

⊙ ⊙ ⊙ ⊙ ⊙

In 1930, the same year Raichō became head of the cooperative, she joined the Proletarian Women's Arts Alliance (Musan Fujin Geijutsu Dōmei). Founded by Takamure Itsue in January, the anarchist organization had goals that resonated with her own:[lxvii] as stated in the inaugural issue of *Women's Front* (*Fujin sensen*, March 1930), the organization would oppose all forms of authoritarianism and work toward the realization of an autono-mous society; expose and extirpate all forms of male tyranny in everyday life and use this process to awaken women's social consciousness; and present new ideas and issues from a woman's perspective in order to create a new society and civilization.

Raichō had admired Takamure ever since reading her collection of poems, *Tokyo Has Come Down with a Fever*, and several of her other writings:

> For several days her words and her phrases kept running through my mind and took hold of my heart as though they had been spoken by a lover. And yet it was not her ideas that fascinated me. I could find any number of ideas elsewhere, and for that matter I often disagreed with her. Rather, her pas-sion, the play of her emotions, her freedom and range of expression all im-pressed me.[lxviii]

[lxv] "On Joining *Women's Front*," *Fujin sensen*, April 1930 (*HRC* 5:179–180).
[lxvi] "Weeds in Kinuta Village," *Fujo shinbun*, June 22, 1930 (*HRC* 5:203–208).
[lxvii] Takamure Itsue (1894–1964): Writer and poet known for her pioneering studies in the history of Japa-nese women. The group initially had 14 members.
[lxviii] "Takamure Itsue," original publication unknown (*HRC* 4:221–222).

She became more admiring still after reading *The Creation of Romantic Love*, Takamure's collection of essays about feminism and love. She found the essays difficult to read, but felt they "contained truths that had spilled out of the treasure house of woman's subconscious."[lxix]

Raichō contributed two essays to the organization's journal. In the first, she called the journal the "second Seitō," traced in detail her intellectual journey from Seitō to the New Women's Association, her rising interest in the consumer cooperative movement, and stated on the last page her reasons for joining the organization.

> Given my views on the importance of motherhood and my hopes for an economically autonomous society based on cooperative organizations, I naturally have an interest in and sympathy for the anarchist vision of society. Indeed, I remain convinced that the cooperative movement in various parts of the world will develop further, be more thoroughly established, and eventually reach its full potential when it is led forward, or at least aided by anarchist theory.... Twenty years ago, Japanese women embarked on a quest for individual self-awareness as human beings. Now, as socially awakened women and as members of the proletariat, they have risen again to build a new self-governing society and create a new civilization based on maternalism (*bosei bunka*).[lxx]

Her second short essay curtly dismissed Yamada Waka for urging working women to return to their proper sphere—the home: "Many women have no choice but to work for low wages, even if it means destroying their homes and losing their claim to motherhood.... Her words apply only to a minority of bourgeois women."[lxxi]

⊚ ⊚ ⊚ ⊚ ⊚

Clouds, Grass, People (*Kumo, kusa, hito*), a collection of Raichō's essays, was published in July 1933. On November 6, friends and former members of Seitō gathered for a celebration. Two days later, Raichō received a package from Yasuda Satsuki, the Seitō member who had been a central figure in the debate over chastity and abortion. The package contained Yasuda's will, seal,

---

[lxix] "On Reading Takamure Itsue's *Creation of Romantic Love*," original publication unknown (*HRC* 4:223).

[lxx] "On Joining *Women's Front*" (*HRC* 5:181–182.)

[lxxi] "A Couple of Reactionary Women," *Fujin sensen*, June 1930 (*HRC* 5:201). *Women's Front* was discontinued in June 1931. Itsue severed all social ties and spent the next thirty years researching matrilineal and matrilocal marriage in ancient Japan.

keys, and notes. She had decided to die. Raichō remembered how she herself had felt twenty-five years earlier.

> I, too, sent a package to a friend, asking her to take care of everything after my death.... I was then barely twenty, my life as a woman unlived, my head full of dreams. This was also after I had attained kenshō, a time of Great Affirmation. At that time, I felt that life was good, and death equally so. Satsuki's case was different. She was in her forties and had experienced life. Illness, poverty, a marriage in ruins, and the responsibility for a child conspired to drive her to suicide.

A month later Raichō was notified by the police that a woman's body had been found in the Hakone Mountains. Certain it was Satsuki, she went immediately, her heart heavy with the "burden of pain placed on the living by those who die."[lxxii]

In October 1938, Naganuma Chieko, who had drawn the cover for the first issue of *Seitō*, died in a mental hospital. Like Raichō, she had been an atypical home economics student in college.

> Just as I was searching ... for spiritual freedom and self-liberation in philosophy and religion, Chieko was searching for the same things in art and beauty. She took up Western art seriously after graduation, but then suddenly married the artist Takamura Kōtarō. I knew nothing of the circumstances leading to their marriage, but I assumed it would not be a disadvantage to her in pursuing her career. From that time on, however, she retreated from me and from the world. Chieko and her husband dedicated themselves to the creation of beauty and love in their own private world.
>
> I then heard some years later that she had become mentally unbalanced. I was not altogether surprised. Nor did this news strike me as tragic, as it might have had it been an ordinary person. I somehow felt that even in her madness and suffering, she had within her a solid core of happiness. When I heard about her death, I also rejoiced for her—a free spirit reborn in the realm of pure thought. And so when I saw her husband to offer my condolences, I could not bring myself to utter the usual platitudes.[lxxiii]

In February 1939, the Lower House passed the National Eugenics Act (Kokumin Yūsei-hō, enacted 1940). Designed to "protect the superior natural endowments of the Japanese people," the act recommended the sterilization of

---

[lxxii] "A Friend's Last Testament," original publication unknown (*HRC* 5:352–355).

[lxxiii] "Takamura Kōtarō and Chieko," *Fujin kōron*, August 1951 (*HRC* 7:182–183). For more about Chieko and her husband, see Phyllis Birnbaum, *Modern Girls, Shining Stars, the Skies of Tokyo*, 55–101.

the "mentally retarded, epileptics, schizophrenics, manic depressives, and others who suffered from 'inherited disorders.'" Even those with severe physical deformities or hereditary blindness or deafness were not exempt. Raichō approved; in the past she had often spoken of "improving the racial stock." But she was not enthusiastic and felt that sterilization was a negative, if unavoidable, measure. She hoped that in the future "advances in medical science and improvements in society and the way of life would render such measures unnecessary."[lxxiv]

The following year, in June, Raichō and Okumura made a trip to western Japan, and on the way back visited the Hiratsuka ancestral grave in Wakayama. In keeping with her father's wishes, she also arranged to have a memorial stone built for Hiratsuka Tamehiro, the ancestor who had died in the epic battle of Sekigahara in 1600. She explained her growing interest in family history.

> [Until recently] I never thought about my ancestors nor had any interest in my antecedents. This was because I came of age when individualism held sway in Japan.... In fact, well into my thirties and forties, not to mention my twenties, I rebelled against the veneration of ancestors and the family system and lived thinking that I somehow came into this world on my own, without benefit of ancestors. But now I feel differently. Offering my prayers to the gods (*kami*) and ancestors each day seems the most natural thing to do. Ancestors are our past; we are the extension of our ancestors.[lxxv]

In February 1941, Raichō's eighty-three-year-old father died of a cerebral hemorrhage. In Raichō's youth, he had been the archetypal authority figure, yet for that era, he had been surprisingly tolerant. Most fathers would have disowned a daughter who lived with a younger lover and bore children out of wedlock. She was moved to write a tribute.

> I had been aware for some time that in his old age, my father was subconsciously longing for death. As might be expected of a descendant of the warrior Hiratsuka Tamehiro, he had something of the old samurai spirit about him to the end. He seemed to feel that he should not be receiving a government pension so long after his retirement, especially when he was no longer serving the emperor.
> ... Almost to the end, he kept to his daily morning ritual of rinsing his mouth first and reading aloud the command given by the Sun Goddess to her grandson on the occasion of his descent to Japan[lxxvi] and the 1890 edict on education. (He

---

[lxxiv] "Regarding the National Eugenics Act," original publication unknown (*HRC* 6:289–290).
[lxxv] "About My Ancestors," original publication unknown (*HRC* 5:316).
[lxxvi] The command given by the Sun Goddess to her grandson to rule Japan, as recorded in the seventh-century chronicle *Kojiki*.

gave up only after he felt his shortness of breath prevented him from reading the texts properly.) Much as I have finally come to appreciate Japan's unique political structure, and to some degree assent to the fact that the emperor is the descendant of the Sun Goddess and a living god (*arahitogami*), the depth of my father's reverence for the imperial house, his single-minded devotion, and his sense of oneness (*kiitsu*) with the emperor are beyond my imagining.[lxxvii]

Even assuming that she wrote this in a moment of grief, the last sentence comes as a complete surprise, for she had earlier adamantly opposed the emperor-centered, patriarchal nation-state. According to Raichō scholar Yoneda Sayoko, the sentence was heavily crossed out in Raichō's copy of the article.[6]

◎ ◎ ◎ ◎ ◎

By the summer of 1941, relations with the United States had deteriorated to the point that war seemed inevitable. Raichō's son Atsubumi was in his final year at Waseda University. Raichō was concerned that if he were conscripted, his "illegitimate" status would bar him from taking the examinations to become an officer. Consequently, Raichō and Okumura formally registered their marriage on August 14. Twenty-seven years had passed since they started living together. Raichō and her son took the name Okumura. Their daughter Akemi, who had married in 1938, lived in Tottori Prefecture.

War broke out on December 8. Atsubumi was called up two months later and subsequently commissioned as an officer in the aeronautical engineering corps. The following April, Raichō and Okumura sold their possessions, rented out the house, and moved to Todai, a village in Ibaraki Prefecture. This was at the insistence of her sister, Taka, who had built a house there because years earlier, a religious figure had prophesied that a great war would break out and Tokyo would be reduced to ashes.[lxxviii]

There is no recorded instance of Raichō speaking out against the war. Kobayashi Tomie wrote that Raichō's move to the countryside was an "act of passive noncooperation with the war (*shōkyokuteki na sensō hikyōryoku*)."[lxxix] Whatever this means, it holds true for many Japanese intellectuals at the time.

[lxxvii] "In Memory of My Father," *Fujin kōron*, May 1941 (HRC 6:341–343).

[lxxviii] "Communication from Ogai River," *Shomotsu tenbō*, May 1944 (HRC 6:395).

[lxxix] Kobayashi Tomie, *Hiratsuka Raichō: Hito to shisō*, 191. The last time Raichō openly criticized the government was in January 1936, when she reproved the Diet for allocating 47 percent of the budget to the military and neglecting the needs of the people. "Direct Your Gaze and Energies Inward," original publication unknown (HRC 6:87).

But it should also be noted that former colleagues in the suffrage movement like Ichikawa Fusae, Oku Mumeo, and Yamada Waka accepted appointments to semigovernment committees.[7]

⊚ ⊚ ⊚ ⊚ ⊚

Raichō spent the war years farming. She grew vegetables—she and Okumura were confirmed vegetarians—kept a goat, and made cheese. Okumura sketched and worked on his novel about their youthful romance. In the village, women, children, and the elderly were pressed into service to build a bridge over a tributary of the Tone River.[lxxx] Japan's situation steadily worsened. Tokyo and other cities were systematically destroyed in aerial bombings, and in April 1945, Raichō's childhood home in Akebono-chō was burned to the ground.

On August 15, the entire nation was instructed to listen to the radio at noon. In an unprecedented broadcast, the emperor read the edict announcing the end of the war. For Japan, defeat was total and devastating. Exhorted to fight to the end, the Japanese did not know what to expect. Raichō wrote:

> Even as I was swept by grief and indignation at the thought that Japan had lost its independence, I read the terms of the Potsdam Declaration over and over.... Reading one of the terms, I could foresee the day when Japanese women would be emancipated and given the right to vote.[lxxxi] ... Still, the prospect of suddenly being handed the vote by a foreign occupying force was a shock.... I thought of the sweeping changes that were about to take place in Japan and was overcome with complex and contradictory feelings.
>
> ...I remembered going to the Diet in 1920 to ask Nagai Ryūtarō, the liberal Kenseikai politician, to present our petition to amend Article 5. He consented, of course, but then, in a more serious tone, he asked, "Now that you've started this movement, how long do you think it will take to get the vote?" I answered, "I realize it won't be easy. At the earliest, I should think in ten years." I was then thirty-four and assumed that by the time I was fifty, Japanese women would certainly have the vote and that other issues affecting us would also have been settled. I was now past sixty. Suddenly, along with the humiliation of defeat, the right to vote was to be handed to women on a platter, through no efforts of their

---

[lxxx] *Path* 267–268.

[lxxxi] Raichō referred to the statement: "The Japanese government shall remove all obstacles to the revival and strengthening of democratic tendencies among the Japanese people. Freedom of speech, of religion, and of thought, as well as respect for the fundamental human rights shall be established." The declaration, signed by the United States, Britain, and China, stipulated the terms for unconditional surrender.

own. How ironic! When I thought back to the twenty-odd-year efforts of feminists that underlay this turn of events, I could not bring myself to accept the gift
with good grace and unmitigated joy.[lxxxii]

Meanwhile, in Tokyo, women quickly took action. On November 3, 1945,
less than three months after the surrender, Ichikawa Fusae and other veter-
ans of the suffrage movement formed the New Japan Women's League (Shin
Nihon Fujin Dōmei) with the aim of educating women voters. Raichō was
invited to join. She declined, saying she would remain in the countryside for
the present, and sent a congratulatory message instead.

If Raichō was ambivalent about being "handed the vote on a platter," she
had no doubt in her mind about the new constitution (November 1946). It
brought about a "bloodless revolution"; she even admitted that she was "glad
that Japan had lost the war." She was elated in particular by Article 9, the
so-called no war clause by which Japan "forever renounced war as a sover-
eign right of the nation and the threat or use of force as a means of settling
international disputes." Women's cherished hope for peace had become the
law of the land.[lxxxiii]

Her reaction to Articles 14 and 24, which established equality under the law
and equality in marriage, was no less euphoric.[lxxxiv] "The two articles eliminated in one stroke the feudalistic discrimination to which women had been
subjected for ages. Indeed, these articles largely realized the goals for which
the feminist movement had fought until now."[lxxxv]

As to the new Civil Code (January 1, 1948), it "fairly took her breath away."
She had been unhappy about the old code ever since she attended lectures on
the subject in college, but now, the changes in family law and inheritance, in
particular, "overturned Japan's traditional family system once and for all."[lxxxvi]

In 1911, when I was twenty-six, I wrote "In the beginning, woman was the sun.
Now she is the moon, a wan and sickly moon, dependent on another." Thirty-

---

[lxxxii] *Path* 268–269.

[lxxxiii] Ibid. 274–275.

[lxxxiv] Article 14: All the people are equal under the law and there shall be no discrimination in political,
economic, or social relations because of race, creed, sex, social status, or family origin. Article
24: Marriage shall be based only on the mutual consent of both sexes and it shall be maintained
through mutual cooperation with the equal rights of husband and wife as a basis. With regard to
choice of spouse, property rights, inheritance, choice of domicile, divorce, and other matters per-
taining to marriage and the family, laws shall be enacted from the standpoint of individual dignity
and the essential equality of the sexes. For the complete text of the 1947 constitution, see *Sources of
Japanese Tradition* 2:1031–1036.

[lxxxv] *Path* 275.

[lxxxvi] Ibid.

seven years later, my heart bursting for joy, I could shout, "Behold, behold, the day has come. The big, big sun has risen from deep within the hearts of the liberated women of Japan!"[lxxxvii]

Raichō resolved to devote herself thenceforth to the cause of world peace. On returning to Tokyo in the spring of 1947, she read assiduously on the peace movement. She then heard of *One World* (*Hitotsu no sekai*), a magazine published by such prewar liberals as Ozaki Yukio, Matsuoka Komakichi, and Inagaki Morikatsu. Inagaki had been a supporting member of the New Women's Association. Raichō promptly took out a subscription; this was her introduction to the world federation movement. Convinced that world government was the surest solution to world peace, she joined the League for the Establishment of a World Federation in 1949 and was subsequently appointed a director. She began studying Esperanto.

On April 10, 1949, at a Women's Day convocation sponsored by the Labor Ministry's Bureau of Women and Minors (Yamakawa Kikue was the first director of the newly established office), Raichō, Ichikawa Fusae, and Sakai Tameko[lxxxviii] were officially recognized for their contributions to women's rights. In her acceptance speech, Raichō acknowledged her debts to former colleagues who had died young and to her family and mother, and took the occasion to urge women to "use their liberated powers in the cause of world peace" and "the awakening of a new human consciousness."[lxxxix]

In the midst of a worsening relations between the United States and the Soviet Union, a peace treaty was signed on September 8, 1951 (China, the Soviet Union, and India refused). The same day, Japan also signed a mutual security treaty with the United States that provided for the continuation of American military bases in Japan. On the grounds that this was in violation of Japan's peace constitution, Raichō, Ichikawa Fusae, and Jōdai Tano sent individual letters to members of the U.S. Senate requesting them not to ratify the two treaties.[xc] To form a united front for peace, in April 1953, Raichō founded the Federation of Japan Women's Organizations (Nihon Fujin Dantai Rengōkai, also known as Fudanren). Its stated goals were to call for the removal of American military bases in Japan and to oppose the manufacture and use of nuclear weapons. In her capacity as president, she established ties with the Women's International Democratic Federation, an organization founded in Paris in 1945.

[lxxxvii] Ibid. 276. In 1948 Raichō wrote a long essay describing her reaction to the new changes. "Have My Dreams Come True?" *Josei kaizō*, October 1948 (*HRC* 7:29–44).

[lxxxviii] Sakai Tameko (1872–1959) was Sakai Toshihiko's second wife. Together with Fukuda Hideko and other women socialists, she participated in the earlier movement to amend Article 5.

[lxxxix] "On Receiving an Award on Women's Day," manuscript (*HRC* 7:65–67).

[xc] *Path* 292–293.

Unlike her former colleagues in the women's movement, Raichō did not run for office. Oku Mumeo was elected to the House of Councilors in 1947 and served three terms as an advocate of consumers' rights. Ichikawa Fusae was elected to the House of Councilors in 1953, and apart from one defeat in 1971, she served until her death in 1981 at age eighty-seven, her reputation for rectitude unsullied. Kamichika Ichiko, despite the Hikage Inn scandal and subsequent imprisonment, was elected on the socialist ticket to the House of Representatives in 1953 and served four terms. Raichō's own sympathies were for the left-wing socialists, and on the eve of the October 1952 elections, she urged women to vote for the parties that "absolutely opposed rearmament and vowed to defend the peace constitution to the last."[xci]

In 1955, Raichō published her first autobiography, *The Path I Took*.[8] She was sixty-nine, or seventy by Japanese count. She dedicated it to her mother, who had died the previous year at age ninety. At the end of the year, pleading old age, Raichō resigned from the Federation of Japan Women's Organizations.

In October 1961, on the occasion of the fiftieth anniversary of Seitō, friends gathered for a memorial service for deceased members. Present were Raichō, Otake Kōkichi, Kamichika Ichiko, Kobayashi Katsu, Nishizaki Hanayo, and several other women. Among those who had died were Araki Ikuko, Itō Noe, Iwano Kiyoko, Okamoto Kanoko, Katō Midori, Kiuchi Teiko, Sakamoto Makoto, Tamura Toshiko, Yasumochi Yoshiko, Yasuda Satsuki, and Yamada Waka.

Once denounced and pilloried, Seitō had become synonymous with the early women's movement and Raichō a feminist icon. Students and scholars of women's history came to borrow her dusty copies of *Seitō*, photographs, and other materials. In November Raichō published an essay entitled "Looking Back at Fifty Years of the Women's Movement."

> [When we started the journal] we were still in our twenties—Otake Kōkichi, Kobayashi Katsu, and Itō Noe were in their teens—and not always fully aware of the consequences of our actions.... In many instances, we acted because we were driven by an irrepressible inner force. As to the manifesto, "In the Beginning, Woman Was the Sun," I little imagined it would resonate so strongly in the hearts and minds of women, or that it would be remembered in women's history as women's first "declaration of their status as human beings" or "declaration of woman's rights." ... Indeed, I am surprised, even a little awed, by the magnitude of the response to my words.
>
> But in retrospect, perhaps this was to be expected. Trampled and despised for generations in a male-dominated world, Japanese women were ready to

---

[xci] "An Appeal to All Women Who Hope for Peace," 1952 *Minami Nihon shinbun*, October 1, 1952 (HRC 7:229).

explode, and I happened to be the escape valve. I was no doubt the right person, for I had practiced Zen for several years and freed myself of preconceptions and reached that realm where there is no Self....

The movement launched by Seitō was not the kind that demanded this right or that. Rather, it was an eruption of life itself, of the lives of all down-trodden women. It was a movement that encompassed the totality of things and called on women to recover their "status as human beings (*ningensei*)" by their own efforts.

...We were inevitably criticized for our actions and had no choice but to fight back.... Yet unlike women today, we did not think of launching an orga-nized movement. We would not have known how to do such a thing even if we had thought of it. Our only recourse was for each of us to speak out and act on our convictions.... It was only in 1919, after World War I, that I launched a large-scale organized movement for women's liberation and proclaimed the importance of collective action. The right time had not yet come during the Seitō years.[xcii]

Raichō's sister, Taka, died in 1962. Sometime during the same year, Raichō began writing her second and more detailed autobiography. She asked her friend Kobayashi Tomie to help gather materials. She kept few personal records, but fortunately, there were copies of her published writings. Accord-ing to Kobayashi, she took down Raichō's oral narrative, showed her the tran-scription so that Raichō could add her emendations, then made a clean copy and showed her the revised version for further emendations. If Raichō was unhappy with the manuscript, she rewrote whole sections.[xciii] When she tired, she often excused herself, faced the wall, and sat in quiet meditation:

Sensei was perfectly motionless. Looking at her from the back, I knew she was "recharging" her inner reserves—the "Absolute Self" she attained from her Zen training as a youth—and I realized anew the centrality of Zen in her "inner life."[xciv]

Okumura died in February 1964 at age seventy-three of aplastic anemia. He and Raichō had been together fifty years. Until the day he died, he sketched the flowers and fruit their friends brought and the scenery outside his hospital

---

[xcii] "Looking Back at Fifty Years of the Women's Movement," *Fujin kōron*, November 1961 (HRC 7:393, 397). For a historical overview of women's rights discourse in Meiji and Taishō Japan, see Barbara Molony, "Women's Rights and the Japanese State, 1880–1925," in *Public Spheres, Private Lives in Modern Japan, 1600–1950*, ed. Gail Lee Bernstein, Andrew Gordon, and Kate Wildman Nakai.
[xciii] "Raichō Sensei and I," *Genshi* 2:296, 305.
[xciv] Ibid. 297.

room. The following year, with financial help from friends, Raichō arranged for Heibonsha to publish a book of Okumura's nude sketches.[xcv]

Despite failing health, Raichō kept up her activities for world peace. She protested the continued presence of American forces in Okinawa and the war in Vietnam. A photograph taken in June 1970 shows her marching at the head of a small group of women holding banners demanding the abrogation of the U.S.–Japan security treaty. Despite her walking stick, her posture is erect, her expression bright and resolute. But she could only manage a ten-minute walk in the neighborhood.

Raichō was hospitalized in August 1970 and again in November; she was diagnosed with cancer. She died on May 24, 1971, at age eighty-five. She was cremated and buried next to Okumura in Shunjūen Cemetery in Ikuta, Kanagawa Prefecture. The gravestone reads OKUMURA HARUKO.

[xcv] "About Okumura Hiroshi's Nude Sketches," *Bungaku sanpo*, September 1964 (HRC 7:419–421).

Notes

Introduction

1. Volumes 3 and 4, which cover the years from 1917 to 1964, were written in the first person singular by Kobayashi Tomie (1917–2004), Raichō's friend and secretary. As Kobayashi wrote in her postscript to volume 3: "One-third of this volume is taken from Raichō Sensei's earlier work *Watakushi no aruita michi* [*The Path I Took*, Shinhyōron-sha, 1955], to which I made some additions, and the rest is based on Sensei's published articles, notes, memos, and conversations I had with Sensei" (p. 333, 1992 edition; p. 305, 1971–73 edition). Kobayashi also wrote in her postscript to volume 2 of the 1971–73 edition: "For Sensei's life after Seitō, I shall have to write a supplementary volume in the form of a biography (*hyōden*). I have already written a rough draft of the postwar years, which will be published by Ōtsuki Shoten in the near future" (pp. 628–629).

2. Kobayashi, "Raichō Sensei and I," *Genshi, josei wa taiyō de atta* (vol. 2, p. 305, 1992 edition).

1. Childhood

1. Translator's note: Raichō's account also mentions rank names, religious names, family crests, and a scroll about the origins of the shrine that was confiscated by the ruling daimyo. This reflects the importance she placed on her ancestry, but I have omitted some of the minor details.

4. The Years After College

1. Yamakawa's first impression of Raichō was more flattering: "Of the fifteen or so members of the Keishū Literary Society, one person stood out for her beauty and elegance, erect posture, and understated but tasteful kimono. When I asked who she was, I was told she was Hiratsuka Haruko, a graduate of the Japan Women's College" (Yamakawa, *Onna nidai no ki*, 128).

2. Yamakawa remembered Raichō's story. "It stayed in my mind because in sharp contrast to most heroines, who were depicted as passive, her heroine was modern and positive…. It may be intentional or a matter of pure coincidence, but Hiratsuka-san is the kind of person who likes to take society by surprise" (Ibid. 130–131).

3. Translator's note: I have omitted a short passage about a commemorative stone marker that was subsequently built at Ichiyō's house.

4. The Japanese for "my life convictions" is *waga shōgai no taikei*, literally, "the system of my life." Raichō uses literary Japanese and the English word "cause."

5. Raichō's motives are difficult to understand. On one hand she says that she intended to die for her "cause" and to "carry through her life convictions." But what she meant by "cause" and "life convictions" is unclear. Was she talking about her freedom and independence as a human being? Or a Zen-like nonattachment? On the other hand, she says that Morita "stirred her latent, irresponsible sense of mischief," that she was "curious to see what would happen," and, later in the narrative, that she didn't think Morita would go through with his plan. In *The Pass* (*Tōge*), the unfinished autobiographical novel that Raichō wrote in 1915, she has the narrator explain why she decided to meet Kojima (Morita) after receiving his (first) letter: "As a result of having practiced zazen for two years, I was overflowing with boundless energy. I was in a state of tension, my mind and heart ready to take on every challenge that came my way, be it large or small. I was waiting unceasingly yet quietly for something to happen to me. I felt there was nothing I had to evade in this world. I only knew that, come what may, I would go forth. Such being the state of my mind, I had no hesitation whatsoever about going [to the station]. Indeed, it seemed the most natural thing to do" (*Hiratsuka Raichō chosakushū* 2:62). Years afterward, in answer to Kobayashi Tomie's asking why she ran away with Morita, Raichō said much the same thing: "I had achieved kenshō and was in a state of exhilaration. Things like life and death were nothing out of the ordinary, nothing to get upset about. I was also attracted to Morita—after all, I continued to see him afterward. Also, I didn't have to worry about earning a livelihood, I had time to spare, I was full of energy, I had achieved kenshō but had no particular purpose in life at the time. So I did exactly what Morita told me to do. I suppose I was eager to please him. It was certainly an adventure of my youth" (Kobayashi, *Hiratsuka Raichō: Hito to shisō*, 66).

6. The *Tokyo Asahi* of March 25, 1908 carried a picture of Raichō with the caption "Naturalism Carried to an Extreme: Unsuccessful Double Suicide by a Gentleman and a Lady: The Man, A University Graduate and Novelist, The Woman, a College Graduate." The article gave the particulars of the incident and opined: "Since ancient times, double suicides have not been unheard of, but this is the first time a highly educated gentleman and lady have imitated the stupid behavior of illiterate men and women. One can only say that this unprecedented occurrence is the result of Naturalism and Free Love carried to the extreme. Even more outrageous is the temerity of the couple, who, on being apprehended by policemen at Obana Pass, said, 'Our act is an expression of the sacredness of romantic love. We have nothing to be ashamed of.'" The Naturalist school of literature in Japan called for unfettered personal fulfillment.

7. Sasaki Shigetsu (Sōkei-an) founded the Zen Institute in New York in 1931. After World War II, Ruth Fuller Sasaki trained with Gotō Sōseki (Zuigan) and was ordained abbess of Ryōsen-an, a subtemple of Daitokuji.

8. Translator's note: I have omitted a short passage about Nantenbō-rōshi having an altercation with a nurse for not being allowed "one more drink."

9. The novel, which generally follows the facts of the incident, is written from the viewpoint of Kojima Yōkichi (Morita), who is "passive" and "yields to every temptation." Manabe Tomoko (Raichō) is portrayed as the stronger one in the relationship, and Yōkichi "feels humiliated" at every turn. He even wonders if she is asexual (he completely misinterprets her remark about being "neither woman nor man"), obsessed with death (in one of her letters, she writes, "Death is the only way I can attain Buddhahood"), or simply "insane." Tomoko nevertheless consents to follow his plan, though the novel gives the impression that the two are really playacting (Yōkichi: "Our love—let me call it love—do you sometimes feel it's like something in an Ibsen play?"). The novel ends with Yōkichi burning the letters and throwing the knife away. *Black Smoke* brought Morita overnight fame (an advertisement for the seventh printing appears in the June 1914 *Seitō*), and without obtaining permission from the Hiratsuka family, Morita wrote a sequel called *Autobiography* (*Jiden*), which was serialized in the *Tokyo Asahi* from April to July 1911 and published as a book in 1915. The novel picks up the story with the narrator ("I") and "that woman" (who is never named) being discovered by the police, and ends with "I" returning to his home village to visit his sick mother, who fails to recognize him. In the sequel, the narrator is contemptuous of "that woman," who "not once showed any kindness and inflicted only pain and humiliation," and, quoting many of her letters, tries to analyze her motives. In the end he decides they never really understood each other. The two novels are no longer much read.

5. Seitō

1. As of 1898, Raichō's father's yearly salary was 1,400 yen from his government job, and 100 yen was the equivalent of his yearly bonus (Kobayashi, *Hiratsuka Raichō: Ai to hangyaku no seishun*, 74).

2. The rest of the statutes covered such matters as the address of the organization, different categories of membership, the journal, fees (30 sen a month), and related activities. For the English text of the statutes, see Bardsley, "Introduction," in *The Bluestockings of Japan: New Women Essays and Fiction from Seitō, 1911–1916*.

3. Translator's note: I have omitted Raichō's summary of an article by a Japanese scholar on Seitō and the rise and function of the literary salon in Western Europe (Tanaka Hisako, "Seitō to yōroppa no burusutokkingu ni tsuite," *Kokugo to kokubungaku* [July 1965]).

4. For the English translation of the series of twelve verses, see Bardsley, *The Bluestockings of Japan*. Akiko contributed other poems until 1915.

5. I have omitted an untranslatable haiku that Sōseki supposedly made when Morita Sōhei remarked that Sugimoto Masao had a face like a gourd. The haiku is: "*Sōhei ni fukarete kaeru hechima kana.*"

6. The advertisements in the first issue were varied: fountain pens (Maruzen); *Subaru*, *Joshi bundan*, *Kokoro no hana*, *Haimi*, and other literary journals; a sectional bookcase with an English caption, "It grows with your library. It fits anyplace"; Ikuta Chōkō's translation of *Thus Spake Zarathustra*; a hospital for children; hair oil.

7. For the full text in English, see Bardsley, *The Bluestockings of Japan*. For the Japanese text, see *Hiratsuka Raicho chosakushū* (hereafter *HRC*), 1:14–27.

8. Though Raichō refers directly to Zen only once (*zenjōryoku*, or the power of Zen meditation), she uses other Buddhist terms such as *shinshō no hito* (a true or authentic person, i.e., someone who has attained satori); *kyomu* or *komu* (nothingness); *shinkū* (true void); *kegen* (Buddha as he appears in this world in physical form in order to save people). She also refers to the historical Buddha's Great Enlightenment.

9. The first precept was "When meeting a man, a suitable third person should always be present. If this is not possible, the man and woman should meet in an open place." As quoted in Horiba Kiyoko, *Seitō no jidai*, 39.

10. Besides Brandes (*Eminent Authors of the Nineteenth Century: Ibsen and Björnson*); Shaw (*Quintessence of Ibsenism: Dramatic Opinions and Essays*); and Merezhkovski, (*The Life Work of Ibsen*), the list of 26 European critics included George Moore and Lou Andreas-Salomé.

11. Actually, the other contributors were sympathetic. Katō Midori: "I hope that both the awakened and yet-to-be awakened Noras in Japan will think more seriously about women's position." Ueno Yōko: "It is my hope that Nora's self-awakening will be the self-awakening of all women. But now that she is awakened, she will need to be strong-willed to survive.... Nora, do not lose heart. Do not give up. Do not forget that every honest and sincere person is behind you." Ueda Kimiko: "Nora speaks for the millions of women in the world who are sacrificed to men. The greater tragedy is not in leaving the house but in living for eight years like a doll, a pet bird, to please her husband." Yasumochi Yoshiko: "I admire and appreciate her courage and determination... . I do not understand why she should be criticized. Nora's problem is also Helmut's problem, and by extension society's problem, and ultimately a religious problem."

12. Araki's story may be found in Bardsley, *The Bluestockings of Japan*.

13. Kōkichi made no attempt to hide her feelings. As she wrote in "From My Diary" (vol. 2, no. 6): "For this older woman ... I am willing to become a slave ("DOREI"), a living sacrifice, as long as I am favored by her embraces and kisses."

14. Okumura's novel, *Meguriai* (*Chance Encounter*) was published in 1956. It is an autobiographical novel with the characters thinly disguised (Okumura is the narrator, Ono Hiroshi; Raichō is Hirooka Teruko; Otake Kōkichi is Sassa Shigeri) and traces Hiroshi's childhood, his platonic love affair with a consumptive young girl, his decision to leave home to study art in Tokyo, and his fateful meeting with Teruko; it ends with their decision to live together. The facts closely follow Raichō's autobiography, but the story is presented in a more romantic light, with the characters drenched in tears of longing and raindrops reminding the sensitive narrator of a Chopin prelude and frequent use of French words such as *clair, aventure, complicité*.

15. In Okumura's novel, Shigeri (Kōkichi) threatens to write an exposé and signs her letter "Monster" (*Chance Encounter* 60).

16. Judging from the feverish tone of the first essay, Raichō's feelings for Kōkichi were more intense than she admits in her autobiography. Referring to the "memorable" night of the Seitō meeting on May 13 (the particulars of which are unknown): "I wanted to make you part of my world, I held you in my arms, and oh, how violently I kissed you." Or, after Kōkichi is diagnosed with tuberculosis: "If you're sick, I want to be sick, too. We'll go to Chigasaki together ... and on a starlit night, we'll row out to

an island, just the two of us." Then, after Kōkichi leaves for the sanatorium: "I want to fly to you, throw my emotions at my young boy, embrace you with all my strength, kiss you until my lips bleed." In the essay she refers several times to Kōkichi as "my young boy (*watashi no shōnen*)" ("Chigasaki e," *HRC* 1:76–108). In "One Year," Raichō mainly quotes from Kokichi's letters. Members were aware of the unusually close relationship between Raichō and Kōkichi. The Editors' Notes for the October 1912 issue (vol. 2, no. 10) includes a ditty by Tamura Toshiko: "Kōkichi, you look pale, just like a dried-up lotus leaf. When you slashed your arm for R, did the blood flow a bright red? Kōkichi, my, but you're big. When you get together with R, who hugs who?" Given the hothouse atmosphere of a group composed of only women and the penchant for experimentation, defiance of convention, and self-dramatization, intense friendships were perhaps to be expected. But it remains an open question whether their relationship was on the order of schoolgirl crushes, common in Japan, or went beyond.

17. Translator's note: I have omitted a third quotation about the inferior quality of normal schools where students are discouraged from thinking independently.

18. Kamichika first learned about Seitō when she read the inaugural issue at the Ōhashi Library. "I was lonely, I had no one to talk to openly about my literary ambitions. I felt that the people at Seitō would satisfy what I was seeking." She also set down her first impression of Raichō in her memoirs: "Ensconced in the middle of the room, her eyes flashed with a light that seemed to tease the younger members. Even though I felt I could not look her in the face, I kept gazing with unbearable pleasure." Kamichika also admits that she became hopelessly drunk at the party (Kamichika, *Waga ai, waga tatakai*, 100–101).

19. "A Cold Monster" is about a baby who is born blind and fated to die soon. In "Mingling in the Crowd," Kōkichi wallows in self-pity: "I told many lies," "I was but a child, utterly without awareness or understanding," "I write this with my eyes clouded with tears, good-bye, good-bye."

20. "Obsession," a story by Katō Midori, is included in Bardsley, *The Bluestockings of Japan*.

21. Ogasawara actually died in 1988, at the ripe old age of one hundred. Her story "Eastern Breeze" is included in Bardsley, *The Bluestockings of Japan*.

22. Raichō puts a good face on the facts. The baby was born before the formal marriage, and before the breakup, Yoshiko, her husband, and his mistress set up a *ménage à trois*.

6. A New Direction for Seitō

1. Ellen Key (1849–1926) was the daughter of a liberal member of the Swedish parliament. Educated at home by French, German, and Swedish tutors (her mother was one of the richest women in Sweden), she traveled widely with her father, acting as his secretary. She became a teacher at a girls' school and later taught at the Popular University of Stockholm. In her numerous writings (she wrote five books on women and marriage between 1909 and 1914, all translated into English), Kay glorified heterosexual love as a "divine" evolutionary force that ideally led to marriage and the procreation of healthy children. Less known is her role in the Swedish arts and crafts

movement, in which she called for the fashioning of simple and beautiful objects that would enhance the home environment. Raichō's piece in the January supplement is actually a translation of Havelock Ellis's preface to Key's book.

2. Raichō's assessment of the essay is puzzling since Fukuda endorses a communist system (*kyōsansei*) several times on the ground that it is "the surest key to women's emancipation" and will usher in a "truly beautiful earthly paradise for men and women." Considering the recent clampdown on leftists following the Great Treason Incident, it is not surprising that the essay ran afoul of the censors. See Bardsley, *The Bluestockings of Japan* for the full text of the essay.

3. *Women of the World (Sekai fujin)* was an eight-page semimonthly pamphlet that dealt with such issues as the Ashio Copper Mine Incident, the plight of women workers, women's rights and suffrage, and women's movements abroad. It was banned in 1909.

4. For excerpts from Fukuda's autobiography, see Mikiso Hane, *Reflections on the Way to the Gallows: Rebel Women in Prewar Japan.*

5. Iwano Kiyoko's talk may be found in Bardsley, *The Bluestockings of Japan.*

6. Raichō criticized Nishikawa Fumiko for giving precedence to men in her views on women's emancipation. She also made personal attacks on Nishikawa, calling her a "busybody housewife," the "kind of woman who changes her kimono to keep up with the current fashion." Raichō never mentions that Nishikawa was a participant in the earlier movement to revise Article 5 in the Police Security Regulations ("On Nishikawa Fumiko's *Fujin kaihōron*," *HRC* 1:307–312). Tomida Hiroko gives a more positive assessment of the Real New Women's Association: "[The association] did not restrict its interest to women's issues but extended [its activities] to more general causes including charity and relief work." She also writes that Nishikawa (1882–1960) was "an activist rather than a theorist," "open-minded and keen to learn tactics and strategy from women's movements in the West" (Tomida, *Hiratsuka Raichō and Early Japanese Feminism*, 213–216).

7. After her marriage, Kōkichi (now Tomimoto Kazue) lived in Nara with her husband, who became a very successful ceramicist. They had three children but separated later. After World War II, Kōkichi supported herself by writing children's stories. She died in 1966 (*Seitō jinbutsu jiten* 68–69).

8. In her essay, Raichō did not mince her words: "How many wives today have married without love to obtain financial security and then spend their entire lives as servants and prostitutes in the service of their husbands? … Even if we do not oppose the institution of marriage as such, we will never submit to present-day ideas about marriage or to the prevailing system of marriage. Under the social system as it exists today, is not marriage a life-long relationship in which one party must submit to another's power and authority? Are not wives treated like minors or cripples? … We do not wish to marry if it means submitting to this wrongful and unreasonable system" ("To the Women of the World," *HRC* 1:220–221). See Bardsley, *The Bluestockings of Japan* for the full text of the essay.

9. The full text of the letter, dated April 26, was printed in the Editors' Notes of the May 1913 issue. According to the letter, the White Caps had 34 members, including six elderly men, seven women and two young girls. Disguised as "gentlemen, spinsters, peasants, young ladies, merchants, rickshaw pullers, and students," they intended to use drugs and resort to physical violence or pistols to carry out their threat, beginning on May 1 and continuing for three days.

10. The "sketches" ranged in tone from positive to hostile. Tamura Toshiko: "She struck me as someone who wants to distract herself from her inner solitude." Otake Kōkichi: "Hiratsuka-san and I were bound by a love that was a step beyond the ordinary, so I can no longer see her objectively. People say she is like a man, but they are wrong. She is kind and gentle, a woman of strong emotions. But she is not good at delegating work." Baba Kochō: "Her writing style tends to strive for rhetorical effect." Iwano Kiyoko: "She is overly influenced by Zen and talks about attaining a state of nonself, but it is hard for me to imagine a world without the self.... She is still unfinished, but she is always striving and thinking. I have no doubt she will be an exceptional woman." "She has a strong sense of pride and tends to be overly cerebral." "One can't measure her by ordinary standards." Iwano Hōmei: "She's too caught up with pedestrian Buddhist thought." In Satō Haruo's case, the antagonism seems to have been mutual. Of the time he first saw Raichō: "She walked like a man ... and had a face like a mask ... a face you don't forget." Recalling a conversation he had with Raichō, Yasumochi Yoshiko, and Otake Kōkichi about Higuchi Ichiyō: "She was intent on showing off her opinions and didn't listen to others." "Her prose style is that of a third-year middle school student describing Napoleon's heroic achievements." Yosano Akiko: "I've heard first hand from the person who wrote the novel about Hiratsuka Raichō that she is not a virgin.... I can scarcely bring myself to write about the other rumors about her, but since I would like to know the truth about her ... I shall reveal one or two.... Namely that she was involved with a man at a coastal summer resort and with another man on the night of Seitō's New Year's party...." Akiko also praised Raichō: "I can think of no other woman who expresses her ideas with such boldness and brilliant logic.... Her prose vibrates with a force that overwhelms other women." But then Akiko added: "One somehow gets the impression that she is merely regurgitating the ideas she picked up from foreign books." Their rivalry would continue into the 1920s.

11. In the letter, in which the principals are identified as N, R, and H(iroshi), Raichō recounts the actual situation in detail, denounces N for his treachery ("You tried to separate R from H, her beloved younger brother"; "There is nothing like jealousy to render a person stupid"), and dares him to make public what he knows about R and H ("You will only be hurting yourself").

12. Shūgaku (real name Nagai Yūjirō) turned to drink, openly lived with a mistress half his age, and died of diabetes in 1928 at age 51 (Kobayashi Tomie, *Hiratsuka Raichō: Ai to hangyaku no seishun*, 224–225).

13. In his novel, Hiroshi (Okumura) is offended by Teruko's (Raichō) letter and writes to her, "To be honest, I was repelled by the list of conditions. I felt as though I were being put to a test.... Was ever a man subjected to such questions by a woman?" He also resists the idea of not having children, though he is "willing to wait" (*Chance Encounter* 178–179).

14. Translator's note: In *Seitō*, the title is "Love and Morality." I have been unable to identify the name of the author of "The Shadow of an Echo' (*Hibiki no kage*).

15. Noe admits that she was flattered by Kimura's letters but neglected to tell him about her relationship with T[suji]. She is even tempted to leave T, and finds herself in a quandary. The situation is resolved when T, who discovers a letter she is about to send to Kimura, demands a showdown and she realizes that she cannot leave him. The "affair" lasted seven days. In her review, Raichō, who thought Noe was too emotional, criticized her for not telling Kimura about Tsuji at the outset.

16. Yamada Waka (1879–1957) was an "Ameyuki-san," one of hundreds of young Japanese women who were shipped to the West Coast under false pretenses and forced to work as prostitutes. She was actually rescued by a Japanese newspaperman who then tried to push her back into prostitution in San Francisco. There, she sought refuge at Cameron House, a rehabilitation center for ex-prostitutes, and met Kakichi at his small language school. For more information about Waka, see Yamazaki Tomoko, *Yamada Waka: From Prostitute to Feminist Pioneer.*

17. The letter, dated January 10, 1914, runs to more than ten pages. After apologizing to her parents for causing them pain and thanking them for their tolerance, Raichō writes she has fallen in love with "H," a painter who is five years younger, "five parts child, three parts female, two parts male, and irresistibly endearing." She has decided to "take the path of love" and live with him, "see what course it takes and where it will lead," and even if this decision turns out to be a mistake, she promises not to trouble her parents. She also writes that since the present marriage system is so detrimental to women, she and H feel no need to go through with a formal marriage. "When H and I are out walking, he gets very angry when people call us 'Mr. and Mrs.'" He says he prefers "older sister" and "younger brother." Nor do they feel obliged to have children. There is nothing known about how her parents, or for that matter Okumura, felt about the letter being published. See Bardsley, *The Bluestockings of Japan,* for the entire text of the letter.

18. Noe starts her essay by criticizing the age-old injunction that "a chaste woman should not marry twice": "If a man is allowed to marry twice, even three times, it is not fair to forbid a widow from marrying. If chastity is not required of a man, it should not be required of a woman." After questioning whether virginity is as precious as it is made out to be, Noe says that she sees nothing shameful in a woman voluntarily giving up her virginity before marriage and that the loss of virginity should not disqualify a woman from marrying or preclude a happy marriage. On this count, men, who are seldom virgins before marriage, have no right to criticize women. She ends her essay with an exhortation: "Destroy convention, destroy convention! This is the only way we can be saved. Cursed to live in misery, we shall not bear our lot forever. Soon, soon."

19. Based on his reading of Ellis, Lombroso, and other European writers, Ogura (1882–1941) wrote that Noe's intense emotional reaction to Kimura's love letters (he attributed this to the fact that women have fewer white blood corpuscles than men), her lack of forethought and perseverance, and her tendency to tire easily were "typical female characteristics." He added that these characteristics were particularly pronounced in Noe's case, since she was pregnant and the weather was unusually hot at the time of the incident.

20. In order to avoid a ban, Sakamoto omitted some passages in her translation.

21. In spite of two indictments for "corrupting public morals," Ogura's society lasted until 1944. His wife continued his work after his sudden death in 1941 (*Seitō jinbutsu jiten* 199).

22. The register of members seems to have been irretrievably lost. According to Horiba Kiyoko's calculations, membership rose from the original 23 to 38 in January 1912, to about 73 in October that same year, and reached a peak of about 87 in May 1914 (*Seitō no jidai,* Appendix). Contributors were not necessarily members, as in the case of Nogami Yaeko, who published translations of Musset and Sonya Kovalevsky's memoirs.

23. In "*Seitō* and I," Raichō lists her reasons for relinquishing the journal—her physical

exhaustion, Seitō's financial problems, her need to "be true to herself," and, quoting Noe's letters verbatim, describes how the two reached their final decision. She ends her piece on an elegiac note describing a dream Tsuji had: Raichō, who is riding a horse near a cliff, throws herself into a lake and drowns. Tsuji happens to see the horse prancing wildly, drags her corpse out of the water, and resuscitates her. She writes: "I thought of the dream and felt as if I were bidding farewell to my past." By contrast, the tone of Noe's essay, "On Taking Over *Seitō*," is defiant. She writes about the changing relations among the people on the staff and her growing interest in social issues. She assures the readers that she will continue *Seitō* "with the last ounce of my strength," "even if it's only two or three pages." "People will wonder about what a child like me can do … but please wait and see what this country bumpkin is capable of." She also declares that under her leadership, *Seitō* will "have no regulations, no set editorial policy or position, and be open to all women." Noe (1895–1923) was twenty at the time.

24. The last installment was on April 21. The autobiographical novel begins with "H" receiving a letter from Kojima (Raichō uses the same name as in Morita's *Black Smoke*) and ends with "H" going over the events of the day when they took their first walk in Ueno Park. Kojima is depicted as "unmanly," "an overgrown baby," with buckteeth and a weak mouth. "H," who admits to being arrogant, takes a superior attitude and laughs inwardly at everything Kojima says, but finds that her curiosity is piqued and that she is "ready for anything" ("The Mountain Pass," *Jiji shinpō*, April 1–21, 1915 [*HRC* 2:61–105]).

25. The passages are part of the woman's response to an interrogation by the judge. For the full text, see Bardsley, *The Bluestockings of Japan*.

26. Raichō spelled out her views in a 1917 essay. In principle she was in favor of limiting children, but feared that artificial birth control of the kind advocated by Margaret Sanger would lead to sexual indulgence and ultimately to moral decadence. Rather, she hoped that women would take the lead and "raise men's natural instincts to a higher level." For Raichō, abstinence was the only method "worthy of human dignity" ("The Pros and Cons of Contraception," *Nihon hyōron*, September 1917; *HRC* 2:337, 340). Much later she changed her views, joined Katō Shidzue's Birth Control League of Japan in 1931, and urged the government to establish clinics to disseminate correct information on contraception ("Birth Control Clinics," original publication unknown; *HRC* 5:259–260).

27. Waka also translated Key's *The Century of the Child* (vol. 5, nos. 7, 9, 10, 11; vol. 6, nos. 1 and 2).

28. Saiga's story is about a sixteen-year-old girl whose husband is at the front and who is so distraught with worry and the burden of taking care of her senile father-in-law that she goes out of her mind and kills herself.

29. In the same article (December 24, 1915) Fukushima wrote: "The case merely proves how powerless a wife is in the face of her husband's high-handed behavior. It is as if the court has announced to the public that the law is unable to do anything when a husband abandons his wife and lives with his mistress. How can any woman rejoice over the results of this case?" *Fujo shinbun* (*Women's Newspaper*) was a progressive weekly started by Fukushima in 1900.

30. Translator's note: I have omitted Raichō's account of how she was cheered when Tokunaga Yuki, a young woman who worked at a nursery school for the poor, dropped

by with a gift for the baby. Thereafter she came each year with a birthday present until Akemi graduated from high school. Apparently the woman told someone that she worked in the slums because she had been inspired by Raicho's "uncompromising attitude toward life."

31. Translator's note: I have omitted some of the details about the couple's complete disregard for the dangers of infection.

32. Asadori, who translated Ladislas Reymont's *The Peasants*, received the Gold Order of Merit from the Polish government in 1930. There is no record that Asadori was nominated to the academy. Personal communication from Anna Elliott.

33. Raichō's description of Noe is inconsistent with what she said about Noe's face being "full of youthful promise" in October 1914, when Noe took responsibility for the November and December issues.

34. Noe's comments about Ōsugi and Arahata are in the Editors' Notes of the November issue (vol. 4, no. 10). Her criticisms of their wives and fellow socialists are in her short essay "Miscellaneous Thoughts" in the December issue (vol. 4, no. 11). There was no September issue.

35. Noe wrote that she was deeply hurt and saddened that the affair had destroyed the trust between her and her husband (she does not name Tsuji), but still loved him and wanted to believe that the affair was a momentary aberration. She also said that she was troubled because she was "more famous" than her husband, who was often "put in the shade," though of course worldly fame meant nothing to her. The essay ends on an inconclusive note.

36. There were all together 52 issues. Although Raichō does not mention it, the December (vol. 5, no. 11), January, and February issues (vol. 6, no. 1; no. 2) carried a spirited exchange between Noe and Yamakawa Kikue on the question of prostitution. In "Regarding the Arrogant, Narrow-Minded, and Half-Baked Public Service Activities by Japanese Women," Noe criticized the antiprostitution campaigns by upper- and middle-class women as hypocritical and nothing more than charity work to flatter their vanity. She was particularly disdainful of the JWCTU's campaign to eliminate licensed prostitution within six years. "Prostitution has its own reason for existing … it is firmly rooted in history, and the innate needs of men cannot be eradicated in the space of six or even ten years." She then admonished the "Bible Women" not to look down on prostitutes as fallen women but to try to educate them. Yamakawa ("In Response to Itō Noe's Remarks on the Social Work of Japanese Women") reproached Noe for being too harsh on the JWCTU's work to eliminate licensed prostitution, which was a vestige of Japan's feudal system and in many cases more exploitative of women than private prostitution. She then took Noe to task for saying that prostitution was unavoidable because it answered "the innate needs of men." "If you say it is impossible to eliminate an evil system just because it is rooted in history, you might as well say that it is better for women who have been enslaved since time immemorial to stay put since there is no point in resisting. Prostitution exists as a by-product of the unnatural system of relationships between men and women. It exists not because of man's innate nature but because of the unnatural social system.… All social systems are made by human beings.… History proves that a system made by human beings can always be changed by human beings, if people make the effort … and so I believe it is possible to eliminate licensed prostitution." Ever practical, Yamakawa proposed setting up job training

centers for former prostitutes at prefectural offices. In the same issue, Noe responded that she still believed prostitution existed because of "the innate needs of men" and that in many cases prostitution was the only way some women could earn a living. She agreed that prostitution was evil and also conceded that licensed prostitution could be eliminated. Throughout the debate, Yamakawa cites figures and is cool and logical, while Noe's argument is muddled and often emotional. A translation of Noe's December essay, as well as some of her other essays, may be found in Hane, *Peasants, Rebels, Women, and Outcastes: The Underside of Modern Japan.*

37.   "So-Called Free Love and Its Limits," *Osaka mainichi shinbun*, January 4, 1917. The entire text may be found in *HRC* 2:255–261.

38.   Ōsugi, who was stabbed in the throat, quickly recovered from his wound, but was ostracized by his fellow socialists, who disapproved of his private life. Noe and Tsuji were divorced in September 1917. Kamichika's sentence was later commuted to two years. For details of the affair see Stanley, *Ōsugi Sakae, Anarchist in Taishō Japan*, 91–110; also Kamichika, *Waga ai, waga tatakai*, 154–165. Tsuji died during World War II, in 1944, some say from severe malnutrition.

Translator's Afterword

1.   The story ends as Keiko (Raichō) gazes at her dead grandmother's face and says, "Now she's gone back to the good grandmother she used to be." Her mother replies, "Yes, how lovely she looks, even her wrinkles are gone. That's what happens when human beings get rid of their desires and resentments" ("Dying of Old Age," *Chūō kōron*, September 1918 [*HRC* 2:374–399]).

2.   Ichikawa Fusae (1893–1981) was a graduate of Aichi Prefectural Normal School. She wrote in her autobiography that she read a copy of *Seitō* in 1915 but was not impressed. She first met Raichō in 1919, when she was studying English with Yamada Kakichi: "Raichō was beautiful, quiet, and spoke slowly in a soft voice. I could not believe that she was the original 'New Woman'" (Ichikawa, *Ichikawa Fusae jiden: Senzen-hen*, 40).

3.   For "human race," Raichō uses the word *shuzoku*, which is closer to "racial stock." The second petition was in line with Raichō's ideas on eugenics, which she doubtless absorbed from Key, for whom "race improvement" was a "new ethical principle" that called for a "strict selection of the human material" (*The Renaissance of Motherhood* 77, 81). In essays written in 1917, 1919, and 1920, Raichō advocated legal restrictions on people with hereditary mental and physical diseases ("On the Pros and Cons of Contraception," *Nihon hyōron*, September 1917 [*HRC* 2:340]; "Women Under the Prevailing Law," original publication unknown [*HRC* 3:115]; "On the Revision of Article 5 and the Prohibition of Marriage for Men with Venereal Disease," original publication unknown [*HRC* 3:209–211]). For a discussion of Raichō's "maternalist eugenics," see Sumiko Otsubo, "Engendering Eugenics: Feminists and Marriage Restriction Legislation in the 1920s," in Molony and Uno, eds., *Gendering Modern Japanese History*.

4.   Quoting figures from a study by Yamakawa Kikue, Tabuchi referred to the growing numbers of women who had joined the workforce and were no longer content to be just good wives and wise mothers. "As human beings, they want to go as far as they

can, experience freedom and equality, and spread their overflowing love to the whole world." He then said that "democracy" did not mean equality or sameness but the strong helping the weak, and that since women, too, were "subjects of Imperial Japan," they should not be discriminated against and forbidden from attending or organizing political meetings (Diet Record [*Nihon fujin mondai* 2:163–164]).

5. "A Letter on the Occasion of the Dissolution of the New Women's Association," *Nihon fujin mondai*, 2:196–199. Yamanouchi Mina, a former textile worker who was temporarily helping out, was incensed by Raichō's decision and accused her of treating the association as her "private possession." Mina, who admired Ichikawa, also criticized Raichō for being autocratic and self-centered (*Yamanouchi Mina jiden: Jūni-sai no bōseki jokō kara no shōgai* 92–94). From March to July 1923, Raichō wrote a series of short essays in *Fujin kōron* entitled "Reflections on the New Women's Association." The essays start with a brief account of the founding of the association but soon turn into a mean-spirited account of her personal relationship with Ichikawa. She writes that Ichikawa was "ambitious for worldly success," "easily swayed by others' opinions," and, "having never fallen in love or married," unsympathetic to her living arrangement with Okumura. *Fujin kōron*, March to July 1923 (*HRC* 3:270–323). In response, Ichikawa, who returned to Japan in January 1924, simply stated in the April 1925 *Fujin kōron* that she regretted that Raichō misunderstood her, and that despite all the criticisms, she would always respect her former colleague. In her autobiography, which was published after Raichō's death, she was more candid: "In my opinion, Raichō wasn't really suited for group action, particularly when the women's movement or politics were concerned. To this day, I think I was wise to leave and strike out on my own in a new direction. Still, I am pained to think that the work into which I poured all my youthful energies turned out this way" (Ichikawa, *Jiden*, 100).

6. Yoneda's Notes to Raichō's essay in *HRC* 6:422. This statement was not an isolated instance. Referring to the imperial rescript read at the sixty-ninth Diet two months after the abortive military coup in February 1936, Raichō wrote: "The tears of awe and gratitude shed by those who heard His Majesty's words, their selfless, pure-hearted, spontaneous vow to reflect as one upon His Majesty's virtue and renew government, can only be ascribed to the effulgent glory of his Imperial Person. The men in the Diet were not the only ones so moved. All Japanese, including women, who are still excluded from politics, were no less stirred by the occasion. I feel more strongly than ever my good fortune in having been born in a nation presided over by an emperor who is a living god and with whom his myriad subjects can immediately be at one (*kiitsu*) at any given moment and in any circumstance.... In submission to the Imperial Will ... women, too, fervently hope to do their best, however indirectly" "Women are Deeply Moved," *Yomiuri shinbun*, May 7, 1936 (*HRC* 6:123–124). Again, in reference to the Konoe cabinet's announcement of a "New Political Order" in 1940: "To be at one (*kiitsu*) with the Sun Goddess Amaterasu and with her descendant, the emperor, who is a living god—is this not the all-encompassing basis of the New Order? Let there be no useless fretting over technical or minor matters" ("Excerpts from a Diary," *Fujo shinbun* October 27, 1940 [*HRC* 6:330]). Ōmori Kaoru discovered a short essay by Raichō in the October 1937 issue of *Kagayaku*, a pamphlet begun by Hasegawa Shigure in 1933 to cheer soldiers a the front: "In giving up their lives for the emperor, who is a living god, the soldiers of the Imperial Army transcend life and death and reach a realm

of absolute religious certainty (*shūkyōteki zettaichi*) that is not easily attained. It must be true that at the moment of death, the soldiers shout 'Long live the emperor' with a smile on their lips" (Ōmori, *Hiratsuka Raichō: Hikari to kage*, 153). Even given the temper of the times, Raichō's exalted vision of the emperor is baffling. Yoneda finds Raichō's repeated use of *kiitsu* suggestive and sees a link between Raichō's view of Japan as a family-state (*kazoku kokka*) with the emperor as the head and her growing sense of oneness with her ancestors (Yoneda Sayoko, *Hiratsuka Raichō: Kindai Nihon no demokurashii to jendā*, 220–223). Another writer connects Raichō's worshipful view of the emperor with her lifelong fascination with self-transcendence and the nonrational (Shindō Ken, *Joseishi to shite no jiden*, 35).

7. As early as September 1937, following the announcement of the National Spiritual Mobilization Act, Ichikawa Fusae formed the Japanese Federation of Women's Organizations (Nihon Fujin Dantai Renmei). Comprised of the League for Securing Women Suffrage, the YWCA, the JWCTU, and other liberal groups, the organization's professed goal was "to enable women to manifest their true worth by cooperating with the government's effort to shore up the defense of the homeland during an unprecedented national emergency" (*Nihon fujin mondai* 2:497).

8. The years from 1923 to 1945 are omitted entirely in this much shorter autobiography. Raichō gave no explanation for the omission. She wrote in the foreword that she made great strides in her ideas during this "turbulent" twenty-year period and briefly alluded to her growing sympathy for proletarian parties, the consumer cooperative movement, and anarchism. She also wrote that she hoped to write about this period in the future, but she never did. There may be two possible reasons. First, as she herself acknowledged, after the dissolution of the New Women's Association she was no longer in the forefront of the feminist movement. She did not "lose all intellectual curiosity," as her contemporary Nogami Yaeko cruelly remarked (quoted in Yoneda, *Hiratsuka Raichō: Kindai Nihon no demokurashii to jendā*, 237–238), but she retreated completely from public life. Second, she may have regretted some of the statements she made during the late 1930s, such as her avowals of reverence for the emperor or approval of government eugenics policies. When she wrote her 1955 autobiography, she may not yet have come to terms with her abrupt shifts in ideas, or she may have simply wished to avoid bringing these facts to public attention. In her reconstruction of Raichō's life in volumes 3 and 4, Kobayashi makes no mention of her views on the emperor or eugenics.

Bibliography

Bardsley, Jan. *The Bluestockings of Japan: New Women Essays and Fiction from Seitō, 1911–1916*. Ann Arbor, MI: Center for Japanese Studies, 2006.

Birnbaum, Phyllis. *Modern Girls, Shining Stars, the Skies of Tokyo*. New York: Columbia University Press, 1999.

Frühstück, Sabine. *Colonizing Sex: Sexology and Social Control in Modern Japan*. Berkeley: University of California Press, 2003.

Hane, Mikiso. *Reflections on the Way to the Gallows: Rebel Women in Prewar Japan*. Berkeley: University of California Press, 1983.

——.*Peasants, Rebels, Women, and Outcastes: The Underside of Modern Japan*. 2nd ed. Lanham, MD: Rowman and Littlefield, 2003.

Hiratsuka Raichō. *Watakushi no aruita michi*. Tokyo: Shinhyōronsha, 1955.

Hiratsuka Raichō Chosakushū Hensan Iinkai, ed. *Hiratsuka Raichō chosakushū*. 8 vols. Tokyo: Ōtsuki Shoten, 1983–1984.

Horiba Kiyoko. *Seitō josei kaihō ronshū*. Tokyo: Iwanami Shoten, 1991.

——.*Seitō no jidai: Hiratsuka Raichō to atarashii onna*. Iwanami Shinsho Series, no. 15. Tokyo: Iwanami Shoten, 1988.

Ichikawa Fusae. *Ichikawa Fusae jiden: Senzen-hen*. Tokyo: Shinjuku Shobō, 1974.

Ide Fumiko. *Seitō no onnatachi*. Tokyo: Kaien Shobō, 1975.

——. *Hiratsuka Raichō: Kindai to shinpi*. Tokyo: Shinchōsha, 1987.

Inagaki Hisao. *A Glossary of Zen Terms*. Kyoto: Bunshōdō, 1991.

Kamichika Ichiko. *Waga ai, waga tatakai*. Ningen no jiden series. Tokyo: Nihon Tosho Sentā, 1999.

Kapleau, Philip, ed. *Three Pillars of Zen: Teaching, Practice, and Enlightenment*. Tokyo: John Weatherhill, 1965.

Key, Ellen. *Love and Marriage*. Trans. Arthur G. Chater. New York: G. P. Putnam's Sons, 1911.

——. *The Renaissance of Motherhood*. Trans. Anna E. B. Fries. New York: G. P. Putnam's Sons, 1914.

Kobayashi Tomie. *Hiratsuka Raichō*. Hito to shisō series. Tokyo: Shimizu Shoin, 1983.

——. *Hiratsuka Raichō: Ai to hangyaku no seishun*. Tokyo: Ōtsuki Shoten, 1977.

Kraft, Kenneth, ed. *Zen: Tradition and Transition*. New York: Grove Press, 1988.

Molony, Barbara. "Women's Rights and the Japanese State, 1880–1925." In Gail Lee Bernstein, Andrew Gordon, and Kate Nakai Wildman, eds., *Public Spheres, Private Lives in Modern Japan, 1600–1950*. Cambridge, MA: Harvard University Asia Center, 2005.

Molony, Kathleen. "One Woman Who Dared: Ichikawa Fusae and the Japanese Women's Suffrage Movement." Ph.D. diss., University of Michigan, 1980.

Morita Sōhei. *Jiden*. Tokyo: Nichigetsusha, 1915.

——. *Baien*. Gendai Nihon bungaku taikei. Vol. 29. Tokyo: Chikuma Shobō, 1971.

Nakamura Hijime. *Kōsetsu bukkyōgo daijiten*. 4 vols. Tokyo: Tokyo Shoseki, 2001.

Nietzsche, Friedrich. *Thus Spake Zarathustra: A Book for All and None*. Trans. Alexander Tille. New York: Macmillan, 1898–99.

Nihon fujin mondai shiryō shūsei. Vol. 2. Tokyo: Domesu Shuppan, 1977.

Nihon Joshi Daigaku, ed. *Nihon joshi daigaku gakuen jiten: Sōritsu hyakunen no kiseki*. Tokyo: Japan Women's College, 2001.

Oku Mumeo. *Nobi aka aka to*. Ningen no kiroku series. Tokyo: Nihon Tosho Sentā, 1997.

Okumura Hiroshi. *Meguriai*. Tokyo: Gendaisha, 1956.

Ōmori Kaoru. *Hiratsuka Raichō: hikari to kage*. Tokyo: Daiichi Shorin, 1997.

Otsubo, Sumiko. "Engendering Eugenics: Feminists and Marriage Restriction Legislation in the 1920s." In Barbara Molony and Kathleen Uno, eds., *Gendering Modern Japanese History*. Cambridge, MA: Harvard University Asia Center,, 2006.

Raichō Kenkyūkai, ed. *Seitō jinbutsu jiten: 110-nin no gunzō*. Tokyo: Daishūkan Shoten, 2001.

Robins-Mowbry, Dorothy. *The Hidden Sun: Women of Modern Japan*. Boulder, CO: Westview Press, 1983.

Rodd, Laura Rasplica. "Yosano Akiko and the Taishō Debate Over the 'New Woman.'" In Gail Lee Bernstein, ed., *Recreating Japanese Women, 1600–1945*. Berkeley: University of California Press, 1991.

Sasaki, Ruth Fuller and Miura Isshū. *Zen Dust: The History of the Kōan and Kōan Study in Rinzai (Lin-chi) Zen*. Kyoto: The First Zen Institute of America in Japan, 1966.

Schreiner, Olive. *Dreams*. 8th ed. London: T. Fisher Unwin, 1897.

Seitō (September 1911–February 1916). 6 vols. Tokyo: Meiji Bunken, 1968–1970.

Shindō Ken. *Joseishi to shite no jiden*. Kyoto: Mineruba Shoten, 1988.

Sievers, Sharon. *Flowers in Salt: The Beginnings of Feminist Consciousness in Modern Japan*. Stanford: Stanford University Press, 1983.

Sources of Japanese Tradition. Vol. 2. Compiled by Wm Theodore de Bary, Carol Gluck, and Arthur Tiedmann. New York: Columbia University Press, 2005.

Stanley, Thomas A. *Ōsugi Sakae, Anarchist in Taishō Japan: The Creativity of the Ego*. Cambridge, MA: Council on East Asian Studies, Harvard University, 1982.

Tokuza Akiko. *The Rise of the Feminist Movement in Japan*. Tokyo: Keio University Press, 1999.

Tomida, Hiroko. *Hiratsuka Raichō and Early Japanese Feminism*. Leiden and Boston: Brill, 2004.

Ward, Lester. *Pure Sociology: A Treatise on the Origin and Spontaneous Development of Society*. New York: Macmillan, 1903.

Watson, Burton. *The Zen Teachings of Master Lin-chi: A Translation of the Lin-chi-lu*. New York: Columbia University Press, 1993.

Yamakawa Kikue. *Nihon fujin-undō shōshi*. Tokyo: Daiwa Shobō. 1979.

———. *Onna nidai no ki*. Heibonsha tōyō bunko series, no. 203. Tokyo: Heibonsha, 1972.

Yamanouchi Mina. *Yamanouchi Mina jiden; Jūni-sai no bōseki jokō kara no shōgai*. Tokyo: Shinjuku Shobō, 1975.

Yamazaki, Tomoko. *Yamada Waka: From Prostitute to Feminist Pioneer*. Trans. Ann Konsant and Wakako Hironaka. Tokyo: Kodansha International, 1985.

Yanagida Seizan. *Rinzairoku*. Tokyo: Daizō Shuppan, 1972.

Yokoi Yūhō. *The Japanese-English Zen Buddhist Dictionary*. Tokyo: Sankibō Buddhist Bookstore, 1991.

Yoneda Sayoko. *Hiratsuka Raichō: Kindai Nihon no demokurashii to jendā*. Tokyo: Yoshikawa Kōbunkan, 2002.

Yoneda Sayoko and Ikeda Emiko, eds. *Seitō o manabu hito no tame ni*. Kyoto: Sekai Shisō-sha, 1999.

Weatherhead Books on Asia

COLUMBIA UNIVERSITY

Literature

DAVID DER-WEI WANG, EDITOR

Ye Zhaoyan, *Nanjing 1937: A Love Story*, translated by Michael Berry

Makoto Oda, *The Breaking Jewel*, translated by Donald Keene

Han Shaogong, *A Dictionary of Maqiao*, translated by Julia Lovell

Takahashi Takako, *Lonely Woman*, translated by Maryellen Toman Mori

Chen Ran, *A Private Life*, translated by John Howard-Gibbon

Eileen Chang, *Written on Water*, translated by Andrew F. Jones

Amy D. Dooling, editor, *Writing Women in Modern China: The Revolutionary Years, 1936–1976*

Han Bangqing, *The Sing-song Girls of Shanghai*, first translated by Eileen Chang, revised and edited by Eva Hung

Aili Mu, Julie Chiu, and Howard Goldblatt, eds., *Loud Sparrows: Chinese Short-Shorts*

History, Society, and Culture

CAROL GLUCK, EDITOR

Takeuchi Yoshimi, *What Is Modernity? Writings of Takeuchi Yoshimi*, translated by Richard Calichman

Richard Calichman, editor, *Contemporary Japanese Thought*